JAMES BOND
007

THE MAN WITH THE GOLDEN GUN

IAN FLEMING
JIM LAWRENCE ◎ YAROSLAV HORAK

TITANS

JAMES BOND 007:
THE MAN WITH THE GOLDEN GUN
ISBN 1 84023 690 6

Published by Titan Books,
a division of Titan Publishing Group Ltd.
144 Southwark St
London SE1 0UP

A CIP catalogue record for this title is available from the British Library

First edition: February 2004
3 5 7 9 10 8 6 4 2

Printed in Italy

To order from the UK telephone 01536 764 646

Titan Books would like to thank Vince Cosgrove, Lucy Fleming, Marcus Hearn,
Paul Simpson and Zoe Watkins for their help and support in the production of this book.

Introduction by Lucy Fleming © Lucy Fleming 2004

'Bond In Books' article and strip introductions by Paul Simpson © Paul Simpson 2004

Picture credits: Paperback cover for *The Man with the Golden Gun*, published by Pan.
Hardback edition of *The Man with the Golden Gun* published by Jonathan Cape.
Hardback edition of *Octopussy* published by Jonathan Cape.

What did you think of this book? We love to hear from our readers. Please email us at:
readerfeedback@titanemail.com, or write to us at the above address.
You can also visit us at www.titanbooks.com

THE SPY WHO LOVED ME

Introduction by
LUCY FLEMING

When *Casino Royale* was published in 1953 my uncle, Ian Fleming, sent a copy to my father for his comments. I was six years old and, frankly, not remotely interested in such a book. As I grew up I became more aware of the excitement and enjoyment generated by the annual appearance of a proof copy of each of the James Bond novels. I vividly remember my father, the writer Peter Fleming, opening the brown paper parcel at the breakfast table and reading with delight the scribbled (usually ironic) inscription from his brother on the flyleaf of each new book. He then disappeared to his study to digest and scrutinise the latest James Bond adventure. He adopted the pseudonym 'Professor Knittpik', a bibliophile and savant who suggested amendments to the manuscripts that he thought might be useful.

The books were not considered suitable for my sister and I to read, so, naturally, we did our best to sneak a copy away whenever we could. I remember enjoying a delightfully illicit read, under the bed-clothes with a torch, following the man with the grey-blue eyes and the thick comma of black hair round the world on his global missions. I think I learned more about the world from the places that Bond was sent to than from any geography lesson. I certainly learned more about falling in love.

Uncle Ian was a fascinating man: tall and laconic with a fund of extraordinary stories. His arrival at our home was always anticipated with relish and I remember being very impressed by the long, sleek American cars that he used to arrive in. The deep note of the exhaust and the gravel that spat up from the rear wheels on his departure are memories that stick in my mind. Once he had his house, 'Goldeneye', in Jamaica we saw less of him but his visits lit up the family and were occasions filled with laughter.

I am sure that Ian would have revelled in the celebrity that is Bond today. The global success of the character is unique. I believe that, in creating his ruthless agent, he used his experiences during the war, his brilliant imagination and his sharp wit to set a template for a hero who has a universal fascination among all cultures, backgrounds and age groups.

BOND IN BOOKS

"The scent and smoke and sweat of a casino are nauseating at three in the morning."

With those evocative words began the literary career of secret agent James Bond, licensed to kill on behalf of Her Majesty's Government. Seated in front of a gold-plated typewriter in his house in Jamaica, agent 007's creator, Ian Lancaster Fleming, was busily thinking about anything other than his upcoming marriage to Ann Rothermere. He was forty-three years old, about to marry and have his first child. To keep his mind occupied he came up with *Casino Royale* and the world's ultimate escapist hero.

But where did Bond come from? Did he spring to life fully-formed from Fleming's imagination?

It's often said that Bond is Fleming's alter ego, and certainly many of Fleming's own experiences were absorbed into Bond's life. Ian was the second of four boys, born in May 1908 to Valentine and Eve Fleming. His father was elected MP for South Oxfordshire in 1910, and Fleming was initially brought up in Pitt House on Hampstead Heath.

As was customary in those days, Fleming was sent away to boarding school, and it was there that he first experienced the delights of adventure novels. The young boy devoured the exploits of Bulldog Drummond, Richard Hannay and Fu Manchu, alongside the more literary tales of Edgar Allan Poe and Robert Louis Stevenson. Fleming's life was changed when his father was killed in action in May 1917, and the author always kept a framed copy of Winston Churchill's obituary of his father from *The Times* beside him.

Although James Bond was only briefly at Eton (he was expelled for an offence concerning one of the domestic staff), his creator spent many years there, proving himself on the athletics field, if not in the classroom. He won the Victor Ludorum (literally, "Winner of the Games") prize two years in succession. From Eton, Fleming spent a brief time at the Military Academy at Sandhurst, but this wasn't to his taste. Life at the Kitzbühel in the Austrian Tyrol suited him far better, and he went on to study languages in Munich and Geneva.

At the age of twenty-three, Fleming tried to join the British Foreign Office, but was unsuccessful in the entrance examinations and found himself without a career. Wanting to work abroad, he joined the Reuters News Agency, and a few years later was sent to Moscow. This culminated in his coverage of one of the major espionage trials of 1933, involving a group of British engineers. Returning to London he changed track again, becoming a banker and stockbroker in the period leading up to the Second World War.

When war was declared in September 1939 Fleming was commissioned as a Lieutenant Commander in the Royal Navy Volunteer Reserves, and joined the Naval Intelligence Division. He became part of the team at Room 39 at the Admiralty as Personal Assistant to the Director of Naval Intelligence, Admiral John H. Godfrey, whose "damnably clear grey eyes" were only part of his model as Bond's superior, Admiral Sir Miles Messervy, alias M. Fleming became familiar with all aspects of naval intelligence, and played a key role co-ordinating the various elements of special intelligence to ensure the smooth running of the Allied campaigns.

During the war Fleming came into regular contact with the British Secret Intelligence Service, as well as the undercover operations of the Special Operations Executive. Stories abound of Fleming's experiences with members of these organisations, and certain incidents in which Fleming took part reappeared in the Bond canon, notably the sinking of a tanker by a mine placed underwater by Fleming himself.

Fleming and Admiral Godfrey also worked extensively with the American intelligence organisations, liaising regularly with William Stephenson and "Wild Bill" Donovan, men whose joint efforts would lead in the post-war world to the formation of America's formidable Central Intelligence Agency. Fleming also travelled around France, Spain and North Africa, and worked on the creation of Operation Golden Eye, the defence of the island of Gibraltar from a potential German attack.

One of Fleming's greatest contributions to the war effort was the organisation of the 30 Assault Unit, a detachment of intelligence personnel who would accompany troops on raids and concentrate on collecting cipher and weapon information. By the end of the war this unit had expanded to nearly four hundred and fifty people.

When the war ended Fleming returned to civilian life, and became foreign manager for Kemsley Newspapers. He had left Naval Intelligence determined to write 'the spy story to end all spy stories', and he mulled the various elements around in his mind until he sat down in January 1952 to begin. Fleming completed the novel in around two months, but didn't try to get it published for some time afterwards. When his friend William Plomer, who scrutinised manuscripts for UK publisher Jonathan Cape, read the book, he realised its potential, and it was accepted and published for the first time on 13th April 1953.

Fleming enjoyed life. He was a great collector of books, accumulating first editions of everything from Darwin's *On The Origin of Species* to the official rules of table tennis. He loved playing golf, driving fast and unusual cars, and eating. Like his creation, Fleming liked plain food, but of the highest quality. He also took great pleasure in the company of women, although he could be kind or callous as the mood took him.

James Bond took on a life of his own as the years went by. As Bond's popularity increased, there were numerous attempts to bring him into life in other formats. CBS Television in America produced a one hour adaptation of *Casino Royale*, taking a great many liberties with the original story. Bond becomes "Card Sharp Jimmy Bond", an American agent, and the treacherous Vesper Lynd amalgamates with Bond's Deuxième Bureau ally Rene Mathis to become Valerie Mathis. Only Peter Lorre's performance as Le Chiffre rescues the drama from total obscurity.

Fleming looked into the possibility of further adventures for Bond on television, and when these came to nothing he reworked the plots into the collection of short stories, *For Your Eyes Only*. Around the same time, he was approached by the *Daily Express*, who wanted to feature a comic strip adaptation of the novels. Fleming was initially reluctant, and his friend William Plomer advised him not to proceed. However the *Express*' editor, Edward Pickering, promised that the paper would deliver a "Rolls Royce" of a job, which overcame Fleming's objections.

The first strip, *Casino Royale*, appeared forty-five years ago in July 1958, and was adapted by the paper's literary editor, Anthony Hern. The novels, as well as three of the short stories, were adapted in publication order (omitting the unusual entry, *The Spy Who Loved Me*) by Hern's successor, Henry Gammidge, before he in turn handed the pen over to Jim Lawrence in time for the adaptation of *The Man With the Golden Gun* in 1966.

Fleming was sufficiently taken with the work on the comic strips that he acknowledged them obliquely in the later books, switching Bond's allegiance from *The Times* to the *Daily Express*. The paper provided a visual form for Bond for the first time, taking Fleming's description from the book and giving it life — predating Sean Connery's on-screen appearance by four years.

Lawrence's first two strips, illustrated by Yaroslav Horak, are reprinted in this volume. American author Lawrence didn't display the same reverence for Fleming's source material that his predecessor had shown, and his work adapting Fleming's stories paved the way for the original tales of 007 that he would begin writing two years later.

PAUL SIMPSON

THE MEN WITH THE GOLDEN PENS

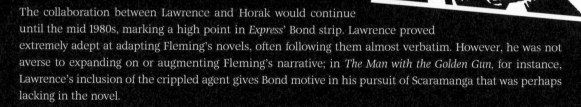

Yaroslav Horak was born in Manchuria (now part of the Republic of China), but later became an Australian citizen. Initially a portrait painter and comic strip writer for a Sidney publishing company, he then enjoyed success as an illustrator. Moving to Melbourne in 1952, he created a series called *The Mask*, which fell foul of Victoria state censors, and later *Mark Steel*, an outback adventure strip that ran daily in the *Sydney Morning Herald*. Horak then moved to London, where the *Daily Express* teamed him up with writer **Jim Lawrence** on the paper's ongoing James Bond strip.

Lawrence had begun his writing career scripting technical training films for the US Armed Forces. He soon graduated to newspaper strips, penning *Buck Rogers* for the National Newspaper Syndicate, before moving onto James Bond in 1963. He also managed to fit in numerous radio dramas and over forty books, including juvenile mystery and adventure stories.

The collaboration between Lawrence and Horak would continue until the mid 1980s, marking a high point in *Express*' Bond strip. Lawrence proved extremely adept at adapting Fleming's novels, often following them almost verbatim. However, he was not averse to expanding on or augmenting Fleming's narrative; in *The Man with the Golden Gun*, for instance, Lawrence's inclusion of the crippled agent gives Bond motive in his pursuit of Scaramanga that was perhaps lacking in the novel.

The duo debuted in the *Daily Express* in January 1966 on *The Man with the Golden Gun*, a mere nine months after the novel's publication in the UK. Their work represented a sharp change in the strip's style. Lawrence's writing toughened up Bond into a more ruthless incarnation of the agent. Horak's crisp and detailed artwork employed an almost cinematic style, using unusual angles and tight close-ups, bringing readers into the heart of the action.

Paradoxically, Horak's tight, angular, almost unreal line work ran counterpoint to panels that could look rough, even unfinished. His use of solid blacks was also considered unusual in its time, yet today gives his artwork a continued contemporary feel. But none of this ever detracted from his realistic portrayals of human figures and faces that gave Horak's art a heart and depth sometimes lacking in his contemporaries.

The duo's virtual reinvention of the Bond strip also portrayed violence more graphically than had previously been seen in newspaper strips, but was in keeping with the trend growing in cinema at the time. The strips hardened, became more gritty and their characterisation more complex. In essence, Lawrence and Horak brought Bond closer to Fleming's concept, even as Lawrence's stories began to diverge from their literary origins.

This last factor did not seem to trouble the public, with readers and critics heaping considerable praise on Lawrence and Horak's work. However, the ultimate accolade must surely have been that from the Fleming Trust who, impressed by Lawrence's writing, gave him permission to generate original stories for the *Express*. Praise from Caesar indeed.

THE MAN WITH THE GOLDEN GUN

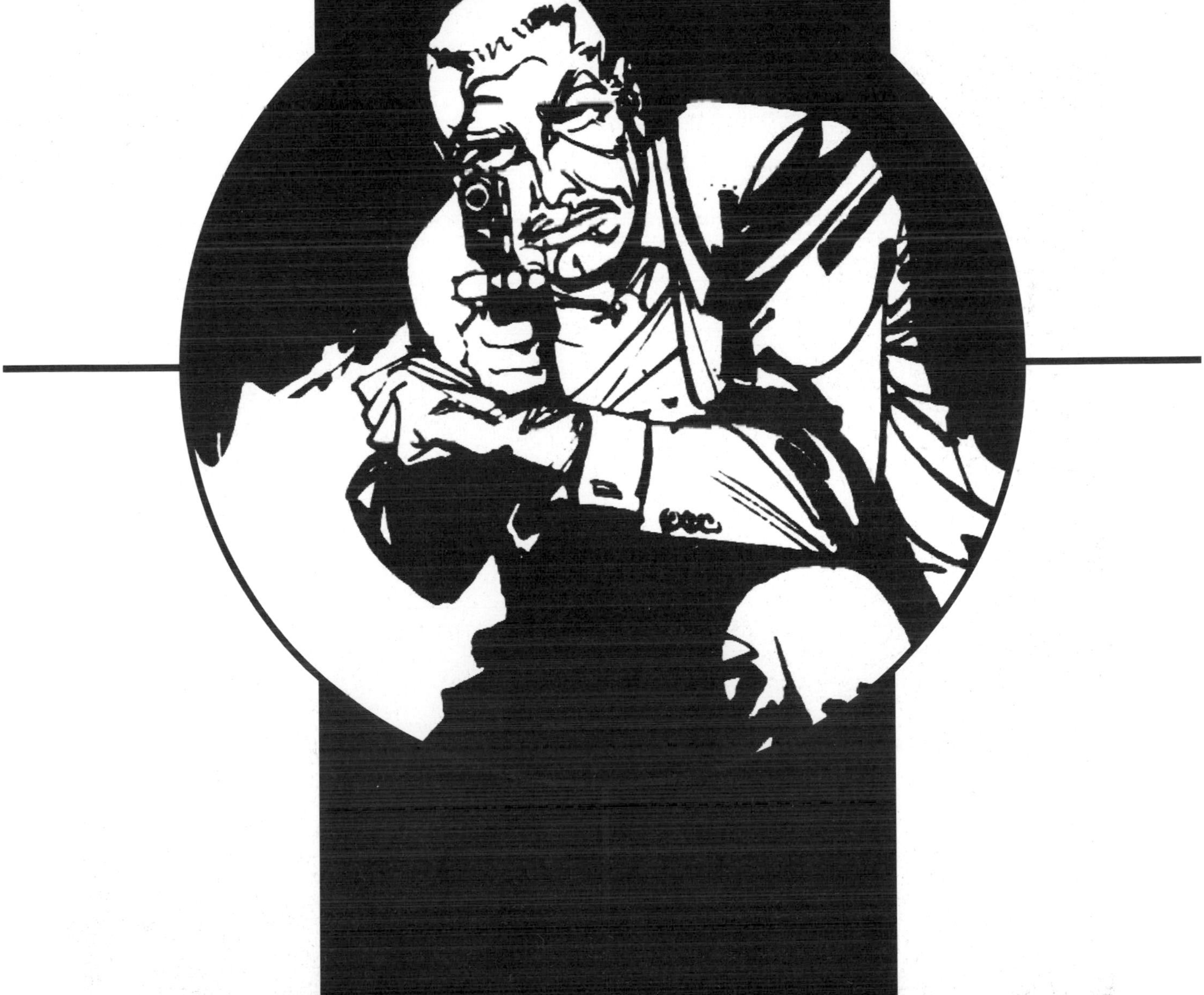

PAN books X527
JAMES BOND
THE MAN WITH THE GOLDEN GUN
BY IAN FLEMING
ALL OVER THE WORLD
NAME Scaramanga

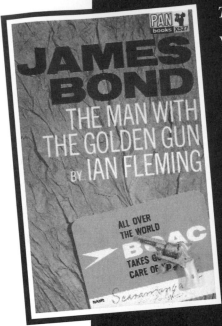

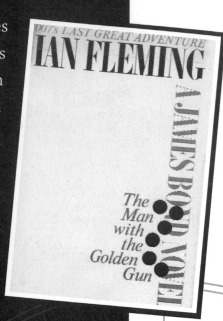

The Man With the Golden Gun combines various elements from Ian Fleming's previous stories, and features a villain who amounts to little more than a sadistic hoodlum, quite unlike the megalomaniac Auric Goldfingers or Ernst Stavro Blofelds of previous books. The novel's Francisco Scaramanga certainly bears little resemblance to the urbane 'Anti-Bond' of the 1974 film. Lawrence adds the complete subplot at the start of the tale regarding Bond's fellow patient at The Park, which adds to Scaramanga's potency as a villain, as well as giving Bond a personal reason for going after the gunman. Lawrence also adds the femme fatale of 'Taj' Mahal, foreshadowing some of the less subtle names that would join the ranks of the Bond girls in the years to come.

007's LAST GREAT ADVENTURE
IAN FLEMING
A JAMES BOND NOVEL
The Man with the Golden Gun

PREVIOUSLY...

James Bond
BY IAN FLEMING
DRAWING BY HORAK
FRIENDLESS, UNARMED, WITHOUT EVEN A MEMORY, JAMES BOND PICKED HIS WAY NORTH — CLINGING DESPERATELY TO THE ONLY TWO WORDS HE KNEW THAT CONNECTED HIM TO HIS PAST...
V-L-A-D-I-V-O-S-T-O-K! R-U-S-S-I-A... R-U-S-S-I-A!
THESE TWO WORDS WOULD, HE KNEW, SOMEHOW BRING ALIVE AGAIN THE LIFE HE COULD NOT REMEMBER...
...AND THEY DID!
SEE HOW—IN THE GREAT NEW BOND STORY THAT BEGINS ON MONDAY!
475

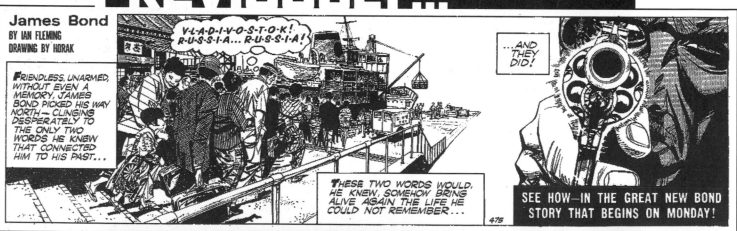

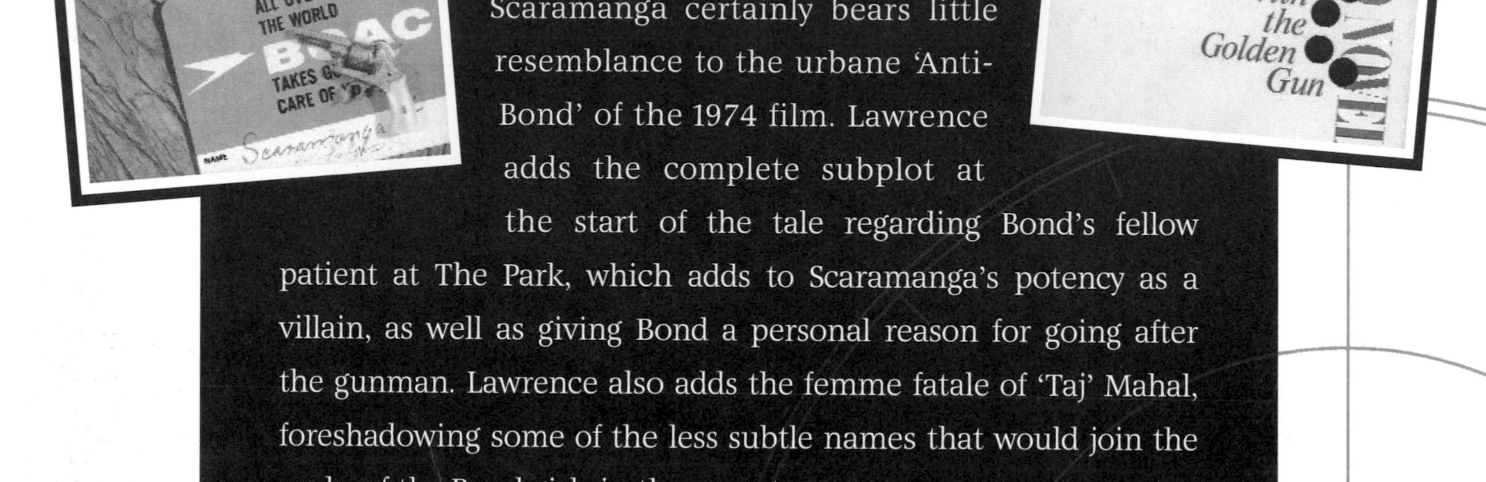

At the end of *You Only Live Twice*, Bond has amnesia, as a result of a fall during his final battle with Blofeld. On the Japanese island where he is living with Kissy Suzuki, he discovers a piece of paper with one simple word, Vladivostok, on it...

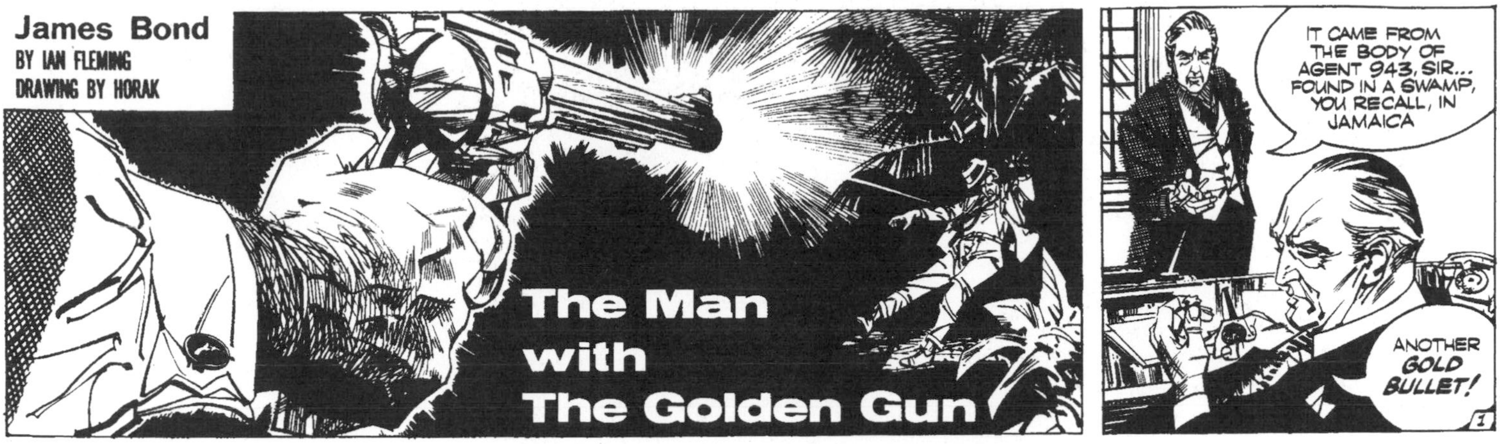
James Bond
BY IAN FLEMING
DRAWING BY HORAK
The Man with The Golden Gun
IT CAME FROM THE BODY OF AGENT 943, SIR... FOUND IN A SWAMP, YOU RECALL, IN JAMAICA
ANOTHER GOLD BULLET!
1

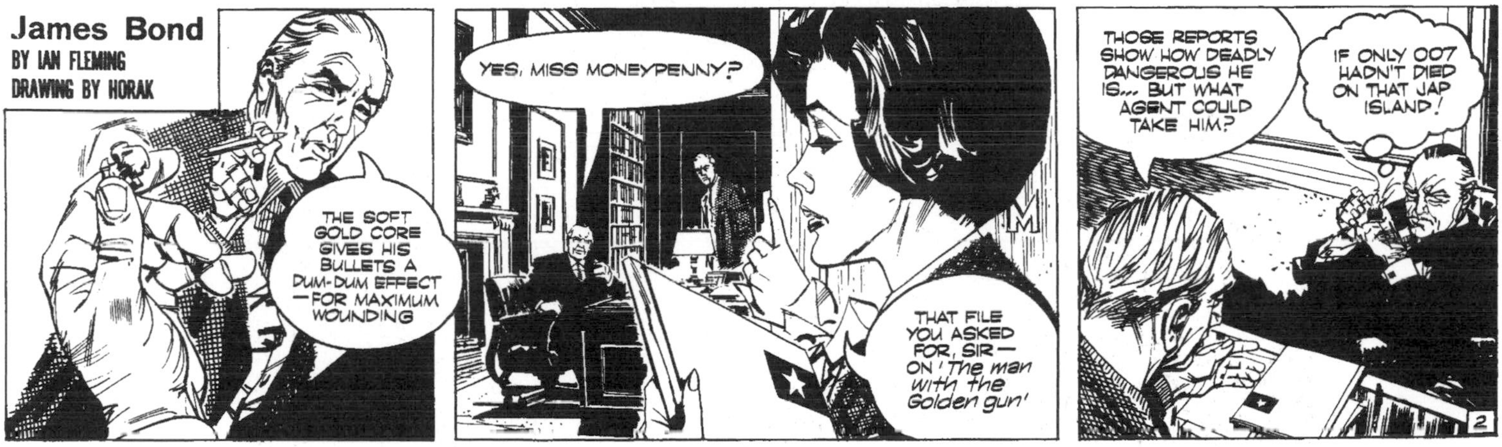
James Bond
BY IAN FLEMING
DRAWING BY HORAK
THE SOFT GOLD CORE GIVES HIS BULLETS A DUM-DUM EFFECT —FOR MAXIMUM WOUNDING
YES, MISS MONEYPENNY?
THAT FILE YOU ASKED FOR, SIR — ON 'The man with the Golden gun'
THOSE REPORTS SHOW HOW DEADLY DANGEROUS HE IS... BUT WHAT AGENT COULD TAKE HIM?
IF ONLY 007 HADN'T DIED ON THAT JAP ISLAND!
2

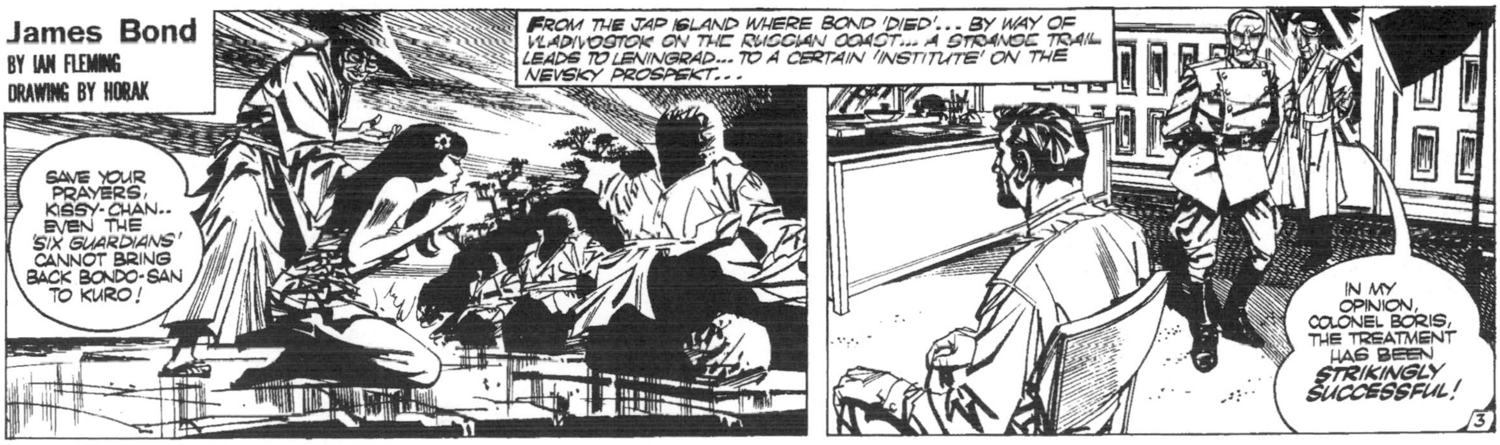
James Bond
BY IAN FLEMING
DRAWING BY HORAK
FROM THE JAP ISLAND WHERE BOND 'DIED'... BY WAY OF VLADIVOSTOK ON THE RUSSIAN COAST... A STRANGE TRAIL LEADS TO LENINGRAD... TO A CERTAIN 'INSTITUTE' ON THE NEVSKY PROSPEKT...
SAVE YOUR PRAYERS, KISSY-CHAN.. EVEN THE 'SIX GUARDIANS' CANNOT BRING BACK BONDO-SAN TO KURO!
IN MY OPINION, COLONEL BORIS, THE TREATMENT HAS BEEN STRIKINGLY SUCCESSFUL!
3

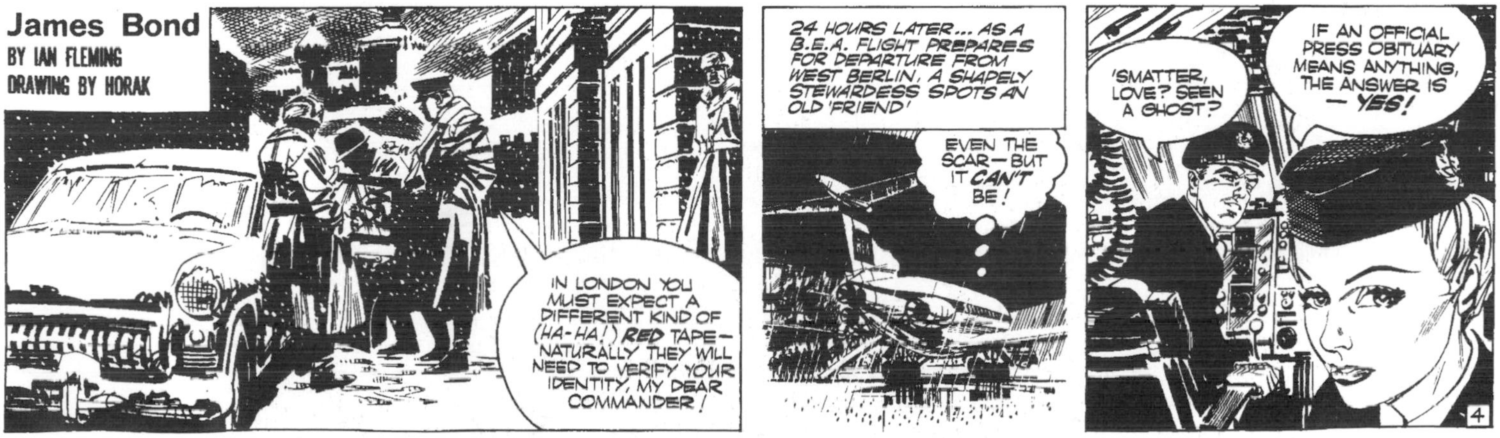
James Bond
BY IAN FLEMING
DRAWING BY HORAK
IN LONDON YOU MUST EXPECT A DIFFERENT KIND OF (HA-HA!) RED TAPE— NATURALLY THEY WILL NEED TO VERIFY YOUR IDENTITY, MY DEAR COMMANDER!
24 HOURS LATER... AS A B.E.A. FLIGHT PREPARES FOR DEPARTURE FROM WEST BERLIN, A SHAPELY STEWARDESS SPOTS AN OLD 'FRIEND'
EVEN THE SCAR—BUT IT CAN'T BE!
'SMATTER, LOVE? SEEN A GHOST?
IF AN OFFICIAL PRESS OBITUARY MEANS ANYTHING, THE ANSWER IS — YES!
4

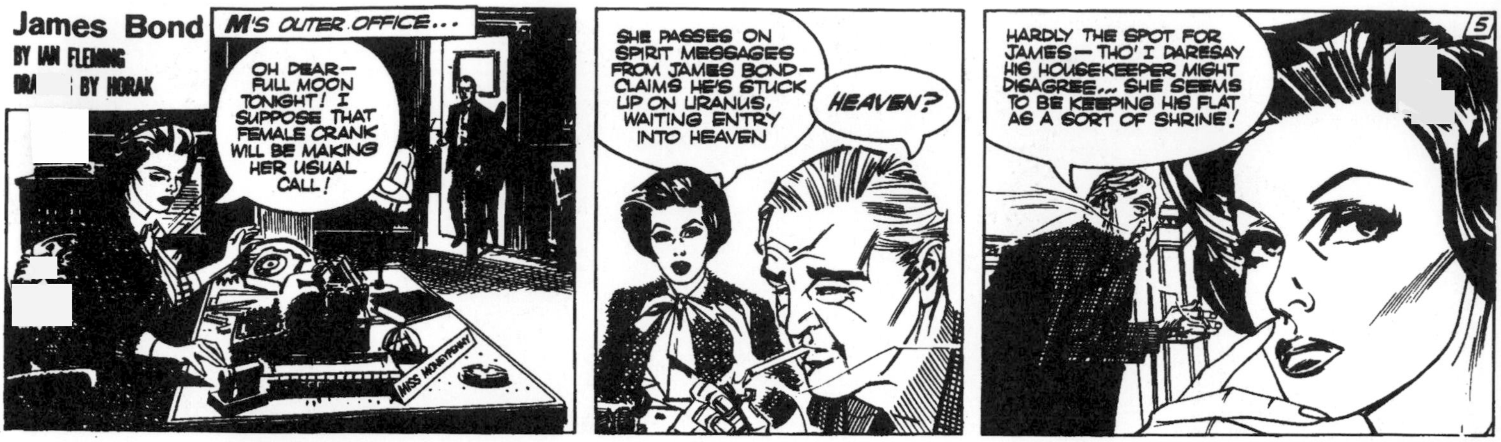
James Bond
BY IAN FLEMING
DRA BY HORAK
M'S OUTER OFFICE...
OH DEAR—FULL MOON TONIGHT! I SUPPOSE THAT FEMALE CRANK WILL BE MAKING HER USUAL CALL!
MISS MONEYPENNY
SHE PASSES ON SPIRIT MESSAGES FROM JAMES BOND—CLAIMS HE'S STUCK UP ON URANUS, WAITING ENTRY INTO HEAVEN
HEAVEN?
5
HARDLY THE SPOT FOR JAMES—THO' I DARESAY HIS HOUSEKEEPER MIGHT DISAGREE... SHE SEEMS TO BE KEEPING HIS FLAT AS A SORT OF SHRINE!

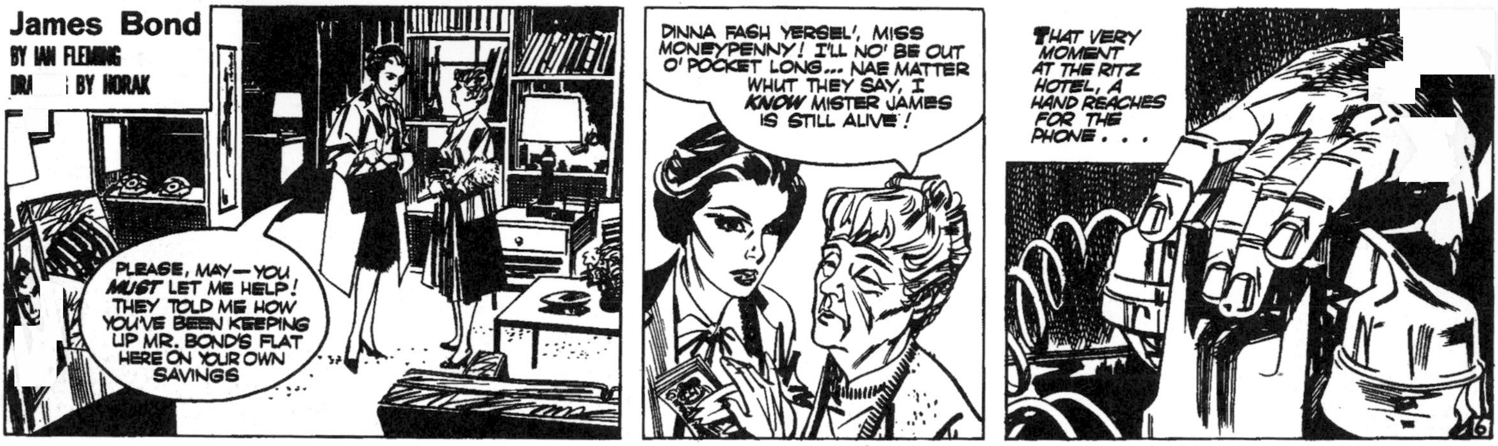
James Bond
BY IAN FLEMING
DRA BY HORAK
PLEASE, MAY—YOU MUST LET ME HELP! THEY TOLD ME HOW YOU'VE BEEN KEEPING UP MR. BOND'S FLAT HERE ON YOUR OWN SAVINGS
DINNA FASH YERSEL', MISS MONEYPENNY! I'LL NO' BE OUT O' POCKET LONG... NAE MATTER WHUT THEY SAY, I KNOW MISTER JAMES IS STILL ALIVE!
THAT VERY MOMENT AT THE RITZ HOTEL, A HAND REACHES FOR THE PHONE . . .
6

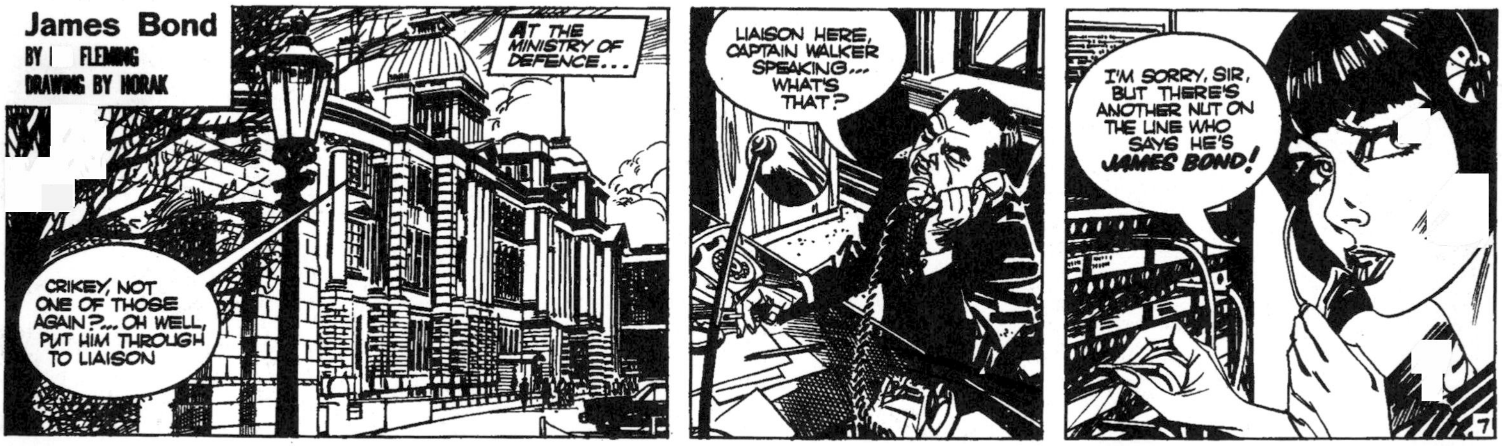
James Bond
BY I FLEMING
DRAWING BY HORAK
AT THE MINISTRY OF DEFENCE...
CRIKEY, NOT ONE OF THOSE AGAIN?... OH WELL, PUT HIM THROUGH TO LIAISON
LIAISON HERE, CAPTAIN WALKER SPEAKING... WHAT'S THAT?
I'M SORRY, SIR, BUT THERE'S ANOTHER NUT ON THE LINE WHO SAYS HE'S JAMES BOND!
7

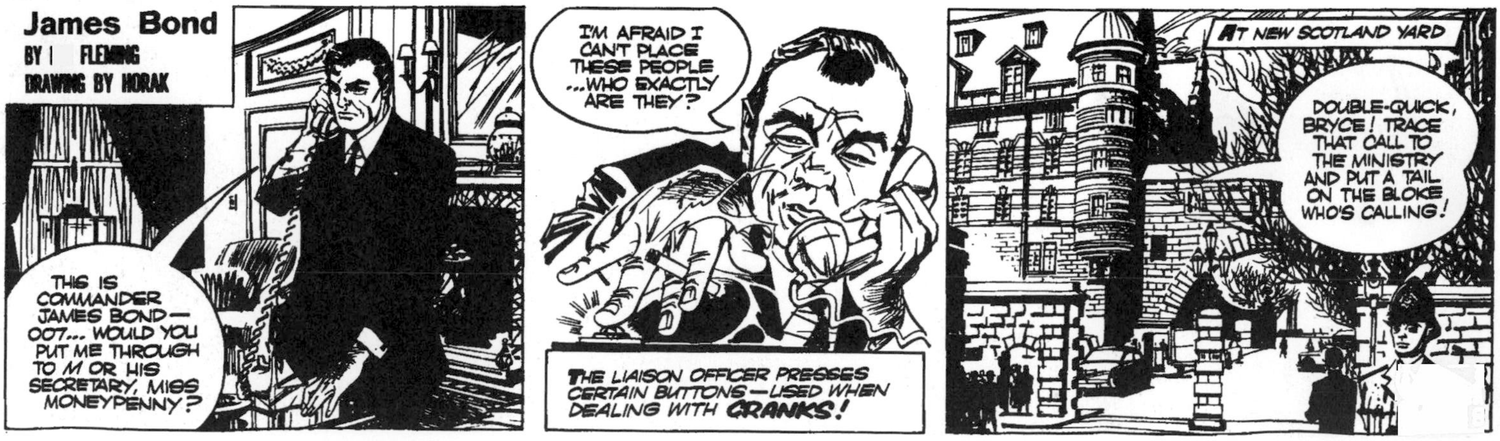
James Bond
BY I FLEMING
DRAWING BY HORAK
THIS IS COMMANDER JAMES BOND—007... WOULD YOU PUT ME THROUGH TO M OR HIS SECRETARY, MISS MONEYPENNY?
I'M AFRAID I CAN'T PLACE THESE PEOPLE ...WHO EXACTLY ARE THEY?
THE LIAISON OFFICER PRESSES CERTAIN BUTTONS—USED WHEN DEALING WITH CRANKS!
AT NEW SCOTLAND YARD
DOUBLE-QUICK, BRYCE! TRACE THAT CALL TO THE MINISTRY AND PUT A TAIL ON THE BLOKE WHO'S CALLING!

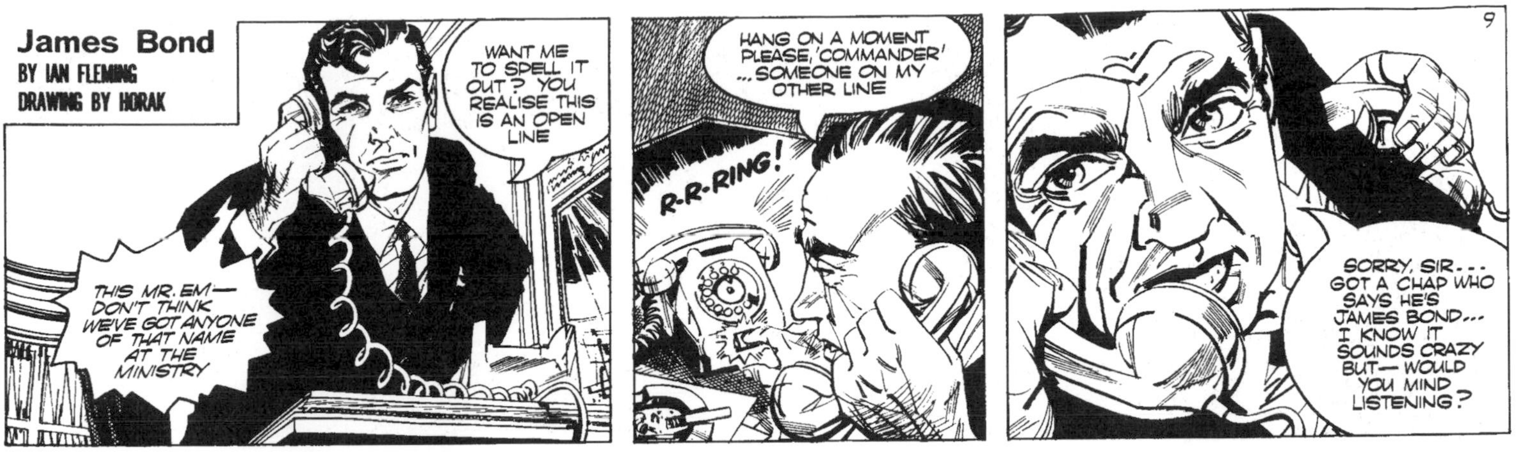
James Bond
BY IAN FLEMING
DRAWING BY HORAK
WANT ME TO SPELL IT OUT? YOU REALISE THIS IS AN OPEN LINE
THIS MR. EM— DON'T THINK WE'VE GOT ANYONE OF THAT NAME AT THE MINISTRY
HANG ON A MOMENT PLEASE, 'COMMANDER' ...SOMEONE ON MY OTHER LINE
R-R-RING!
9
SORRY, SIR--- GOT A CHAP WHO SAYS HE'S JAMES BOND... I KNOW IT SOUNDS CRAZY BUT— WOULD YOU MIND LISTENING?

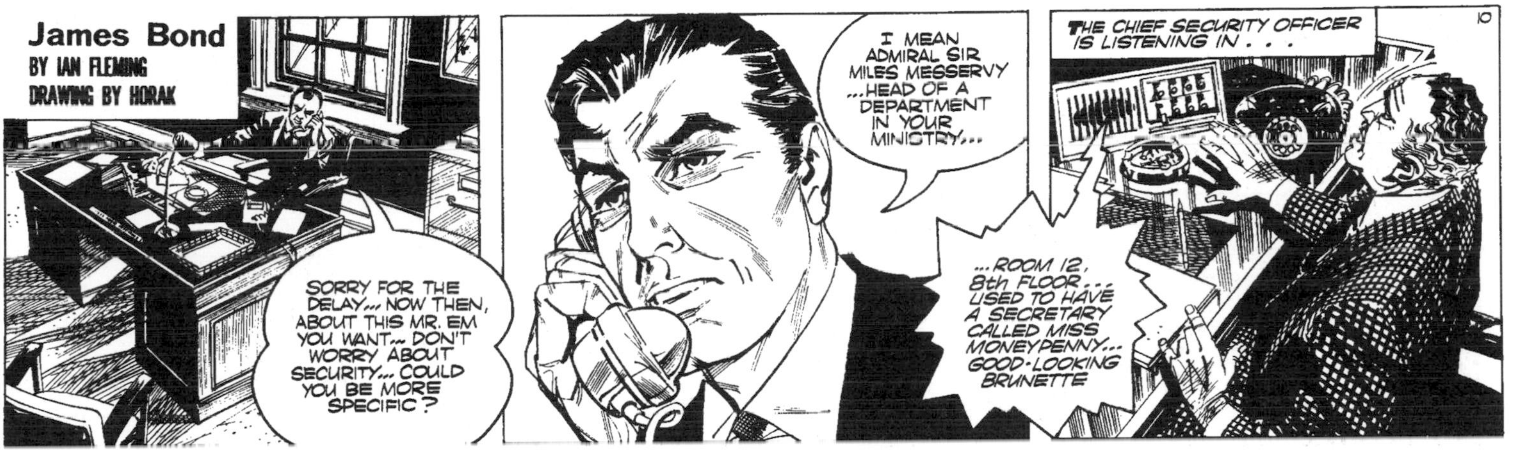
James Bond
BY IAN FLEMING
DRAWING BY HORAK
SORRY FOR THE DELAY... NOW THEN, ABOUT THIS MR. EM YOU WANT... DON'T WORRY ABOUT SECURITY... COULD YOU BE MORE SPECIFIC?
I MEAN ADMIRAL SIR MILES MESSERVY ...HEAD OF A DEPARTMENT IN YOUR MINISTRY...
10
THE CHIEF SECURITY OFFICER IS LISTENING IN . . .
...ROOM 12, 8th FLOOR... USED TO HAVE A SECRETARY CALLED MISS MONEYPENNY... GOOD-LOOKING BRUNETTE

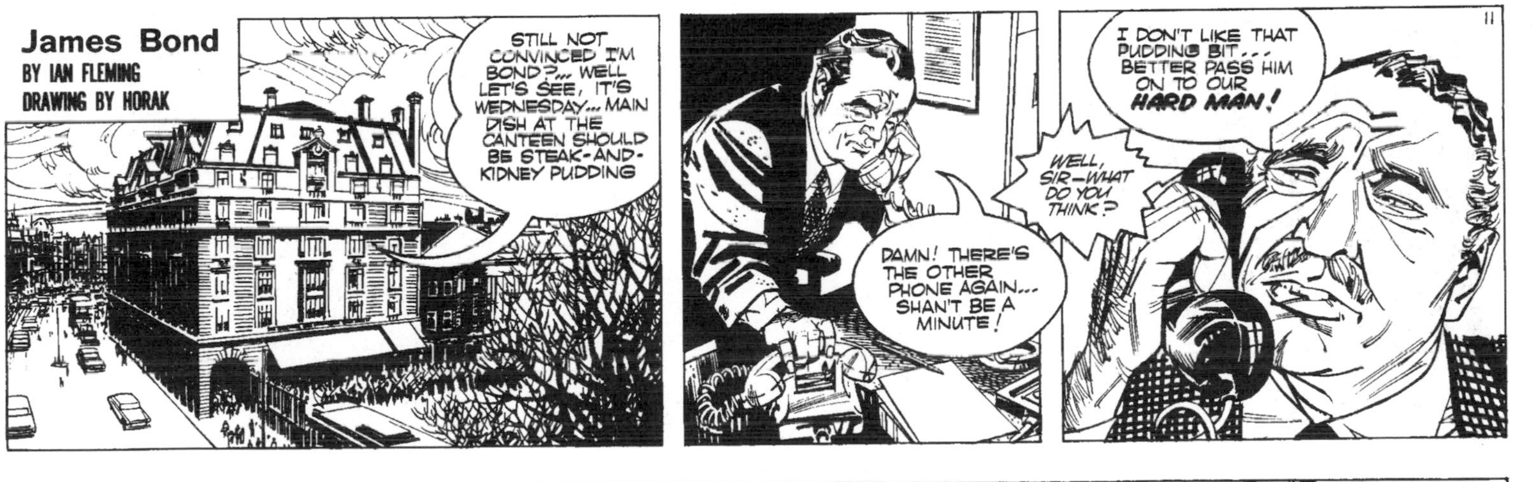
James Bond
BY IAN FLEMING
DRAWING BY HORAK
STILL NOT CONVINCED I'M BOND?... WELL LET'S SEE, IT'S WEDNESDAY... MAIN DISH AT THE CANTEEN SHOULD BE STEAK-AND-KIDNEY PUDDING
DAMN! THERE'S THE OTHER PHONE AGAIN... SHAN'T BE A MINUTE!
11
WELL, SIR—WHAT DO YOU THINK?
I DON'T LIKE THAT PUDDING BIT... BETTER PASS HIM ON TO OUR HARD MAN!

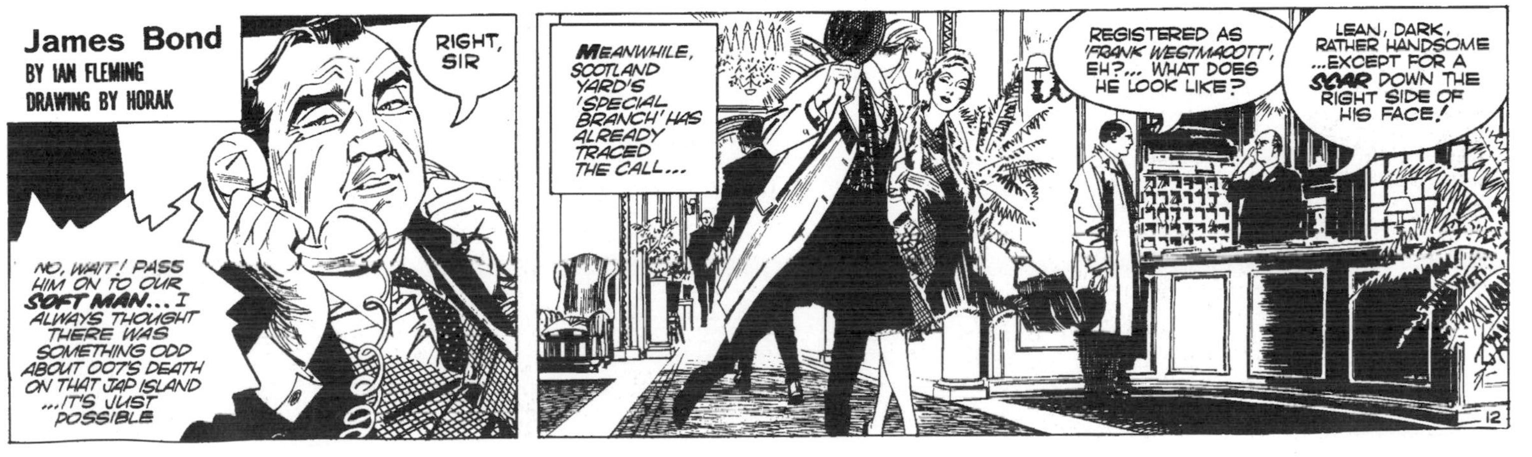
James Bond
BY IAN FLEMING
DRAWING BY HORAK
RIGHT, SIR
NO, WAIT! PASS HIM ON TO OUR SOFT MAN... I ALWAYS THOUGHT THERE WAS SOMETHING ODD ABOUT 007'S DEATH ON THAT JAP ISLAND ...IT'S JUST POSSIBLE
MEANWHILE, SCOTLAND YARD'S 'SPECIAL BRANCH' HAS ALREADY TRACED THE CALL...
REGISTERED AS 'FRANK WESTMACOTT', EH?... WHAT DOES HE LOOK LIKE?
LEAN, DARK, RATHER HANDSOME ...EXCEPT FOR A SCAR DOWN THE RIGHT SIDE OF HIS FACE!
12

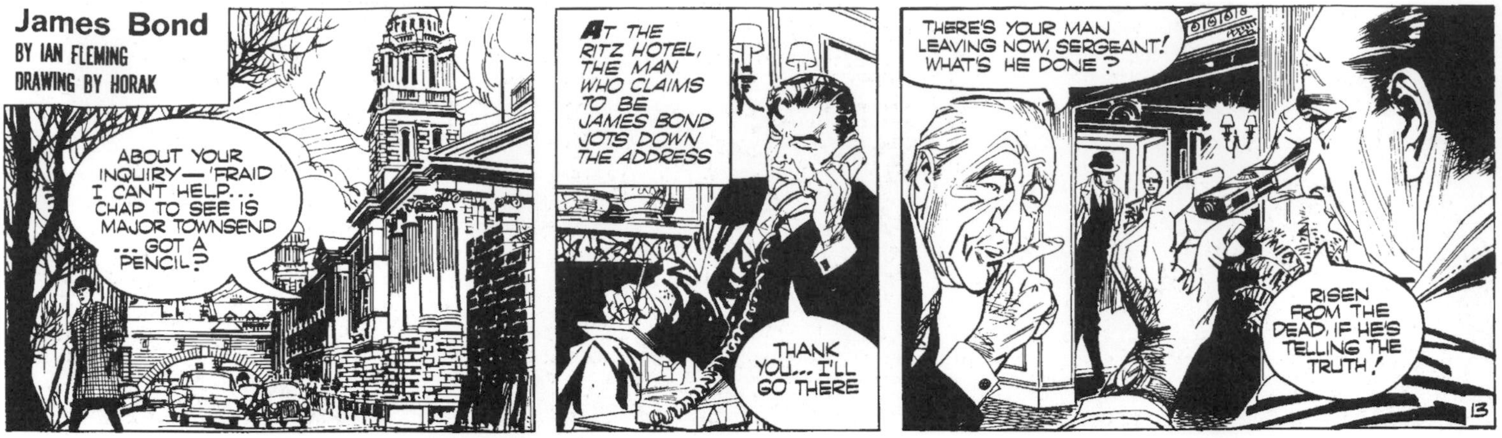
James Bond
BY IAN FLEMING
DRAWING BY HORAK
ABOUT YOUR INQUIRY—'FRAID I CAN'T HELP... CHAP TO SEE IS MAJOR TOWNSEND ... GOT A PENCIL?
AT THE RITZ HOTEL, THE MAN WHO CLAIMS TO BE JAMES BOND JOTS DOWN THE ADDRESS
THANK YOU... I'LL GO THERE
THERE'S YOUR MAN LEAVING NOW, SERGEANT! WHAT'S HE DONE?
RISEN FROM THE DEAD, IF HE'S TELLING THE TRUTH!
13

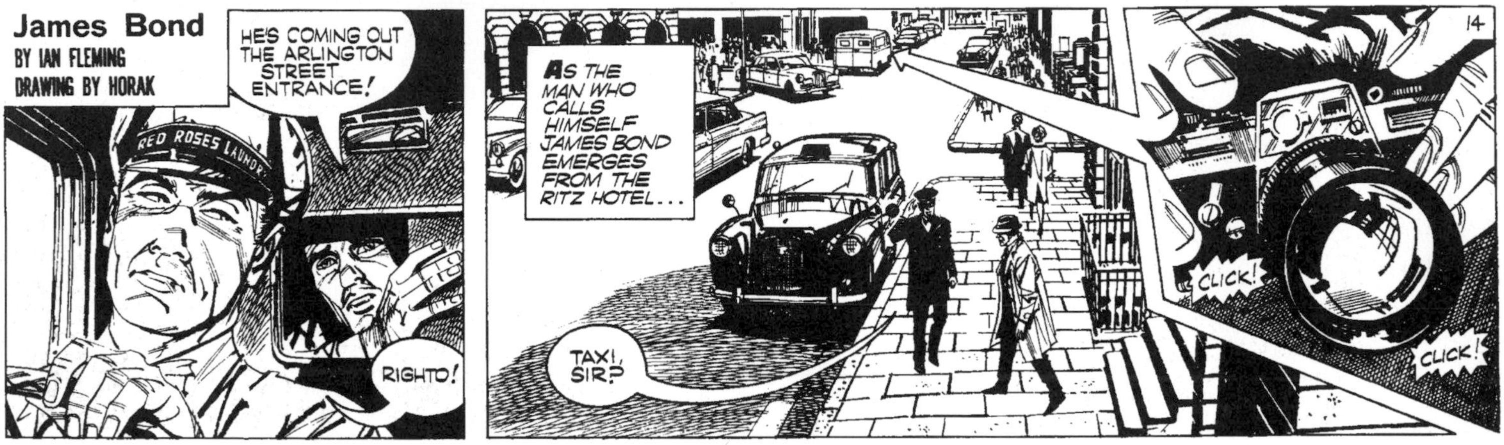
James Bond
BY IAN FLEMING
DRAWING BY HORAK
HE'S COMING OUT THE ARLINGTON STREET ENTRANCE!
RED ROSES LAUNDRY
RIGHTO!
AS THE MAN WHO CALLS HIMSELF JAMES BOND EMERGES FROM THE RITZ HOTEL...
TAXI!, SIR?
14
CLICK!
CLICK!

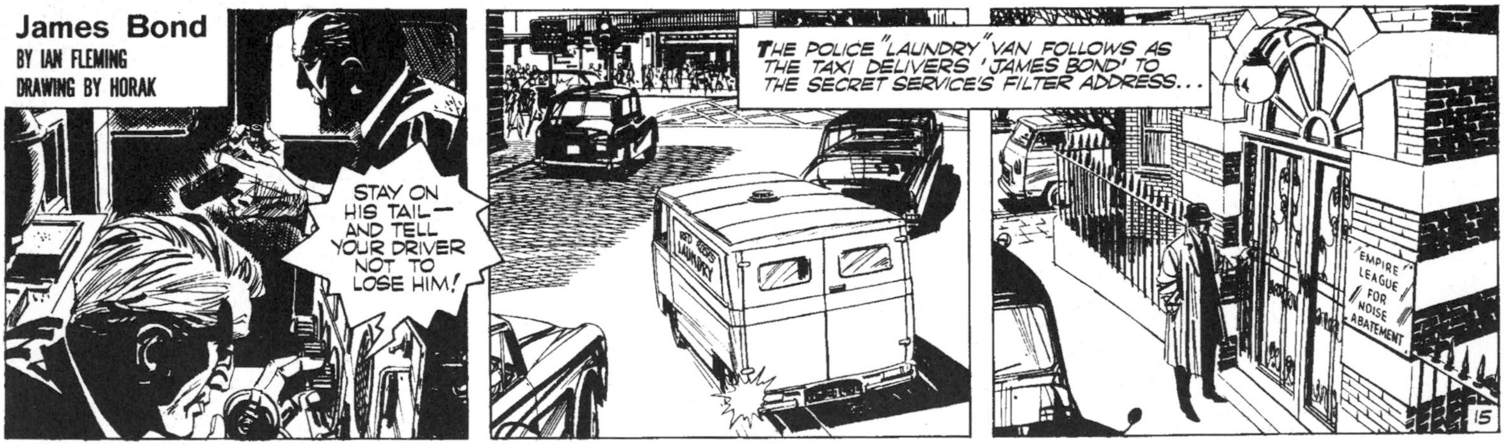
James Bond
BY IAN FLEMING
DRAWING BY HORAK
STAY ON HIS TAIL—AND TELL YOUR DRIVER NOT TO LOSE HIM!
THE POLICE "LAUNDRY" VAN FOLLOWS AS THE TAXI DELIVERS 'JAMES BOND' TO THE SECRET SERVICE'S FILTER ADDRESS...
EMPIRE LEAGUE FOR NOISE ABATEMENT
15

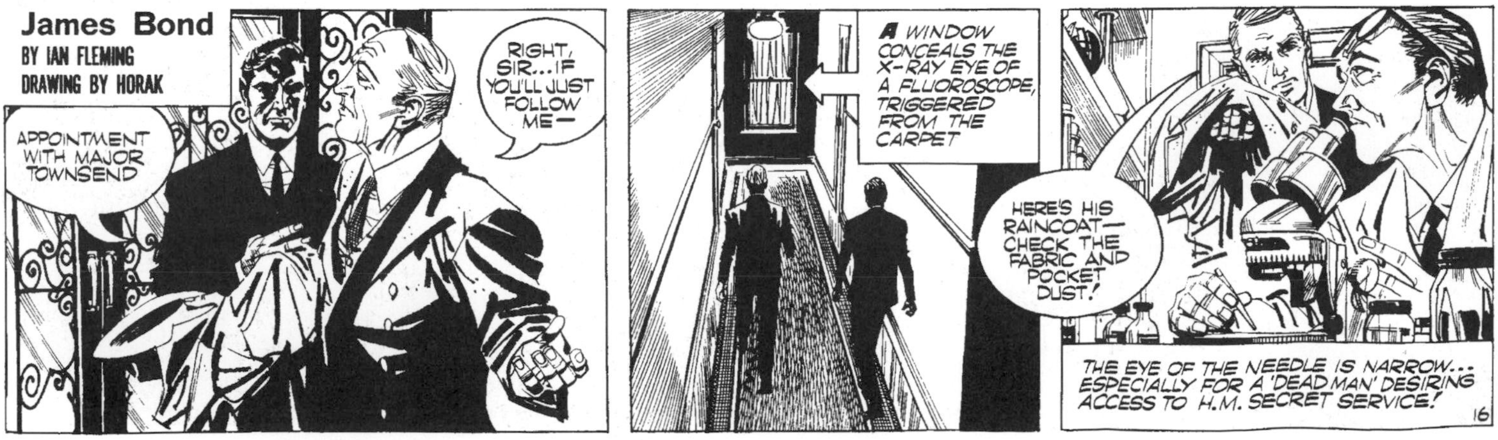
James Bond
BY IAN FLEMING
DRAWING BY HORAK
APPOINTMENT WITH MAJOR TOWNSEND
RIGHT, SIR... IF YOU'LL JUST FOLLOW ME—
A WINDOW CONCEALS THE X-RAY EYE OF A FLUOROSCOPE, TRIGGERED FROM THE CARPET
HERE'S HIS RAINCOAT—CHECK THE FABRIC AND POCKET DUST!
THE EYE OF THE NEEDLE IS NARROW... ESPECIALLY FOR A 'DEAD MAN' DESIRING ACCESS TO H.M. SECRET SERVICE!
16

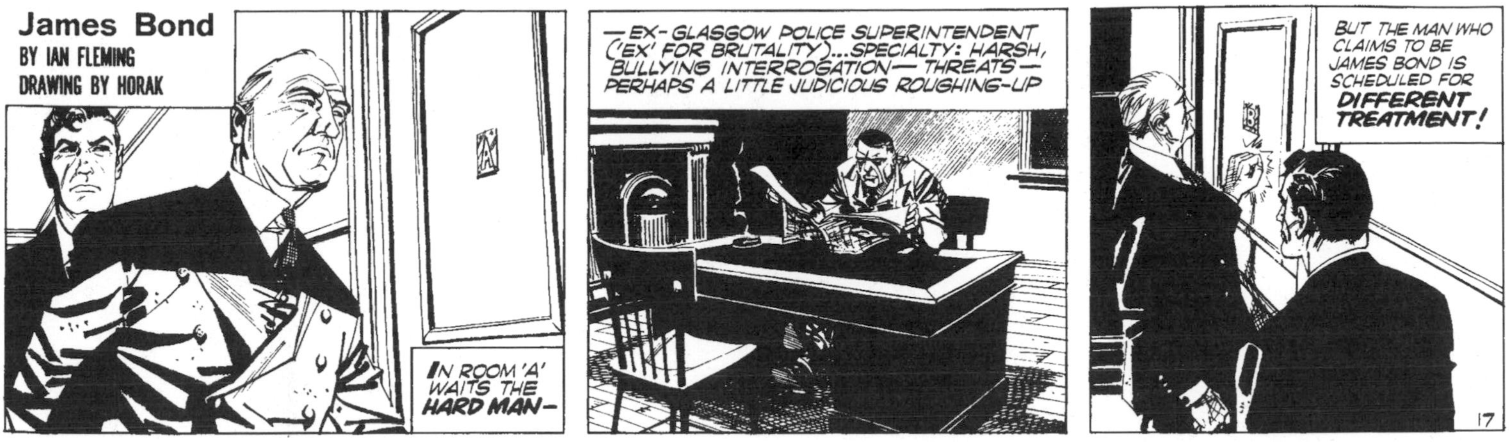
James Bond
BY IAN FLEMING
DRAWING BY HORAK
IN ROOM 'A' WAITS THE HARD MAN—
—EX-GLASGOW POLICE SUPERINTENDENT ('EX' FOR BRUTALITY)...SPECIALTY: HARSH, BULLYING INTERROGATION— THREATS— PERHAPS A LITTLE JUDICIOUS ROUGHING-UP
BUT THE MAN WHO CLAIMS TO BE JAMES BOND IS SCHEDULED FOR DIFFERENT TREATMENT!
17

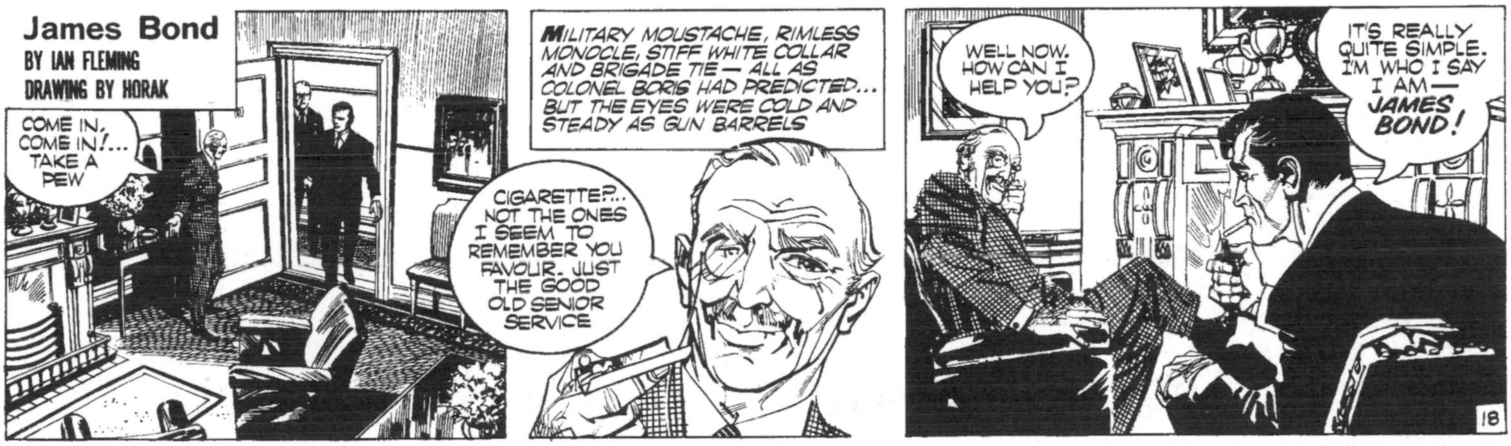
James Bond
BY IAN FLEMING
DRAWING BY HORAK
COME IN, COME IN!... TAKE A PEW
MILITARY MOUSTACHE, RIMLESS MONOCLE, STIFF WHITE COLLAR AND BRIGADE TIE— ALL AS COLONEL BORIS HAD PREDICTED... BUT THE EYES WERE COLD AND STEADY AS GUN BARRELS
CIGARETTE?... NOT THE ONES I SEEM TO REMEMBER YOU FAVOUR. JUST THE GOOD OLD SENIOR SERVICE
WELL NOW. HOW CAN I HELP YOU?
IT'S REALLY QUITE SIMPLE. I'M WHO I SAY I AM— JAMES BOND!
18

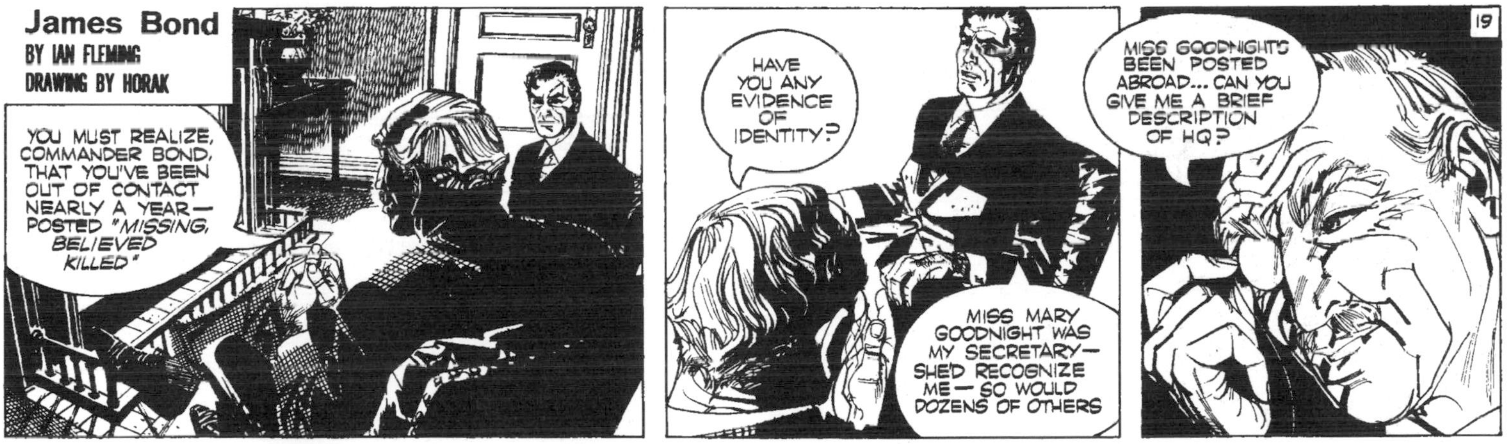
James Bond
BY IAN FLEMING
DRAWING BY HORAK
YOU MUST REALIZE, COMMANDER BOND, THAT YOU'VE BEEN OUT OF CONTACT NEARLY A YEAR— POSTED "MISSING, BELIEVED KILLED"
HAVE YOU ANY EVIDENCE OF IDENTITY?
MISS MARY GOODNIGHT WAS MY SECRETARY— SHE'D RECOGNIZE ME— SO WOULD DOZENS OF OTHERS
19
MISS GOODNIGHT'S BEEN POSTED ABROAD... CAN YOU GIVE ME A BRIEF DESCRIPTION OF HQ?

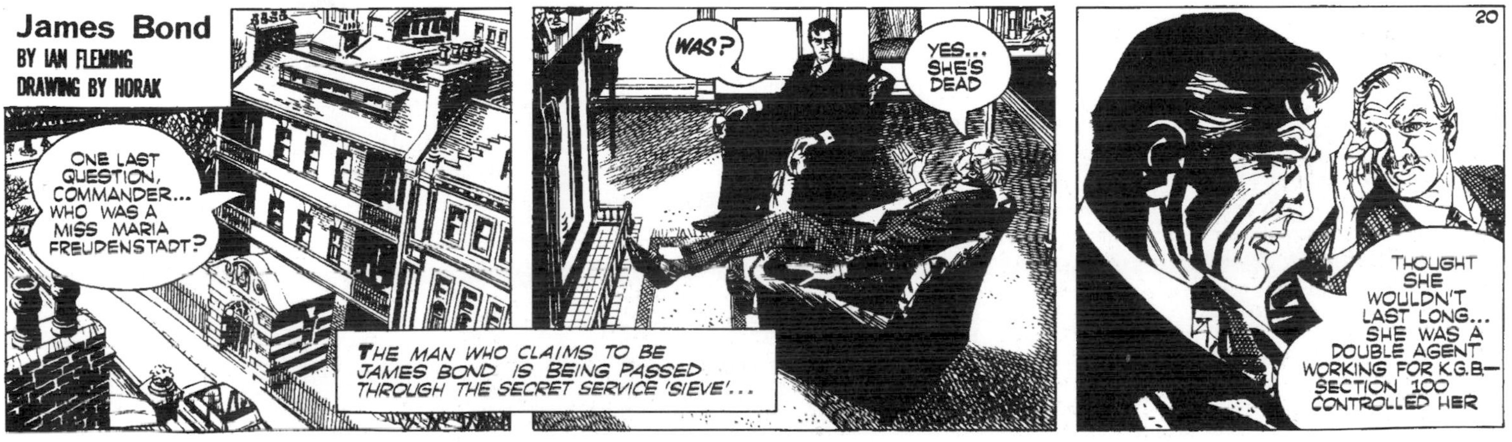
James Bond
BY IAN FLEMING
DRAWING BY HORAK
ONE LAST QUESTION, COMMANDER... WHO WAS A MISS MARIA FREUDENSTADT?
WAS?
YES... SHE'S DEAD
THE MAN WHO CLAIMS TO BE JAMES BOND IS BEING PASSED THROUGH THE SECRET SERVICE 'SIEVE'...
20
THOUGHT SHE WOULDN'T LAST LONG... SHE WAS A DOUBLE AGENT WORKING FOR K.G.B.— SECTION 100 CONTROLLED HER

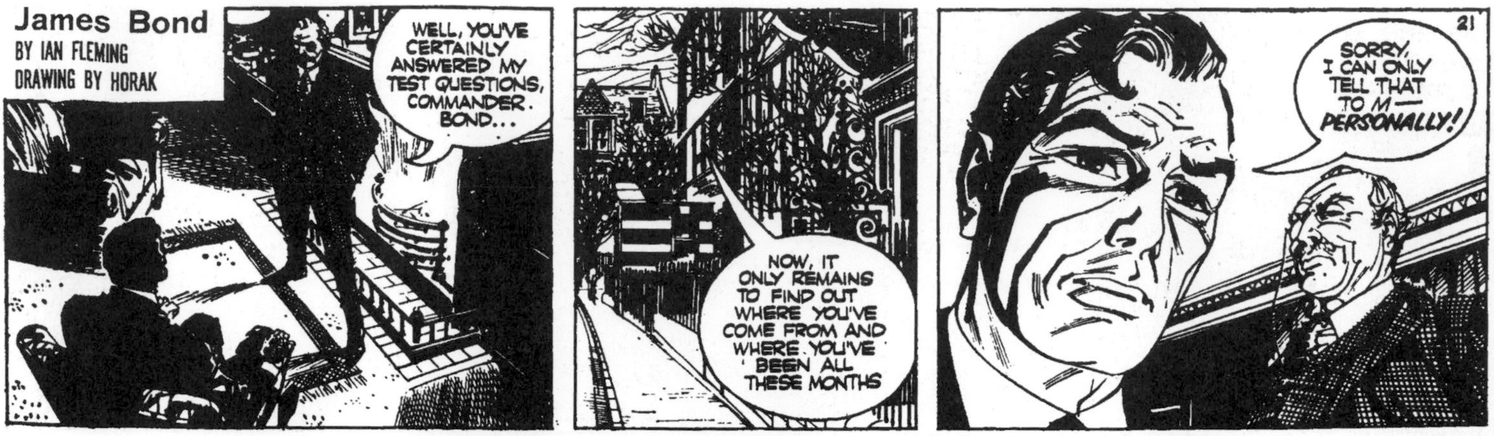
James Bond
BY IAN FLEMING
DRAWING BY HORAK
WELL, YOU'VE CERTAINLY ANSWERED MY TEST QUESTIONS, COMMANDER BOND...
NOW, IT ONLY REMAINS TO FIND OUT WHERE YOU'VE COME FROM AND WHERE YOU'VE BEEN ALL THESE MONTHS
21
SORRY, I CAN ONLY TELL THAT TO M— *PERSONALLY!*

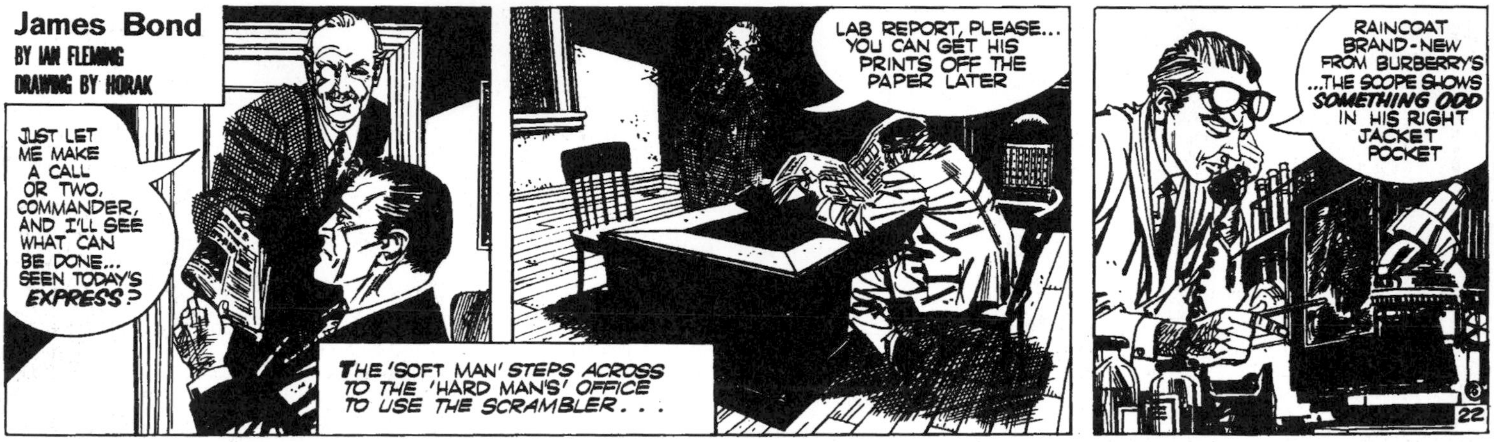
James Bond
BY IAN FLEMING
DRAWING BY HORAK
JUST LET ME MAKE A CALL OR TWO, COMMANDER, AND I'LL SEE WHAT CAN BE DONE... SEEN TODAY'S *EXPRESS*?
THE 'SOFT MAN' STEPS ACROSS TO THE 'HARD MAN'S' OFFICE TO USE THE SCRAMBLER . . .
LAB REPORT, PLEASE... YOU CAN GET HIS PRINTS OFF THE PAPER LATER
RAINCOAT BRAND-NEW FROM BURBERRY'S ...THE SCOPE SHOWS *SOMETHING ODD* IN HIS RIGHT JACKET POCKET
22

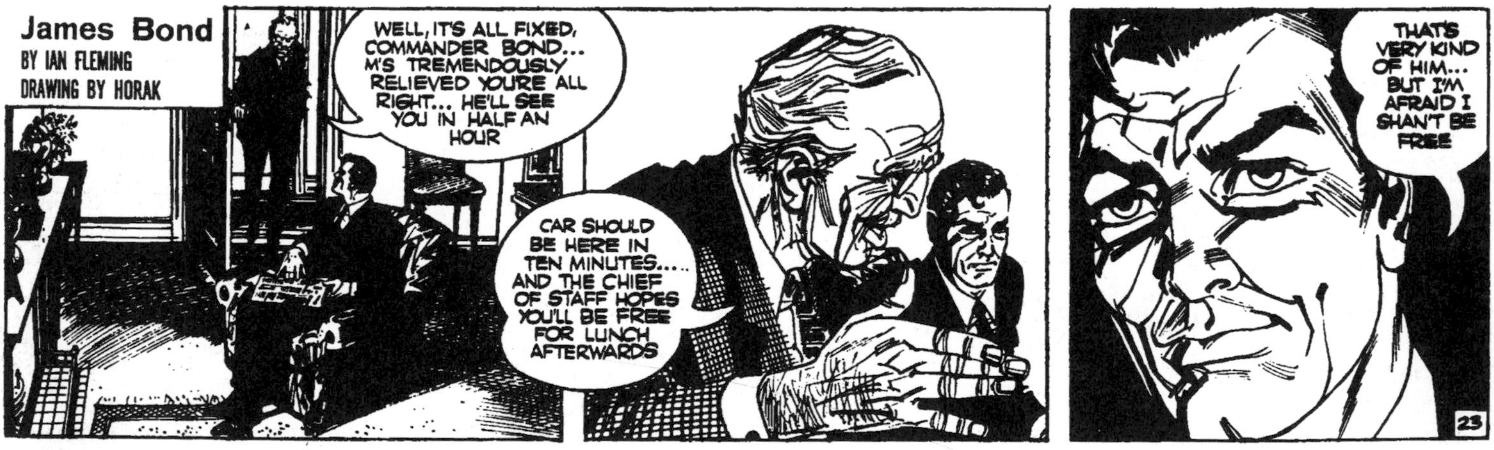
James Bond
BY IAN FLEMING
DRAWING BY HORAK
WELL, IT'S ALL FIXED, COMMANDER BOND... M'S TREMENDOUSLY RELIEVED YOU'RE ALL RIGHT... HE'LL SEE YOU IN HALF AN HOUR
CAR SHOULD BE HERE IN TEN MINUTES.... AND THE CHIEF OF STAFF HOPES YOU'LL BE FREE FOR LUNCH AFTERWARDS
THAT'S VERY KIND OF HIM... BUT I'M AFRAID I SHAN'T BE FREE
23

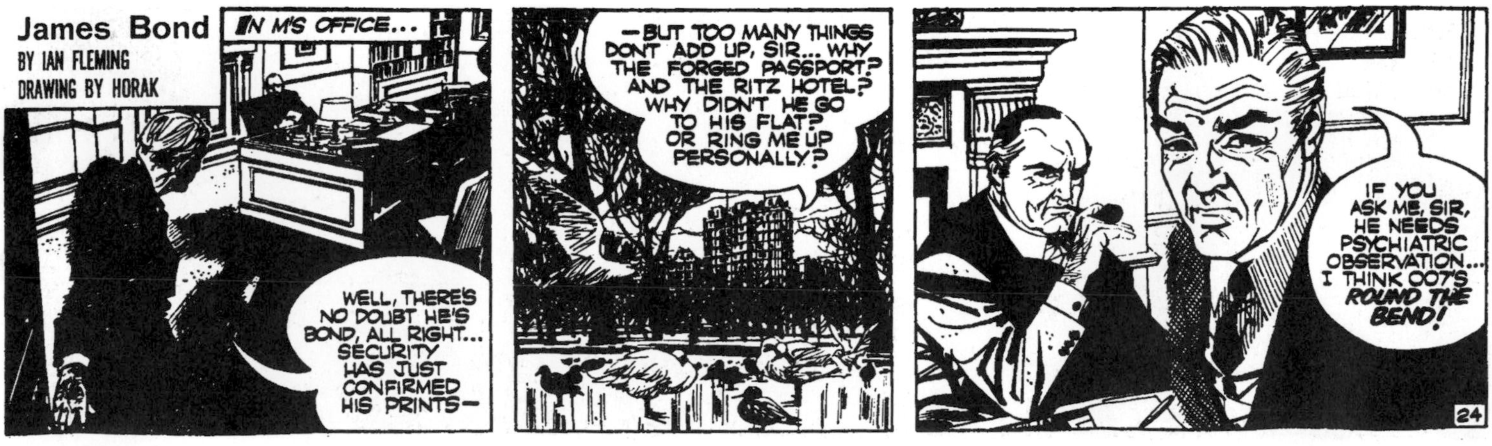
James Bond
BY IAN FLEMING
DRAWING BY HORAK
IN M'S OFFICE...
WELL, THERE'S NO DOUBT HE'S BOND, ALL RIGHT... SECURITY HAS JUST CONFIRMED HIS PRINTS—
—BUT TOO MANY THINGS DON'T ADD UP, SIR... WHY THE FORGED PASSPORT? AND THE RITZ HOTEL? WHY DIDN'T HE GO TO HIS FLAT? OR RING ME UP PERSONALLY?
IF YOU ASK ME, SIR, HE NEEDS PSYCHIATRIC OBSERVATION... I THINK 007'S *ROUND THE BEND!*
24

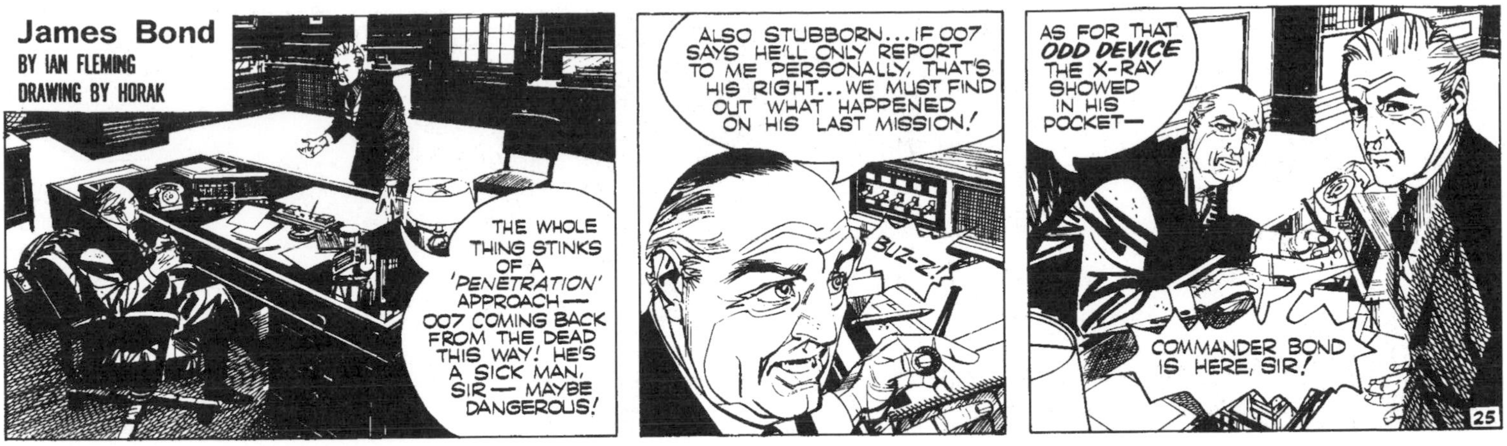
James Bond
BY IAN FLEMING
DRAWING BY HORAK
THE WHOLE THING STINKS OF A 'PENETRATION' APPROACH — 007 COMING BACK FROM THE DEAD THIS WAY! HE'S A SICK MAN, SIR— MAYBE DANGEROUS!
ALSO STUBBORN... IF 007 SAYS HE'LL ONLY REPORT TO ME PERSONALLY, THAT'S HIS RIGHT... WE MUST FIND OUT WHAT HAPPENED ON HIS LAST MISSION!
BUZ-Z!
AS FOR THAT ODD DEVICE THE X-RAY SHOWED IN HIS POCKET—
COMMANDER BOND IS HERE, SIR!
25

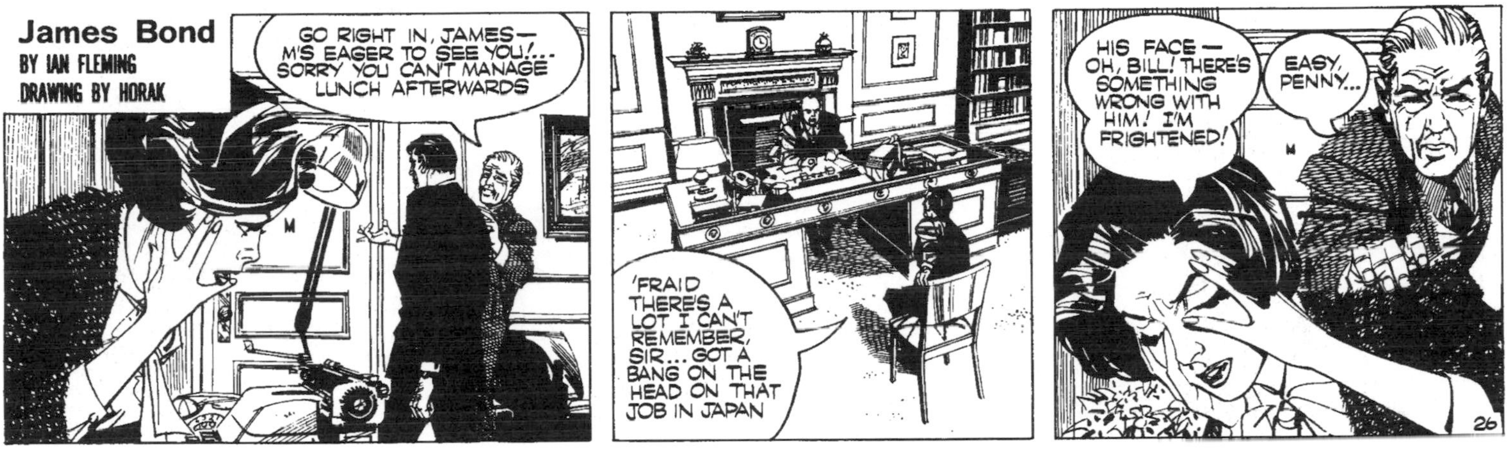
James Bond
BY IAN FLEMING
DRAWING BY HORAK
GO RIGHT IN, JAMES— M'S EAGER TO SEE YOU!... SORRY YOU CAN'T MANAGE LUNCH AFTERWARDS
'FRAID THERE'S A LOT I CAN'T REMEMBER, SIR... GOT A BANG ON THE HEAD ON THAT JOB IN JAPAN
HIS FACE — OH, BILL! THERE'S SOMETHING WRONG WITH HIM! I'M FRIGHTENED!
EASY, PENNY...
26

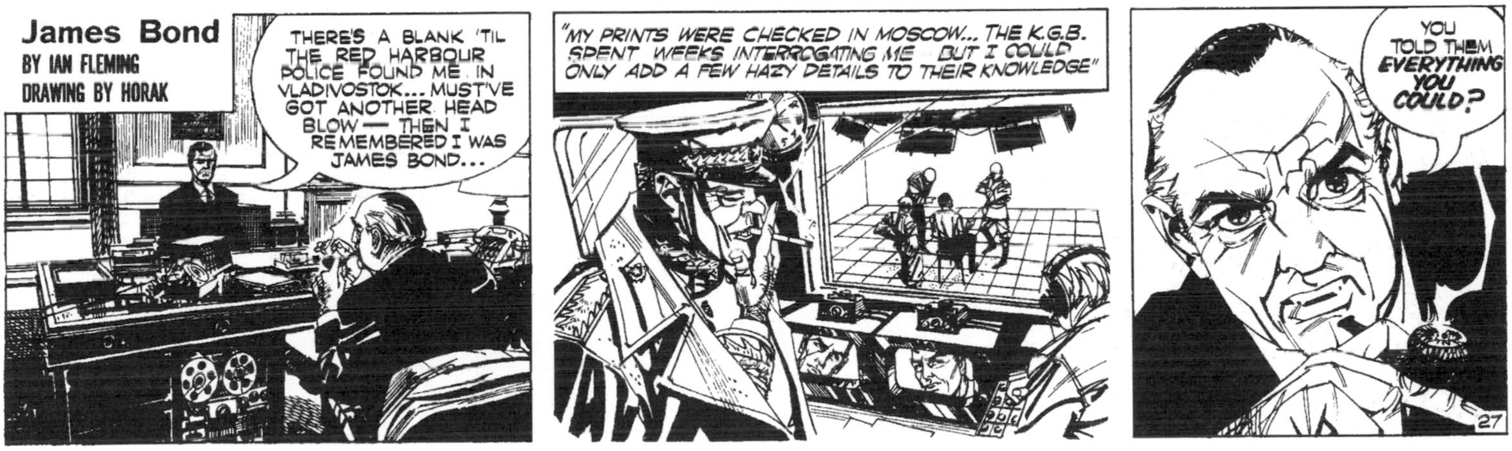
James Bond
BY IAN FLEMING
DRAWING BY HORAK
THERE'S A BLANK 'TIL THE RED HARBOUR POLICE FOUND ME IN VLADIVOSTOK... MUST'VE GOT ANOTHER HEAD BLOW— THEN I REMEMBERED I WAS JAMES BOND...
"MY PRINTS WERE CHECKED IN MOSCOW... THE K.G.B. SPENT WEEKS INTERROGATING ME BUT I COULD ONLY ADD A FEW HAZY DETAILS TO THEIR KNOWLEDGE"
YOU TOLD THEM EVERYTHING YOU COULD?
27

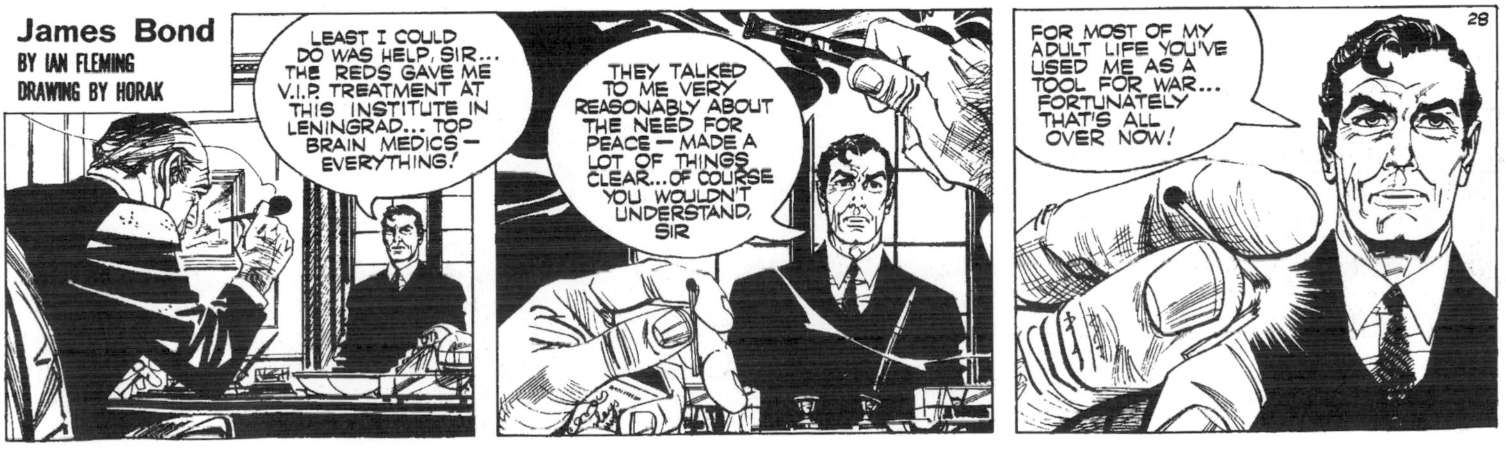
James Bond
BY IAN FLEMING
DRAWING BY HORAK
LEAST I COULD DO WAS HELP, SIR... THE REDS GAVE ME V.I.P. TREATMENT AT THIS INSTITUTE IN LENINGRAD... TOP BRAIN MEDICS— EVERYTHING!
THEY TALKED TO ME VERY REASONABLY ABOUT THE NEED FOR PEACE— MADE A LOT OF THINGS CLEAR... OF COURSE YOU WOULDN'T UNDERSTAND, SIR
FOR MOST OF MY ADULT LIFE YOU'VE USED ME AS A TOOL FOR WAR... FORTUNATELY THAT'S ALL OVER NOW!
28

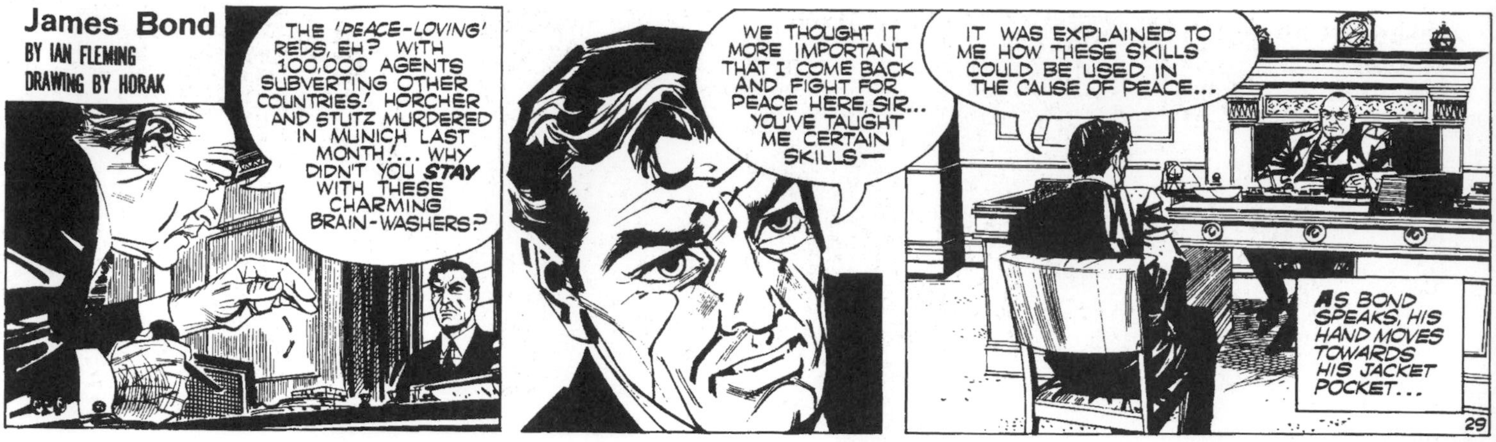
James Bond
BY IAN FLEMING
DRAWING BY HORAK
THE 'PEACE-LOVING' REDS, EH? WITH 100,000 AGENTS SUBVERTING OTHER COUNTRIES! HORCHER AND STUTZ MURDERED IN MUNICH LAST MONTH!... WHY DIDN'T YOU STAY WITH THESE CHARMING BRAIN-WASHERS?
WE THOUGHT IT MORE IMPORTANT THAT I COME BACK AND FIGHT FOR PEACE HERE, SIR... YOU'VE TAUGHT ME CERTAIN SKILLS—
IT WAS EXPLAINED TO ME HOW THESE SKILLS COULD BE USED IN THE CAUSE OF PEACE...
AS BOND SPEAKS, HIS HAND MOVES TOWARDS HIS JACKET POCKET...
29

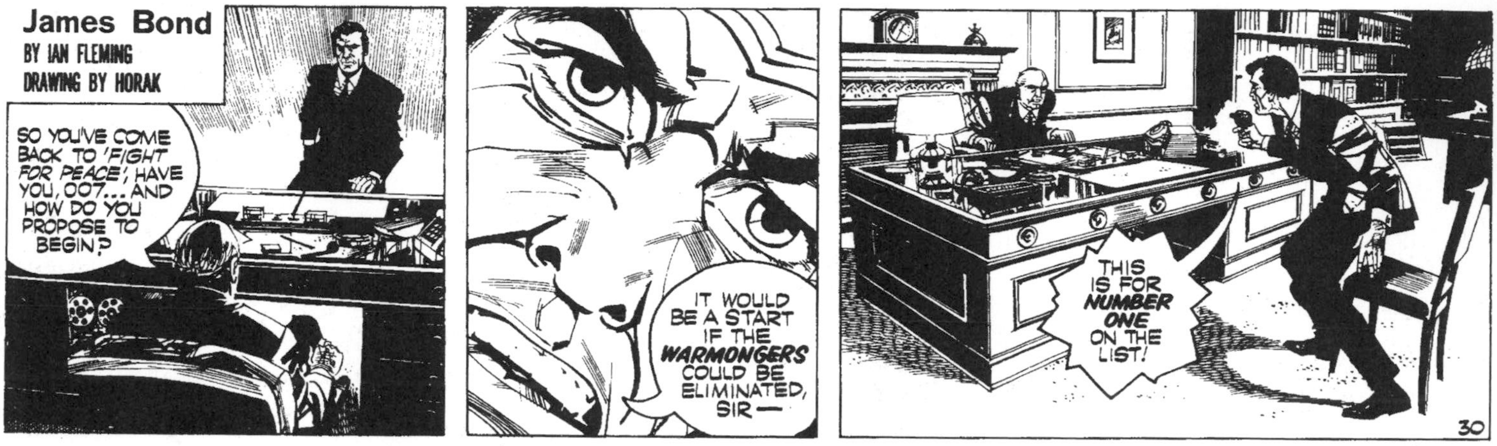
James Bond
BY IAN FLEMING
DRAWING BY HORAK
SO YOU'VE COME BACK TO 'FIGHT FOR PEACE', HAVE YOU, 007... AND HOW DO YOU PROPOSE TO BEGIN?
IT WOULD BE A START IF THE WARMONGERS COULD BE ELIMINATED, SIR—
THIS IS FOR NUMBER ONE ON THE LIST!
30

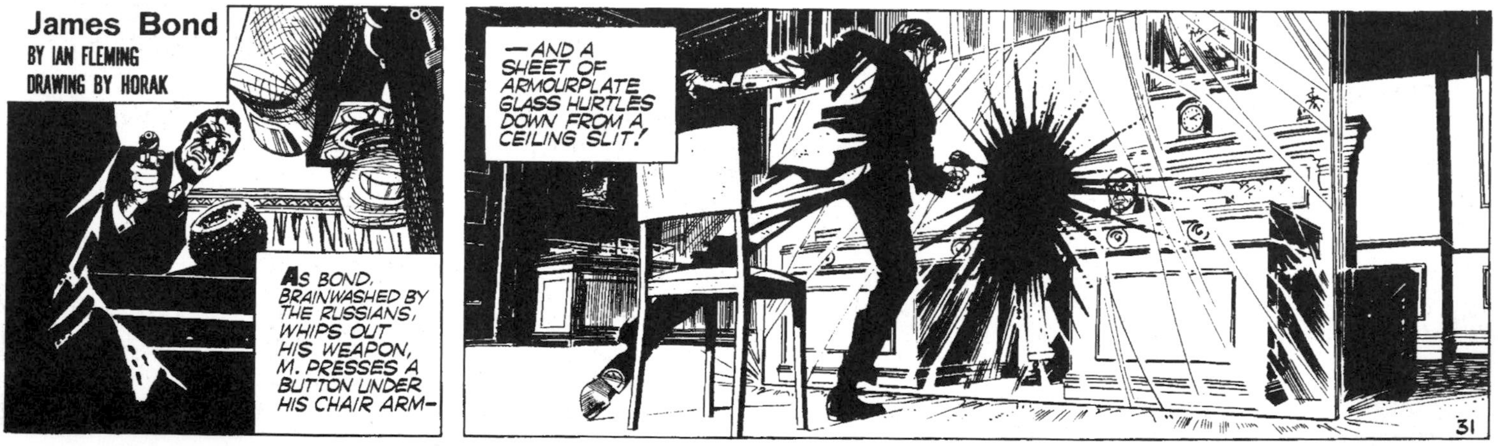
James Bond
BY IAN FLEMING
DRAWING BY HORAK
AS BOND, BRAINWASHED BY THE RUSSIANS, WHIPS OUT HIS WEAPON, M. PRESSES A BUTTON UNDER HIS CHAIR ARM—
—AND A SHEET OF ARMOURPLATE GLASS HURTLES DOWN FROM A CEILING SLIT!
31

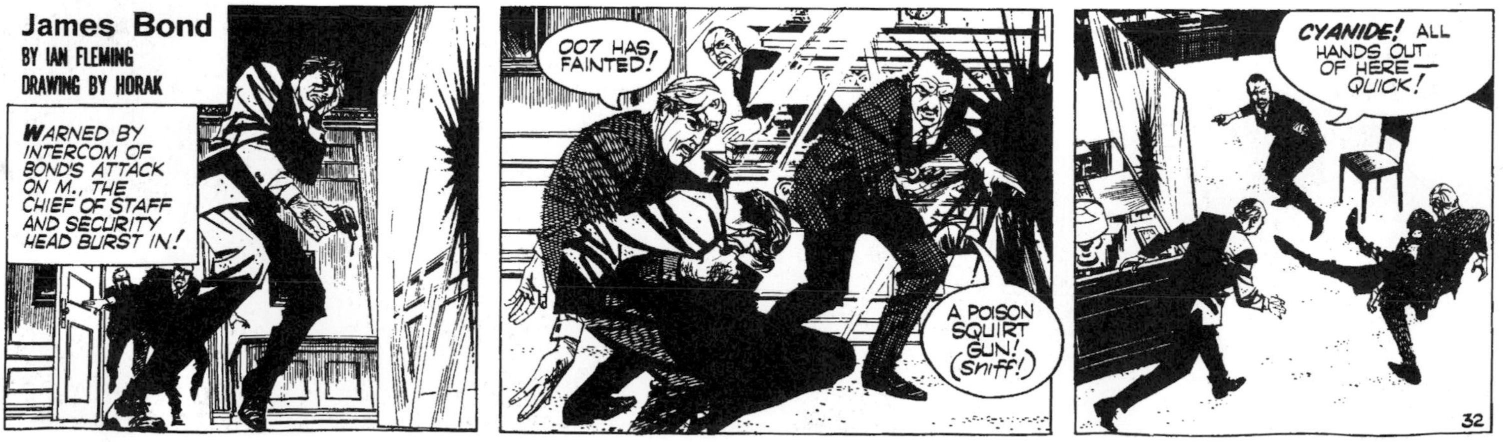
James Bond
BY IAN FLEMING
DRAWING BY HORAK
WARNED BY INTERCOM OF BOND'S ATTACK ON M., THE CHIEF OF STAFF AND SECURITY HEAD BURST IN!
007 HAS FAINTED!
A POISON SQUIRT GUN! (Sniff!)
CYANIDE! ALL HANDS OUT OF HERE— QUICK!
32

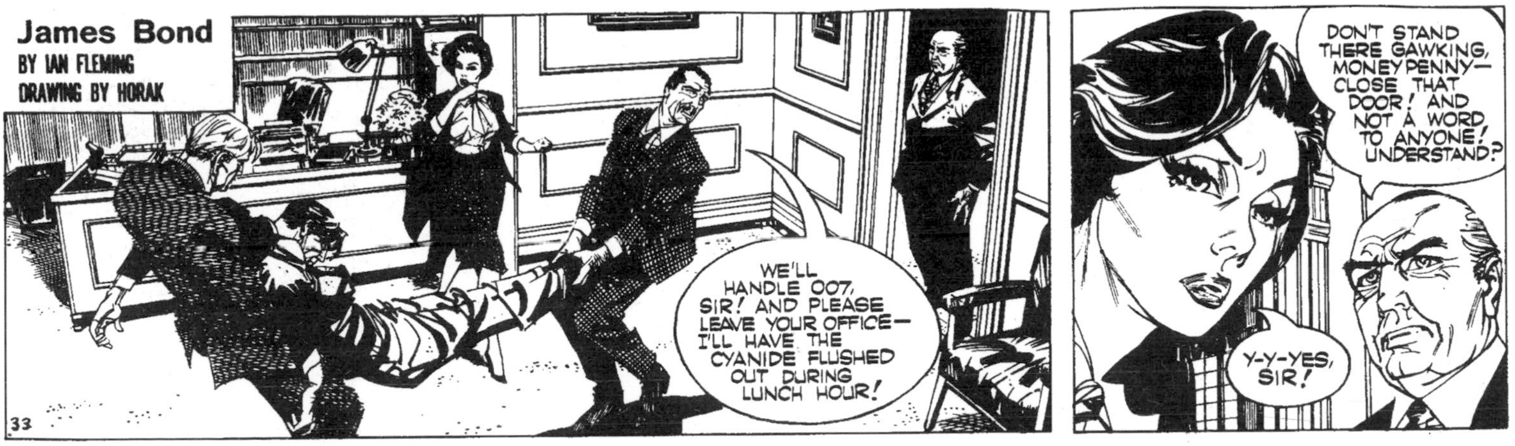

James Bond
BY IAN FLEMING
DRAWING BY HORAK
WE'LL HANDLE 007, SIR! AND PLEASE LEAVE YOUR OFFICE— I'LL HAVE THE CYANIDE FLUSHED OUT DURING LUNCH HOUR!
33
DON'T STAND THERE GAWKING, MONEYPENNY— CLOSE THAT DOOR! AND NOT A WORD TO ANYONE! UNDERSTAND?
Y-Y-YES, SIR!

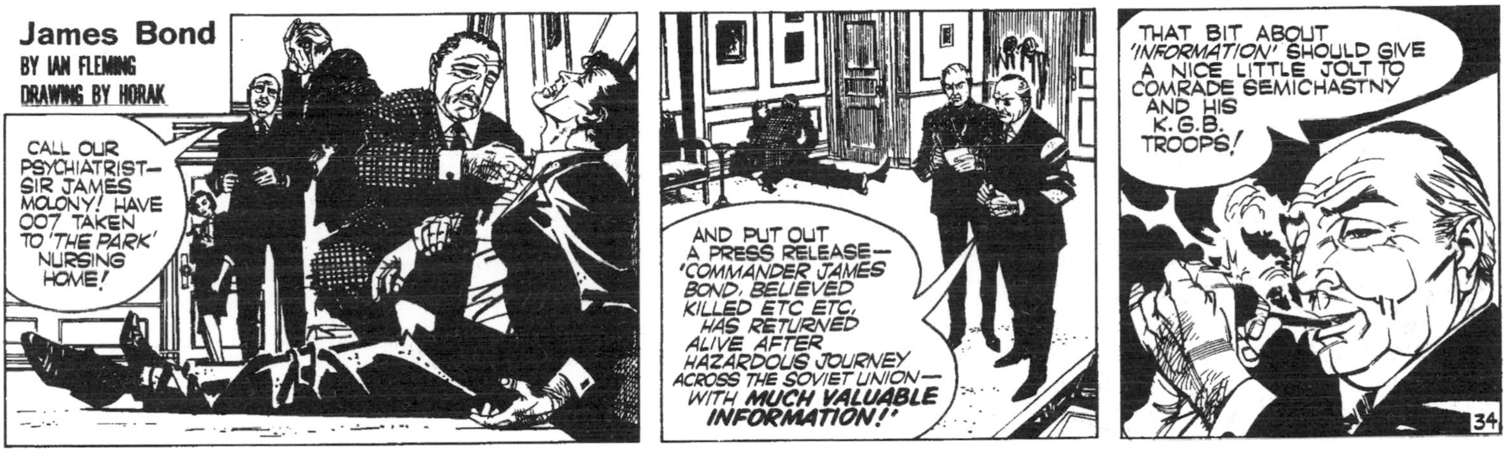

James Bond
BY IAN FLEMING
DRAWING BY HORAK
CALL OUR PSYCHIATRIST— SIR JAMES MOLONY! HAVE 007 TAKEN TO 'THE PARK' NURSING HOME!
AND PUT OUT A PRESS RELEASE— 'COMMANDER JAMES BOND, BELIEVED KILLED ETC ETC, HAS RETURNED ALIVE AFTER HAZARDOUS JOURNEY ACROSS THE SOVIET UNION— WITH MUCH VALUABLE INFORMATION!'
THAT BIT ABOUT 'INFORMATION' SHOULD GIVE A NICE LITTLE JOLT TO COMRADE SEMICHASTNY AND HIS K.G.B. TROOPS!
34

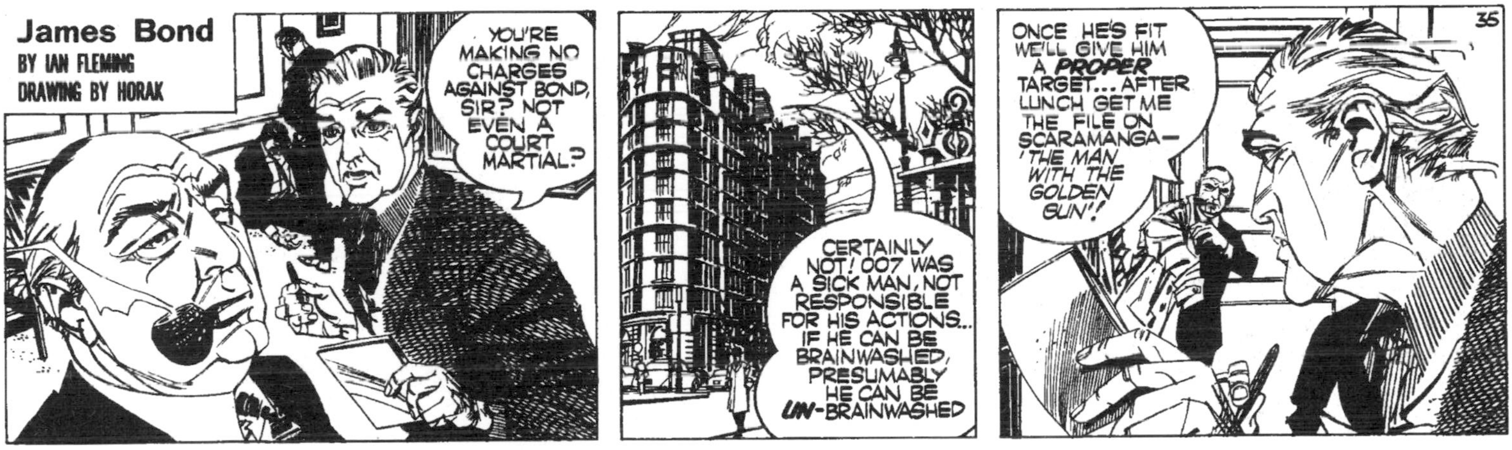

James Bond
BY IAN FLEMING
DRAWING BY HORAK
YOU'RE MAKING NO CHARGES AGAINST BOND, SIR? NOT EVEN A COURT MARTIAL?
CERTAINLY NOT! 007 WAS A SICK MAN, NOT RESPONSIBLE FOR HIS ACTIONS... IF HE CAN BE BRAINWASHED, PRESUMABLY HE CAN BE UN-BRAINWASHED
35
ONCE HE'S FIT WE'LL GIVE HIM A PROPER TARGET... AFTER LUNCH GET ME THE FILE ON SCARAMANGA— 'THE MAN WITH THE GOLDEN GUN'!

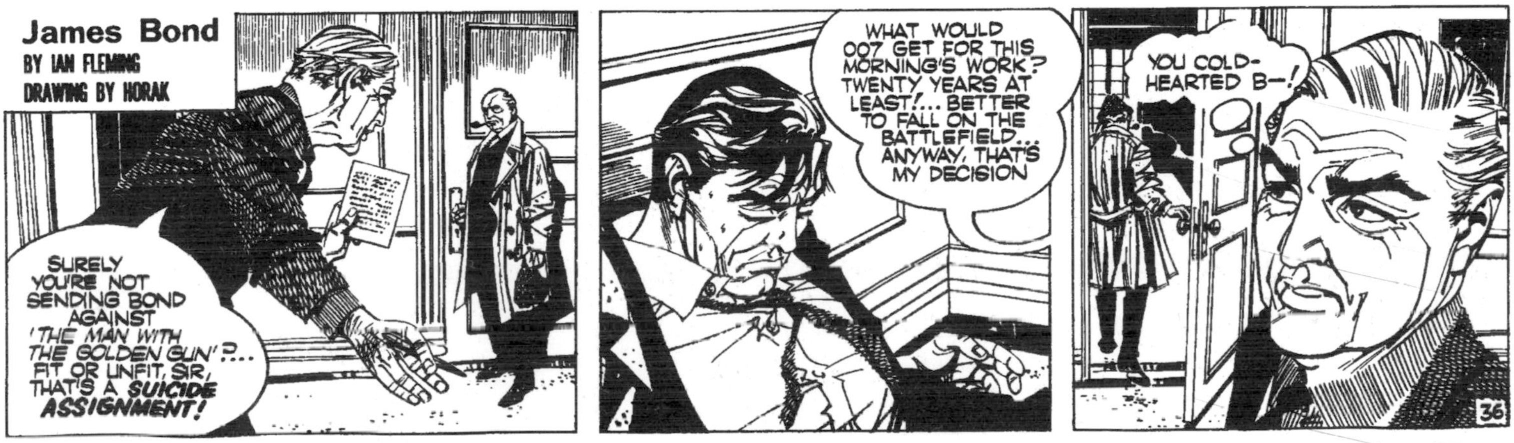

James Bond
BY IAN FLEMING
DRAWING BY HORAK
SURELY YOU'RE NOT SENDING BOND AGAINST 'THE MAN WITH THE GOLDEN GUN'?... FIT OR UNFIT, SIR, THAT'S A SUICIDE ASSIGNMENT!
WHAT WOULD 007 GET FOR THIS MORNING'S WORK? TWENTY YEARS AT LEAST!... BETTER TO FALL ON THE BATTLEFIELD... ANYWAY, THAT'S MY DECISION
YOU COLD-HEARTED B—!
36

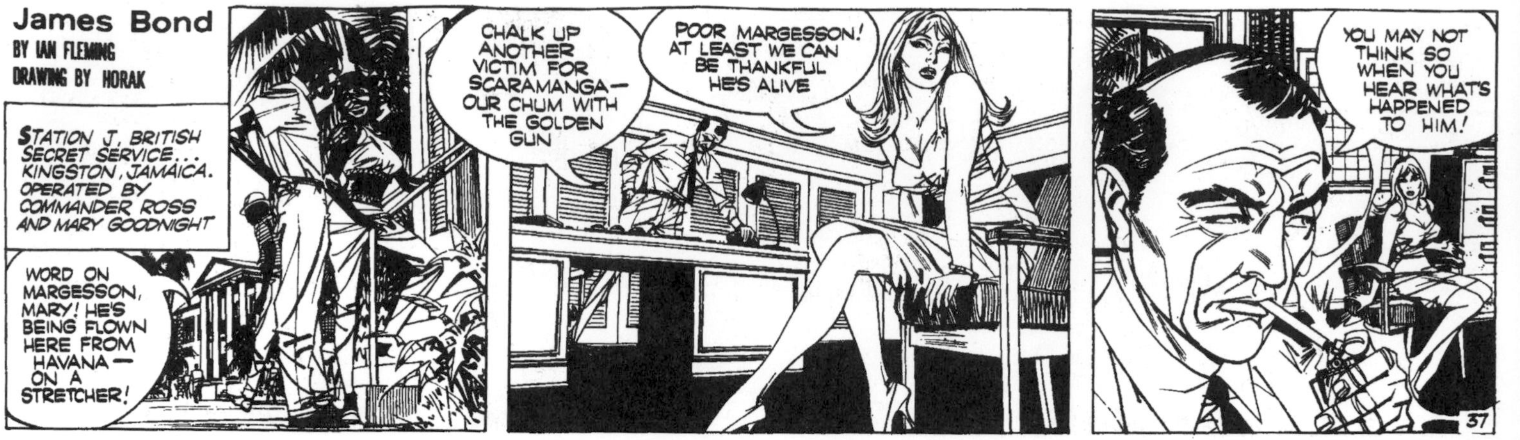
James Bond
BY IAN FLEMING
DRAWING BY HORAK
STATION J, BRITISH SECRET SERVICE... KINGSTON, JAMAICA. OPERATED BY COMMANDER ROSS AND MARY GOODNIGHT
WORD ON MARGESSON, MARY! HE'S BEING FLOWN HERE FROM HAVANA — ON A STRETCHER!
CHALK UP ANOTHER VICTIM FOR SCARAMANGA — OUR CHUM WITH THE GOLDEN GUN
POOR MARGESSON! AT LEAST WE CAN BE THANKFUL HE'S ALIVE
YOU MAY NOT THINK SO WHEN YOU HEAR WHAT'S HAPPENED TO HIM!
37

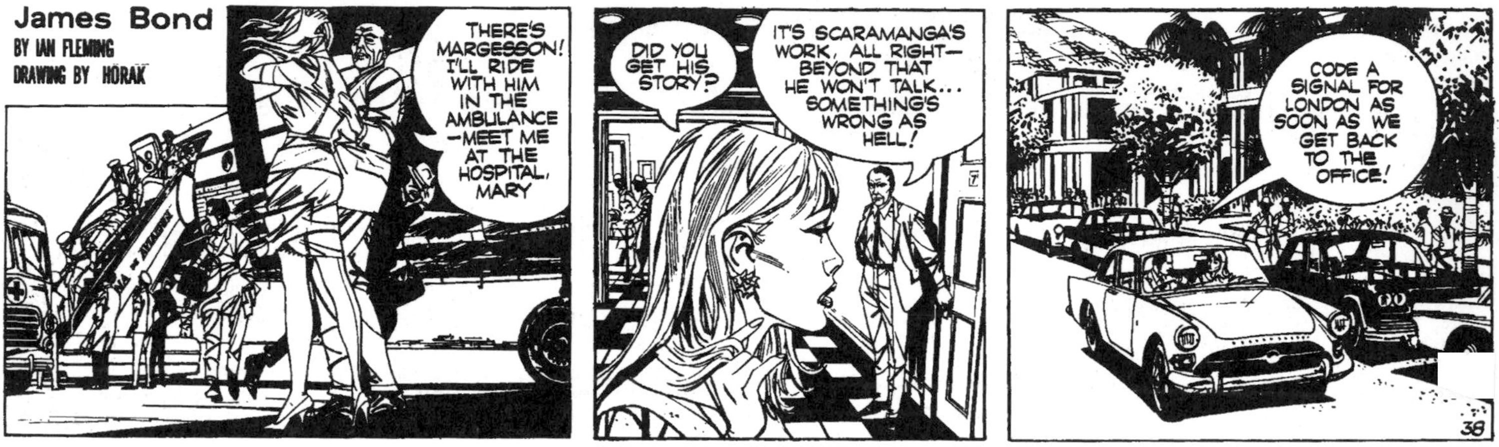
James Bond
BY IAN FLEMING
DRAWING BY HORAK
THERE'S MARGESSON! I'LL RIDE WITH HIM IN THE AMBULANCE — MEET ME AT THE HOSPITAL, MARY
DID YOU GET HIS STORY?
IT'S SCARAMANGA'S WORK, ALL RIGHT — BEYOND THAT HE WON'T TALK... SOMETHING'S WRONG AS HELL!
CODE A SIGNAL FOR LONDON AS SOON AS WE GET BACK TO THE OFFICE!
38

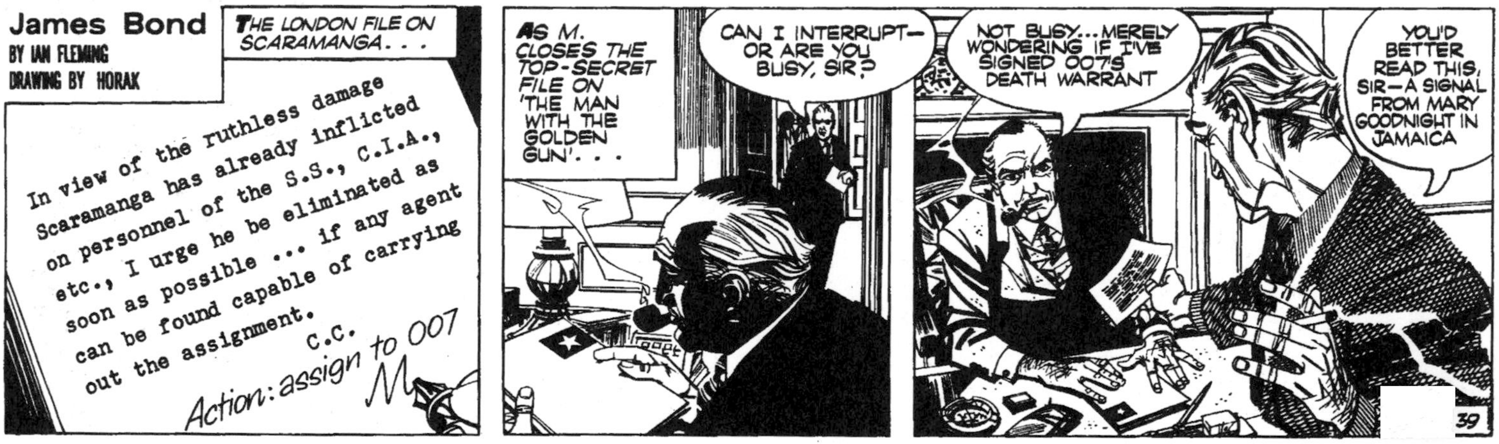
James Bond
BY IAN FLEMING
DRAWING BY HORAK
THE LONDON FILE ON SCARAMANGA...
In view of the ruthless damage Scaramanga has already inflicted on personnel of the S.S., C.I.A., etc., I urge he be eliminated as soon as possible ... if any agent can be found capable of carrying out the assignment.
C.C.
Action: assign to 007
M
AS M. CLOSES THE TOP-SECRET FILE ON 'THE MAN WITH THE GOLDEN GUN'...
CAN I INTERRUPT — OR ARE YOU BUSY, SIR?
NOT BUSY... MERELY WONDERING IF I'VE SIGNED 007'S DEATH WARRANT
YOU'D BETTER READ THIS, SIR — A SIGNAL FROM MARY GOODNIGHT IN JAMAICA
39

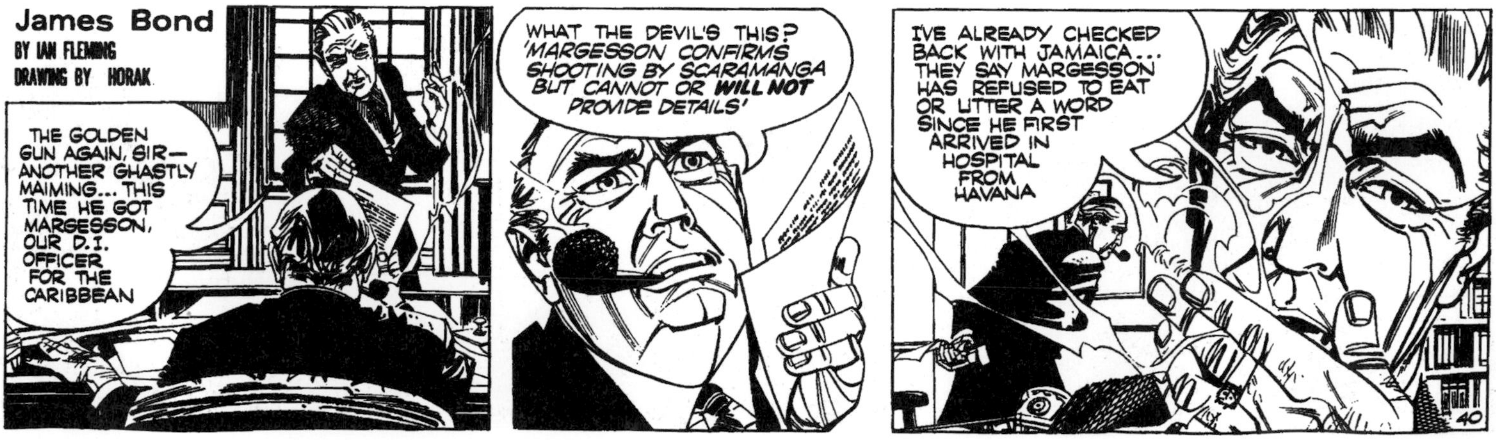
James Bond
BY IAN FLEMING
DRAWING BY HORAK
THE GOLDEN GUN AGAIN, SIR — ANOTHER GHASTLY MAIMING... THIS TIME HE GOT MARGESSON, OUR D.I. OFFICER FOR THE CARIBBEAN
WHAT THE DEVIL'S THIS? 'MARGESSON CONFIRMS SHOOTING BY SCARAMANGA BUT CANNOT OR WILL NOT PROVIDE DETAILS'
I'VE ALREADY CHECKED BACK WITH JAMAICA... THEY SAY MARGESSON HAS REFUSED TO EAT OR UTTER A WORD SINCE HE FIRST ARRIVED IN HOSPITAL FROM HAVANA
40

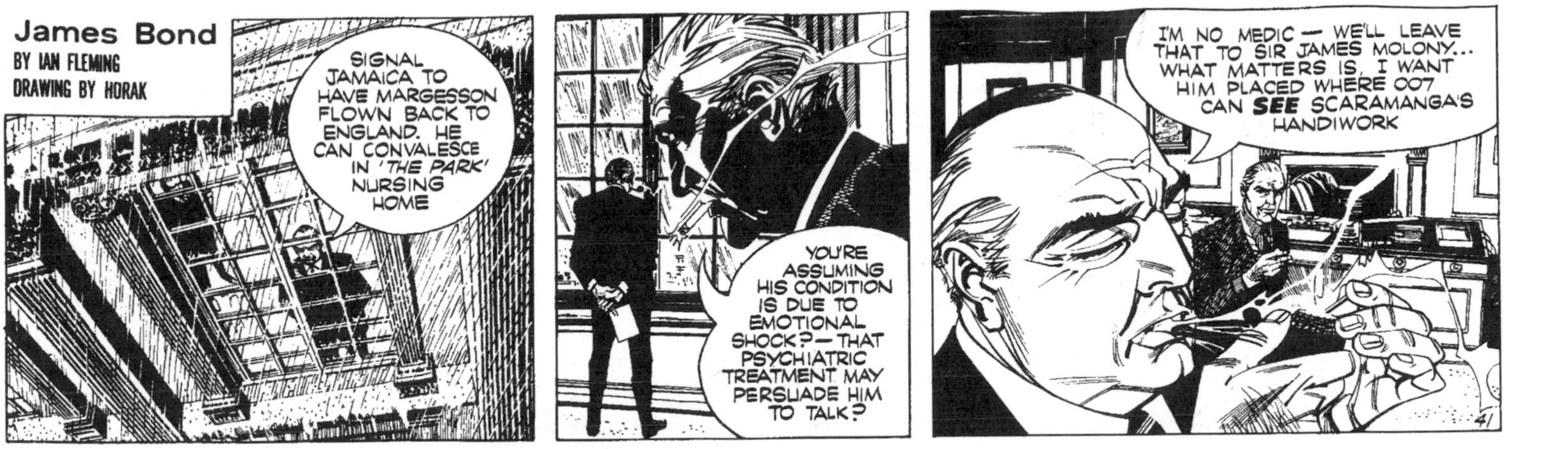
James Bond
BY IAN FLEMING
DRAWING BY HORAK
SIGNAL JAMAICA TO HAVE MARGESSON FLOWN BACK TO ENGLAND. HE CAN CONVALESCE IN 'THE PARK' NURSING HOME
YOU'RE ASSUMING HIS CONDITION IS DUE TO EMOTIONAL SHOCK?— THAT PSYCHIATRIC TREATMENT MAY PERSUADE HIM TO TALK?
I'M NO MEDIC — WE'LL LEAVE THAT TO SIR JAMES MOLONY... WHAT MATTERS IS, I WANT HIM PLACED WHERE 007 CAN SEE SCARAMANGA'S HANDIWORK
41

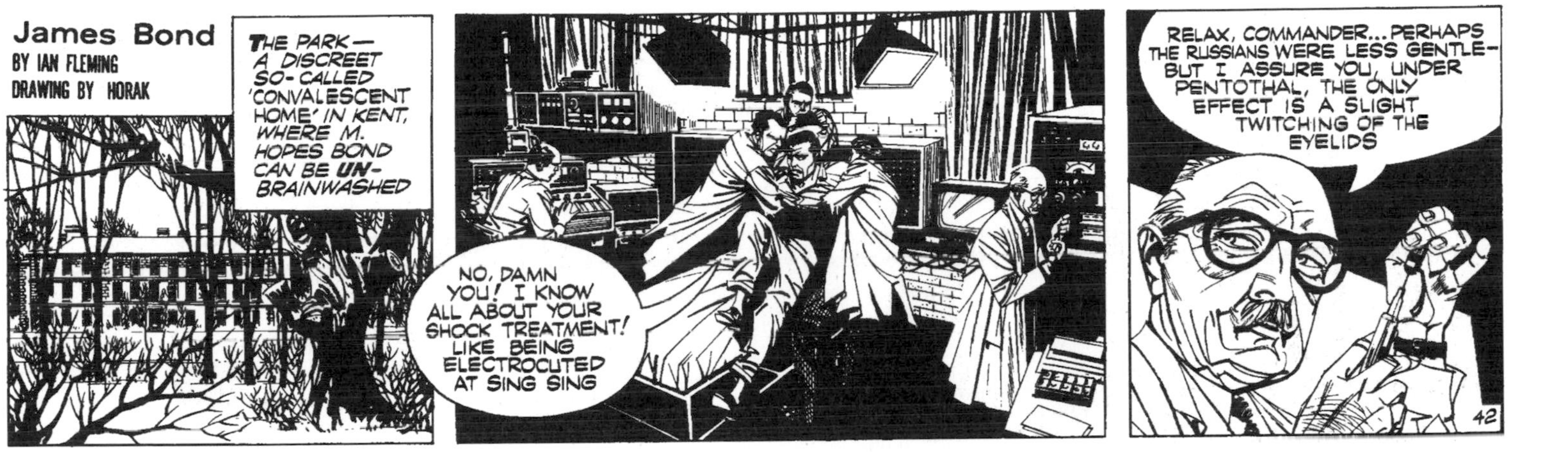
James Bond
BY IAN FLEMING
DRAWING BY HORAK
THE PARK— A DISCREET SO-CALLED 'CONVALESCENT HOME' IN KENT, WHERE M. HOPES BOND CAN BE UN-BRAINWASHED
NO, DAMN YOU! I KNOW ALL ABOUT YOUR SHOCK TREATMENT! LIKE BEING ELECTROCUTED AT SING SING
RELAX, COMMANDER... PERHAPS THE RUSSIANS WERE LESS GENTLE— BUT I ASSURE YOU, UNDER PENTOTHAL, THE ONLY EFFECT IS A SLIGHT TWITCHING OF THE EYELIDS
42

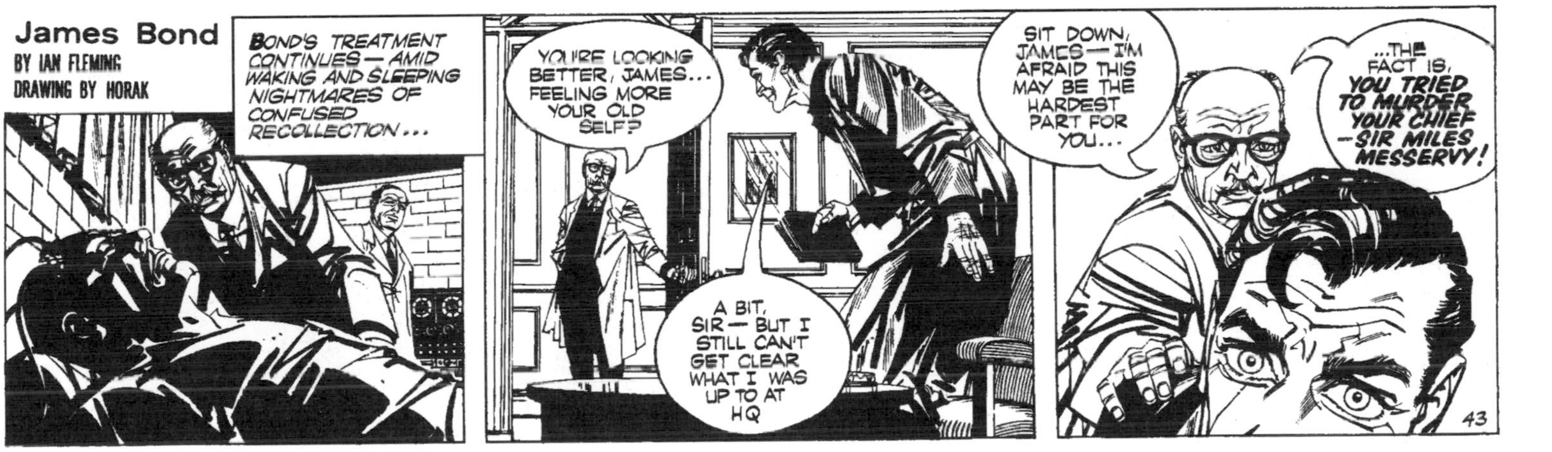
James Bond
BY IAN FLEMING
DRAWING BY HORAK
BOND'S TREATMENT CONTINUES— AMID WAKING AND SLEEPING NIGHTMARES OF CONFUSED RECOLLECTION...
YOU'RE LOOKING BETTER, JAMES... FEELING MORE YOUR OLD SELF?
A BIT, SIR— BUT I STILL CAN'T GET CLEAR WHAT I WAS UP TO AT HQ
SIT DOWN, JAMES— I'M AFRAID THIS MAY BE THE HARDEST PART FOR YOU...
...THE FACT IS, YOU TRIED TO MURDER YOUR CHIEF —SIR MILES MESSERVY!
43

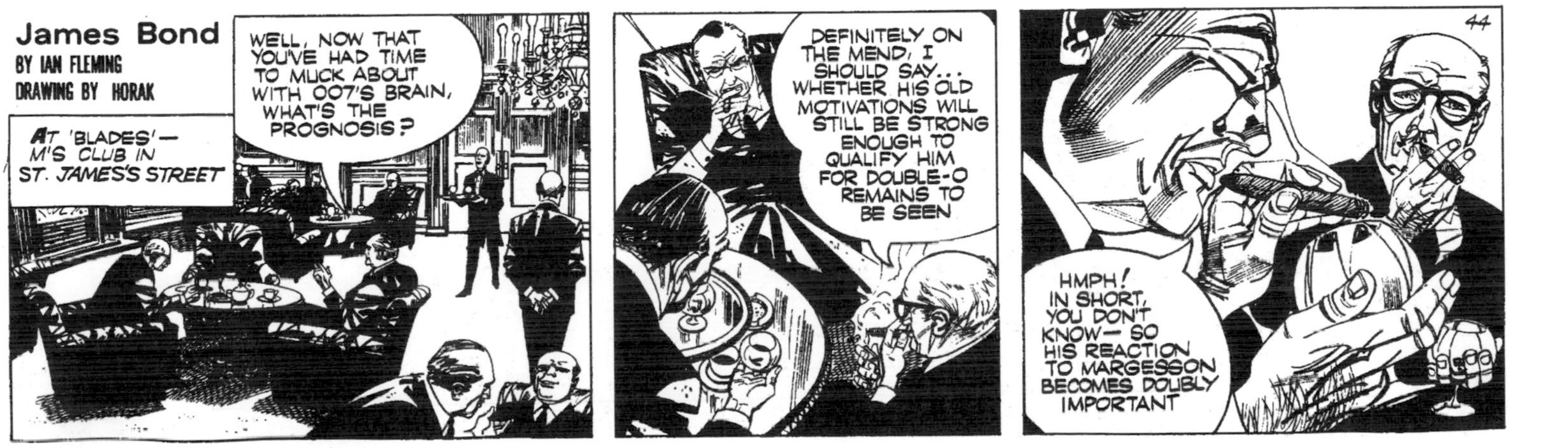
James Bond
BY IAN FLEMING
DRAWING BY HORAK
AT 'BLADES'— M'S CLUB IN ST. JAMES'S STREET
WELL, NOW THAT YOU'VE HAD TIME TO MUCK ABOUT WITH 007'S BRAIN, WHAT'S THE PROGNOSIS?
DEFINITELY ON THE MEND, I SHOULD SAY... WHETHER HIS OLD MOTIVATIONS WILL STILL BE STRONG ENOUGH TO QUALIFY HIM FOR DOUBLE-O REMAINS TO BE SEEN
44
HMPH! IN SHORT, YOU DON'T KNOW— SO HIS REACTION TO MARGESSON BECOMES DOUBLY IMPORTANT

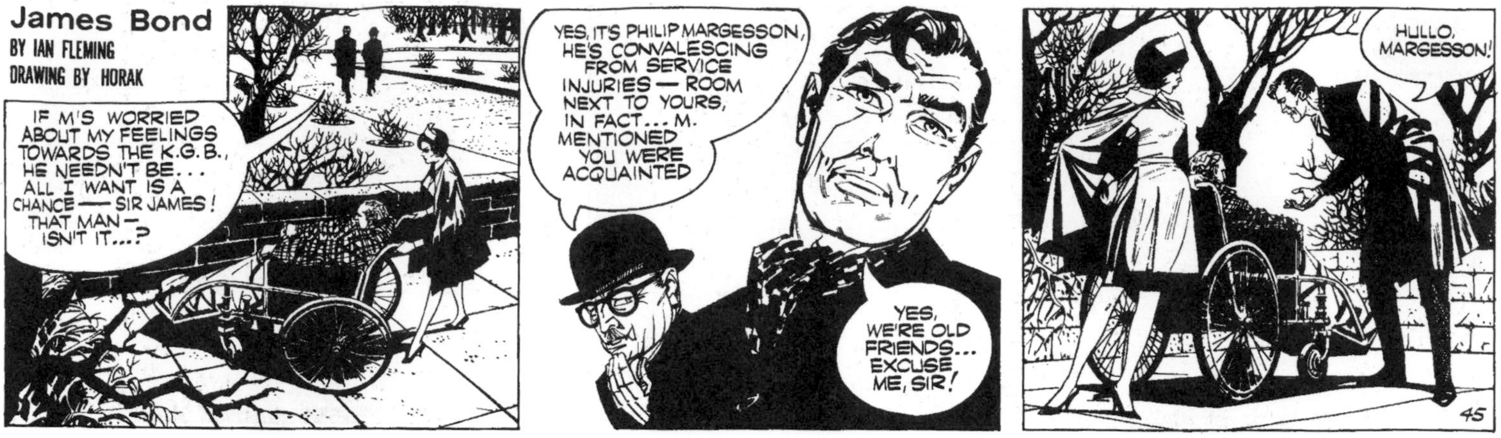
James Bond
BY IAN FLEMING
DRAWING BY HORAK
IF M'S WORRIED ABOUT MY FEELINGS TOWARDS THE K.G.B., HE NEEDN'T BE... ALL I WANT IS A CHANCE — SIR JAMES! THAT MAN — ISN'T IT...?
YES, IT'S PHILIP MARGESSON, HE'S CONVALESCING FROM SERVICE INJURIES — ROOM NEXT TO YOURS, IN FACT... M. MENTIONED YOU WERE ACQUAINTED
YES, WE'RE OLD FRIENDS... EXCUSE ME, SIR!
HULLO, MARGESSON!
45

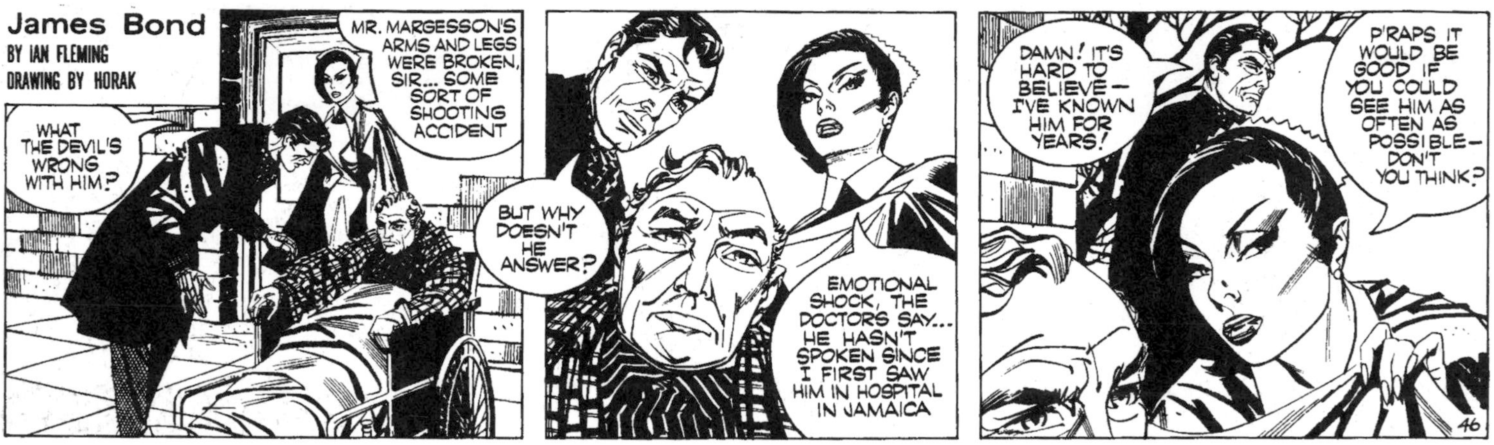
James Bond
BY IAN FLEMING
DRAWING BY HORAK
WHAT THE DEVIL'S WRONG WITH HIM?
MR. MARGESSON'S ARMS AND LEGS WERE BROKEN, SIR... SOME SORT OF SHOOTING ACCIDENT
BUT WHY DOESN'T HE ANSWER?
EMOTIONAL SHOCK, THE DOCTORS SAY... HE HASN'T SPOKEN SINCE I FIRST SAW HIM IN HOSPITAL IN JAMAICA
DAMN! IT'S HARD TO BELIEVE — I'VE KNOWN HIM FOR YEARS!
P'RAPS IT WOULD BE GOOD IF YOU COULD SEE HIM AS OFTEN AS POSSIBLE — DON'T YOU THINK?
46

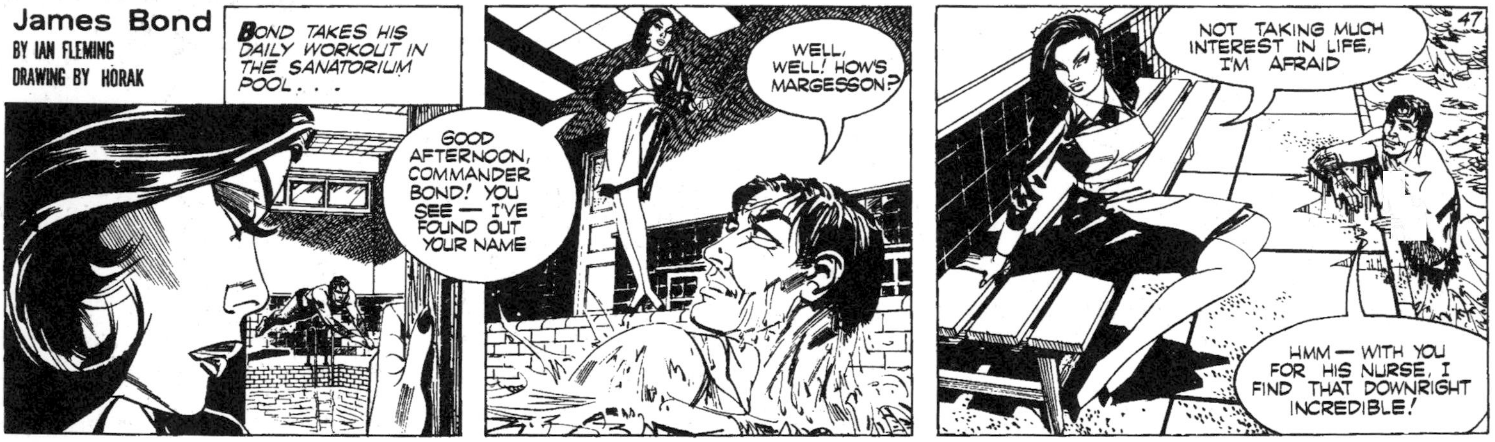
James Bond
BY IAN FLEMING
DRAWING BY HORAK
BOND TAKES HIS DAILY WORKOUT IN THE SANATORIUM POOL...
GOOD AFTERNOON, COMMANDER BOND! YOU SEE — I'VE FOUND OUT YOUR NAME
WELL, WELL! HOW'S MARGESSON?
47
NOT TAKING MUCH INTEREST IN LIFE, I'M AFRAID
HMM — WITH YOU FOR HIS NURSE, I FIND THAT DOWNRIGHT INCREDIBLE!

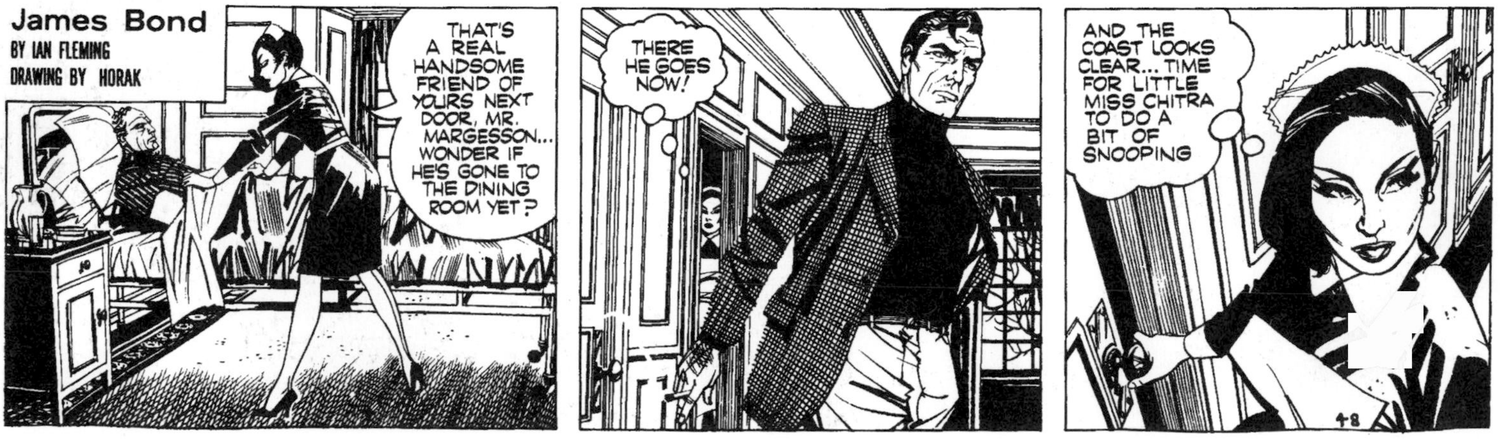
James Bond
BY IAN FLEMING
DRAWING BY HORAK
THAT'S A REAL HANDSOME FRIEND OF YOURS NEXT DOOR, MR. MARGESSON... WONDER IF HE'S GONE TO THE DINING ROOM YET?
THERE HE GOES NOW!
AND THE COAST LOOKS CLEAR... TIME FOR LITTLE MISS CHITRA TO DO A BIT OF SNOOPING
48

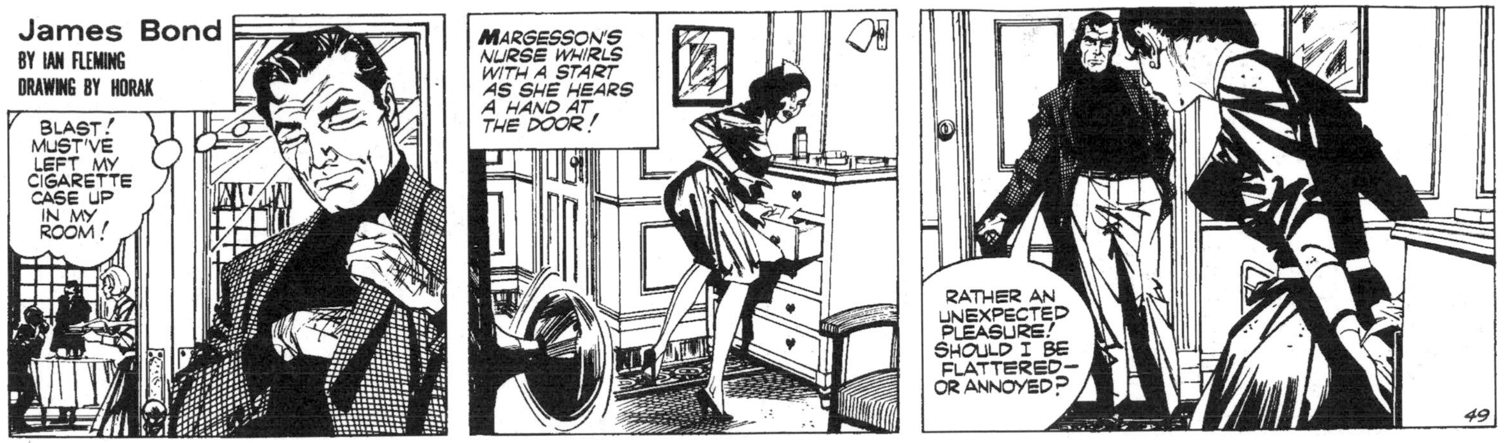
James Bond
BY IAN FLEMING
DRAWING BY HORAK
BLAST! MUST'VE LEFT MY CIGARETTE CASE UP IN MY ROOM!
MARGESSON'S NURSE WHIRLS WITH A START AS SHE HEARS A HAND AT THE DOOR!
RATHER AN UNEXPECTED PLEASURE! SHOULD I BE FLATTERED– OR ANNOYED?
49

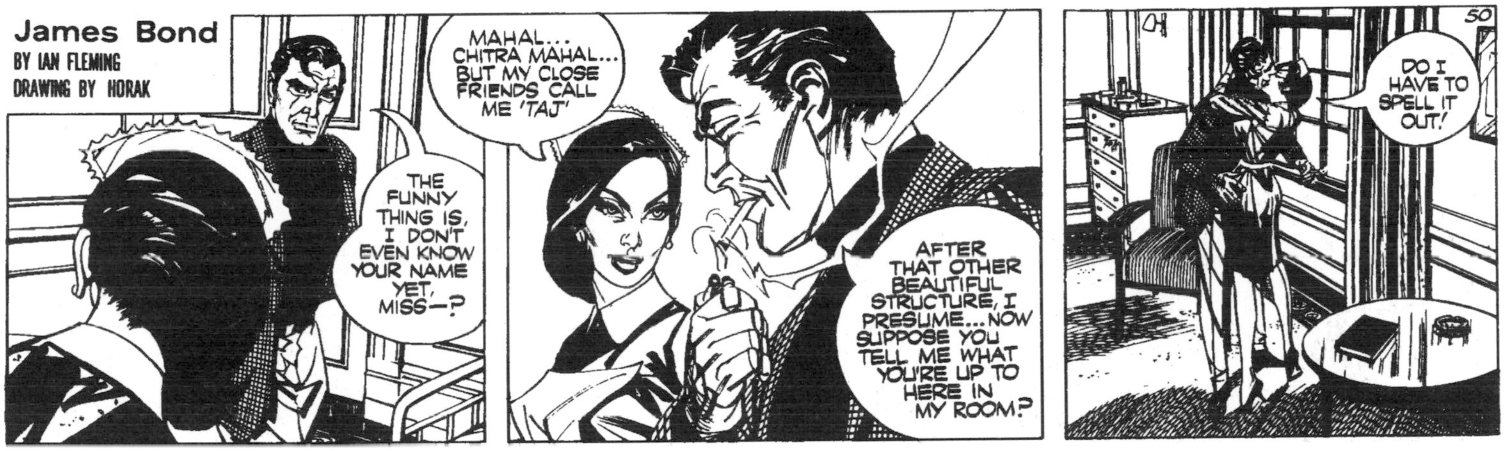
James Bond
BY IAN FLEMING
DRAWING BY HORAK
THE FUNNY THING IS, I DON'T EVEN KNOW YOUR NAME YET, MISS–?
MAHAL... CHITRA MAHAL... BUT MY CLOSE FRIENDS CALL ME 'TAJ'
AFTER THAT OTHER BEAUTIFUL STRUCTURE, I PRESUME... NOW SUPPOSE YOU TELL ME WHAT YOU'RE UP TO HERE IN MY ROOM?
50
DO I HAVE TO SPELL IT OUT!

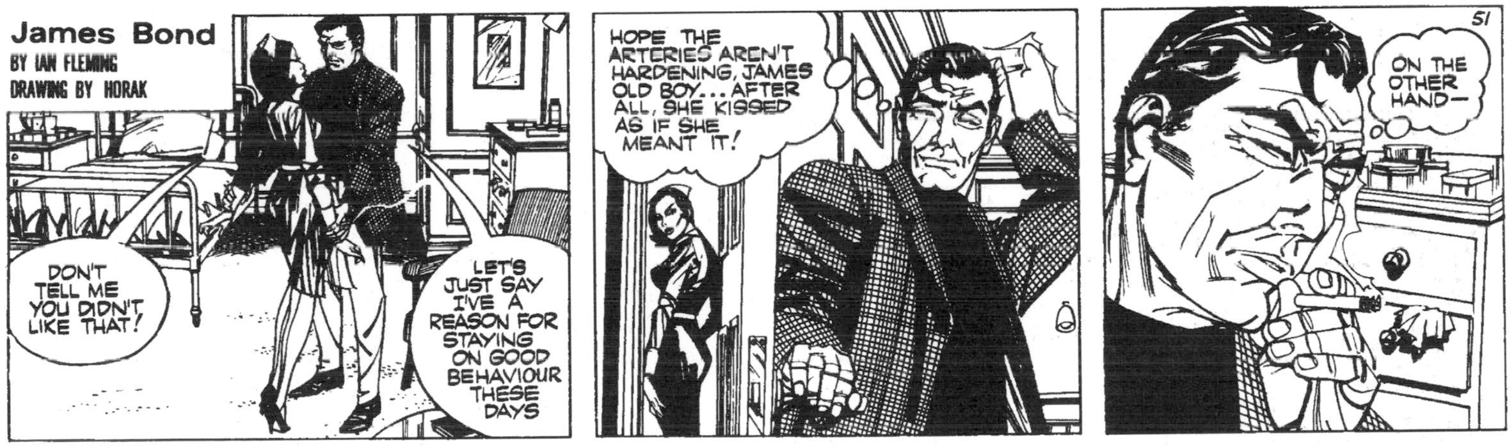
James Bond
BY IAN FLEMING
DRAWING BY HORAK
DON'T TELL ME YOU DIDN'T LIKE THAT!
LET'S JUST SAY I'VE A REASON FOR STAYING ON GOOD BEHAVIOUR THESE DAYS
HOPE THE ARTERIES AREN'T HARDENING, JAMES OLD BOY... AFTER ALL, SHE KISSED AS IF SHE MEANT IT!
51
ON THE OTHER HAND–

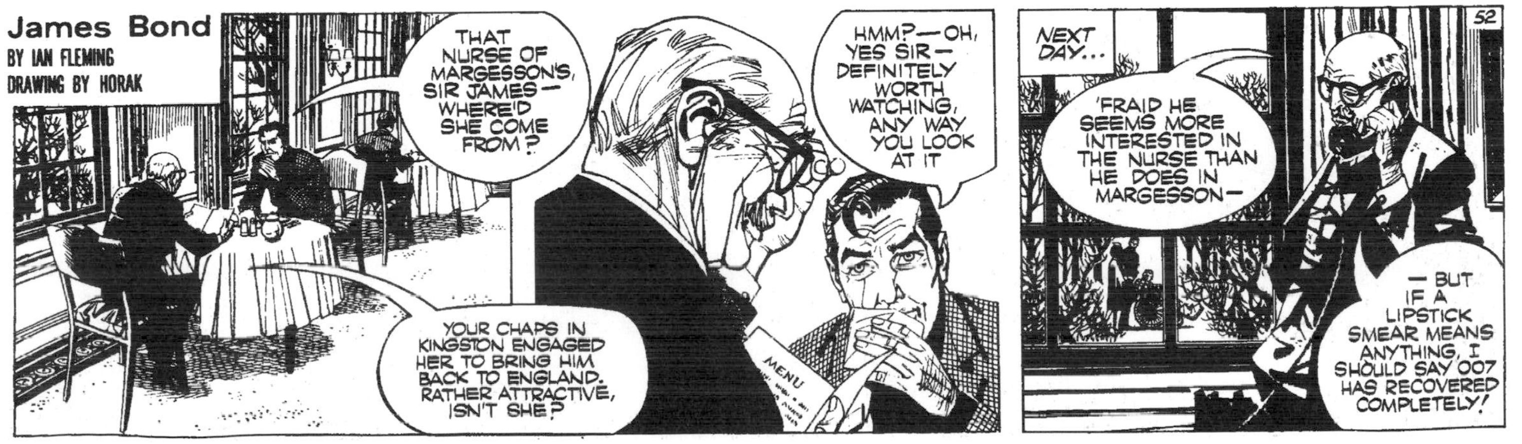
James Bond
BY IAN FLEMING
DRAWING BY HORAK
THAT NURSE OF MARGESSON'S, SIR JAMES– WHERE'D SHE COME FROM?
YOUR CHAPS IN KINGSTON ENGAGED HER TO BRING HIM BACK TO ENGLAND. RATHER ATTRACTIVE, ISN'T SHE?
HMM?–OH, YES SIR– DEFINITELY WORTH WATCHING, ANY WAY YOU LOOK AT IT
MENU
52
NEXT DAY...
'FRAID HE SEEMS MORE INTERESTED IN THE NURSE THAN HE DOES IN MARGESSON–
–BUT IF A LIPSTICK SMEAR MEANS ANYTHING, I SHOULD SAY 007 HAS RECOVERED COMPLETELY!

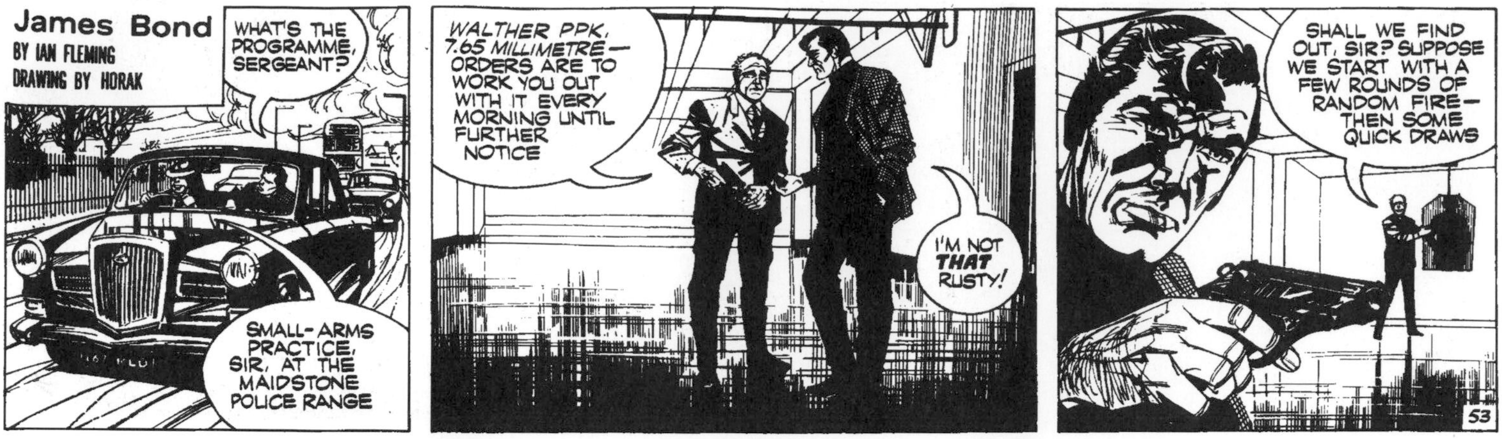
James Bond
BY IAN FLEMING
DRAWING BY HORAK
WHAT'S THE PROGRAMME, SERGEANT?
SMALL-ARMS PRACTICE, SIR, AT THE MAIDSTONE POLICE RANGE
WALTHER PPK, 7.65 MILLIMETRE— ORDERS ARE TO WORK YOU OUT WITH IT EVERY MORNING UNTIL FURTHER NOTICE
I'M NOT THAT RUSTY!
SHALL WE FIND OUT, SIR? SUPPOSE WE START WITH A FEW ROUNDS OF RANDOM FIRE— THEN SOME QUICK DRAWS
53

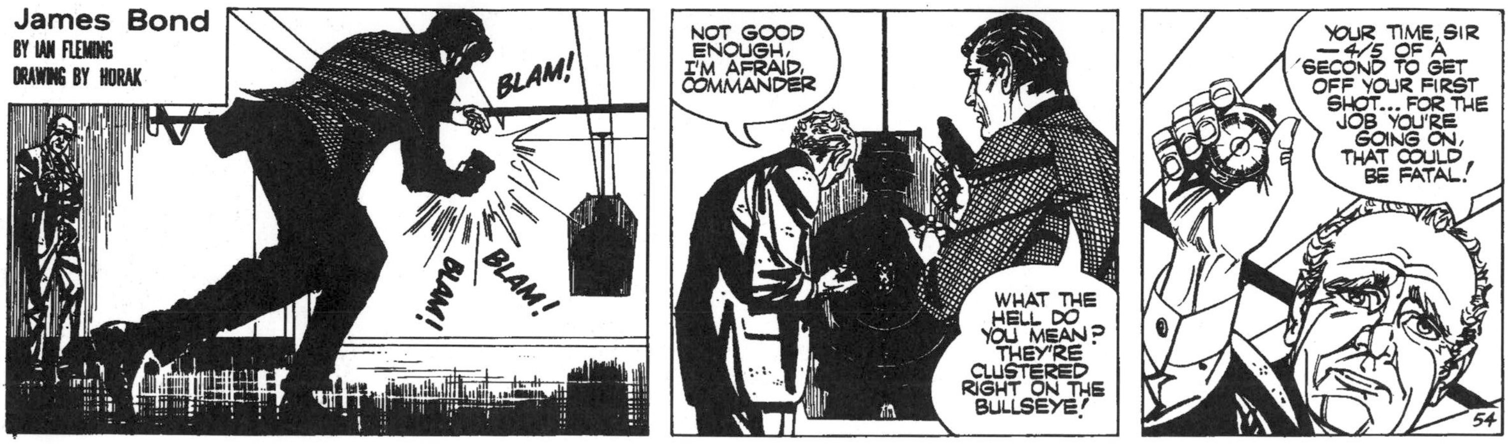
James Bond
BY IAN FLEMING
DRAWING BY HORAK
BLAM!
BLAM!
BLAM!
NOT GOOD ENOUGH, I'M AFRAID, COMMANDER
WHAT THE HELL DO YOU MEAN? THEY'RE CLUSTERED RIGHT ON THE BULLSEYE!
YOUR TIME, SIR —4/5 OF A SECOND TO GET OFF YOUR FIRST SHOT... FOR THE JOB YOU'RE GOING ON, THAT COULD BE FATAL!
54

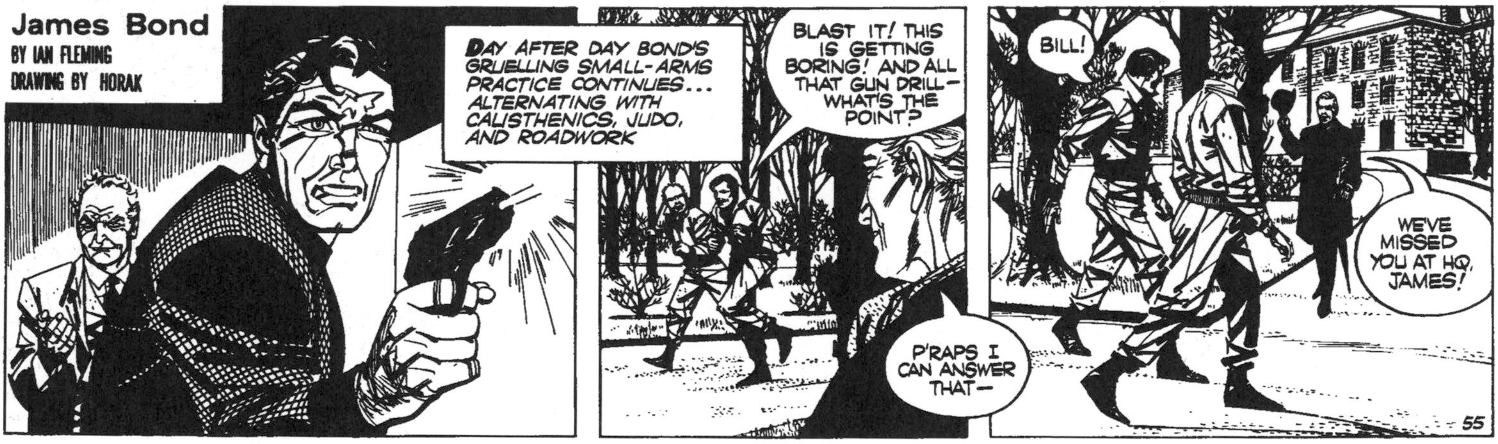
James Bond
BY IAN FLEMING
DRAWING BY HORAK
DAY AFTER DAY BOND'S GRUELLING SMALL-ARMS PRACTICE CONTINUES... ALTERNATING WITH CALISTHENICS, JUDO, AND ROADWORK
BLAST IT! THIS IS GETTING BORING! AND ALL THAT GUN DRILL— WHAT'S THE POINT?
P'RAPS I CAN ANSWER THAT—
BILL!
WE'VE MISSED YOU AT HQ, JAMES!
55

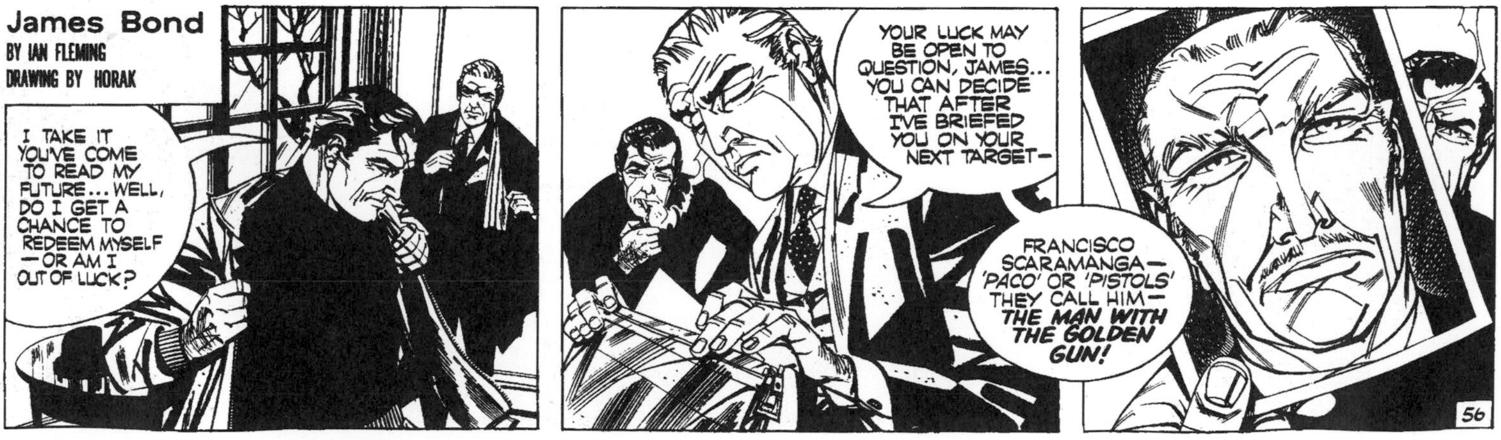
James Bond
BY IAN FLEMING
DRAWING BY HORAK
I TAKE IT YOU'VE COME TO READ MY FUTURE... WELL, DO I GET A CHANCE TO REDEEM MYSELF —OR AM I OUT OF LUCK?
YOUR LUCK MAY BE OPEN TO QUESTION, JAMES... YOU CAN DECIDE THAT AFTER I'VE BRIEFED YOU ON YOUR NEXT TARGET—
FRANCISCO SCARAMANGA— 'PACO' OR 'PISTOLS' THEY CALL HIM— THE MAN WITH THE GOLDEN GUN!
56

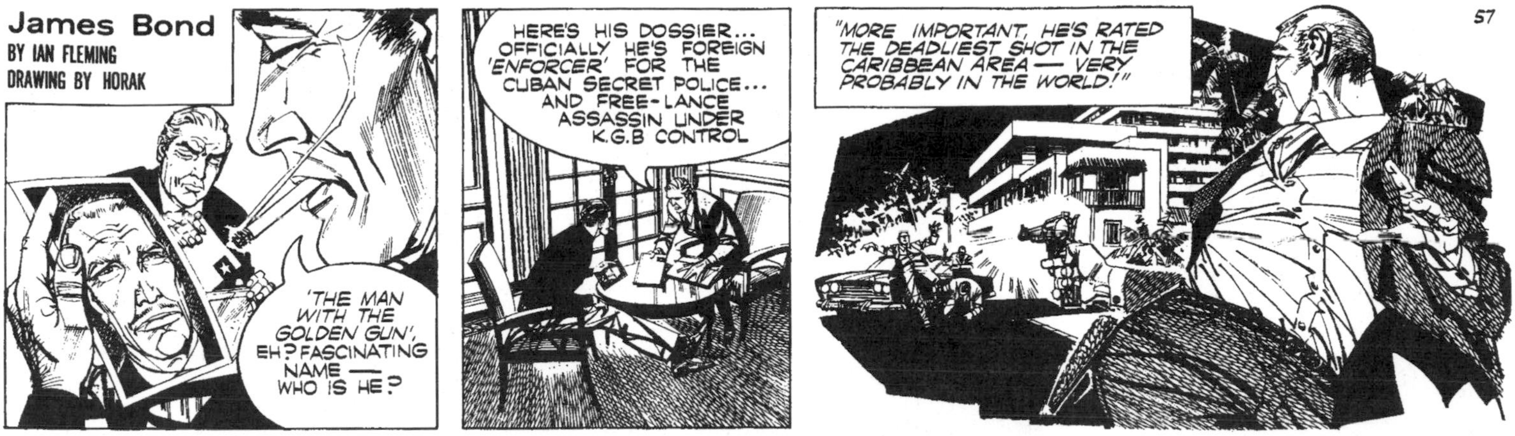
James Bond
BY IAN FLEMING
DRAWING BY HORAK
'THE MAN WITH THE GOLDEN GUN', EH? FASCINATING NAME — WHO IS HE?
HERE'S HIS DOSSIER... OFFICIALLY HE'S FOREIGN 'ENFORCER' FOR THE CUBAN SECRET POLICE... AND FREE-LANCE ASSASSIN UNDER K.G.B CONTROL
"MORE IMPORTANT, HE'S RATED THE DEADLIEST SHOT IN THE CARIBBEAN AREA — VERY PROBABLY IN THE WORLD!"
57

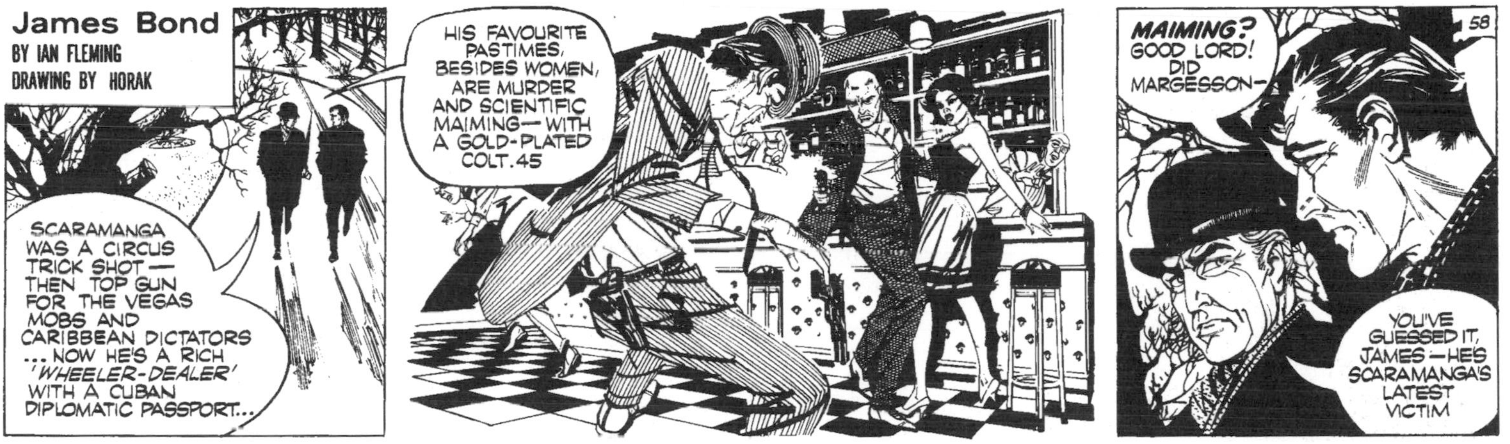
James Bond
BY IAN FLEMING
DRAWING BY HORAK
SCARAMANGA WAS A CIRCUS TRICK SHOT — THEN TOP GUN FOR THE VEGAS MOBS AND CARIBBEAN DICTATORS ... NOW HE'S A RICH 'WHEELER-DEALER' WITH A CUBAN DIPLOMATIC PASSPORT...
HIS FAVOURITE PASTIMES, BESIDES WOMEN, ARE MURDER AND SCIENTIFIC MAIMING — WITH A GOLD-PLATED COLT.45
MAIMING? GOOD LORD! DID MARGESSON—
YOU'VE GUESSED IT, JAMES — HE'S SCARAMANGA'S LATEST VICTIM
58

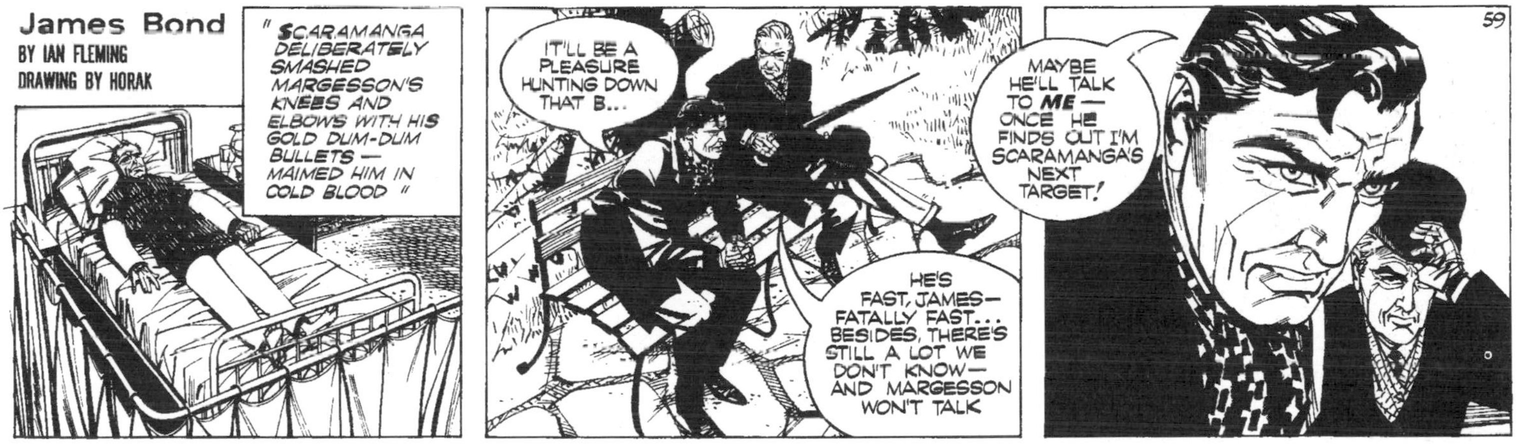
James Bond
BY IAN FLEMING
DRAWING BY HORAK
" SCARAMANGA DELIBERATELY SMASHED MARGESSON'S KNEES AND ELBOWS WITH HIS GOLD DUM-DUM BULLETS — MAIMED HIM IN COLD BLOOD "
IT'LL BE A PLEASURE HUNTING DOWN THAT B...
HE'S FAST, JAMES — FATALLY FAST... BESIDES, THERE'S STILL A LOT WE DON'T KNOW — AND MARGESSON WON'T TALK
MAYBE HE'LL TALK TO ME — ONCE HE FINDS OUT I'M SCARAMANGA'S NEXT TARGET!
59

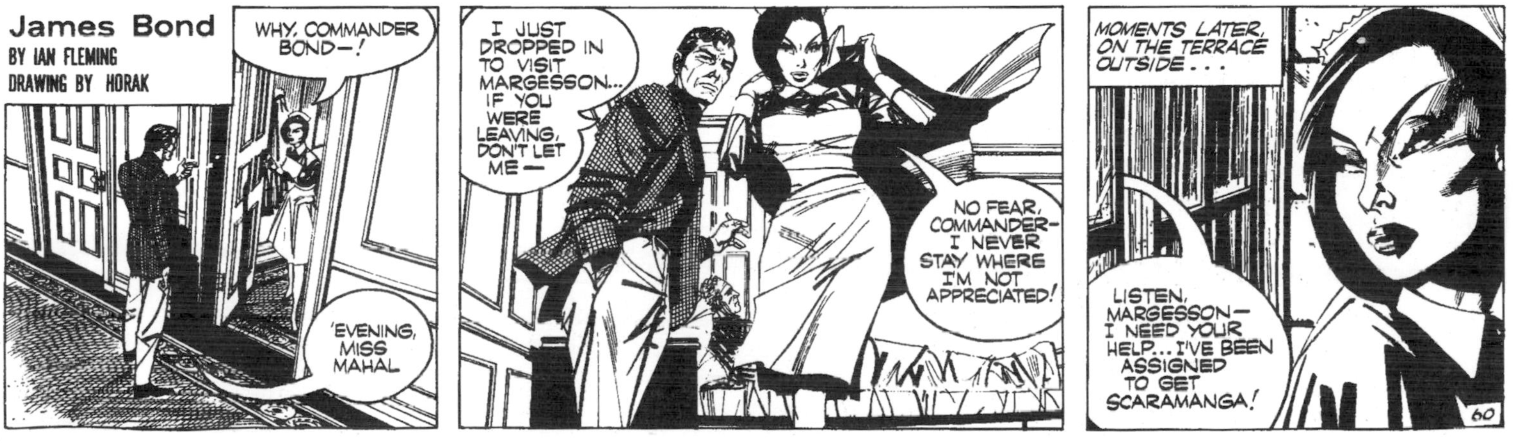
James Bond
BY IAN FLEMING
DRAWING BY HORAK
WHY, COMMANDER BOND—!
'EVENING, MISS MAHAL
I JUST DROPPED IN TO VISIT MARGESSON... IF YOU WERE LEAVING, DON'T LET ME —
NO FEAR, COMMANDER — I NEVER STAY WHERE I'M NOT APPRECIATED!
MOMENTS LATER, ON THE TERRACE OUTSIDE . . .
LISTEN, MARGESSON — I NEED YOUR HELP... I'VE BEEN ASSIGNED TO GET SCARAMANGA!
60

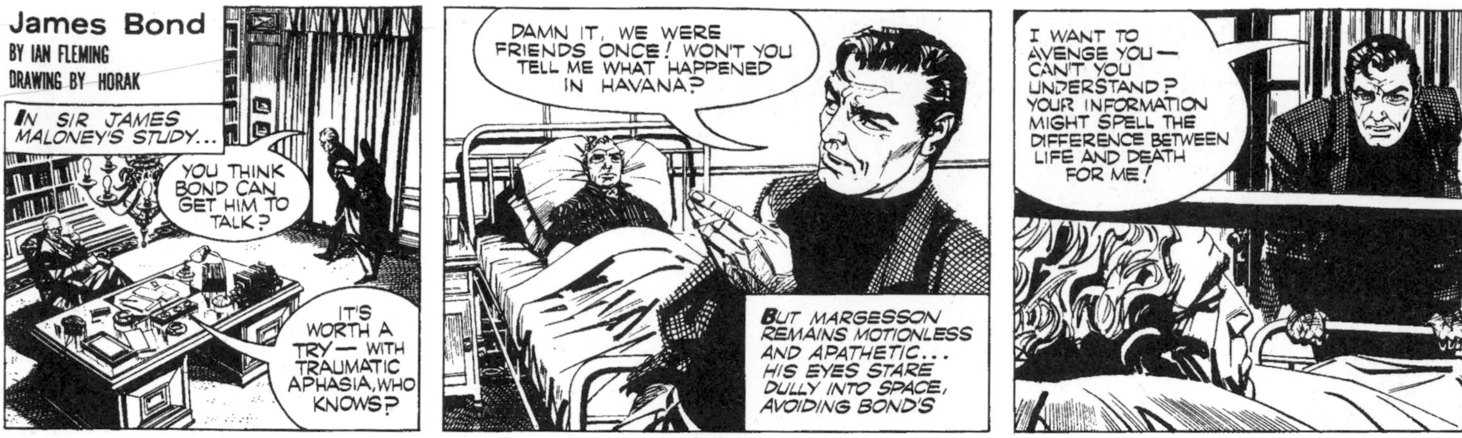
James Bond
BY IAN FLEMING
DRAWING BY HORAK
IN SIR JAMES MALONEY'S STUDY...
YOU THINK BOND CAN GET HIM TO TALK?
IT'S WORTH A TRY — WITH TRAUMATIC APHASIA, WHO KNOWS?
DAMN IT, WE WERE FRIENDS ONCE! WON'T YOU TELL ME WHAT HAPPENED IN HAVANA?
BUT MARGESSON REMAINS MOTIONLESS AND APATHETIC... HIS EYES STARE DULLY INTO SPACE, AVOIDING BOND'S
I WANT TO AVENGE YOU — CAN'T YOU UNDERSTAND? YOUR INFORMATION MIGHT SPELL THE DIFFERENCE BETWEEN LIFE AND DEATH FOR ME!
61

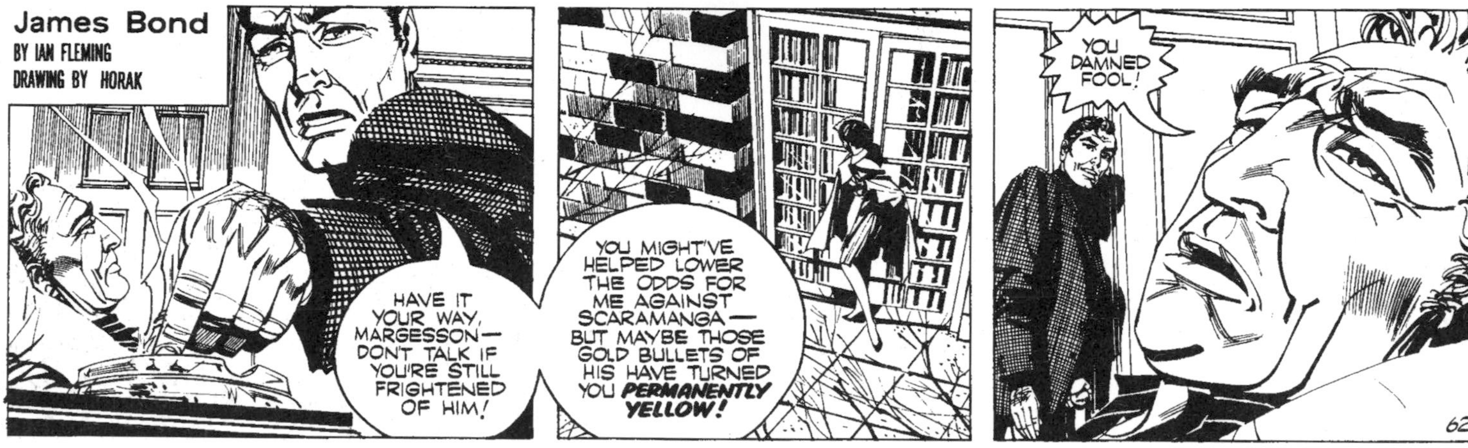
James Bond
BY IAN FLEMING
DRAWING BY HORAK
HAVE IT YOUR WAY, MARGESSON — DON'T TALK IF YOU'RE STILL FRIGHTENED OF HIM!
YOU MIGHT'VE HELPED LOWER THE ODDS FOR ME AGAINST SCARAMANGA — BUT MAYBE THOSE GOLD BULLETS OF HIS HAVE TURNED YOU PERMANENTLY YELLOW!
YOU DAMNED FOOL!
62

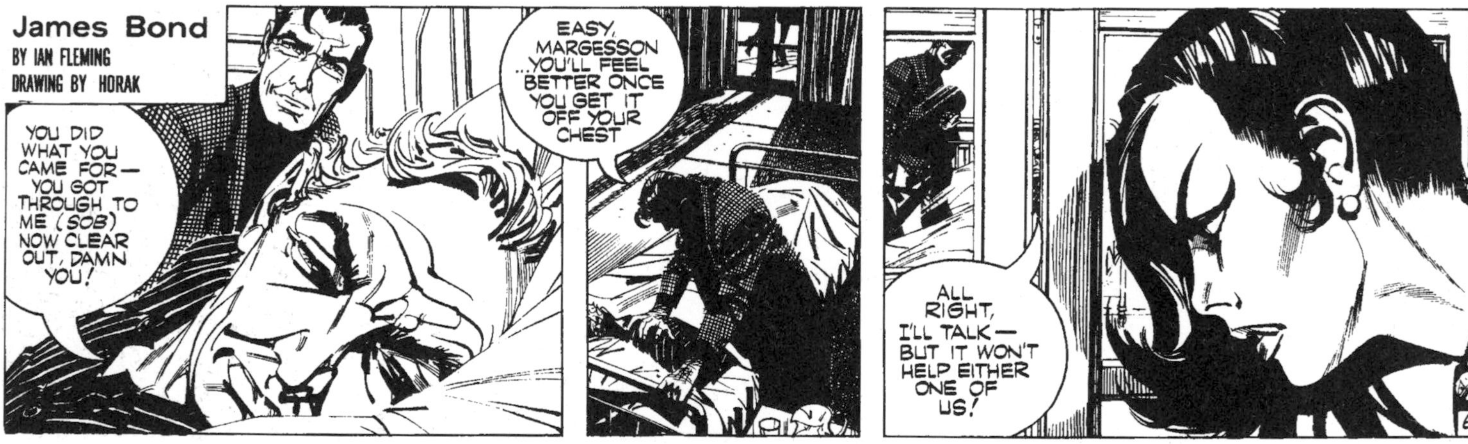
James Bond
BY IAN FLEMING
DRAWING BY HORAK
YOU DID WHAT YOU CAME FOR — YOU GOT THROUGH TO ME (SOB) NOW CLEAR OUT, DAMN YOU!
EASY, MARGESSON ...YOU'LL FEEL BETTER ONCE YOU GET IT OFF YOUR CHEST
ALL RIGHT, I'LL TALK — BUT IT WON'T HELP EITHER ONE OF US!
63

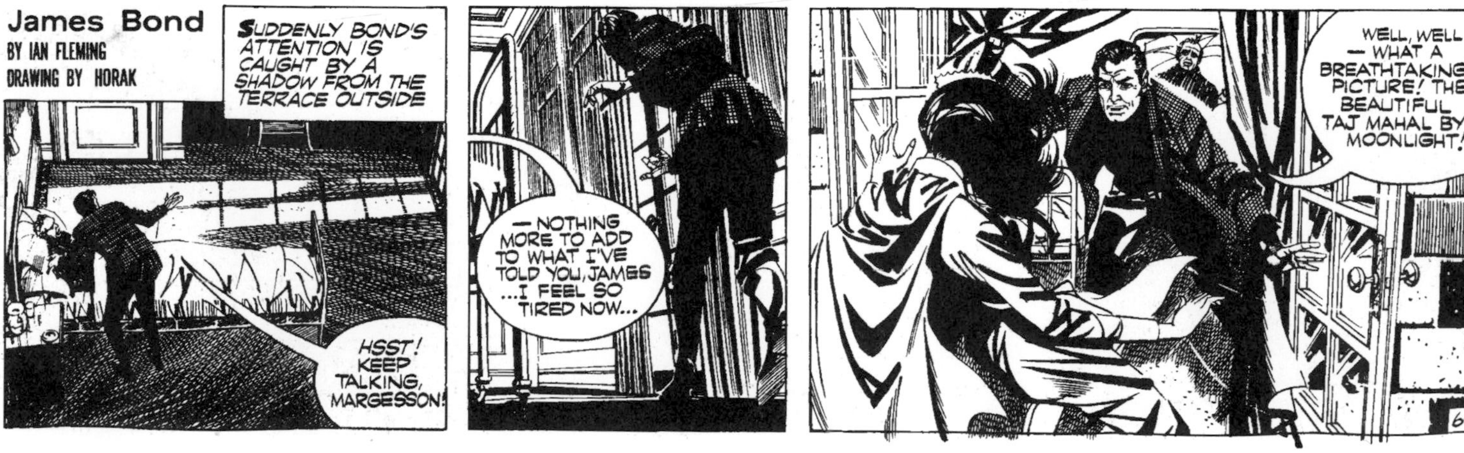
James Bond
BY IAN FLEMING
DRAWING BY HORAK
SUDDENLY BOND'S ATTENTION IS CAUGHT BY A SHADOW FROM THE TERRACE OUTSIDE
HSST! KEEP TALKING, MARGESSON!
— NOTHING MORE TO ADD TO WHAT I'VE TOLD YOU, JAMES ...I FEEL SO TIRED NOW...
WELL, WELL — WHAT A BREATHTAKING PICTURE! THE BEAUTIFUL TAJ MAHAL BY MOONLIGHT!
64

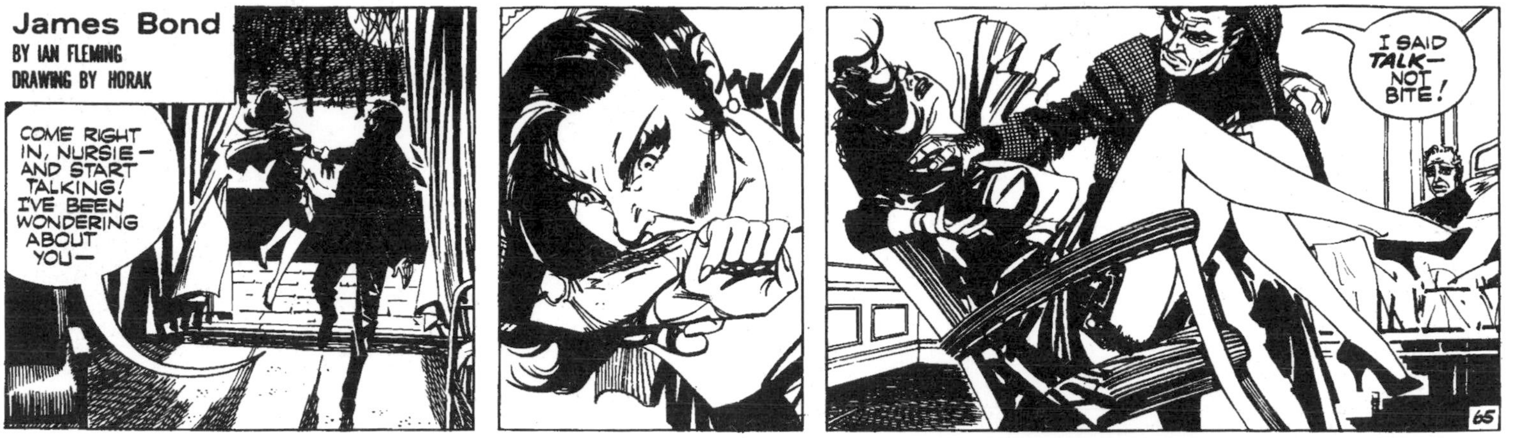
James Bond
BY IAN FLEMING
DRAWING BY HORAK
COME RIGHT IN, NURSIE— AND START TALKING! I'VE BEEN WONDERING ABOUT YOU—
I SAID TALK— NOT BITE!
65

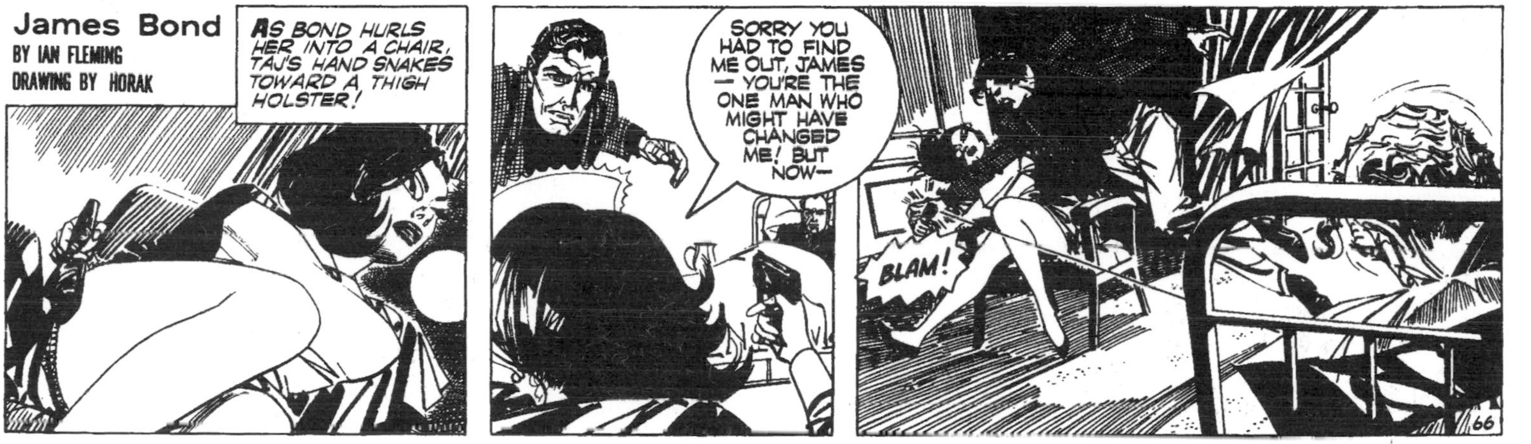
James Bond
BY IAN FLEMING
DRAWING BY HORAK
AS BOND HURLS HER INTO A CHAIR, TAJ'S HAND SNAKES TOWARD A THIGH HOLSTER!
SORRY YOU HAD TO FIND ME OUT, JAMES — YOU'RE THE ONE MAN WHO MIGHT HAVE CHANGED ME! BUT NOW—
BLAM!
66

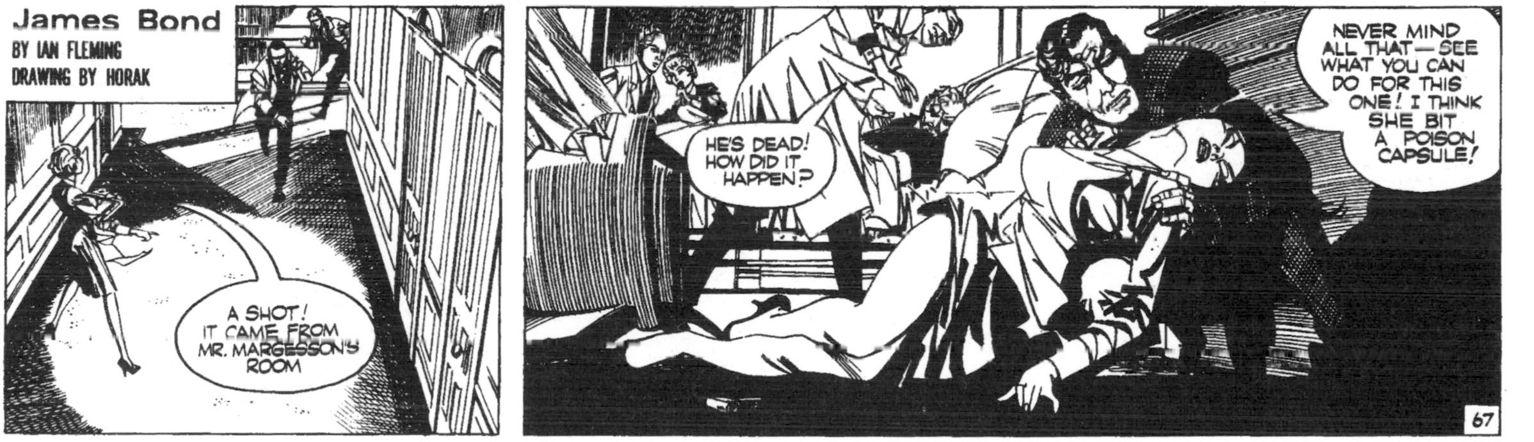
James Bond
BY IAN FLEMING
DRAWING BY HORAK
A SHOT! IT CAME FROM MR. MARGESSON'S ROOM
HE'S DEAD! HOW DID IT HAPPEN?
NEVER MIND ALL THAT— SEE WHAT YOU CAN DO FOR THIS ONE! I THINK SHE BIT A POISON CAPSULE!
67

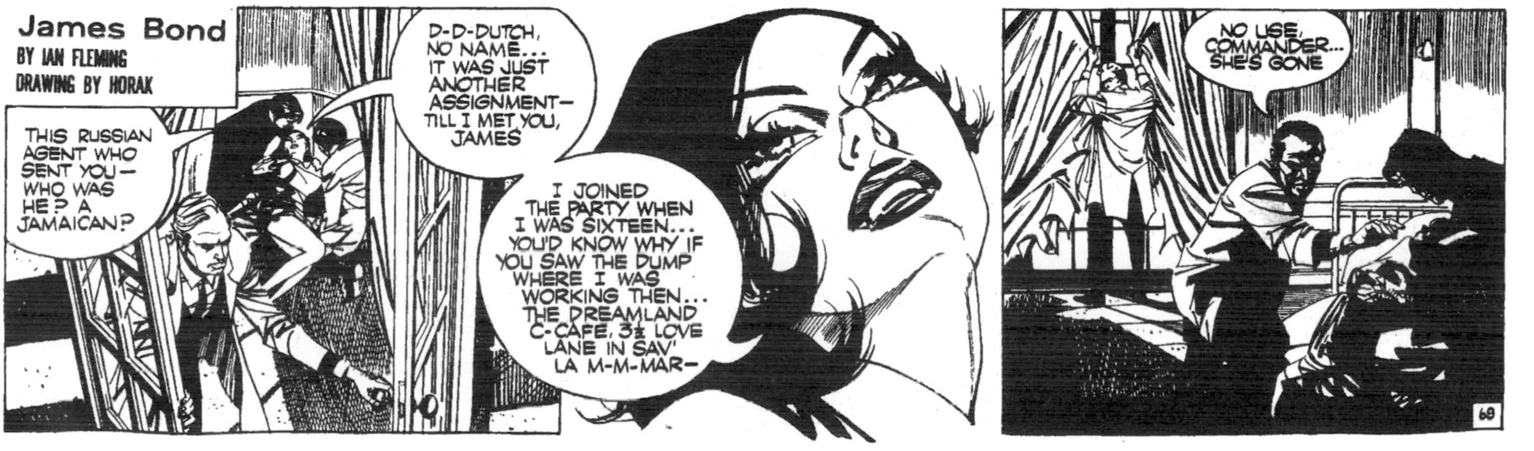
James Bond
BY IAN FLEMING
DRAWING BY HORAK
THIS RUSSIAN AGENT WHO SENT YOU— WHO WAS HE? A JAMAICAN?
D-D-DUTCH, NO NAME... IT WAS JUST ANOTHER ASSIGNMENT— TILL I MET YOU, JAMES
I JOINED THE PARTY WHEN I WAS SIXTEEN... YOU'D KNOW WHY IF YOU SAW THE DUMP WHERE I WAS WORKING THEN... THE DREAMLAND C-CAFE, 3½ LOVE LANE IN SAV' LA M-M-MAR—
NO USE, COMMANDER... SHE'S GONE
68

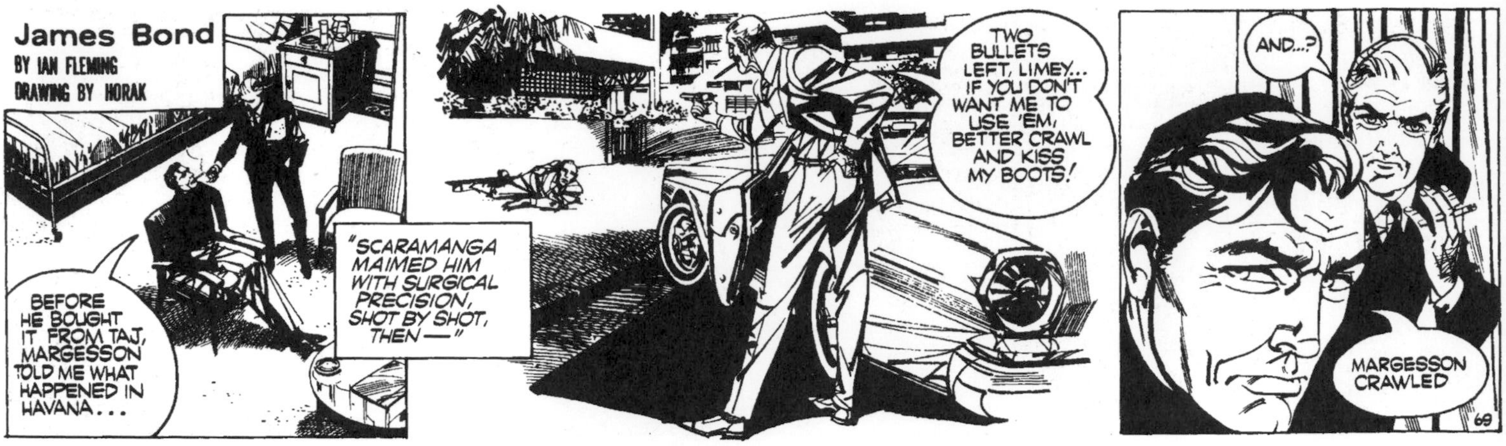
James Bond
BY IAN FLEMING
DRAWING BY HORAK
BEFORE HE BOUGHT IT FROM TAJ, MARGESSON TOLD ME WHAT HAPPENED IN HAVANA...
"SCARAMANGA MAIMED HIM WITH SURGICAL PRECISION, SHOT BY SHOT, THEN—"
TWO BULLETS LEFT, LIMEY... IF YOU DON'T WANT ME TO USE 'EM, BETTER CRAWL AND KISS MY BOOTS!
AND...?
MARGESSON CRAWLED
69

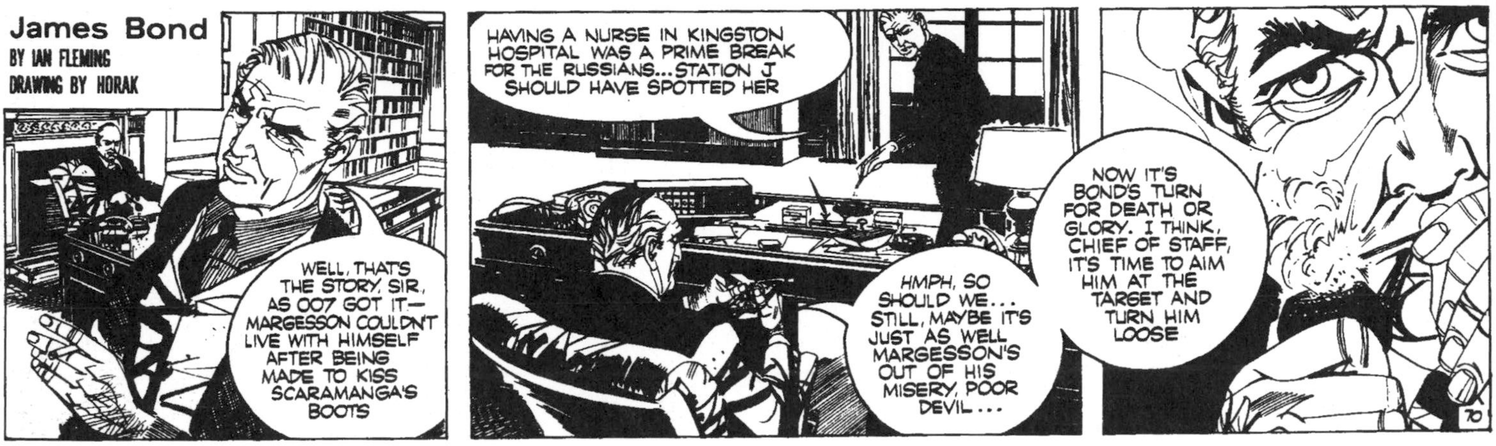
James Bond
BY IAN FLEMING
DRAWING BY HORAK
WELL, THAT'S THE STORY, SIR, AS 007 GOT IT— MARGESSON COULDN'T LIVE WITH HIMSELF AFTER BEING MADE TO KISS SCARAMANGA'S BOOTS
HAVING A NURSE IN KINGSTON HOSPITAL WAS A PRIME BREAK FOR THE RUSSIANS... STATION J SHOULD HAVE SPOTTED HER
HMPH, SO SHOULD WE... STILL, MAYBE IT'S JUST AS WELL MARGESSON'S OUT OF HIS MISERY, POOR DEVIL...
NOW IT'S BOND'S TURN FOR DEATH OR GLORY. I THINK, CHIEF OF STAFF, IT'S TIME TO AIM HIM AT THE TARGET AND TURN HIM LOOSE
70

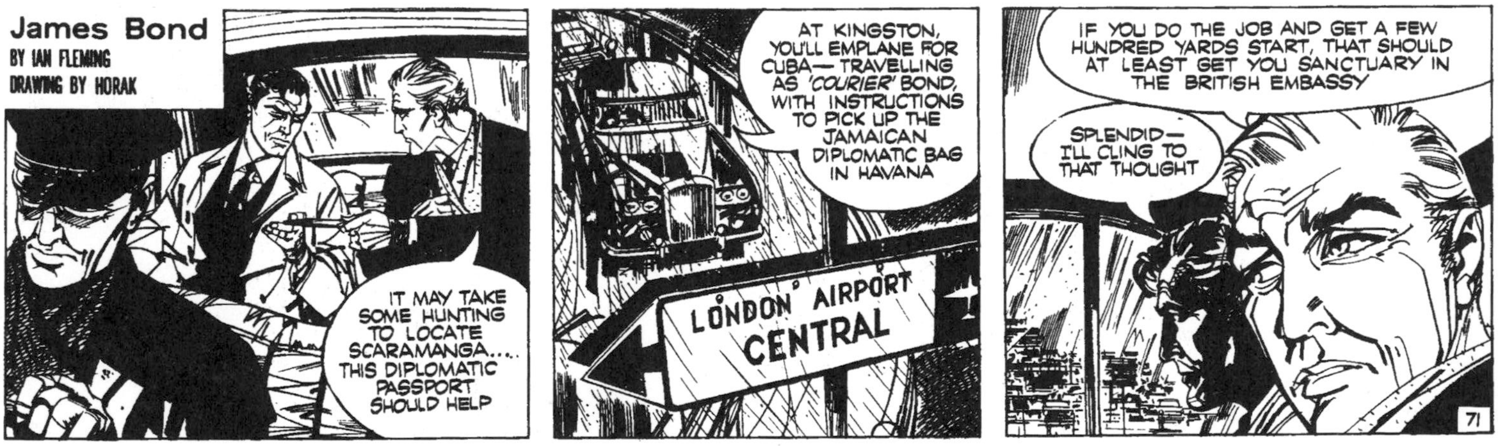
James Bond
BY IAN FLEMING
DRAWING BY HORAK
IT MAY TAKE SOME HUNTING TO LOCATE SCARAMANGA... THIS DIPLOMATIC PASSPORT SHOULD HELP
AT KINGSTON, YOU'LL EMPLANE FOR CUBA— TRAVELLING AS 'COURIER' BOND, WITH INSTRUCTIONS TO PICK UP THE JAMAICAN DIPLOMATIC BAG IN HAVANA
LONDON AIRPORT CENTRAL
IF YOU DO THE JOB AND GET A FEW HUNDRED YARDS START, THAT SHOULD AT LEAST GET YOU SANCTUARY IN THE BRITISH EMBASSY
SPLENDID— I'LL CLING TO THAT THOUGHT
71

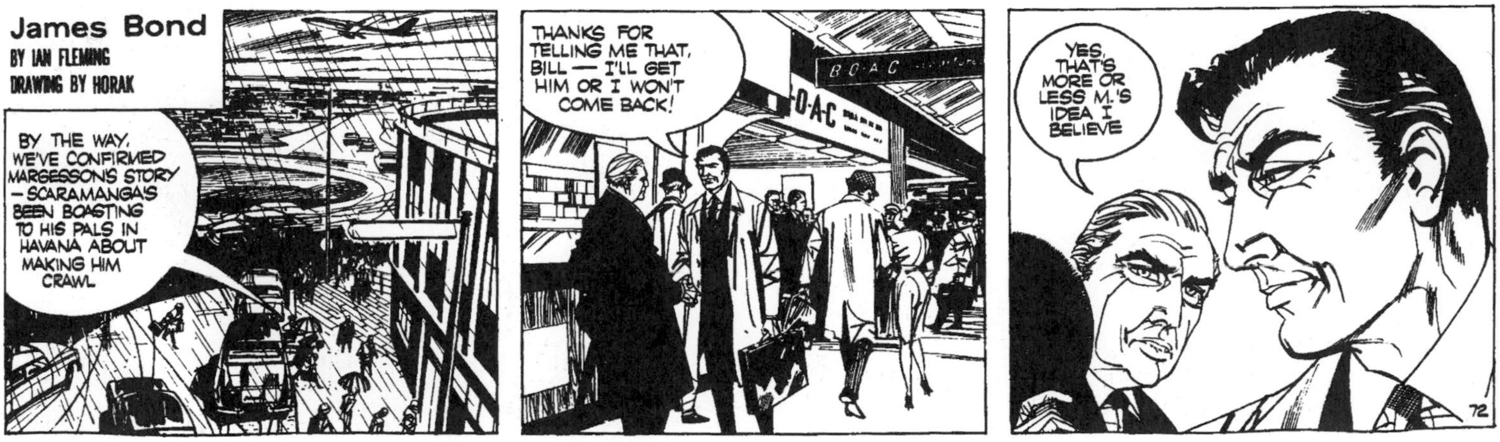
James Bond
BY IAN FLEMING
DRAWING BY HORAK
BY THE WAY, WE'VE CONFIRMED MARGESSON'S STORY —SCARAMANGA'S BEEN BOASTING TO HIS PALS IN HAVANA ABOUT MAKING HIM CRAWL
THANKS FOR TELLING ME THAT, BILL — I'LL GET HIM OR I WON'T COME BACK!
B·O·A·C
YES, THAT'S MORE OR LESS M.'S IDEA I BELIEVE
72

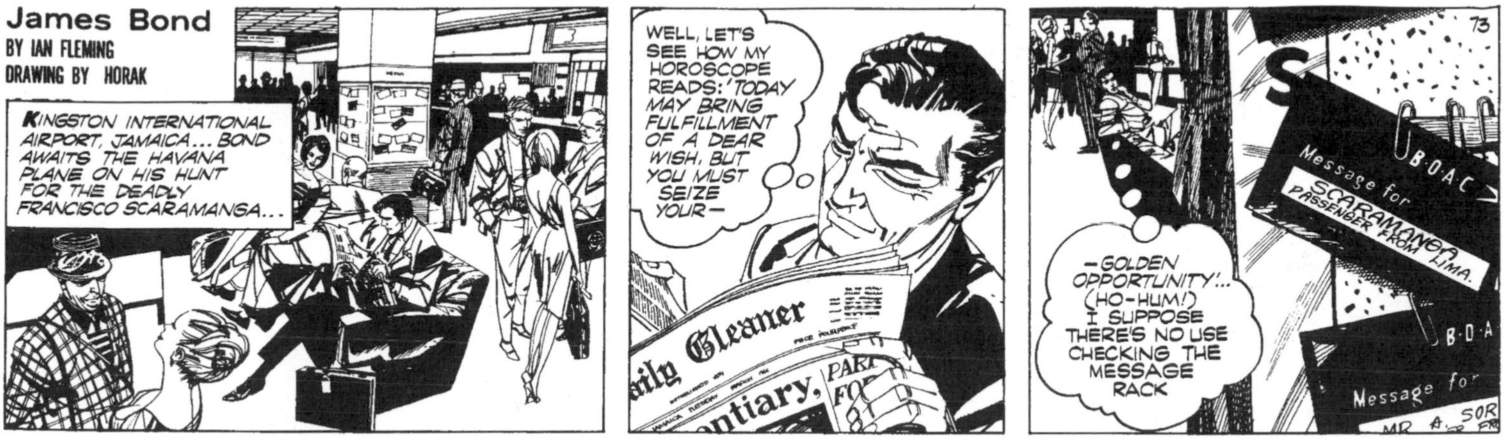
James Bond
BY IAN FLEMING
DRAWING BY HORAK
KINGSTON INTERNATIONAL AIRPORT, JAMAICA... BOND AWAITS THE HAVANA PLANE ON HIS HUNT FOR THE DEADLY FRANCISCO SCARAMANGA...
WELL, LET'S SEE HOW MY HOROSCOPE READS: 'TODAY MAY BRING FULFILLMENT OF A DEAR WISH, BUT YOU MUST SEIZE YOUR—
Daily Gleaner
73
—GOLDEN OPPORTUNITY'... (HO-HUM!) I SUPPOSE THERE'S NO USE CHECKING THE MESSAGE RACK
B.O.A.C
Message for
SCARAMANGA PASSENGER FROM LIMA
Message for

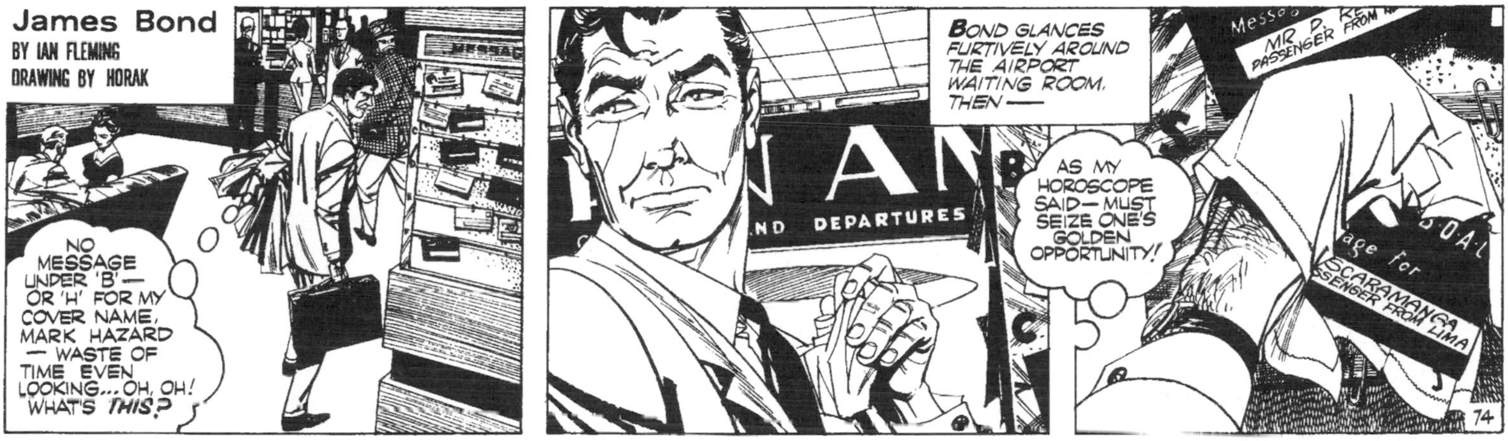
James Bond
BY IAN FLEMING
DRAWING BY HORAK
NO MESSAGE UNDER 'B'— OR 'H' FOR MY COVER NAME, MARK HAZARD — WASTE OF TIME EVEN LOOKING... OH, OH! WHAT'S *THIS?*
DEPARTURES
BOND GLANCES FURTIVELY AROUND THE AIRPORT WAITING ROOM, THEN —
AS MY HOROSCOPE SAID— MUST SEIZE ONE'S GOLDEN OPPORTUNITY!
SCARAMANGA PASSENGER FROM LIMA
74

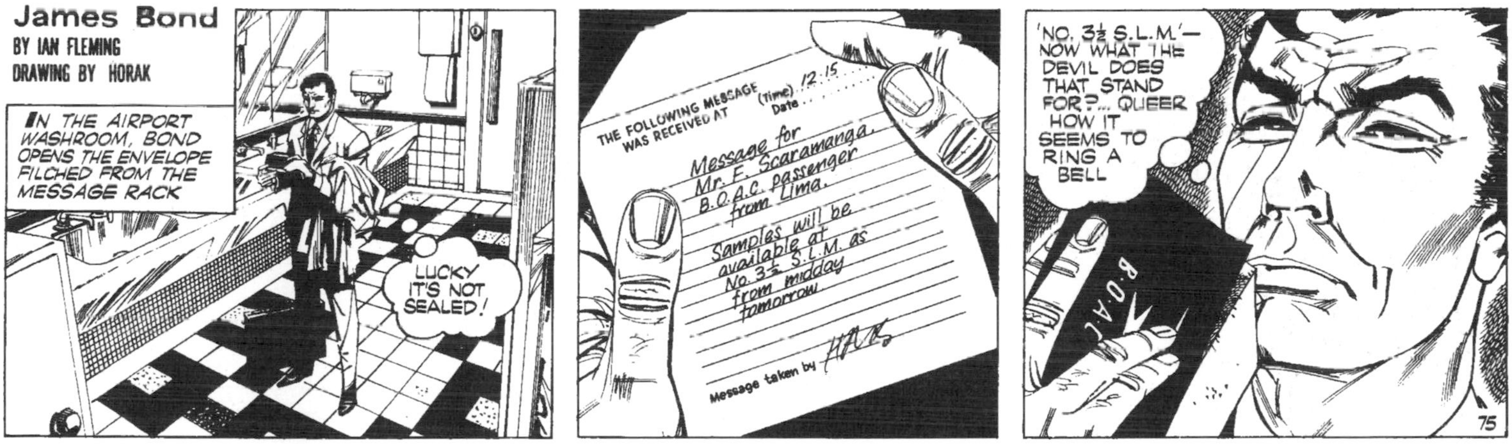
James Bond
BY IAN FLEMING
DRAWING BY HORAK
IN THE AIRPORT WASHROOM, BOND OPENS THE ENVELOPE FILCHED FROM THE MESSAGE RACK
LUCKY IT'S NOT SEALED!
THE FOLLOWING MESSAGE WAS RECEIVED AT (Time) 12:15 Date
Message for Mr. F. Scaramanga. B.O.A.C. passenger from Lima.
Samples will be available at No. 3½ S.L.M. as from midday tomorrow
Message taken by
'NO. 3½ S.L.M.'— NOW WHAT THE DEVIL DOES THAT STAND FOR?... QUEER HOW IT SEEMS TO RING A BELL
B.O.A.C.
75

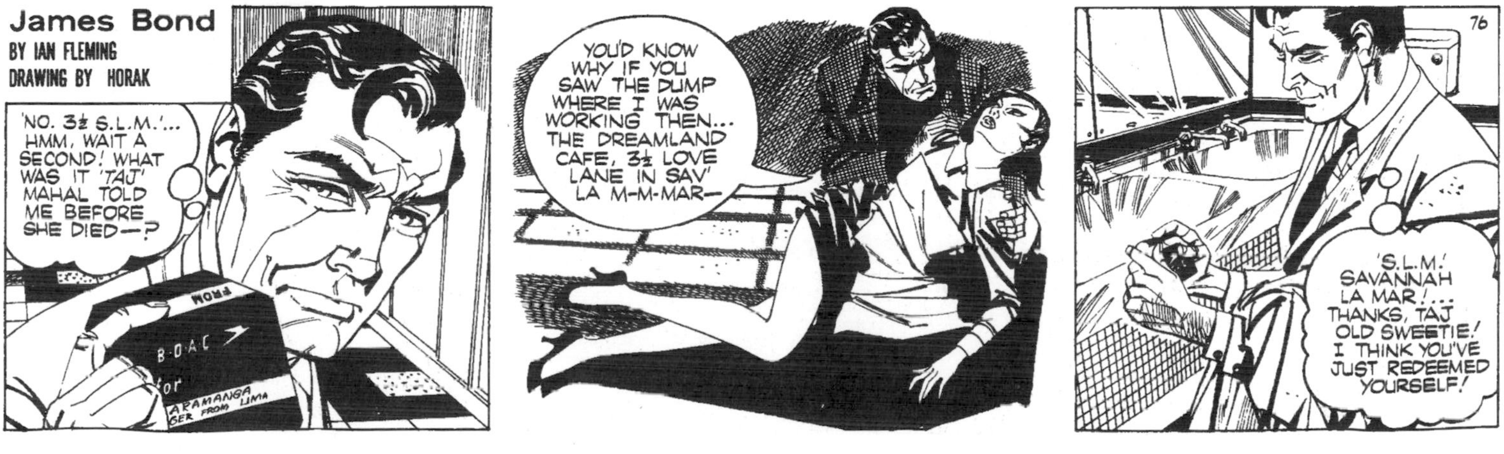
James Bond
BY IAN FLEMING
DRAWING BY HORAK
'NO. 3½ S.L.M.'... HMM, WAIT A SECOND! WHAT WAS IT 'TAJ' MAHAL TOLD ME BEFORE SHE DIED—?
B.O.A.C
YOU'D KNOW WHY IF YOU SAW THE DUMP WHERE I WAS WORKING THEN... THE DREAMLAND CAFE, 3½ LOVE LANE IN SAV' LA M-M-MAR—
76
'S.L.M.' SAVANNAH LA MAR!... THANKS, TAJ OLD SWEETIE! I THINK YOU'VE JUST REDEEMED YOURSELF!

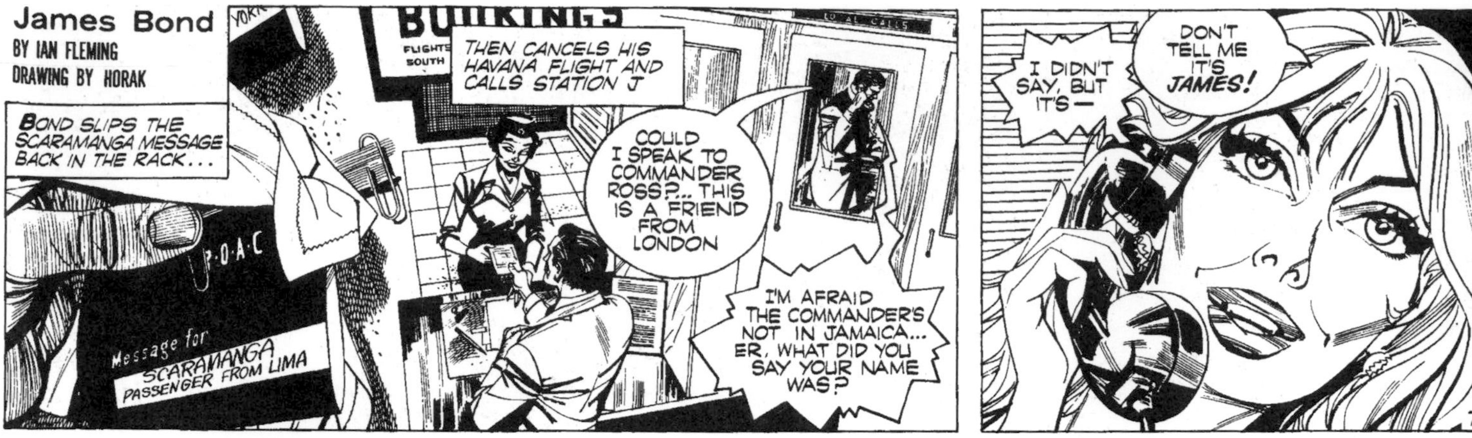
James Bond
BY IAN FLEMING
DRAWING BY HORAK
BOND SLIPS THE SCARAMANGA MESSAGE BACK IN THE RACK...
B.O.A.C
Message for SCARAMANGA PASSENGER FROM LIMA
THEN CANCELS HIS HAVANA FLIGHT AND CALLS STATION J
COULD I SPEAK TO COMMANDER ROSS?... THIS IS A FRIEND FROM LONDON
I'M AFRAID THE COMMANDER'S NOT IN JAMAICA... ER, WHAT DID YOU SAY YOUR NAME WAS?
I DIDN'T SAY, BUT IT'S —
DON'T TELL ME IT'S JAMES!
77

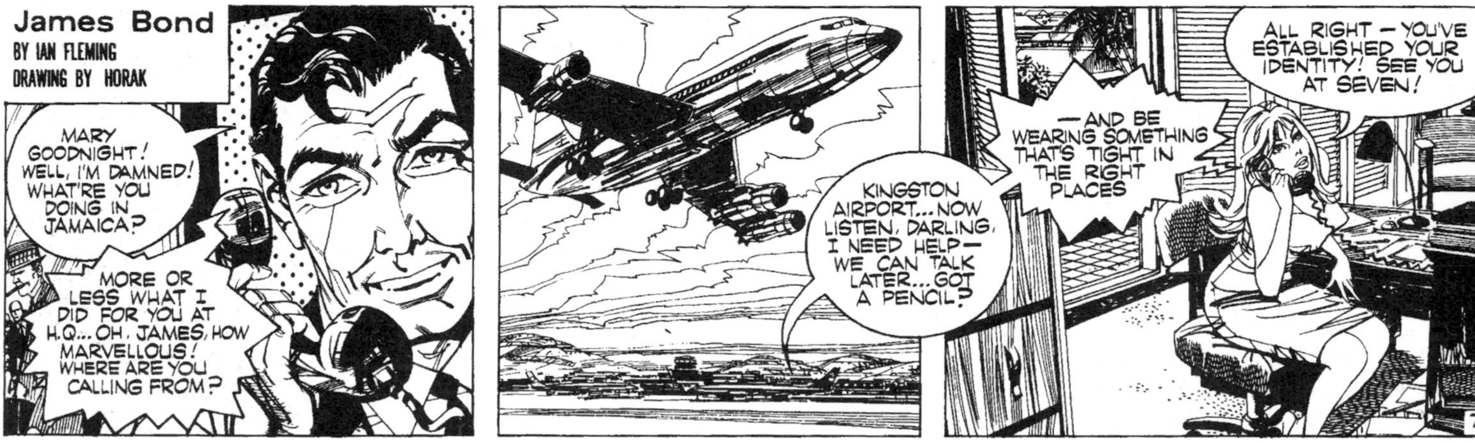
James Bond
BY IAN FLEMING
DRAWING BY HORAK
MARY GOODNIGHT! WELL, I'M DAMNED! WHAT'RE YOU DOING IN JAMAICA?
MORE OR LESS WHAT I DID FOR YOU AT H.Q... OH, JAMES, HOW MARVELLOUS! WHERE ARE YOU CALLING FROM?
KINGSTON AIRPORT... NOW LISTEN, DARLING, I NEED HELP— WE CAN TALK LATER... GOT A PENCIL?
—AND BE WEARING SOMETHING THAT'S TIGHT IN THE RIGHT PLACES
ALL RIGHT — YOU'VE ESTABLISHED YOUR IDENTITY! SEE YOU AT SEVEN!
78

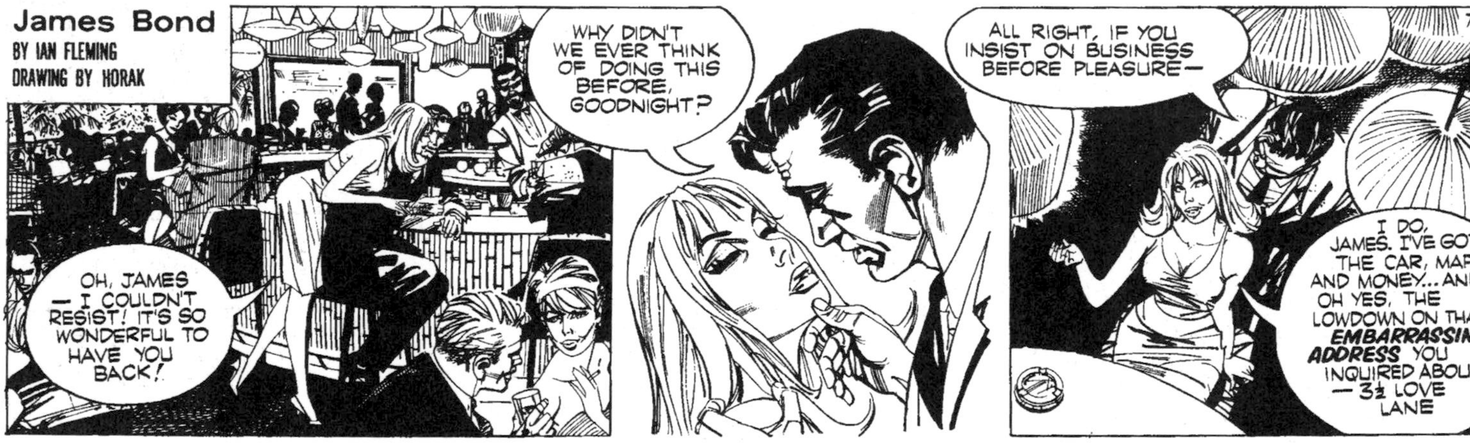
James Bond
BY IAN FLEMING
DRAWING BY HORAK
OH, JAMES — I COULDN'T RESIST! IT'S SO WONDERFUL TO HAVE YOU BACK!
WHY DIDN'T WE EVER THINK OF DOING THIS BEFORE, GOODNIGHT?
ALL RIGHT, IF YOU INSIST ON BUSINESS BEFORE PLEASURE—
I DO, JAMES. I'VE GOT THE CAR, MAP, AND MONEY... AND, OH YES, THE LOWDOWN ON THAT EMBARRASSING ADDRESS YOU INQUIRED ABOUT — 3½ LOVE LANE
79

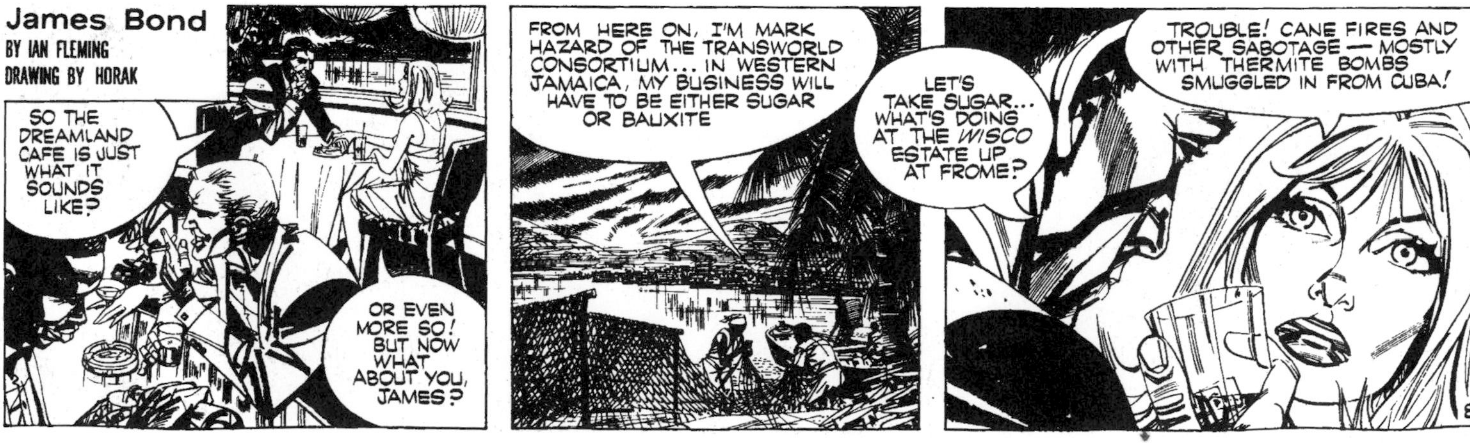
James Bond
BY IAN FLEMING
DRAWING BY HORAK
SO THE DREAMLAND CAFE IS JUST WHAT IT SOUNDS LIKE?
OR EVEN MORE SO! BUT NOW WHAT ABOUT YOU, JAMES?
FROM HERE ON, I'M MARK HAZARD OF THE TRANSWORLD CONSORTIUM... IN WESTERN JAMAICA, MY BUSINESS WILL HAVE TO BE EITHER SUGAR OR BAUXITE
LET'S TAKE SUGAR... WHAT'S DOING AT THE WISCO ESTATE UP AT FROME?
TROUBLE! CANE FIRES AND OTHER SABOTAGE — MOSTLY WITH THERMITE BOMBS SMUGGLED IN FROM CUBA!
80

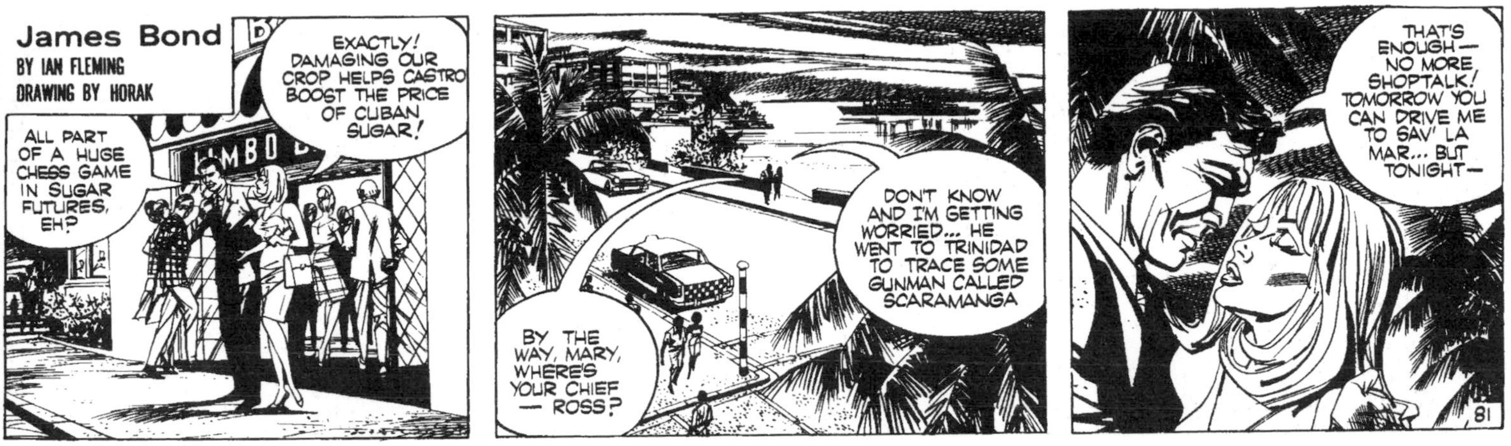
James Bond
BY IAN FLEMING
DRAWING BY HORAK
ALL PART OF A HUGE CHESS GAME IN SUGAR FUTURES, EH?
EXACTLY! DAMAGING OUR CROP HELPS CASTRO BOOST THE PRICE OF CUBAN SUGAR!
BY THE WAY, MARY, WHERE'S YOUR CHIEF — ROSS?
DON'T KNOW AND I'M GETTING WORRIED... HE WENT TO TRINIDAD TO TRACE SOME GUNMAN CALLED SCARAMANGA
THAT'S ENOUGH— NO MORE SHOPTALK! TOMORROW YOU CAN DRIVE ME TO SAV' LA MAR... BUT TONIGHT—
81

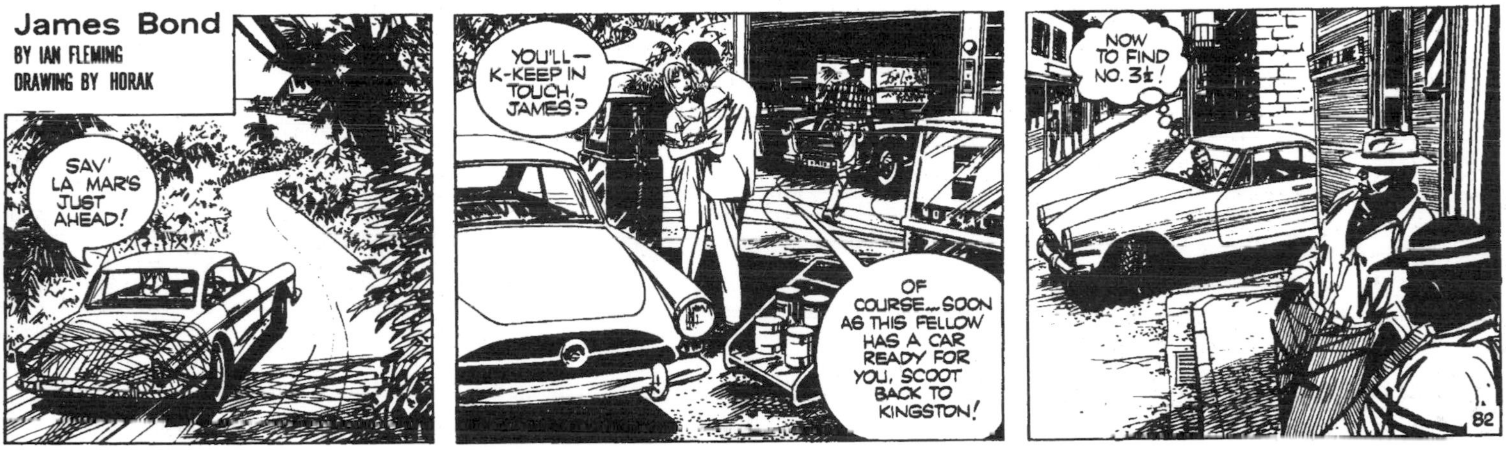
James Bond
BY IAN FLEMING
DRAWING BY HORAK
SAV' LA MAR'S JUST AHEAD!
YOU'LL— K-KEEP IN TOUCH, JAMES?
OF COURSE... SOON AS THIS FELLOW HAS A CAR READY FOR YOU, SCOOT BACK TO KINGSTON!
NOW TO FIND NO. 3½!
82

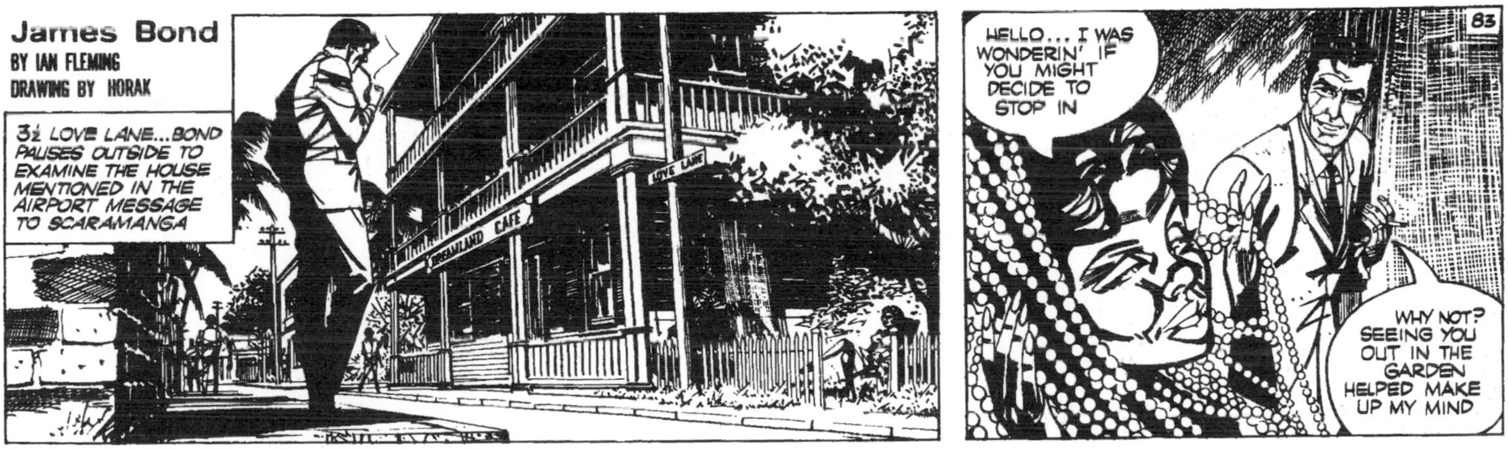
James Bond
BY IAN FLEMING
DRAWING BY HORAK
3½ LOVE LANE... BOND PAUSES OUTSIDE TO EXAMINE THE HOUSE MENTIONED IN THE AIRPORT MESSAGE TO SCARAMANGA
LOVE LANE
DREAMLAND CAFE
83
HELLO... I WAS WONDERIN' IF YOU MIGHT DECIDE TO STOP IN
WHY NOT? SEEING YOU OUT IN THE GARDEN HELPED MAKE UP MY MIND

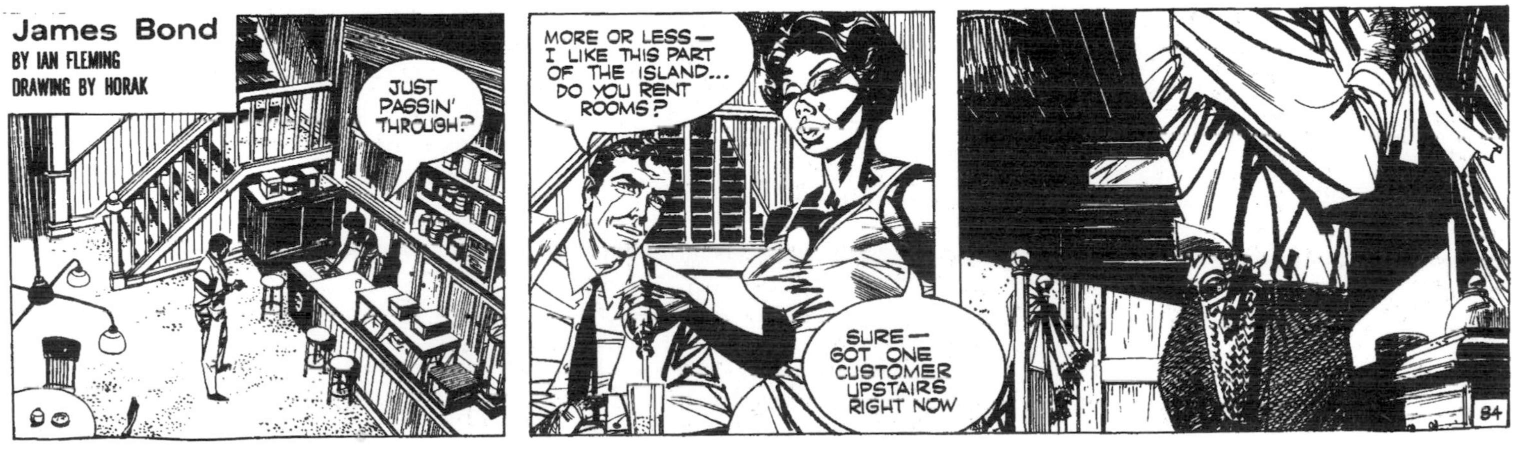
James Bond
BY IAN FLEMING
DRAWING BY HORAK
JUST PASSIN' THROUGH?
MORE OR LESS— I LIKE THIS PART OF THE ISLAND... DO YOU RENT ROOMS?
SURE— GOT ONE CUSTOMER UPSTAIRS RIGHT NOW
84

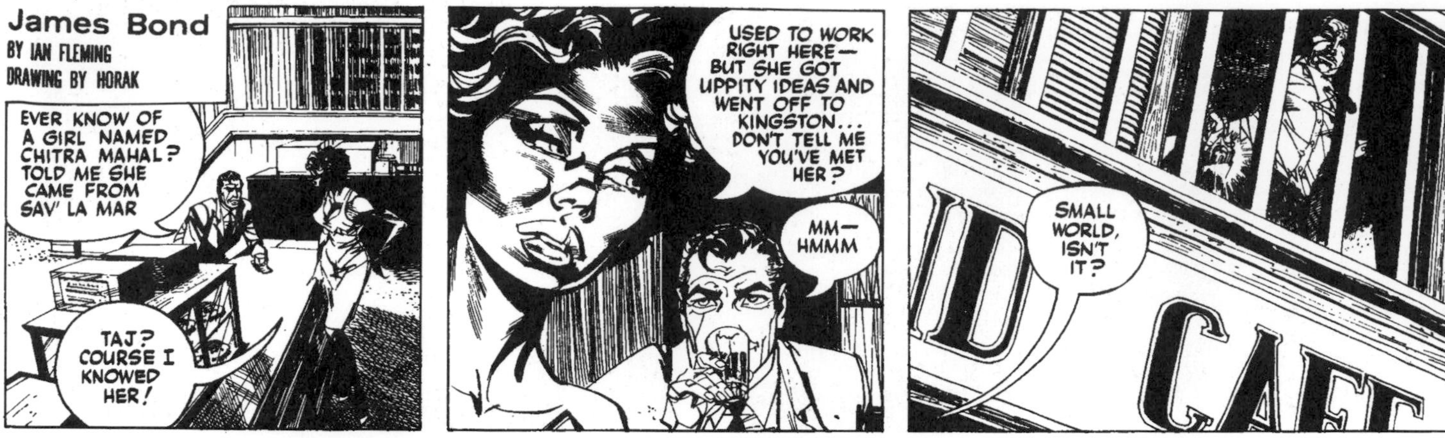
James Bond
BY IAN FLEMING
DRAWING BY HORAK
EVER KNOW OF A GIRL NAMED CHITRA MAHAL? TOLD ME SHE CAME FROM SAV' LA MAR
TAJ? COURSE I KNOWED HER!
USED TO WORK RIGHT HERE— BUT SHE GOT UPPITY IDEAS AND WENT OFF TO KINGSTON... DON'T TELL ME YOU'VE MET HER?
MM— HMMM
SMALL WORLD, ISN'T IT?
85

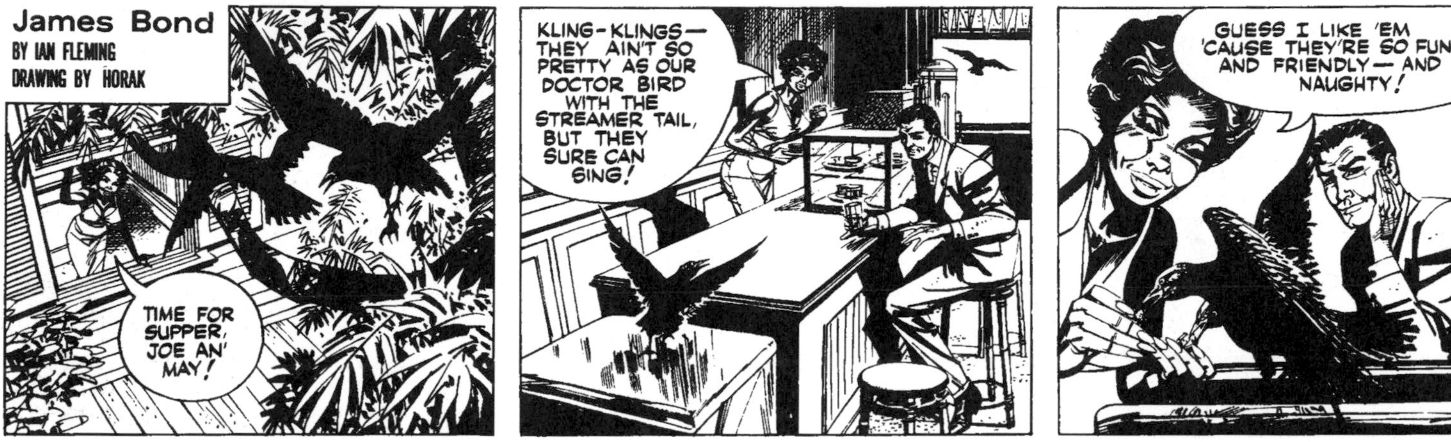
James Bond
BY IAN FLEMING
DRAWING BY HORAK
TIME FOR SUPPER, JOE AN' MAY!
KLING-KLINGS— THEY AIN'T SO PRETTY AS OUR DOCTOR BIRD WITH THE STREAMER TAIL, BUT THEY SURE CAN SING!
GUESS I LIKE 'EM 'CAUSE THEY'RE SO FUNNY AND FRIENDLY— AND NAUGHTY!
86

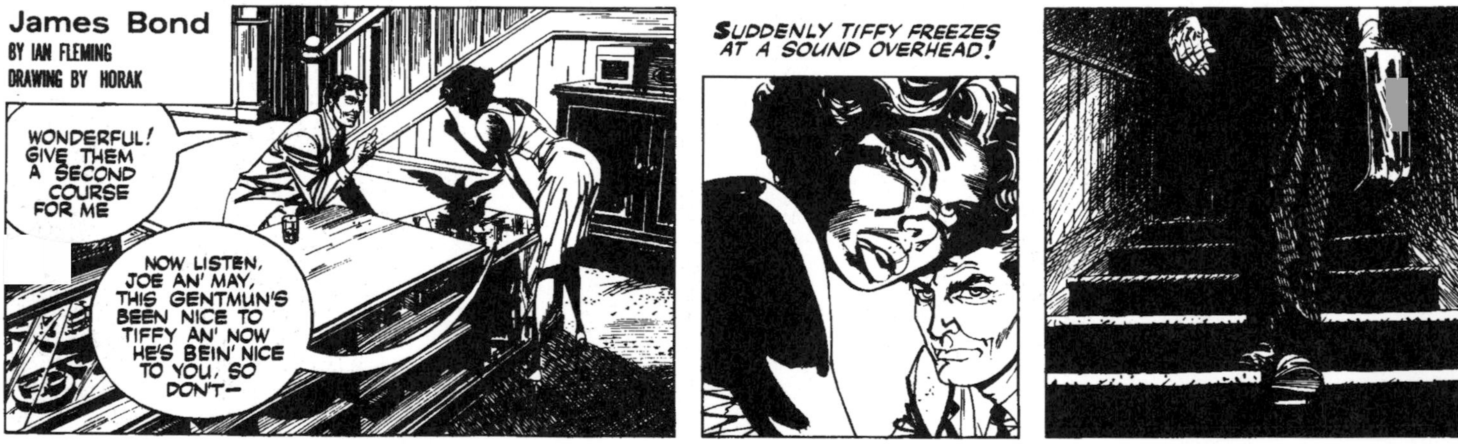
James Bond
BY IAN FLEMING
DRAWING BY HORAK
WONDERFUL! GIVE THEM A SECOND COURSE FOR ME
NOW LISTEN, JOE AN' MAY, THIS GENTMUN'S BEEN NICE TO TIFFY AN' NOW HE'S BEIN' NICE TO YOU, SO DON'T—
SUDDENLY TIFFY FREEZES AT A SOUND OVERHEAD!
87

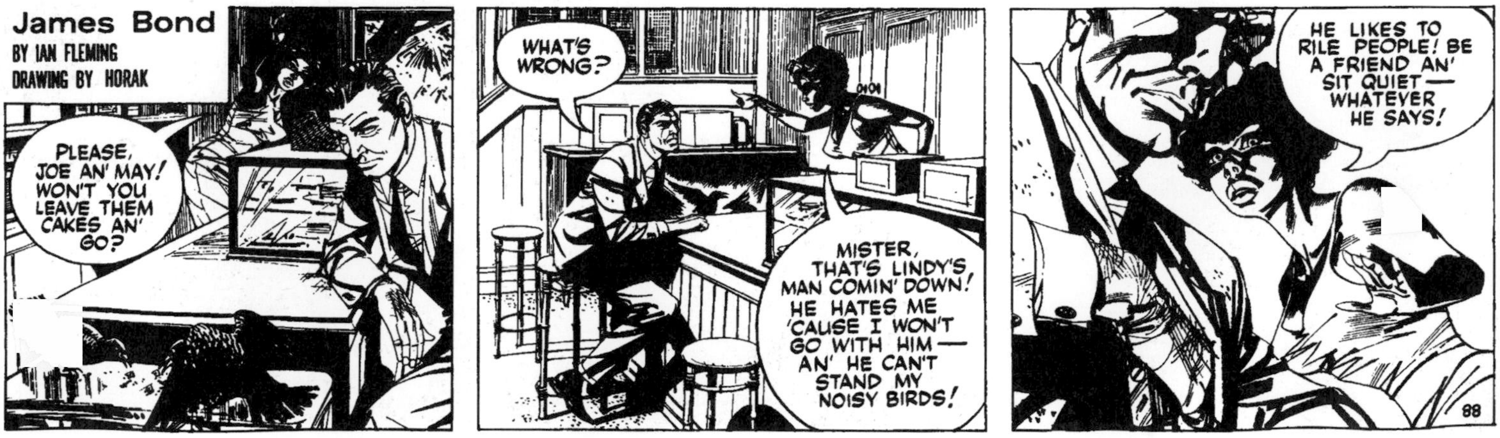
James Bond
BY IAN FLEMING
DRAWING BY HORAK
PLEASE, JOE AN' MAY! WON'T YOU LEAVE THEM CAKES AN' GO?
WHAT'S WRONG?
MISTER, THAT'S LINDY'S MAN COMIN' DOWN! HE HATES ME 'CAUSE I WON'T GO WITH HIM— AN' HE CAN'T STAND MY NOISY BIRDS!
HE LIKES TO RILE PEOPLE! BE A FRIEND AN' SIT QUIET— WHATEVER HE SAYS!
88

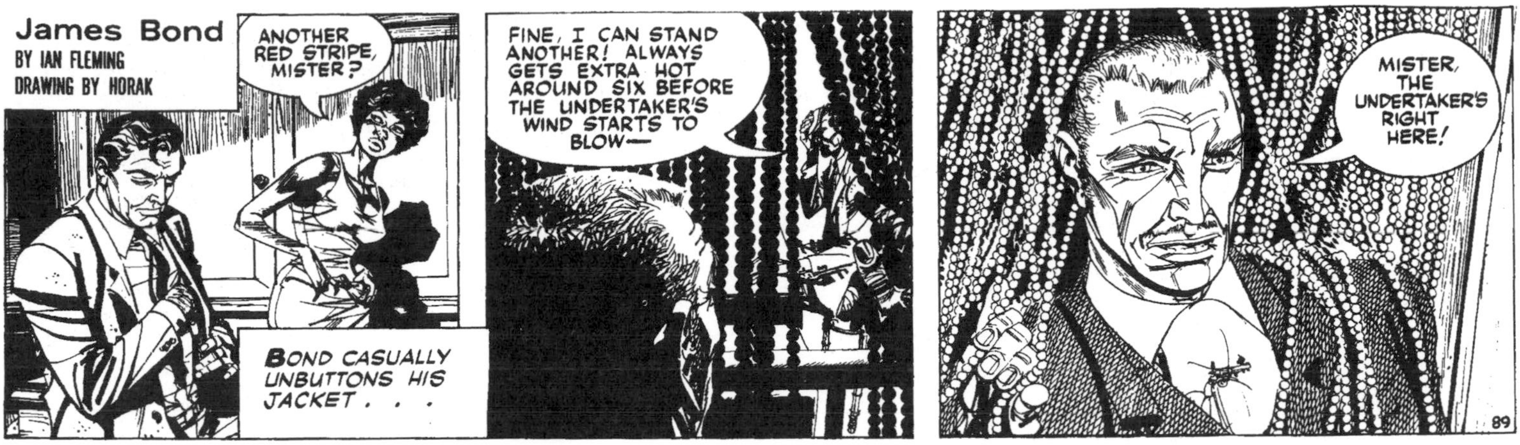
James Bond
BY IAN FLEMING
DRAWING BY HORAK
ANOTHER RED STRIPE, MISTER?
BOND CASUALLY UNBUTTONS HIS JACKET . . .
FINE, I CAN STAND ANOTHER! ALWAYS GETS EXTRA HOT AROUND SIX BEFORE THE UNDERTAKER'S WIND STARTS TO BLOW—
MISTER, THE UNDERTAKER'S RIGHT HERE!
89

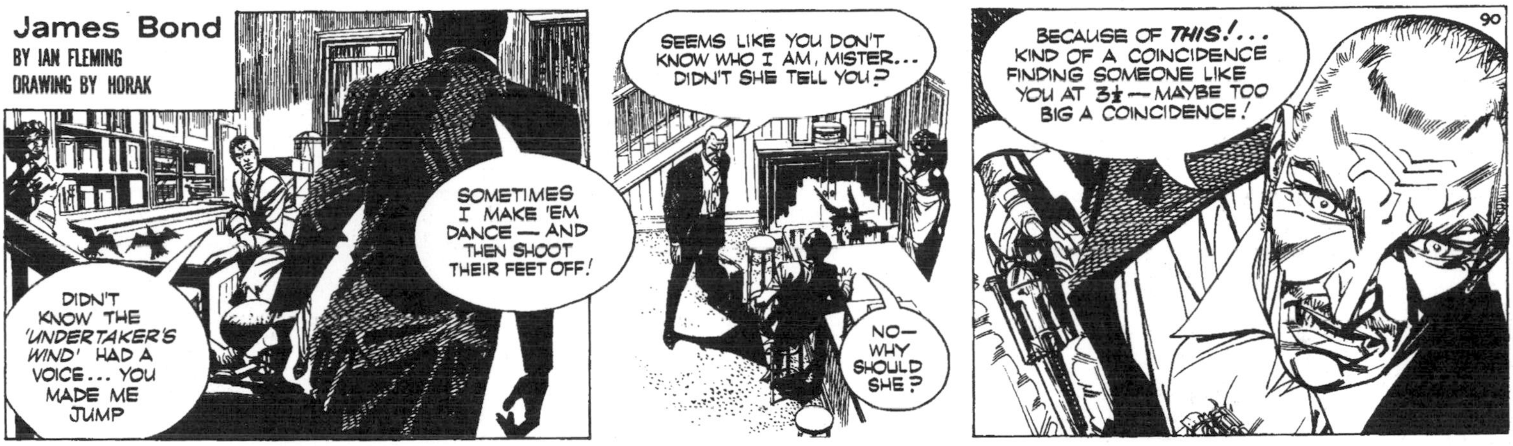
James Bond
BY IAN FLEMING
DRAWING BY HORAK
DIDN'T KNOW THE 'UNDERTAKER'S WIND' HAD A VOICE... YOU MADE ME JUMP
SOMETIMES I MAKE 'EM DANCE — AND THEN SHOOT THEIR FEET OFF!
SEEMS LIKE YOU DON'T KNOW WHO I AM, MISTER... DIDN'T SHE TELL YOU?
NO— WHY SHOULD SHE?
BECAUSE OF THIS!... KIND OF A COINCIDENCE FINDING SOMEONE LIKE YOU AT 3½ — MAYBE TOO BIG A COINCIDENCE!
90

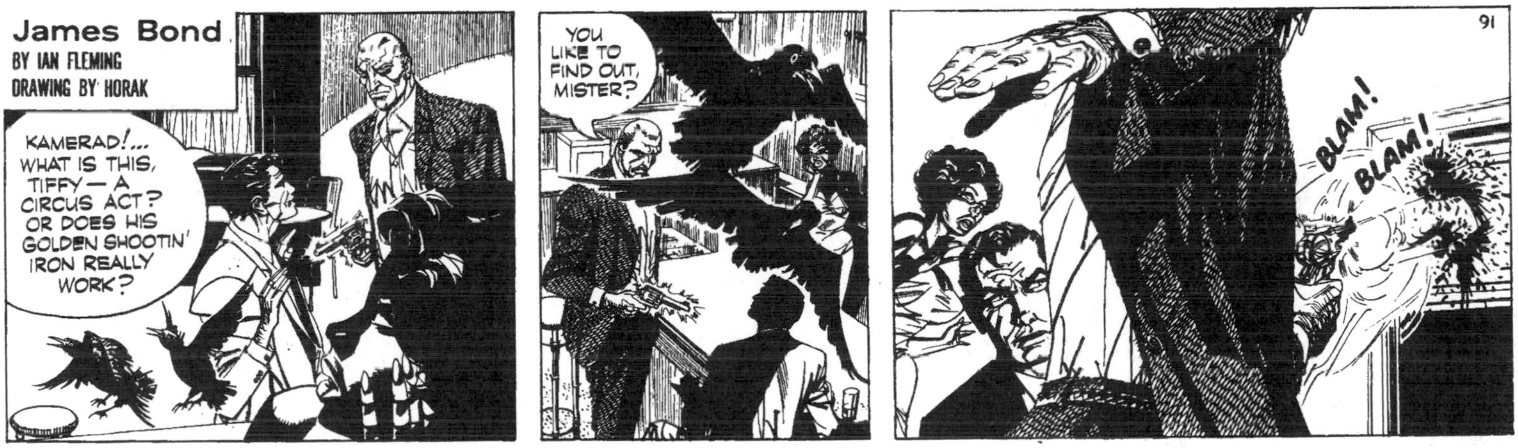
James Bond
BY IAN FLEMING
DRAWING BY HORAK
KAMERAD!... WHAT IS THIS, TIFFY — A CIRCUS ACT? OR DOES HIS GOLDEN SHOOTIN' IRON REALLY WORK?
YOU LIKE TO FIND OUT, MISTER?
BLAM!
BLAM!
91

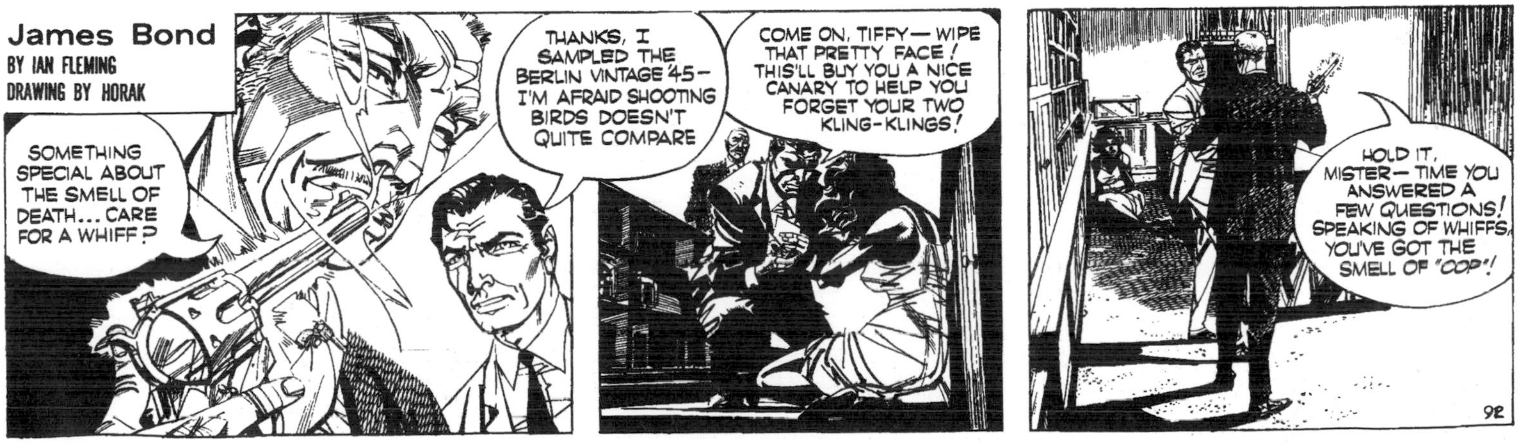
James Bond
BY IAN FLEMING
DRAWING BY HORAK
SOMETHING SPECIAL ABOUT THE SMELL OF DEATH... CARE FOR A WHIFF?
THANKS, I SAMPLED THE BERLIN VINTAGE '45 — I'M AFRAID SHOOTING BIRDS DOESN'T QUITE COMPARE
COME ON, TIFFY — WIPE THAT PRETTY FACE! THIS'LL BUY YOU A NICE CANARY TO HELP YOU FORGET YOUR TWO KLING-KLINGS!
HOLD IT, MISTER— TIME YOU ANSWERED A FEW QUESTIONS! SPEAKING OF WHIFFS, YOU'VE GOT THE SMELL OF 'COP'!
92

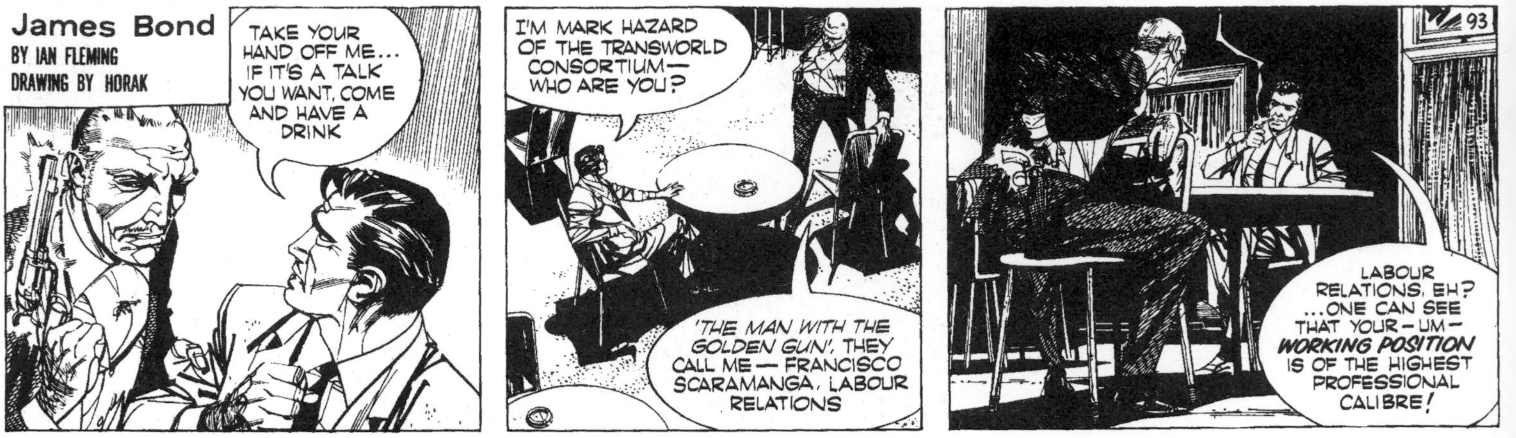
James Bond
BY IAN FLEMING
DRAWING BY HORAK
TAKE YOUR HAND OFF ME... IF IT'S A TALK YOU WANT, COME AND HAVE A DRINK
I'M MARK HAZARD OF THE TRANSWORLD CONSORTIUM— WHO ARE YOU?
'THE MAN WITH THE GOLDEN GUN', THEY CALL ME — FRANCISCO SCARAMANGA, LABOUR RELATIONS
93
LABOUR RELATIONS, EH? ...ONE CAN SEE THAT YOUR—UM— WORKING POSITION IS OF THE HIGHEST PROFESSIONAL CALIBRE!

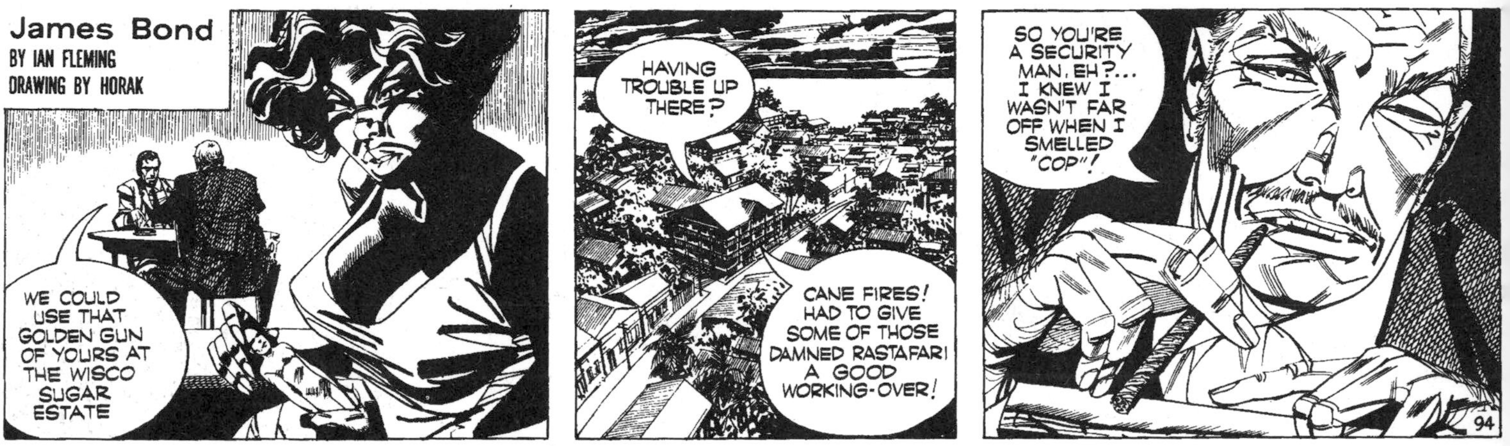
James Bond
BY IAN FLEMING
DRAWING BY HORAK
WE COULD USE THAT GOLDEN GUN OF YOURS AT THE WISCO SUGAR ESTATE
HAVING TROUBLE UP THERE?
CANE FIRES! HAD TO GIVE SOME OF THOSE DAMNED RASTAFARI A GOOD WORKING-OVER!
SO YOU'RE A SECURITY MAN, EH?... I KNEW I WASN'T FAR OFF WHEN I SMELLED "COP"!
94

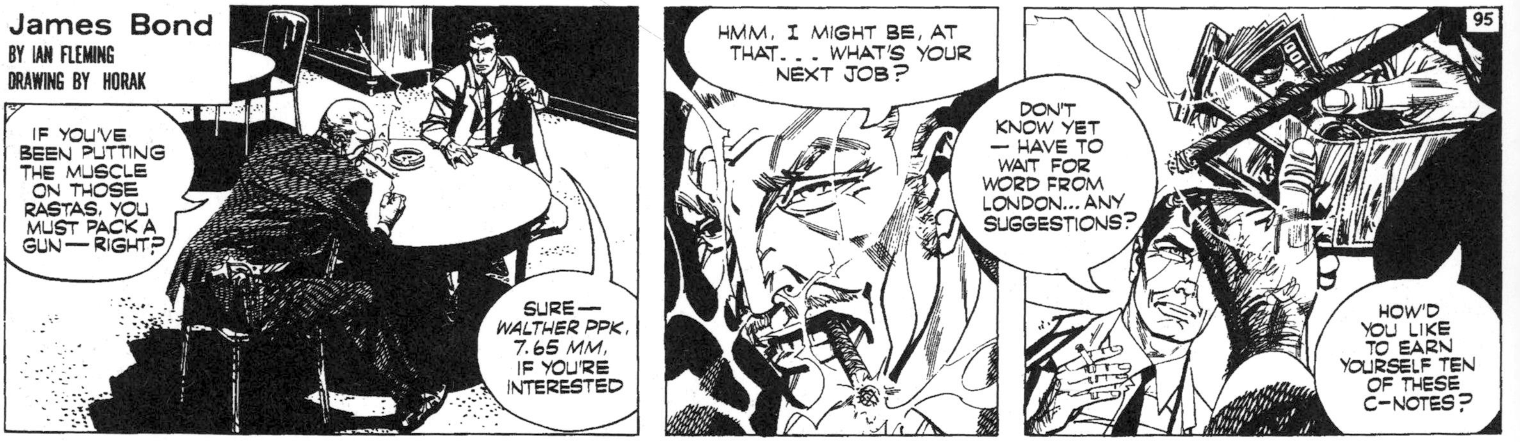
James Bond
BY IAN FLEMING
DRAWING BY HORAK
IF YOU'VE BEEN PUTTING THE MUSCLE ON THOSE RASTAS, YOU MUST PACK A GUN — RIGHT?
SURE— WALTHER PPK, 7.65 MM, IF YOU'RE INTERESTED
HMM, I MIGHT BE, AT THAT... WHAT'S YOUR NEXT JOB?
DON'T KNOW YET — HAVE TO WAIT FOR WORD FROM LONDON... ANY SUGGESTIONS?
95
HOW'D YOU LIKE TO EARN YOURSELF TEN OF THESE C-NOTES?

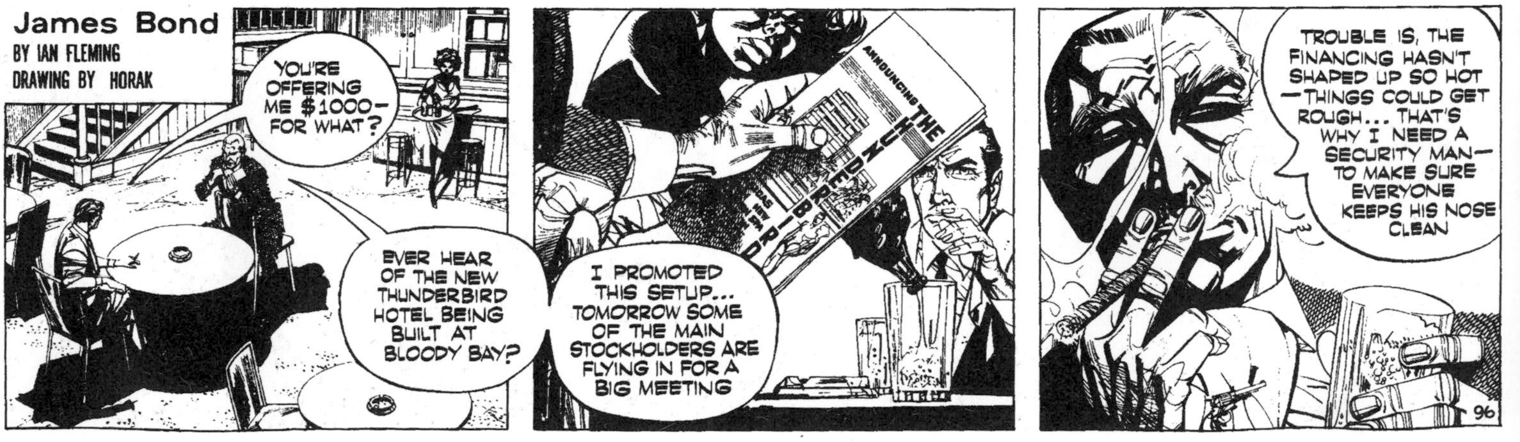
James Bond
BY IAN FLEMING
DRAWING BY HORAK
YOU'RE OFFERING ME $1000— FOR WHAT?
EVER HEAR OF THE NEW THUNDERBIRD HOTEL BEING BUILT AT BLOODY BAY?
ANNOUNCING THE
I PROMOTED THIS SETUP... TOMORROW SOME OF THE MAIN STOCKHOLDERS ARE FLYING IN FOR A BIG MEETING
TROUBLE IS, THE FINANCING HASN'T SHAPED UP SO HOT —THINGS COULD GET ROUGH... THAT'S WHY I NEED A SECURITY MAN— TO MAKE SURE EVERYONE KEEPS HIS NOSE CLEAN
96

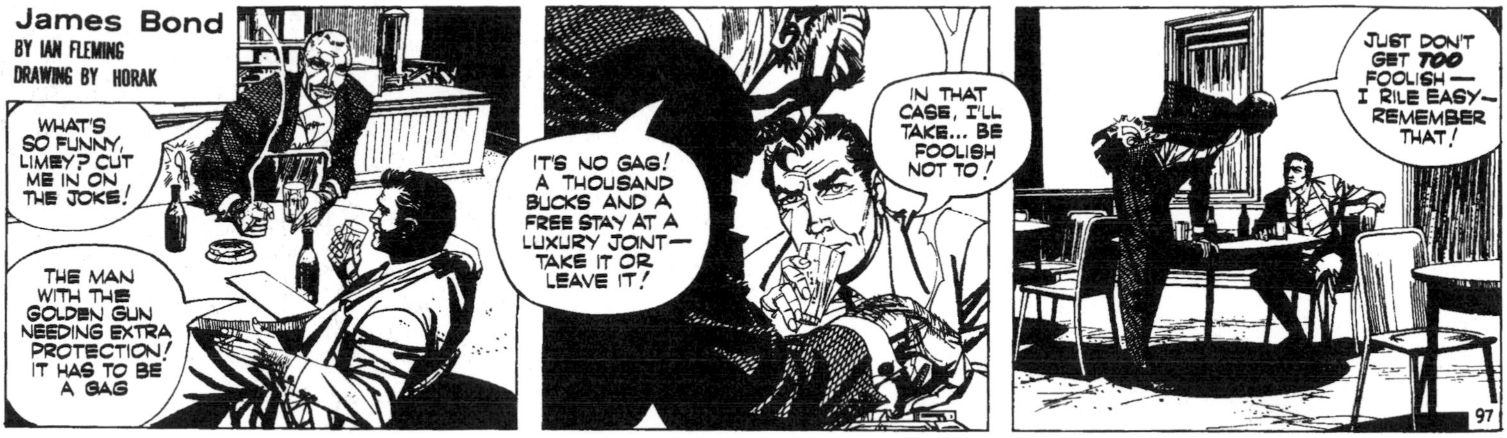
James Bond
BY IAN FLEMING
DRAWING BY HORAK
WHAT'S SO FUNNY, LIMEY? CUT ME IN ON THE JOKE!
THE MAN WITH THE GOLDEN GUN NEEDING EXTRA PROTECTION! IT HAS TO BE A GAG
IT'S NO GAG! A THOUSAND BUCKS AND A FREE STAY AT A LUXURY JOINT— TAKE IT OR LEAVE IT!
IN THAT CASE, I'LL TAKE... BE FOOLISH NOT TO!
JUST DON'T GET TOO FOOLISH — I RILE EASY— REMEMBER THAT!
97

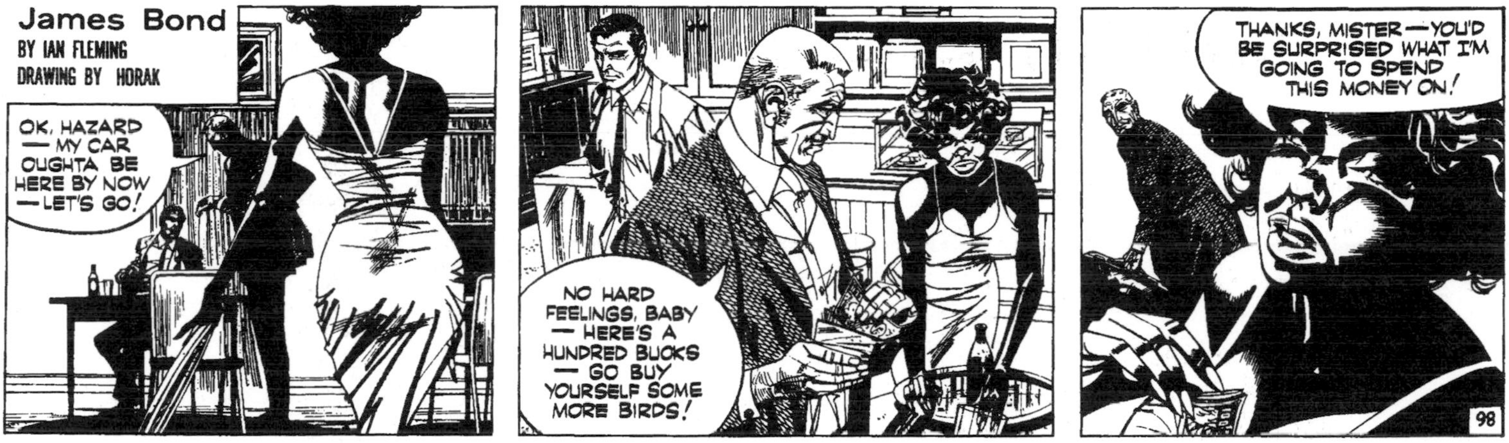
James Bond
BY IAN FLEMING
DRAWING BY HORAK
OK, HAZARD — MY CAR OUGHTA BE HERE BY NOW —LET'S GO!
NO HARD FEELINGS, BABY — HERE'S A HUNDRED BUCKS — GO BUY YOURSELF SOME MORE BIRDS!
THANKS, MISTER —YOU'D BE SURPRISED WHAT I'M GOING TO SPEND THIS MONEY ON!
98

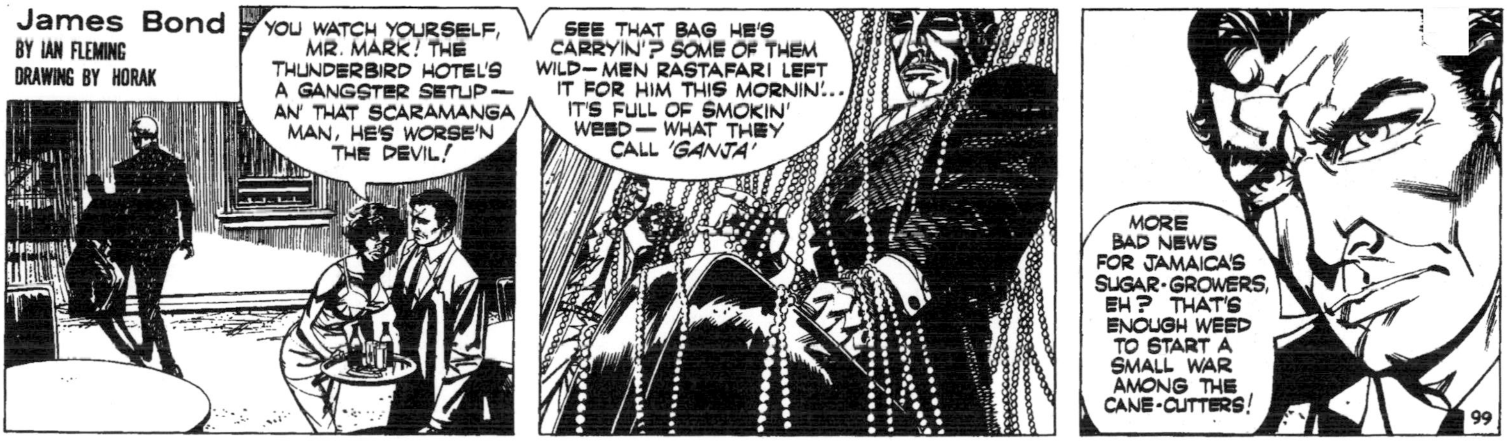
James Bond
BY IAN FLEMING
DRAWING BY HORAK
YOU WATCH YOURSELF, MR. MARK! THE THUNDERBIRD HOTEL'S A GANGSTER SETUP— AN' THAT SCARAMANGA MAN, HE'S WORSE'N THE DEVIL!
SEE THAT BAG HE'S CARRYIN'? SOME OF THEM WILD-MEN RASTAFARI LEFT IT FOR HIM THIS MORNIN'... IT'S FULL OF SMOKIN' WEED — WHAT THEY CALL 'GANJA'
MORE BAD NEWS FOR JAMAICA'S SUGAR-GROWERS, EH? THAT'S ENOUGH WEED TO START A SMALL WAR AMONG THE CANE-CUTTERS!
99

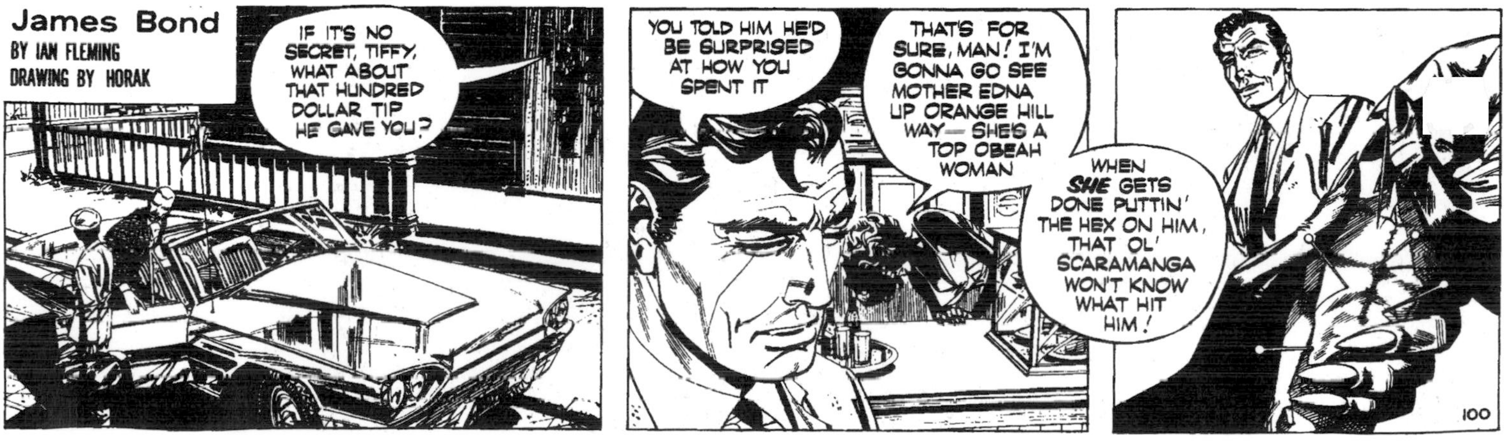
James Bond
BY IAN FLEMING
DRAWING BY HORAK
IF IT'S NO SECRET, TIFFY, WHAT ABOUT THAT HUNDRED DOLLAR TIP HE GAVE YOU?
YOU TOLD HIM HE'D BE SURPRISED AT HOW YOU SPENT IT
THAT'S FOR SURE, MAN! I'M GONNA GO SEE MOTHER EDNA UP ORANGE HILL WAY— SHE'S A TOP OBEAH WOMAN
WHEN SHE GETS DONE PUTTIN' THE HEX ON HIM, THAT OL' SCARAMANGA WON'T KNOW WHAT HIT HIM!
100

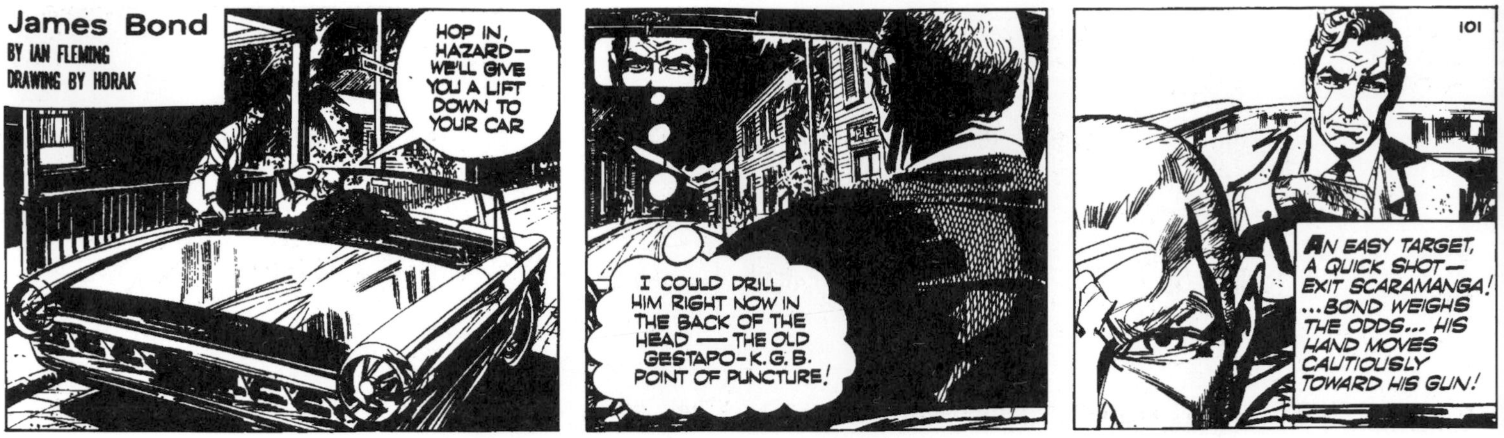
James Bond
BY IAN FLEMING
DRAWING BY HORAK
HOP IN, HAZARD— WE'LL GIVE YOU A LIFT DOWN TO YOUR CAR
I COULD DRILL HIM RIGHT NOW IN THE BACK OF THE HEAD — THE OLD GESTAPO-K.G.B. POINT OF PUNCTURE!
101
AN EASY TARGET, A QUICK SHOT— EXIT SCARAMANGA! ...BOND WEIGHS THE ODDS... HIS HAND MOVES CAUTIOUSLY TOWARD HIS GUN!

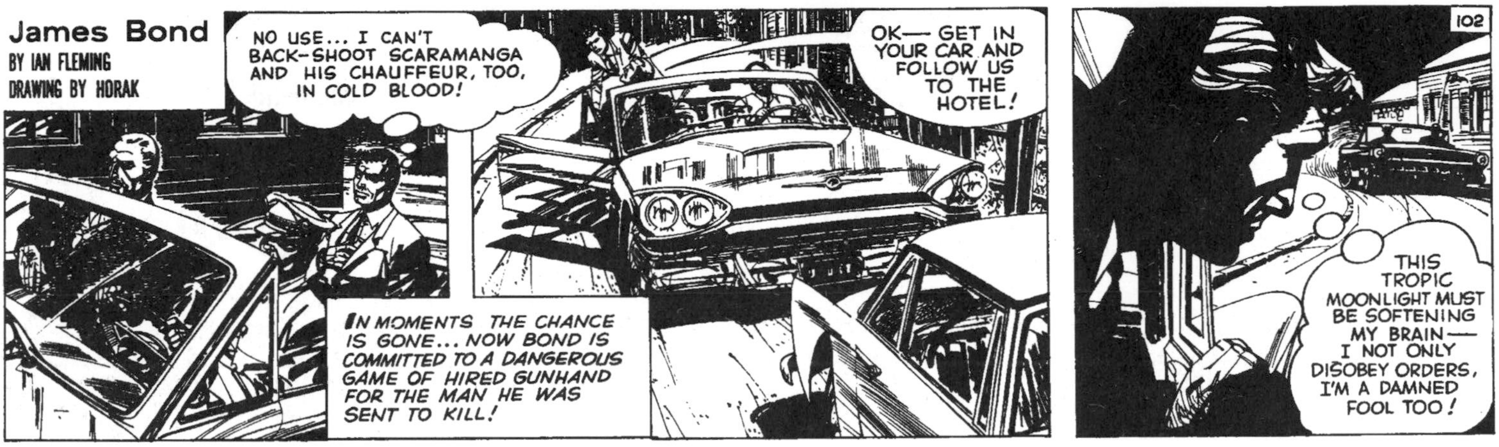
James Bond
BY IAN FLEMING
DRAWING BY HORAK
NO USE... I CAN'T BACK-SHOOT SCARAMANGA AND HIS CHAUFFEUR, TOO, IN COLD BLOOD!
OK— GET IN YOUR CAR AND FOLLOW US TO THE HOTEL!
IN MOMENTS THE CHANCE IS GONE... NOW BOND IS COMMITTED TO A DANGEROUS GAME OF HIRED GUNHAND FOR THE MAN HE WAS SENT TO KILL!
102
THIS TROPIC MOONLIGHT MUST BE SOFTENING MY BRAIN— I NOT ONLY DISOBEY ORDERS, I'M A DAMNED FOOL TOO!

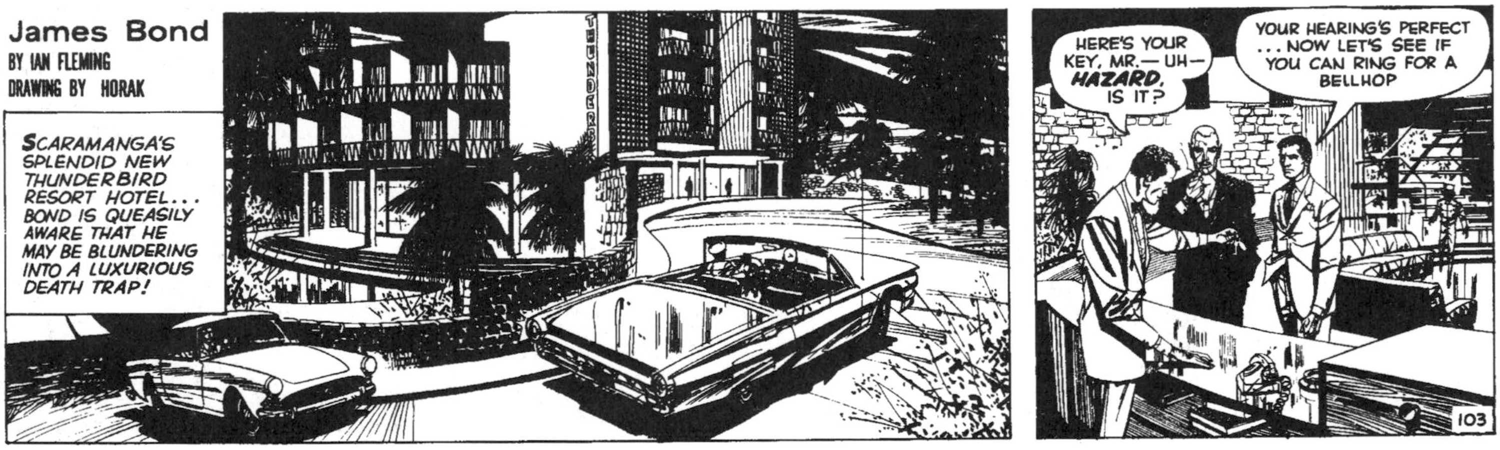
James Bond
BY IAN FLEMING
DRAWING BY HORAK
SCARAMANGA'S SPLENDID NEW THUNDERBIRD RESORT HOTEL... BOND IS QUEASILY AWARE THAT HE MAY BE BLUNDERING INTO A LUXURIOUS DEATH TRAP!
HERE'S YOUR KEY, MR.— UH— HAZARD, IS IT?
YOUR HEARING'S PERFECT ... NOW LET'S SEE IF YOU CAN RING FOR A BELLHOP
103

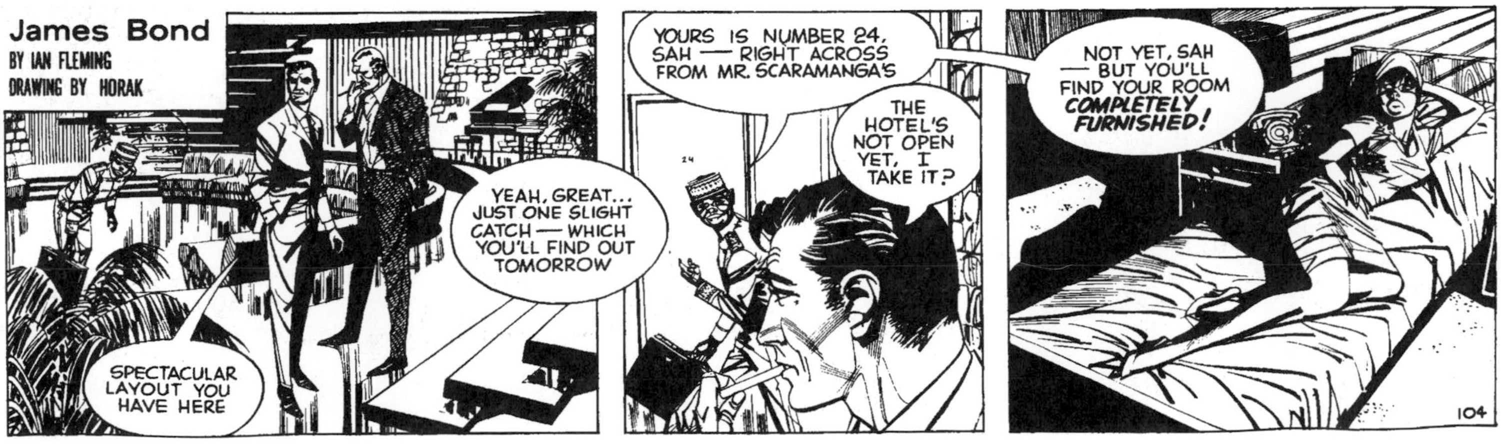
James Bond
BY IAN FLEMING
DRAWING BY HORAK
SPECTACULAR LAYOUT YOU HAVE HERE
YEAH, GREAT... JUST ONE SLIGHT CATCH — WHICH YOU'LL FIND OUT TOMORROW
YOURS IS NUMBER 24, SAH — RIGHT ACROSS FROM MR. SCARAMANGA'S
THE HOTEL'S NOT OPEN YET, I TAKE IT?
NOT YET, SAH — BUT YOU'LL FIND YOUR ROOM COMPLETELY FURNISHED!
104

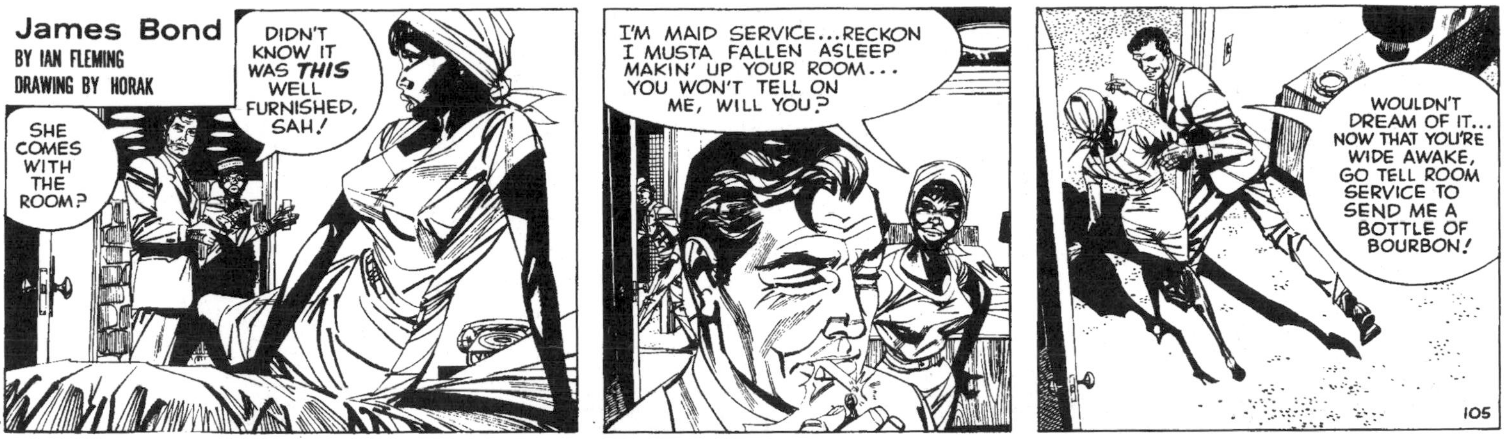
James Bond
BY IAN FLEMING
DRAWING BY HORAK
SHE COMES WITH THE ROOM?
DIDN'T KNOW IT WAS THIS WELL FURNISHED, SAH!
I'M MAID SERVICE...RECKON I MUSTA FALLEN ASLEEP MAKIN' UP YOUR ROOM... YOU WON'T TELL ON ME, WILL YOU?
WOULDN'T DREAM OF IT... NOW THAT YOU'RE WIDE AWAKE, GO TELL ROOM SERVICE TO SEND ME A BOTTLE OF BOURBON!
105

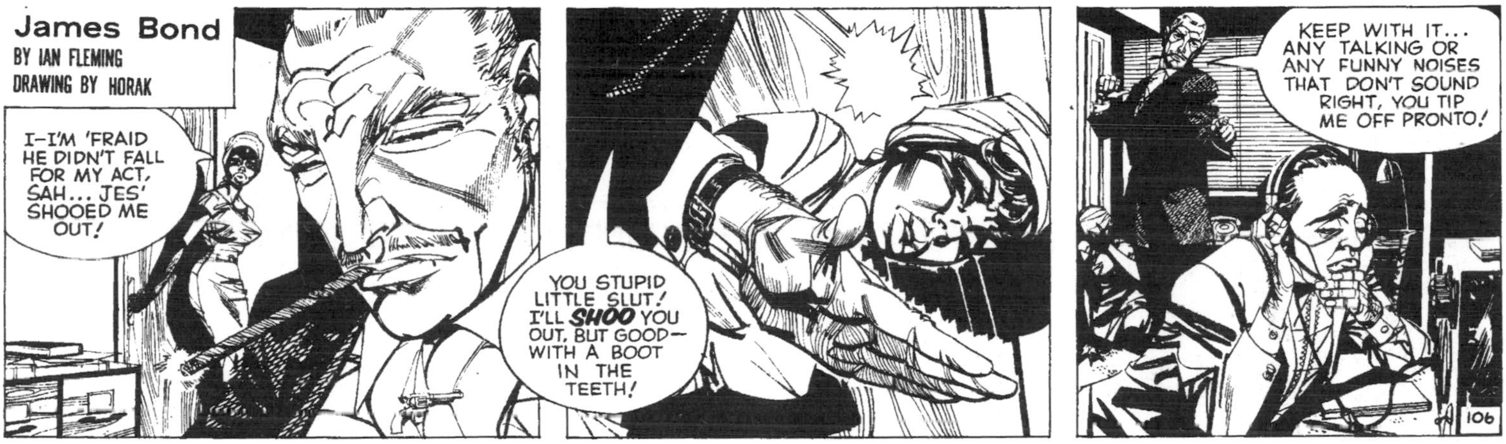
James Bond
BY IAN FLEMING
DRAWING BY HORAK
I-I'M 'FRAID HE DIDN'T FALL FOR MY ACT, SAH... JES' SHOOED ME OUT!
YOU STUPID LITTLE SLUT! I'LL SHOO YOU OUT, BUT GOOD— WITH A BOOT IN THE TEETH!
KEEP WITH IT... ANY TALKING OR ANY FUNNY NOISES THAT DON'T SOUND RIGHT, YOU TIP ME OFF PRONTO!
106

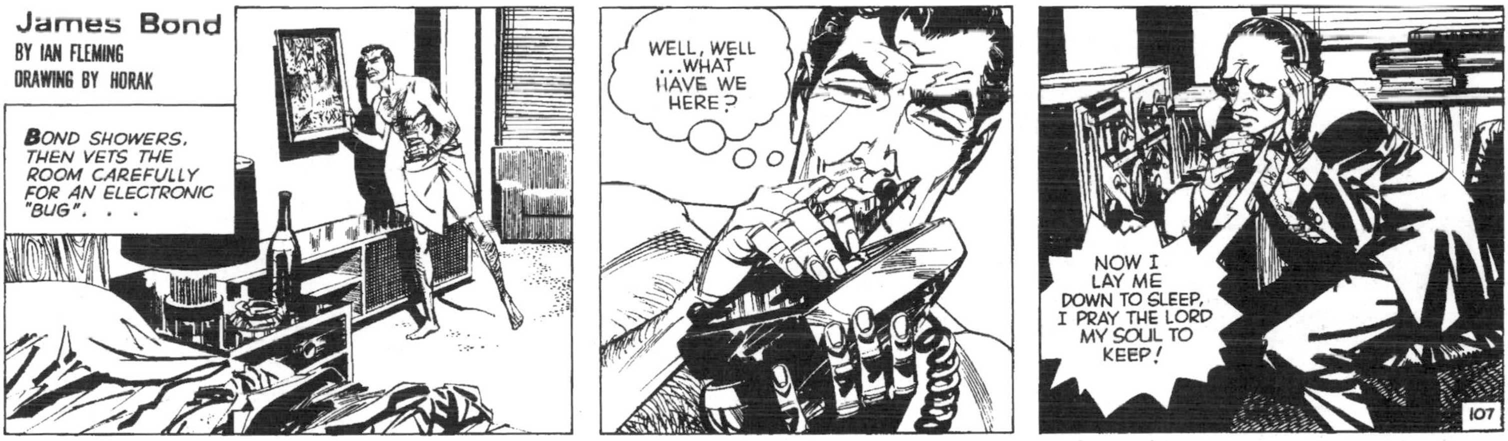
James Bond
BY IAN FLEMING
DRAWING BY HORAK
BOND SHOWERS, THEN VETS THE ROOM CAREFULLY FOR AN ELECTRONIC "BUG". . .
WELL, WELL ...WHAT HAVE WE HERE?
NOW I LAY ME DOWN TO SLEEP, I PRAY THE LORD MY SOUL TO KEEP!
107

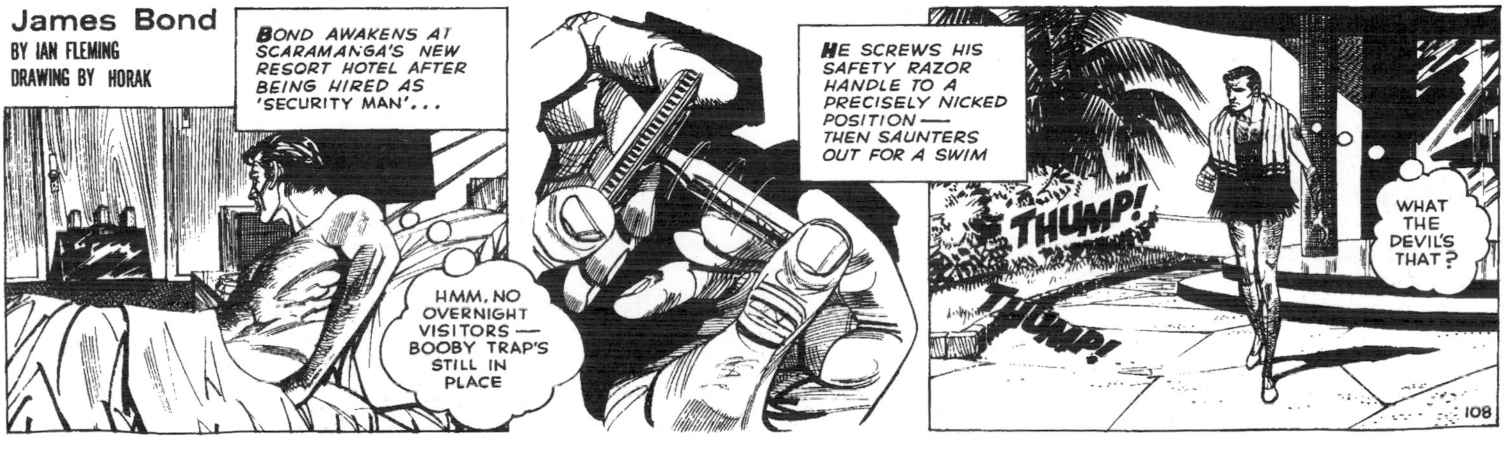
James Bond
BY IAN FLEMING
DRAWING BY HORAK
BOND AWAKENS AT SCARAMANGA'S NEW RESORT HOTEL AFTER BEING HIRED AS 'SECURITY MAN'...
HMM, NO OVERNIGHT VISITORS — BOOBY TRAP'S STILL IN PLACE
HE SCREWS HIS SAFETY RAZOR HANDLE TO A PRECISELY NICKED POSITION — THEN SAUNTERS OUT FOR A SWIM
THUMP!
THUMP!
WHAT THE DEVIL'S THAT?
108

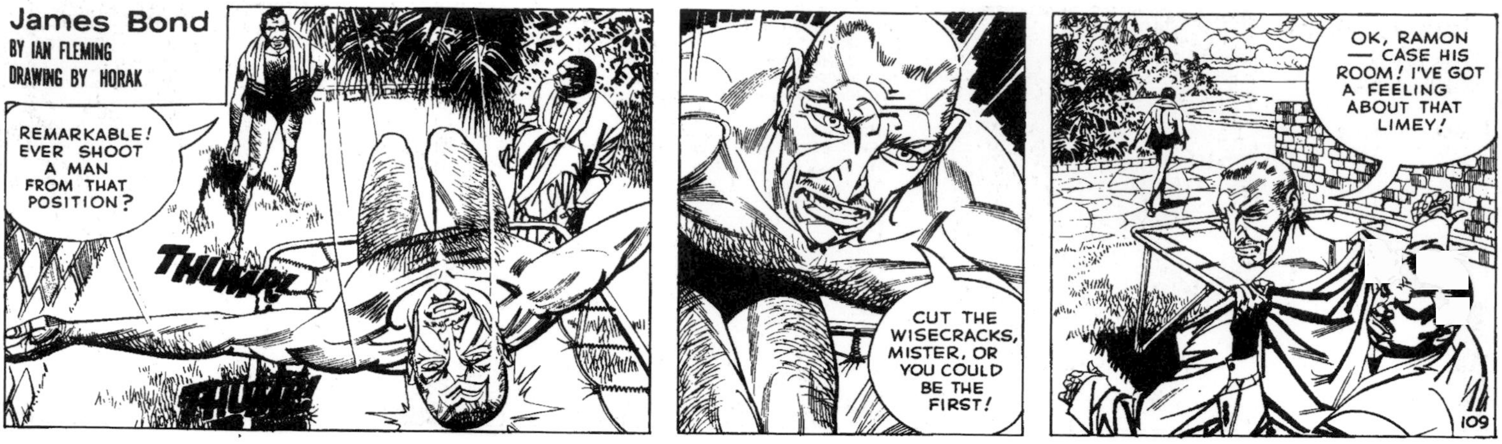
James Bond
BY IAN FLEMING
DRAWING BY HORAK
REMARKABLE! EVER SHOOT A MAN FROM THAT POSITION?
THUMP!
CUT THE WISECRACKS, MISTER, OR YOU COULD BE THE FIRST!
OK, RAMON — CASE HIS ROOM! I'VE GOT A FEELING ABOUT THAT LIMEY!
109

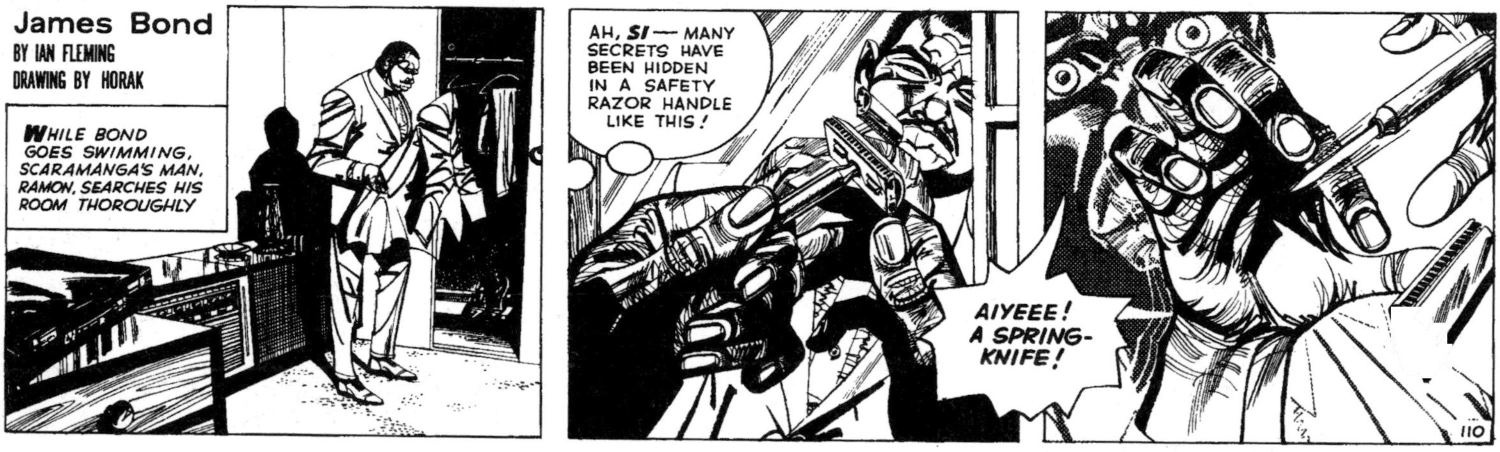
James Bond
BY IAN FLEMING
DRAWING BY HORAK
WHILE BOND GOES SWIMMING, SCARAMANGA'S MAN, RAMON, SEARCHES HIS ROOM THOROUGHLY
AH, SI — MANY SECRETS HAVE BEEN HIDDEN IN A SAFETY RAZOR HANDLE LIKE THIS!
AIYEEE! A SPRING-KNIFE!
110

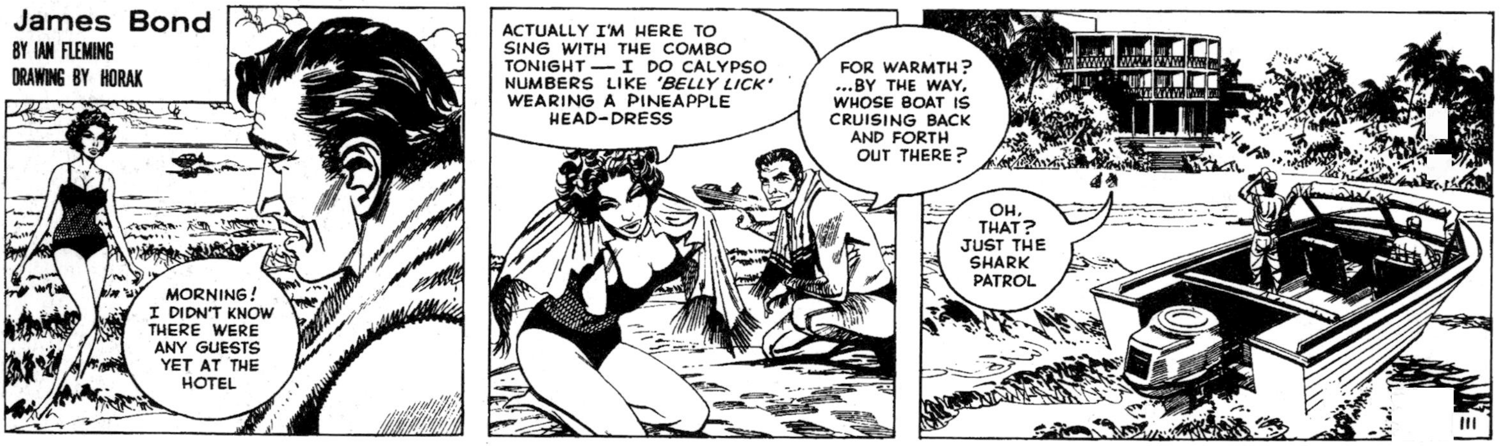
James Bond
BY IAN FLEMING
DRAWING BY HORAK
MORNING! I DIDN'T KNOW THERE WERE ANY GUESTS YET AT THE HOTEL
ACTUALLY I'M HERE TO SING WITH THE COMBO TONIGHT — I DO CALYPSO NUMBERS LIKE 'BELLY LICK' WEARING A PINEAPPLE HEAD-DRESS
FOR WARMTH? ...BY THE WAY, WHOSE BOAT IS CRUISING BACK AND FORTH OUT THERE?
OH, THAT? JUST THE SHARK PATROL
111

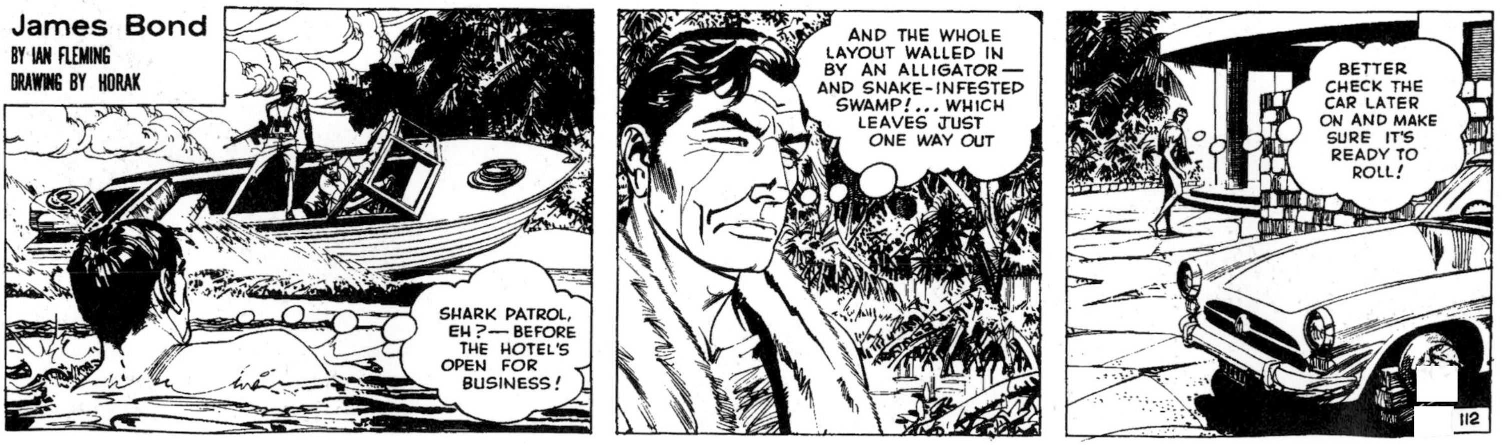
James Bond
BY IAN FLEMING
DRAWING BY HORAK
SHARK PATROL, EH? — BEFORE THE HOTEL'S OPEN FOR BUSINESS!
AND THE WHOLE LAYOUT WALLED IN BY AN ALLIGATOR — AND SNAKE-INFESTED SWAMP!... WHICH LEAVES JUST ONE WAY OUT
BETTER CHECK THE CAR LATER ON AND MAKE SURE IT'S READY TO ROLL!
112

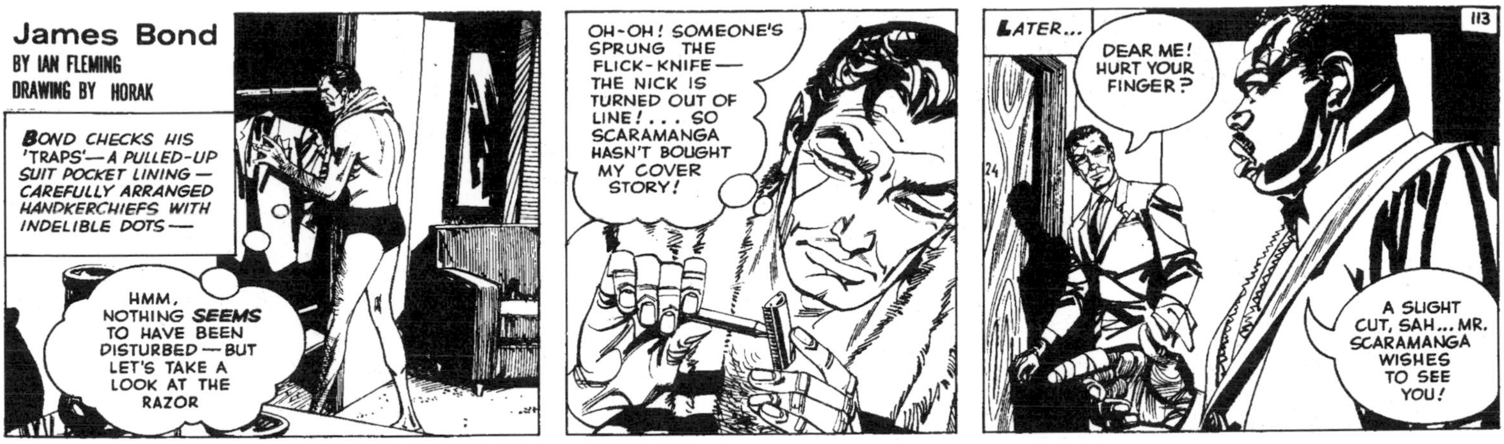
James Bond
BY IAN FLEMING
DRAWING BY HORAK
BOND CHECKS HIS 'TRAPS'—A PULLED-UP SUIT POCKET LINING—CAREFULLY ARRANGED HANDKERCHIEFS WITH INDELIBLE DOTS—
HMM, NOTHING SEEMS TO HAVE BEEN DISTURBED—BUT LET'S TAKE A LOOK AT THE RAZOR
OH-OH! SOMEONE'S SPRUNG THE FLICK-KNIFE—THE NICK IS TURNED OUT OF LINE! . . . SO SCARAMANGA HASN'T BOUGHT MY COVER STORY!
LATER...
113
DEAR ME! HURT YOUR FINGER?
A SLIGHT CUT, SAH... MR. SCARAMANGA WISHES TO SEE YOU!

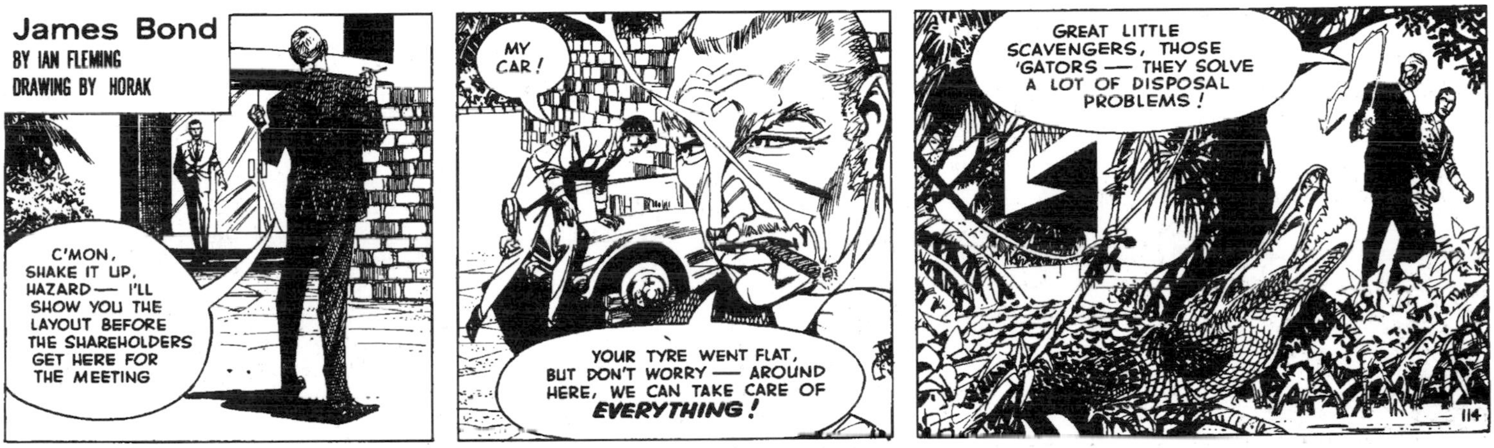
James Bond
BY IAN FLEMING
DRAWING BY HORAK
C'MON, SHAKE IT UP, HAZARD—I'LL SHOW YOU THE LAYOUT BEFORE THE SHAREHOLDERS GET HERE FOR THE MEETING
MY CAR!
YOUR TYRE WENT FLAT, BUT DON'T WORRY—AROUND HERE, WE CAN TAKE CARE OF EVERYTHING!
GREAT LITTLE SCAVENGERS, THOSE 'GATORS—THEY SOLVE A LOT OF DISPOSAL PROBLEMS!
114

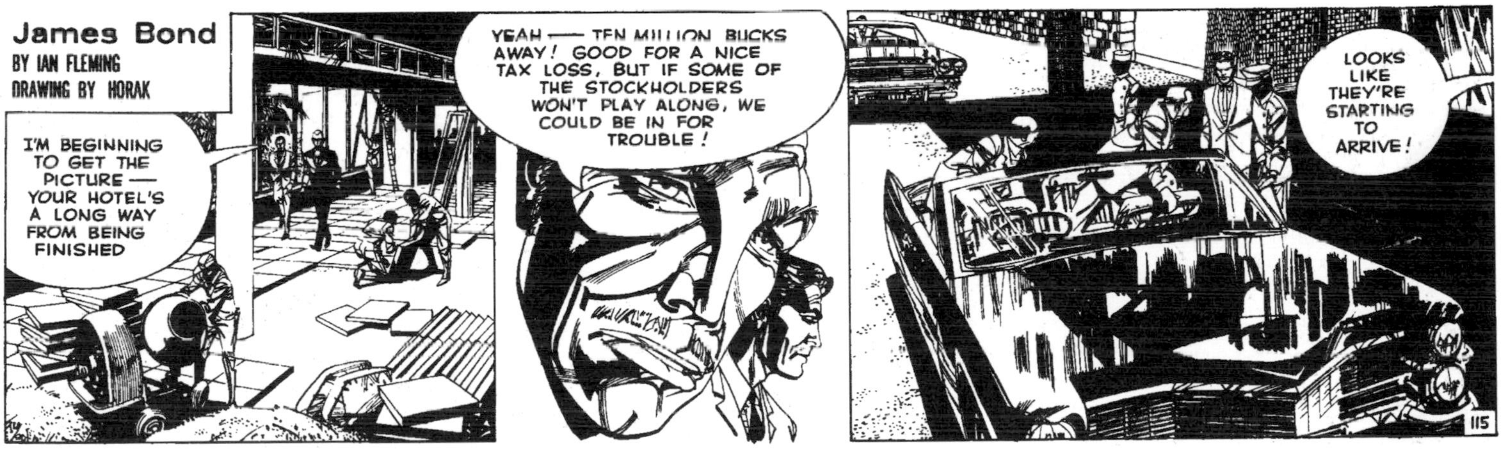
James Bond
BY IAN FLEMING
DRAWING BY HORAK
I'M BEGINNING TO GET THE PICTURE—YOUR HOTEL'S A LONG WAY FROM BEING FINISHED
YEAH—TEN MILLION BUCKS AWAY! GOOD FOR A NICE TAX LOSS, BUT IF SOME OF THE STOCKHOLDERS WON'T PLAY ALONG, WE COULD BE IN FOR TROUBLE!
LOOKS LIKE THEY'RE STARTING TO ARRIVE!
115

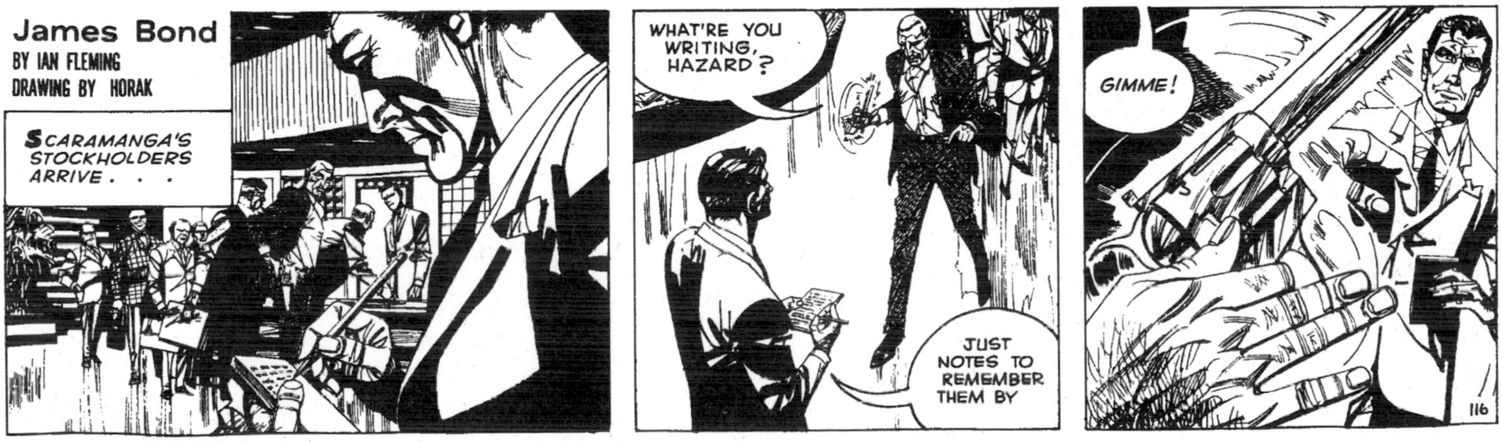
James Bond
BY IAN FLEMING
DRAWING BY HORAK
SCARAMANGA'S STOCKHOLDERS ARRIVE . . .
WHAT'RE YOU WRITING, HAZARD?
JUST NOTES TO REMEMBER THEM BY
GIMME!
116

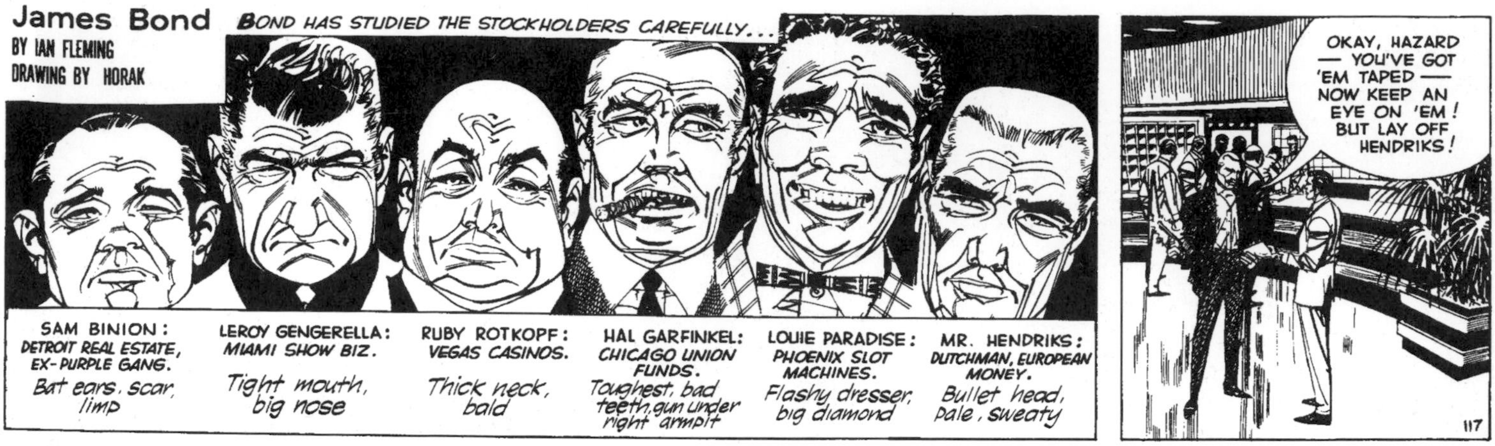
James Bond
BY IAN FLEMING
DRAWING BY HORAK
BOND HAS STUDIED THE STOCKHOLDERS CAREFULLY...
SAM BINION: DETROIT REAL ESTATE, EX-PURPLE GANG. Bat ears, scar, limp
LEROY GENGERELLA: MIAMI SHOW BIZ. Tight mouth, big nose
RUBY ROTKOPF: VEGAS CASINOS. Thick neck, bald
HAL GARFINKEL: CHICAGO UNION FUNDS. Toughest, bad teeth, gun under right armpit
LOUIE PARADISE: PHOENIX SLOT MACHINES. Flashy dresser, big diamond
MR. HENDRIKS: DUTCHMAN, EUROPEAN MONEY. Bullet head, pale, sweaty
OKAY, HAZARD — YOU'VE GOT 'EM TAPED — NOW KEEP AN EYE ON 'EM! BUT LAY OFF HENDRIKS!
117

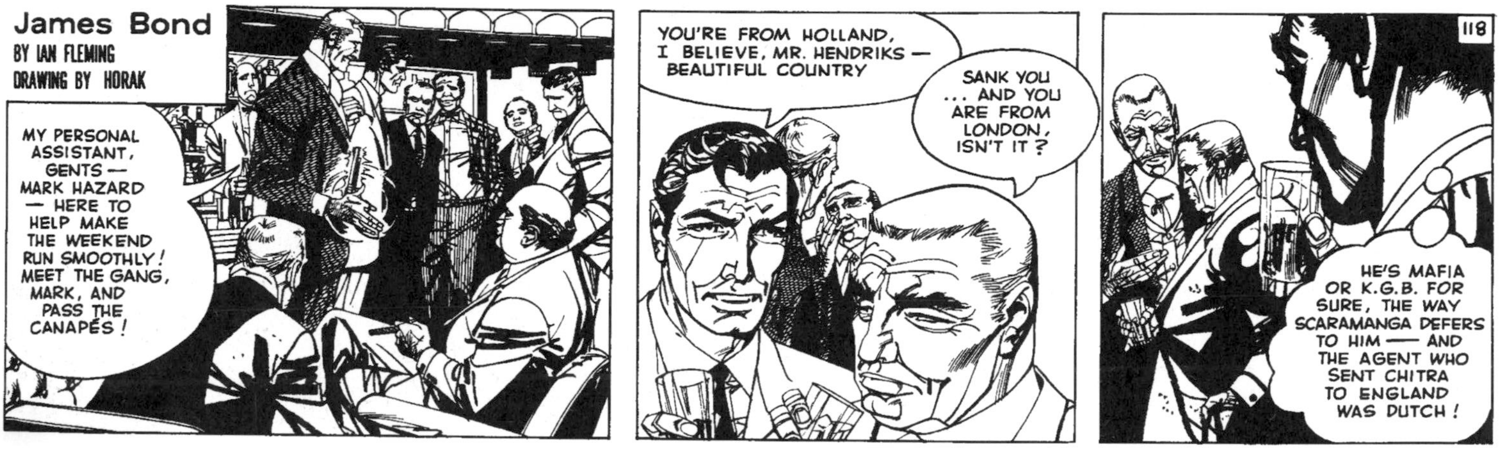
James Bond
BY IAN FLEMING
DRAWING BY HORAK
MY PERSONAL ASSISTANT, GENTS — MARK HAZARD — HERE TO HELP MAKE THE WEEKEND RUN SMOOTHLY! MEET THE GANG, MARK, AND PASS THE CANAPÉS!
YOU'RE FROM HOLLAND, I BELIEVE, MR. HENDRIKS — BEAUTIFUL COUNTRY
SANK YOU ... AND YOU ARE FROM LONDON, ISN'T IT?
118
HE'S MAFIA OR K.G.B. FOR SURE, THE WAY SCARAMANGA DEFERS TO HIM — AND THE AGENT WHO SENT CHITRA TO ENGLAND WAS DUTCH!

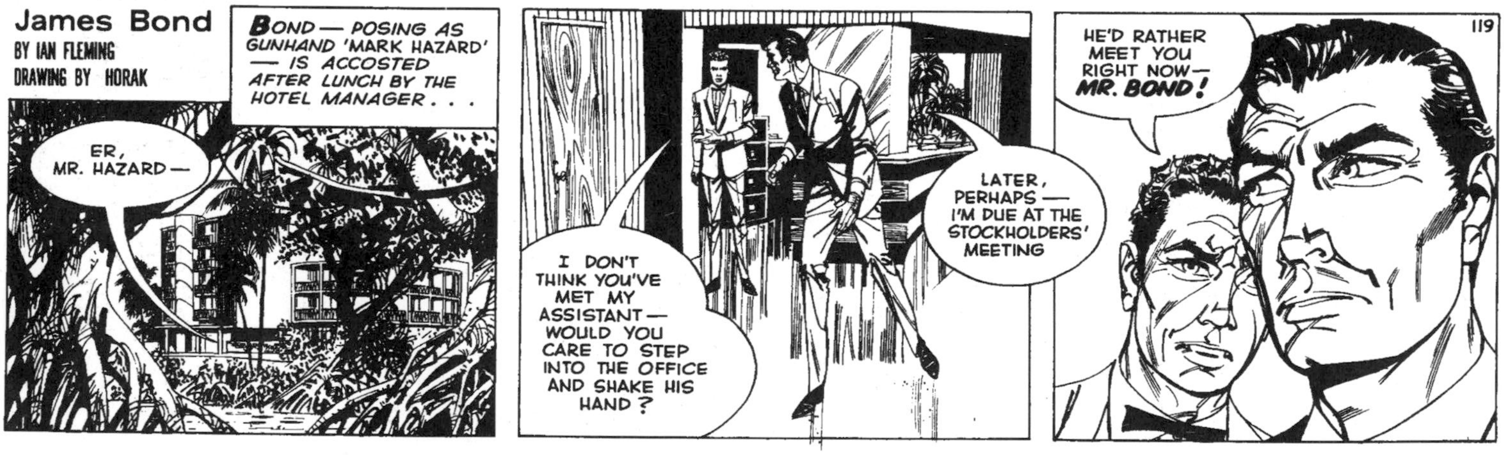
James Bond
BY IAN FLEMING
DRAWING BY HORAK
BOND — POSING AS GUNHAND 'MARK HAZARD' — IS ACCOSTED AFTER LUNCH BY THE HOTEL MANAGER . . .
ER, MR. HAZARD —
I DON'T THINK YOU'VE MET MY ASSISTANT — WOULD YOU CARE TO STEP INTO THE OFFICE AND SHAKE HIS HAND?
LATER, PERHAPS — I'M DUE AT THE STOCKHOLDERS' MEETING
HE'D RATHER MEET YOU RIGHT NOW — MR. BOND!
119

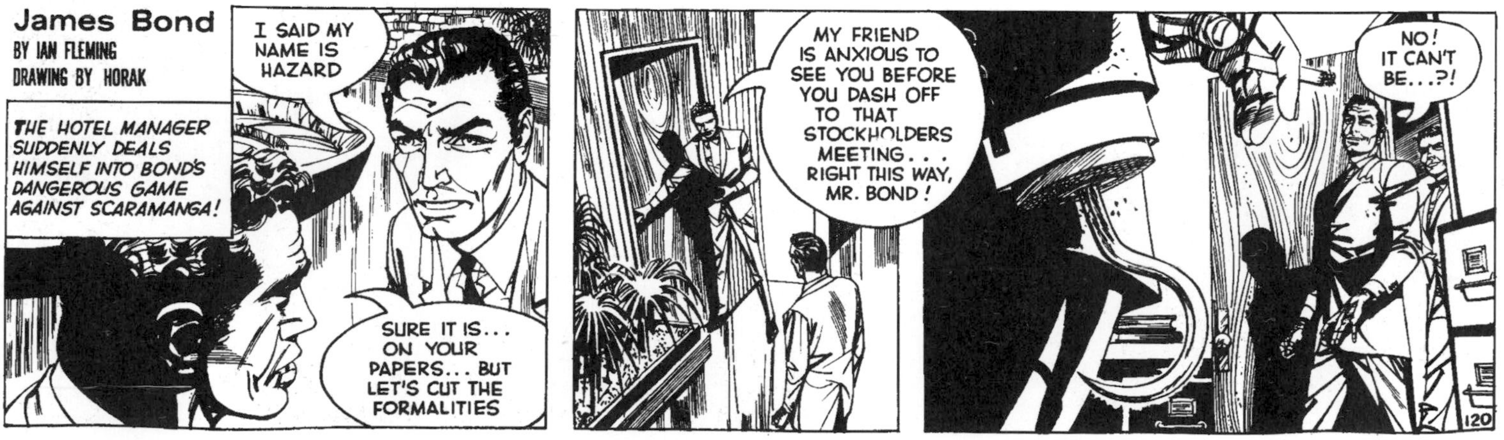
James Bond
BY IAN FLEMING
DRAWING BY HORAK
THE HOTEL MANAGER SUDDENLY DEALS HIMSELF INTO BOND'S DANGEROUS GAME AGAINST SCARAMANGA!
I SAID MY NAME IS HAZARD
SURE IT IS... ON YOUR PAPERS... BUT LET'S CUT THE FORMALITIES
MY FRIEND IS ANXIOUS TO SEE YOU BEFORE YOU DASH OFF TO THAT STOCKHOLDERS MEETING . . . RIGHT THIS WAY, MR. BOND!
NO! IT CAN'T BE...?!
120

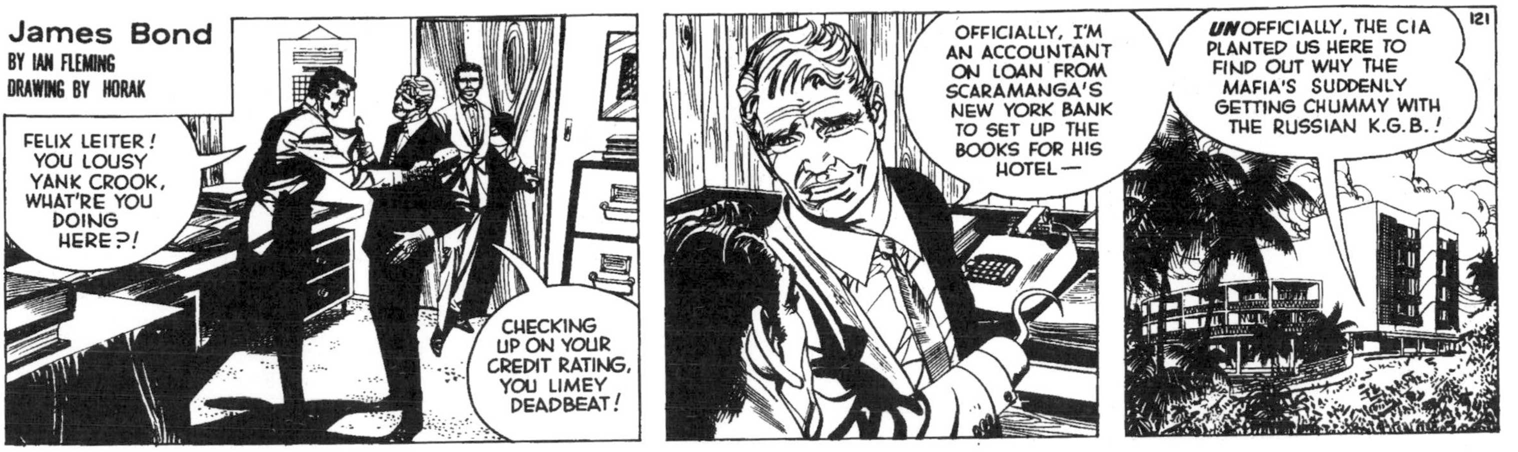
James Bond
BY IAN FLEMING
DRAWING BY HORAK
FELIX LEITER! YOU LOUSY YANK CROOK, WHAT'RE YOU DOING HERE?!
CHECKING UP ON YOUR CREDIT RATING, YOU LIMEY DEADBEAT!
OFFICIALLY, I'M AN ACCOUNTANT ON LOAN FROM SCARAMANGA'S NEW YORK BANK TO SET UP THE BOOKS FOR HIS HOTEL—
UNOFFICIALLY, THE CIA PLANTED US HERE TO FIND OUT WHY THE MAFIA'S SUDDENLY GETTING CHUMMY WITH THE RUSSIAN K.G.B.!
121

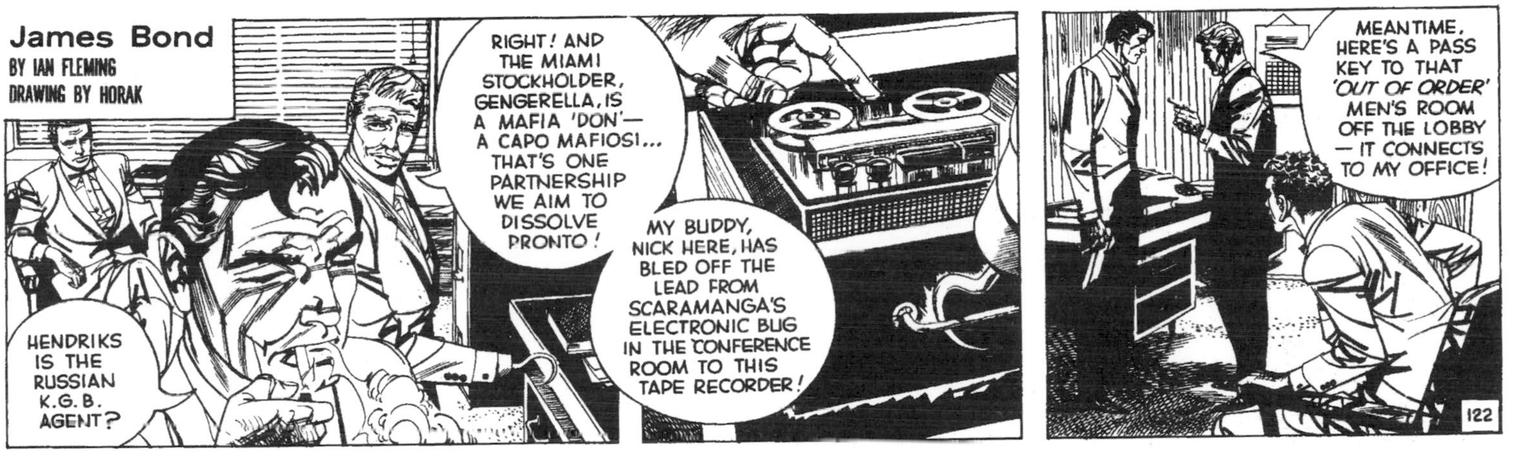
James Bond
BY IAN FLEMING
DRAWING BY HORAK
HENDRIKS IS THE RUSSIAN K.G.B. AGENT?
RIGHT! AND THE MIAMI STOCKHOLDER, GENGERELLA, IS A MAFIA 'DON'— A CAPO MAFIOSI... THAT'S ONE PARTNERSHIP WE AIM TO DISSOLVE PRONTO!
MY BUDDY, NICK HERE, HAS BLED OFF THE LEAD FROM SCARAMANGA'S ELECTRONIC BUG IN THE CONFERENCE ROOM TO THIS TAPE RECORDER!
MEANTIME, HERE'S A PASS KEY TO THAT *'OUT OF ORDER'* MEN'S ROOM OFF THE LOBBY — IT CONNECTS TO MY OFFICE!
122

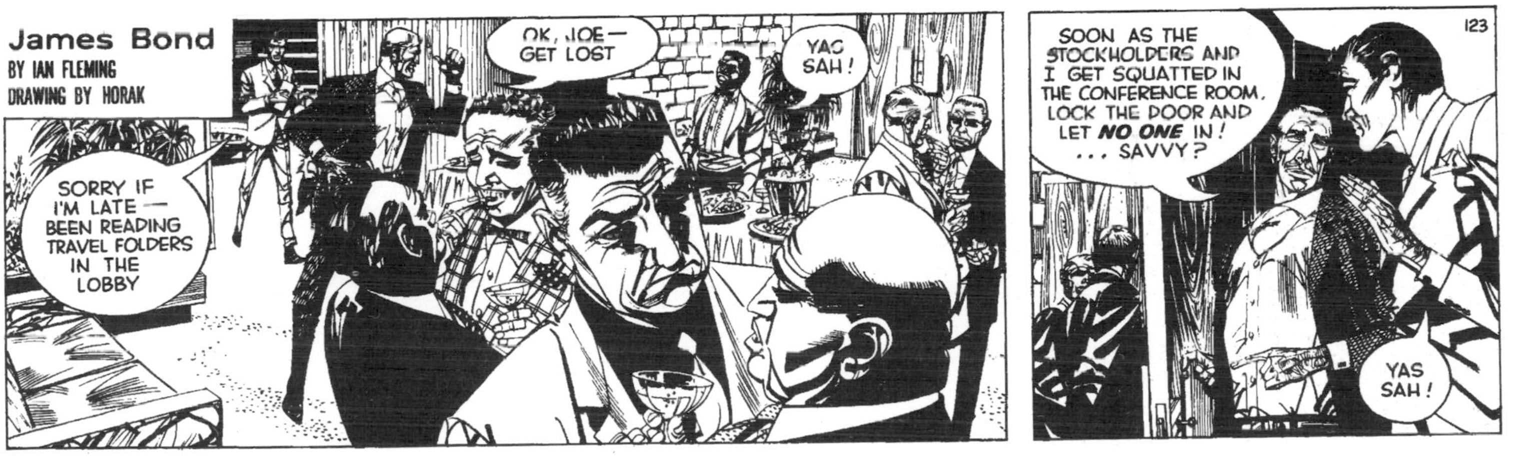
James Bond
BY IAN FLEMING
DRAWING BY HORAK
SORRY IF I'M LATE— BEEN READING TRAVEL FOLDERS IN THE LOBBY
OK, JOE— GET LOST
YAS SAH!
SOON AS THE STOCKHOLDERS AND I GET SQUATTED IN THE CONFERENCE ROOM, LOCK THE DOOR AND LET **NO ONE** IN! ... SAVVY?
YAS SAH!
123

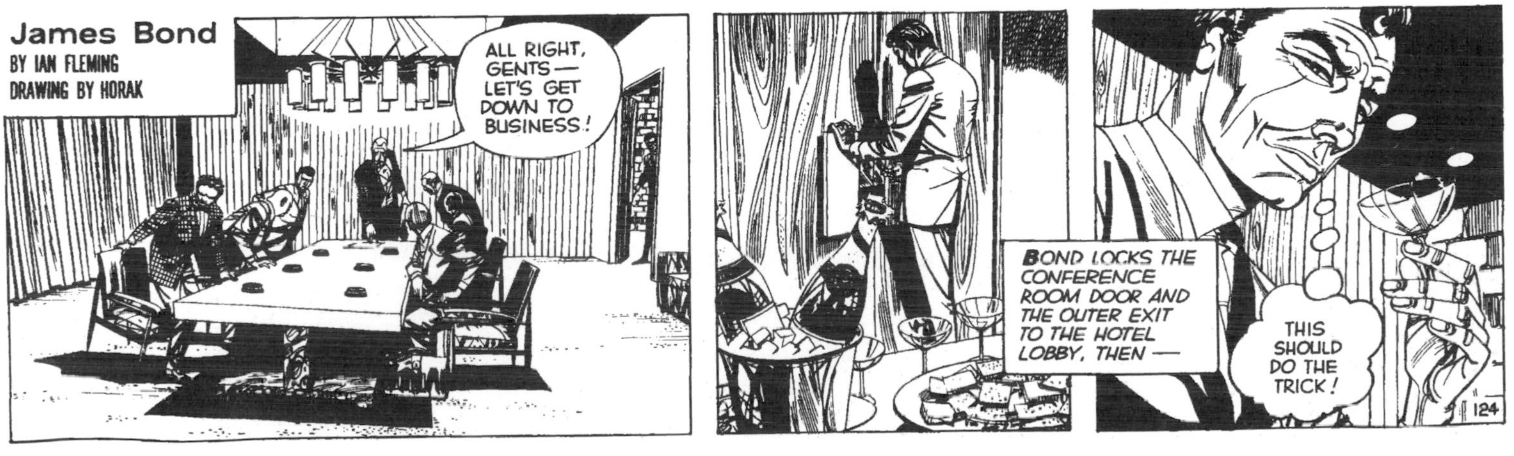
James Bond
BY IAN FLEMING
DRAWING BY HORAK
ALL RIGHT, GENTS— LET'S GET DOWN TO BUSINESS!
BOND LOCKS THE CONFERENCE ROOM DOOR AND THE OUTER EXIT TO THE HOTEL LOBBY, THEN—
THIS SHOULD DO THE TRICK!
124

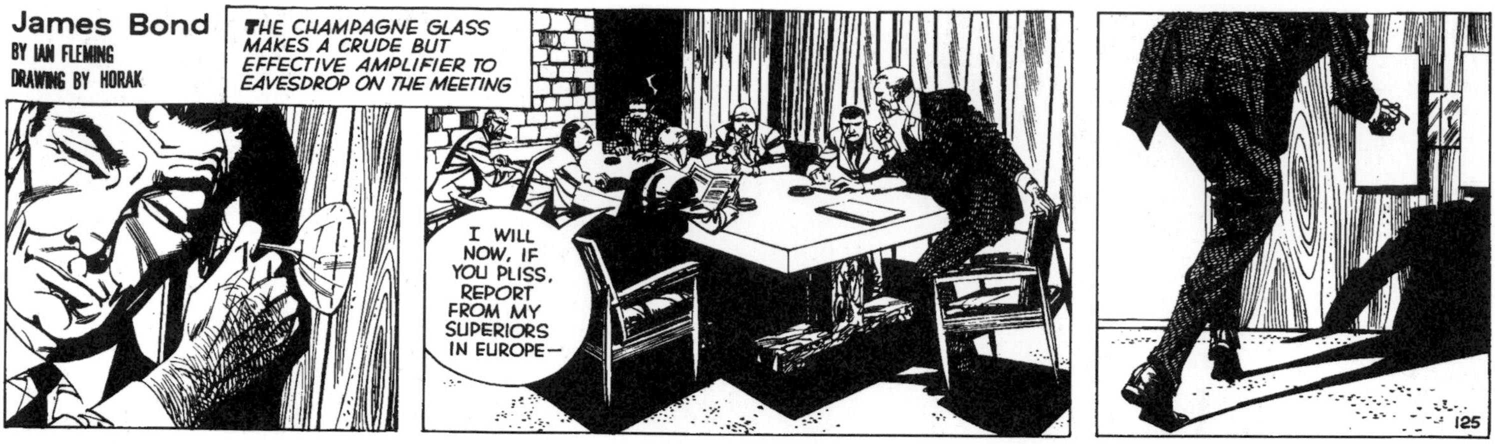
James Bond
BY IAN FLEMING
DRAWING BY HORAK
THE CHAMPAGNE GLASS MAKES A CRUDE BUT EFFECTIVE AMPLIFIER TO EAVESDROP ON THE MEETING
I WILL NOW, IF YOU PLISS, REPORT FROM MY SUPERIORS IN EUROPE—
125

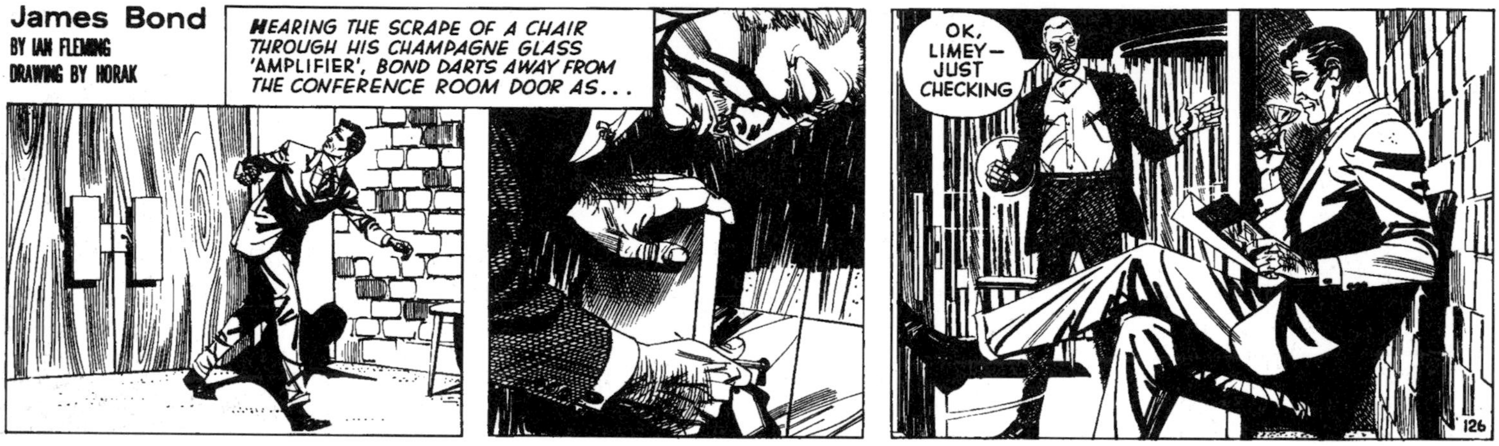
James Bond
BY IAN FLEMING
DRAWING BY HORAK
HEARING THE SCRAPE OF A CHAIR THROUGH HIS CHAMPAGNE GLASS 'AMPLIFIER', BOND DARTS AWAY FROM THE CONFERENCE ROOM DOOR AS . . .
OK, LIMEY— JUST CHECKING
126

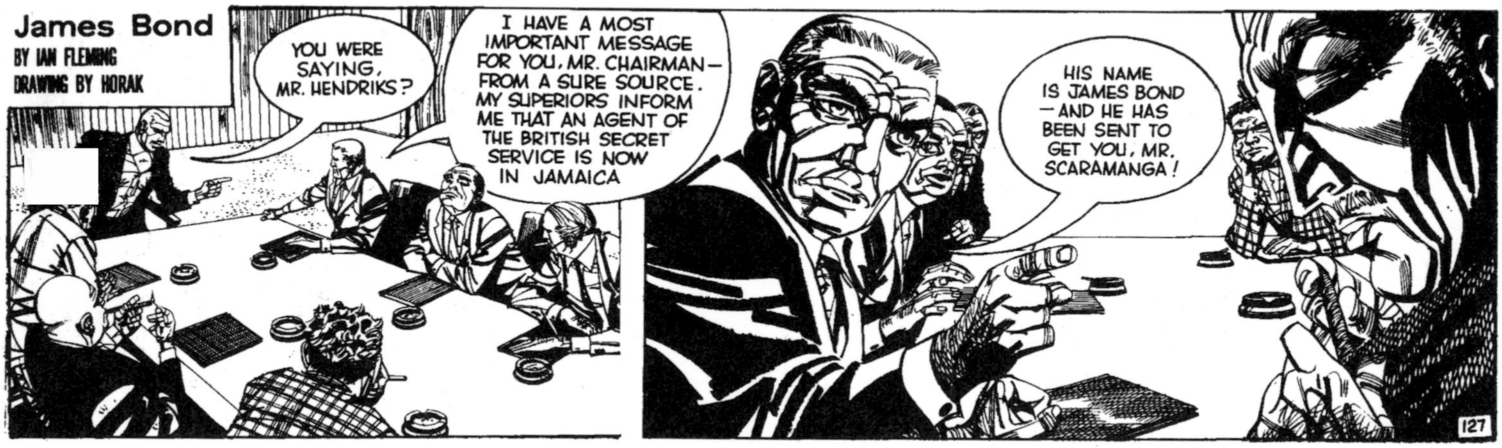
James Bond
BY IAN FLEMING
DRAWING BY HORAK
YOU WERE SAYING, MR. HENDRIKS?
I HAVE A MOST IMPORTANT MESSAGE FOR YOU, MR. CHAIRMAN— FROM A SURE SOURCE. MY SUPERIORS INFORM ME THAT AN AGENT OF THE BRITISH SECRET SERVICE IS NOW IN JAMAICA
HIS NAME IS JAMES BOND —AND HE HAS BEEN SENT TO GET YOU, MR. SCARAMANGA!
127

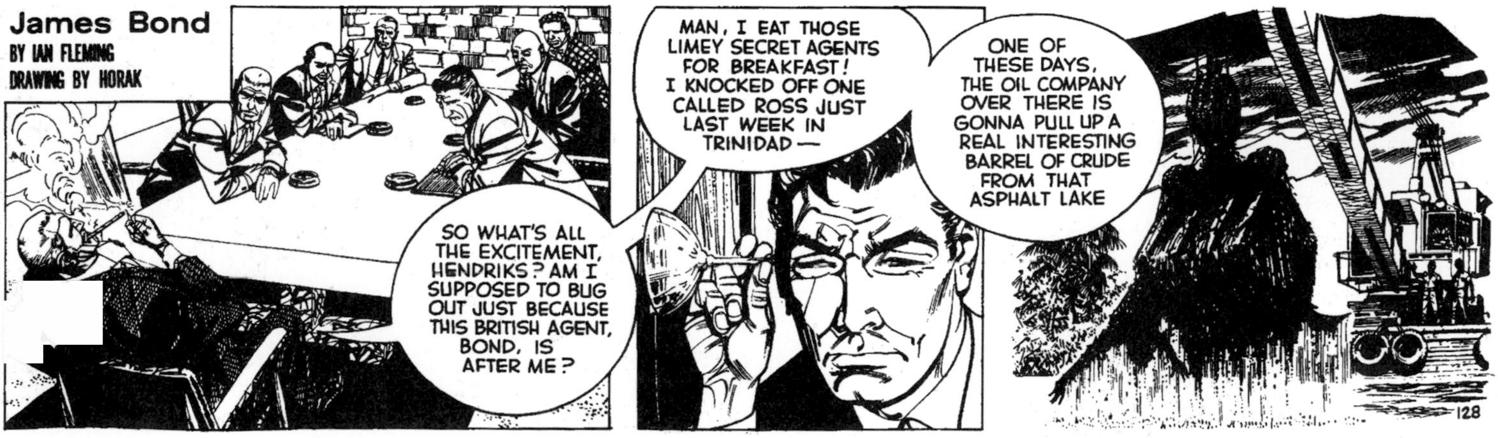
James Bond
BY IAN FLEMING
DRAWING BY HORAK
SO WHAT'S ALL THE EXCITEMENT, HENDRIKS? AM I SUPPOSED TO BUG OUT JUST BECAUSE THIS BRITISH AGENT, BOND, IS AFTER ME?
MAN, I EAT THOSE LIMEY SECRET AGENTS FOR BREAKFAST! I KNOCKED OFF ONE CALLED ROSS JUST LAST WEEK IN TRINIDAD—
ONE OF THESE DAYS, THE OIL COMPANY OVER THERE IS GONNA PULL UP A REAL INTERESTING BARREL OF CRUDE FROM THAT ASPHALT LAKE
128

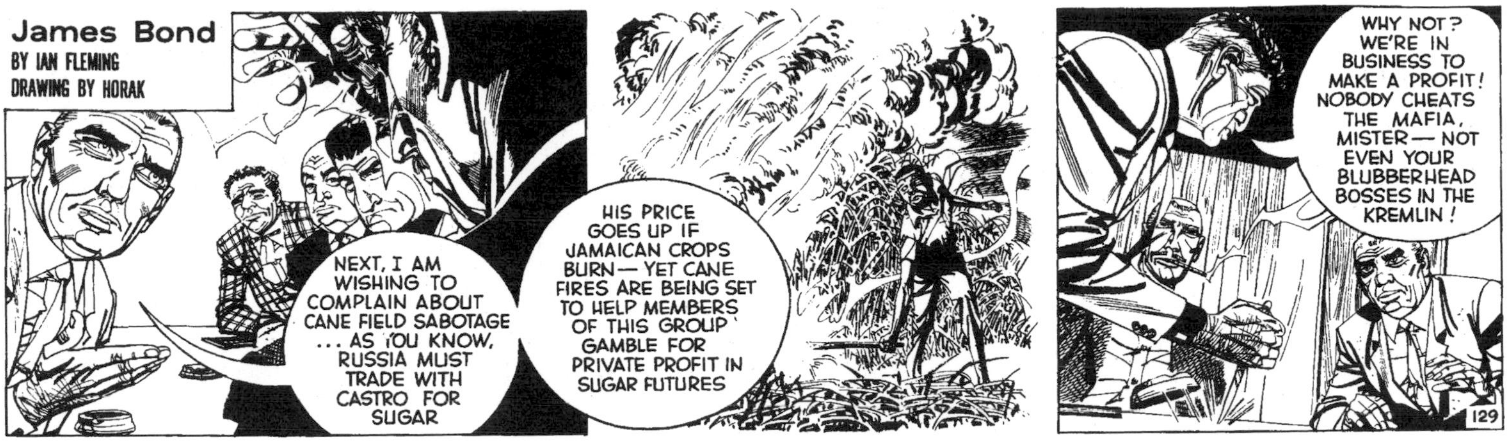
James Bond
BY IAN FLEMING
DRAWING BY HORAK
NEXT, I AM WISHING TO COMPLAIN ABOUT CANE FIELD SABOTAGE ... AS YOU KNOW, RUSSIA MUST TRADE WITH CASTRO FOR SUGAR
HIS PRICE GOES UP IF JAMAICAN CROPS BURN — YET CANE FIRES ARE BEING SET TO HELP MEMBERS OF THIS GROUP GAMBLE FOR PRIVATE PROFIT IN SUGAR FUTURES
WHY NOT? WE'RE IN BUSINESS TO MAKE A PROFIT! NOBODY CHEATS THE MAFIA, MISTER — NOT EVEN YOUR BLUBBERHEAD BOSSES IN THE KREMLIN!
129

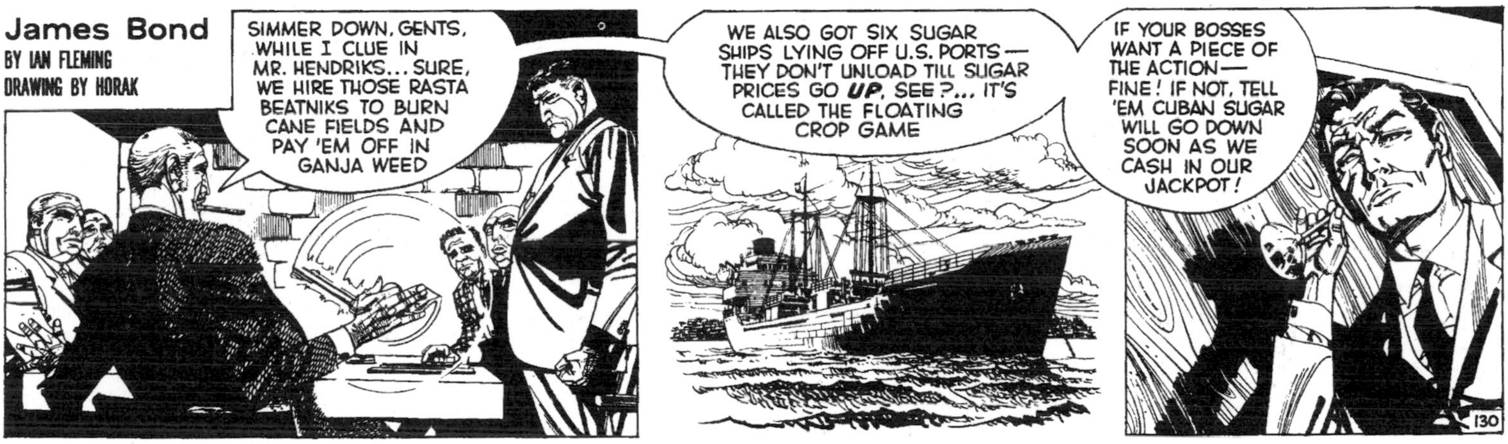
James Bond
BY IAN FLEMING
DRAWING BY HORAK
SIMMER DOWN, GENTS, WHILE I CLUE IN MR. HENDRIKS... SURE, WE HIRE THOSE RASTA BEATNIKS TO BURN CANE FIELDS AND PAY 'EM OFF IN GANJA WEED
WE ALSO GOT SIX SUGAR SHIPS LYING OFF U.S. PORTS — THEY DON'T UNLOAD TILL SUGAR PRICES GO UP, SEE?... IT'S CALLED THE FLOATING CROP GAME
IF YOUR BOSSES WANT A PIECE OF THE ACTION — FINE! IF NOT, TELL 'EM CUBAN SUGAR WILL GO DOWN SOON AS WE CASH IN OUR JACKPOT!
130

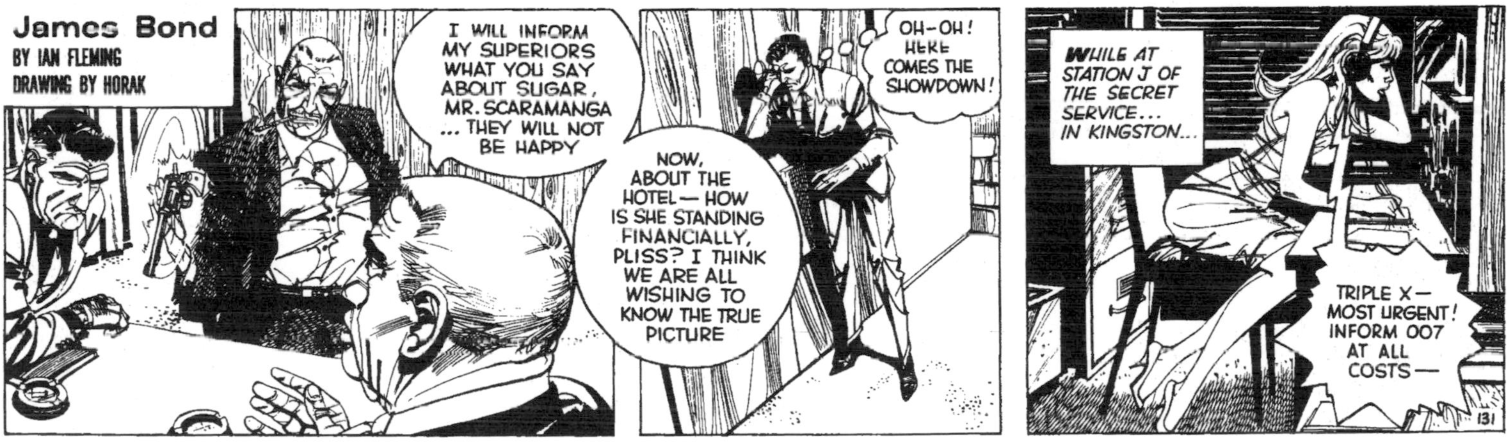
James Bond
BY IAN FLEMING
DRAWING BY HORAK
I WILL INFORM MY SUPERIORS WHAT YOU SAY ABOUT SUGAR, MR. SCARAMANGA ... THEY WILL NOT BE HAPPY
NOW, ABOUT THE HOTEL — HOW IS SHE STANDING FINANCIALLY, PLISS? I THINK WE ARE ALL WISHING TO KNOW THE TRUE PICTURE
OH-OH! HERE COMES THE SHOWDOWN!
WHILE AT STATION J OF THE SECRET SERVICE... IN KINGSTON...
TRIPLE X — MOST URGENT! INFORM 007 AT ALL COSTS —
131

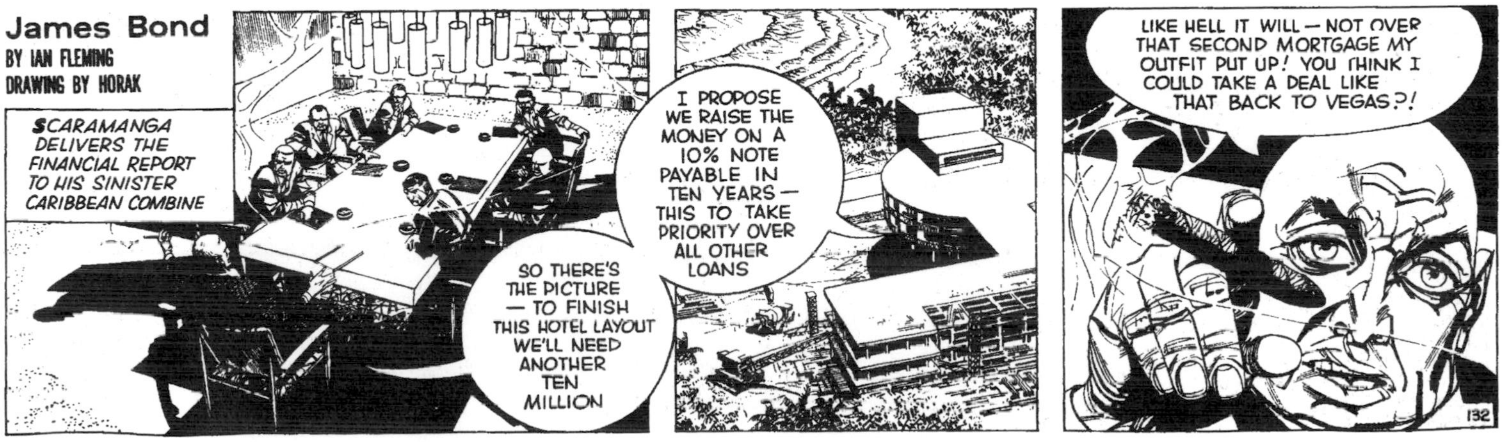
James Bond
BY IAN FLEMING
DRAWING BY HORAK
SCARAMANGA DELIVERS THE FINANCIAL REPORT TO HIS SINISTER CARIBBEAN COMBINE
SO THERE'S THE PICTURE — TO FINISH THIS HOTEL LAYOUT WE'LL NEED ANOTHER TEN MILLION
I PROPOSE WE RAISE THE MONEY ON A 10% NOTE PAYABLE IN TEN YEARS — THIS TO TAKE PRIORITY OVER ALL OTHER LOANS
LIKE HELL IT WILL — NOT OVER THAT SECOND MORTGAGE MY OUTFIT PUT UP! YOU THINK I COULD TAKE A DEAL LIKE THAT BACK TO VEGAS?!
132

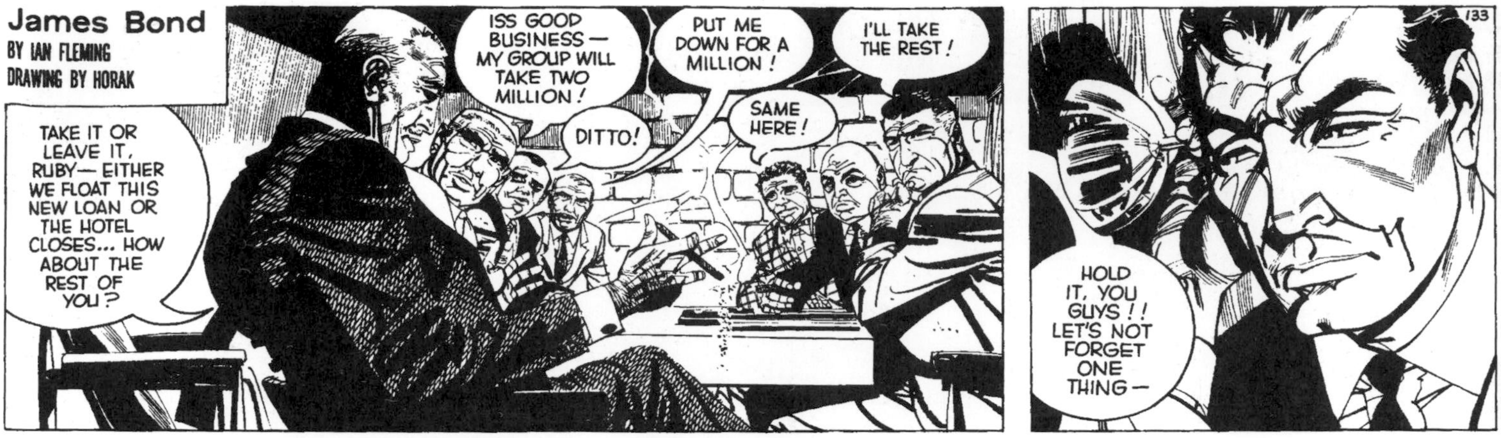
James Bond
BY IAN FLEMING
DRAWING BY HORAK
TAKE IT OR LEAVE IT, RUBY— EITHER WE FLOAT THIS NEW LOAN OR THE HOTEL CLOSES... HOW ABOUT THE REST OF YOU?
ISS GOOD BUSINESS— MY GROUP WILL TAKE TWO MILLION!
DITTO!
PUT ME DOWN FOR A MILLION!
SAME HERE!
I'LL TAKE THE REST!
133
HOLD IT, YOU GUYS!! LET'S NOT FORGET ONE THING—

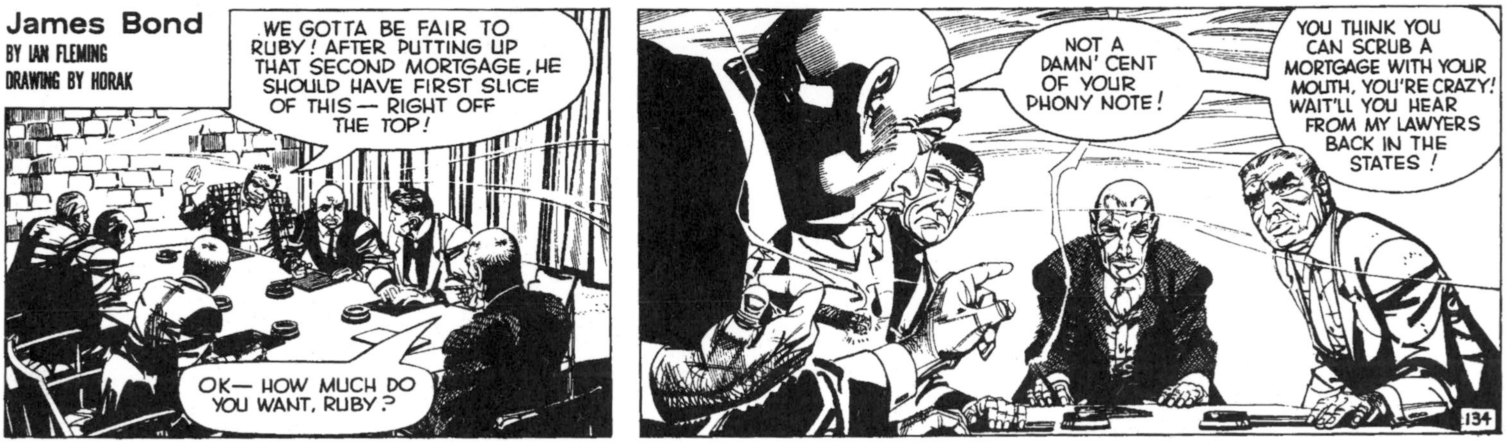
James Bond
BY IAN FLEMING
DRAWING BY HORAK
WE GOTTA BE FAIR TO RUBY! AFTER PUTTING UP THAT SECOND MORTGAGE, HE SHOULD HAVE FIRST SLICE OF THIS— RIGHT OFF THE TOP!
OK— HOW MUCH DO YOU WANT, RUBY?
NOT A DAMN' CENT OF YOUR PHONY NOTE!
YOU THINK YOU CAN SCRUB A MORTGAGE WITH YOUR MOUTH, YOU'RE CRAZY! WAIT'LL YOU HEAR FROM MY LAWYERS BACK IN THE STATES!
134

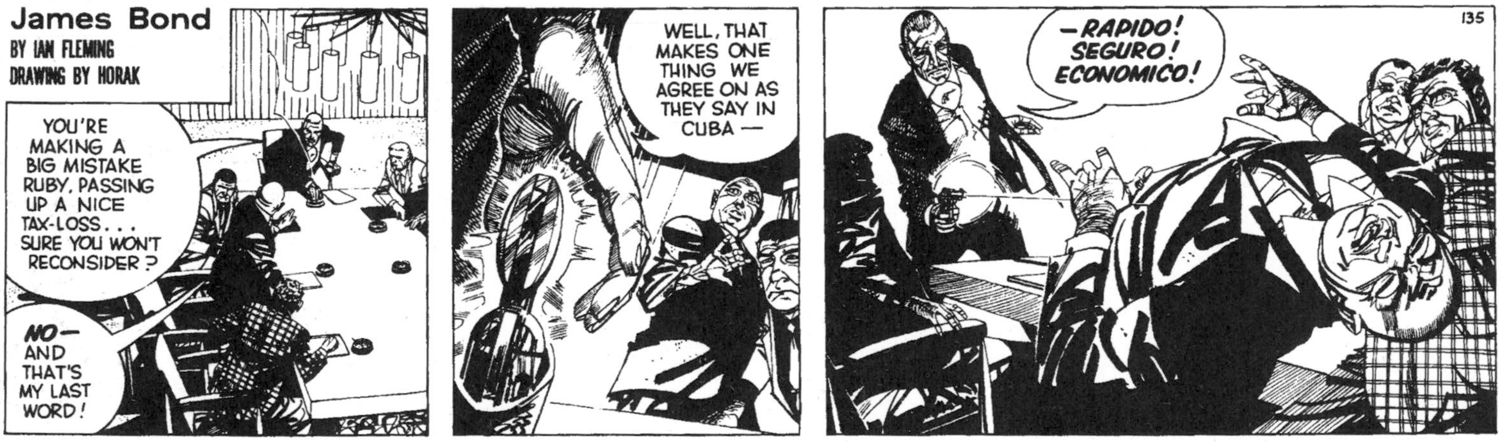
James Bond
BY IAN FLEMING
DRAWING BY HORAK
YOU'RE MAKING A BIG MISTAKE RUBY, PASSING UP A NICE TAX-LOSS... SURE YOU WON'T RECONSIDER?
NO— AND THAT'S MY LAST WORD!
WELL, THAT MAKES ONE THING WE AGREE ON AS THEY SAY IN CUBA—
135
—RAPIDO! SEGURO! ECONOMICO!

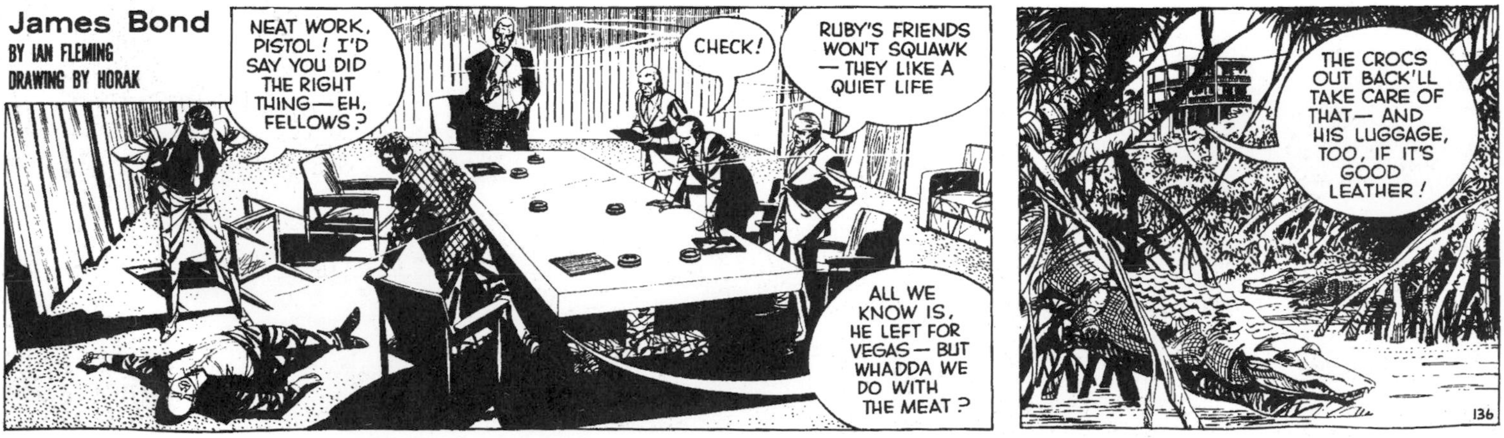
James Bond
BY IAN FLEMING
DRAWING BY HORAK
NEAT WORK, PISTOL! I'D SAY YOU DID THE RIGHT THING— EH, FELLOWS?
CHECK!
RUBY'S FRIENDS WON'T SQUAWK —THEY LIKE A QUIET LIFE
ALL WE KNOW IS, HE LEFT FOR VEGAS— BUT WHADDA WE DO WITH THE MEAT?
THE CROCS OUT BACK'LL TAKE CARE OF THAT— AND HIS LUGGAGE, TOO, IF IT'S GOOD LEATHER!
136

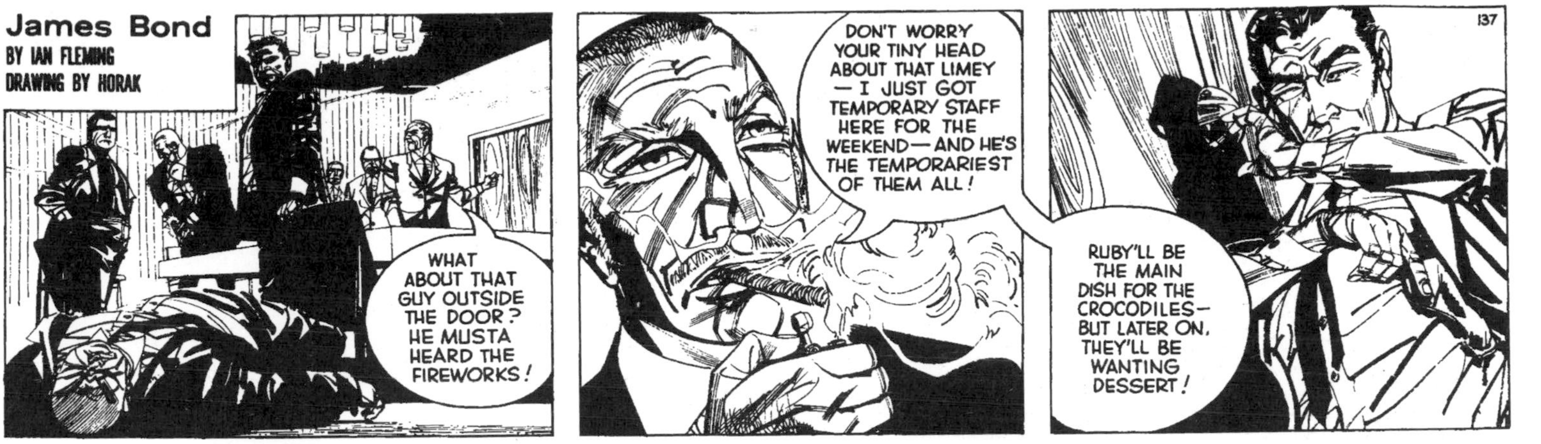
James Bond
BY IAN FLEMING
DRAWING BY HORAK
137
WHAT ABOUT THAT GUY OUTSIDE THE DOOR? HE MUSTA HEARD THE FIREWORKS!
DON'T WORRY YOUR TINY HEAD ABOUT THAT LIMEY — I JUST GOT TEMPORARY STAFF HERE FOR THE WEEKEND — AND HE'S THE TEMPORARIEST OF THEM ALL!
RUBY'LL BE THE MAIN DISH FOR THE CROCODILES— BUT LATER ON, THEY'LL BE WANTING DESSERT!

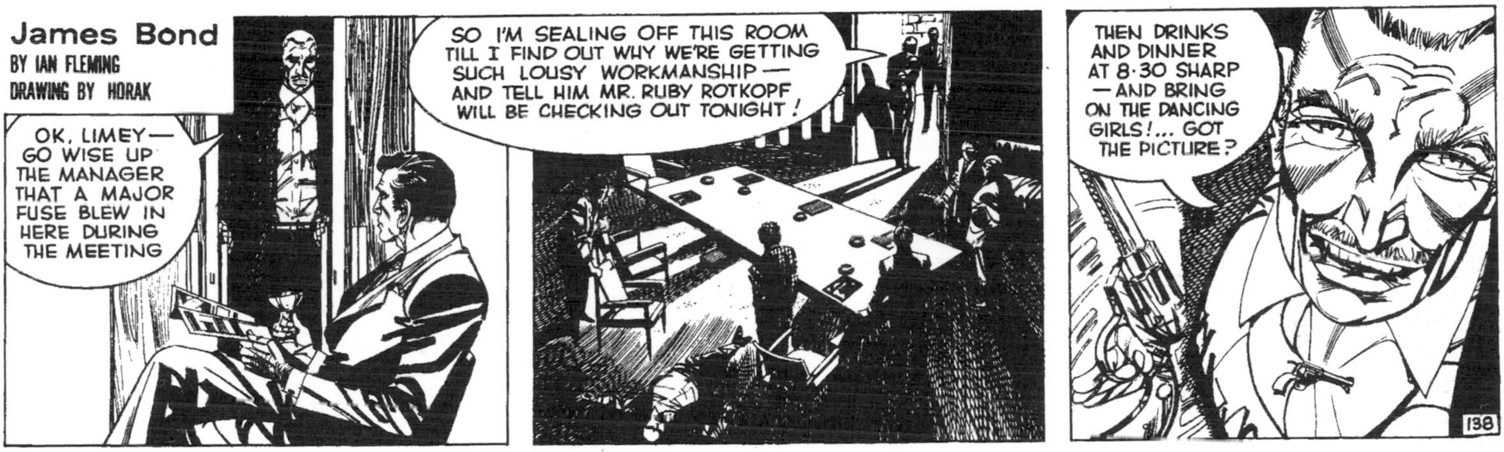
James Bond
BY IAN FLEMING
DRAWING BY HORAK
OK, LIMEY— GO WISE UP THE MANAGER THAT A MAJOR FUSE BLEW IN HERE DURING THE MEETING
SO I'M SEALING OFF THIS ROOM TILL I FIND OUT WHY WE'RE GETTING SUCH LOUSY WORKMANSHIP — AND TELL HIM MR. RUBY ROTKOPF WILL BE CHECKING OUT TONIGHT!
THEN DRINKS AND DINNER AT 8·30 SHARP — AND BRING ON THE DANCING GIRLS!... GOT THE PICTURE?
138

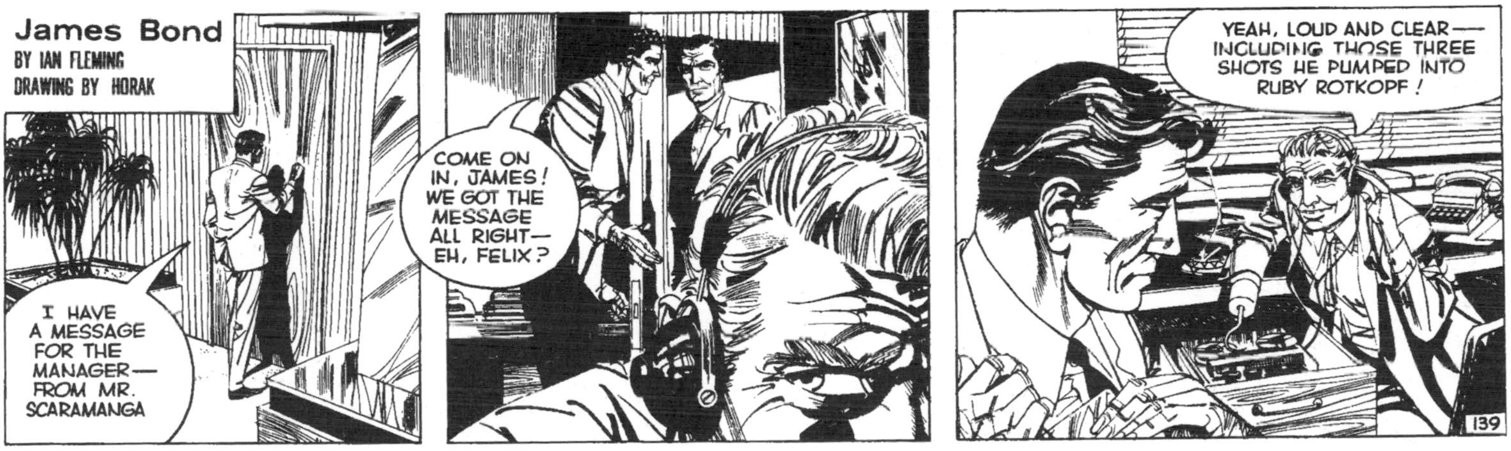
James Bond
BY IAN FLEMING
DRAWING BY HORAK
I HAVE A MESSAGE FOR THE MANAGER— FROM MR. SCARAMANGA
COME ON IN, JAMES! WE GOT THE MESSAGE ALL RIGHT— EH, FELIX?
YEAH, LOUD AND CLEAR— INCLUDING THOSE THREE SHOTS HE PUMPED INTO RUBY ROTKOPF!
139

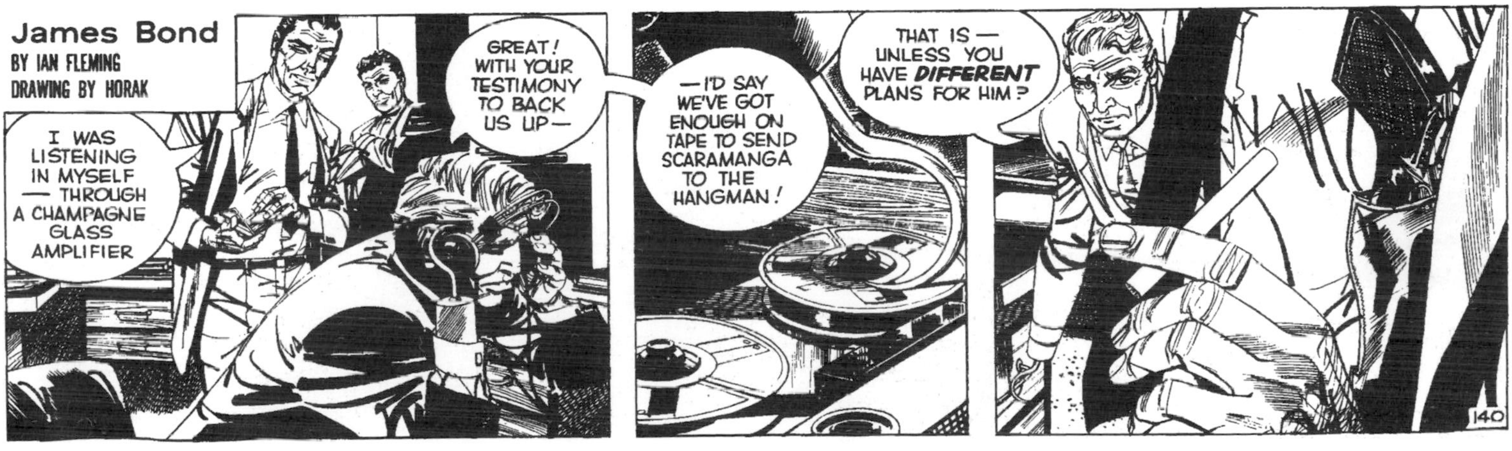
James Bond
BY IAN FLEMING
DRAWING BY HORAK
I WAS LISTENING IN MYSELF — THROUGH A CHAMPAGNE GLASS AMPLIFIER
GREAT! WITH YOUR TESTIMONY TO BACK US UP—
—I'D SAY WE'VE GOT ENOUGH ON TAPE TO SEND SCARAMANGA TO THE HANGMAN!
THAT IS — UNLESS YOU HAVE ***DIFFERENT*** PLANS FOR HIM?
140

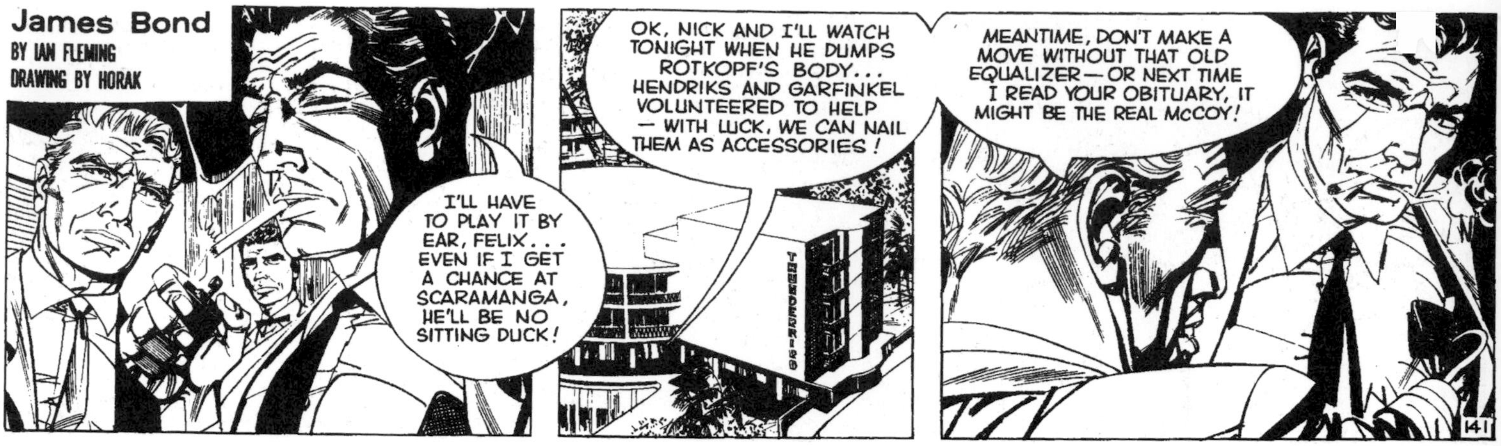
James Bond
BY IAN FLEMING
DRAWING BY HORAK
I'LL HAVE TO PLAY IT BY EAR, FELIX... EVEN IF I GET A CHANCE AT SCARAMANGA, HE'LL BE NO SITTING DUCK!
OK, NICK AND I'LL WATCH TONIGHT WHEN HE DUMPS ROTKOPF'S BODY... HENDRIKS AND GARFINKEL VOLUNTEERED TO HELP — WITH LUCK, WE CAN NAIL THEM AS ACCESSORIES!
MEANTIME, DON'T MAKE A MOVE WITHOUT THAT OLD EQUALIZER — OR NEXT TIME I READ YOUR OBITUARY, IT MIGHT BE THE REAL McCOY!
141

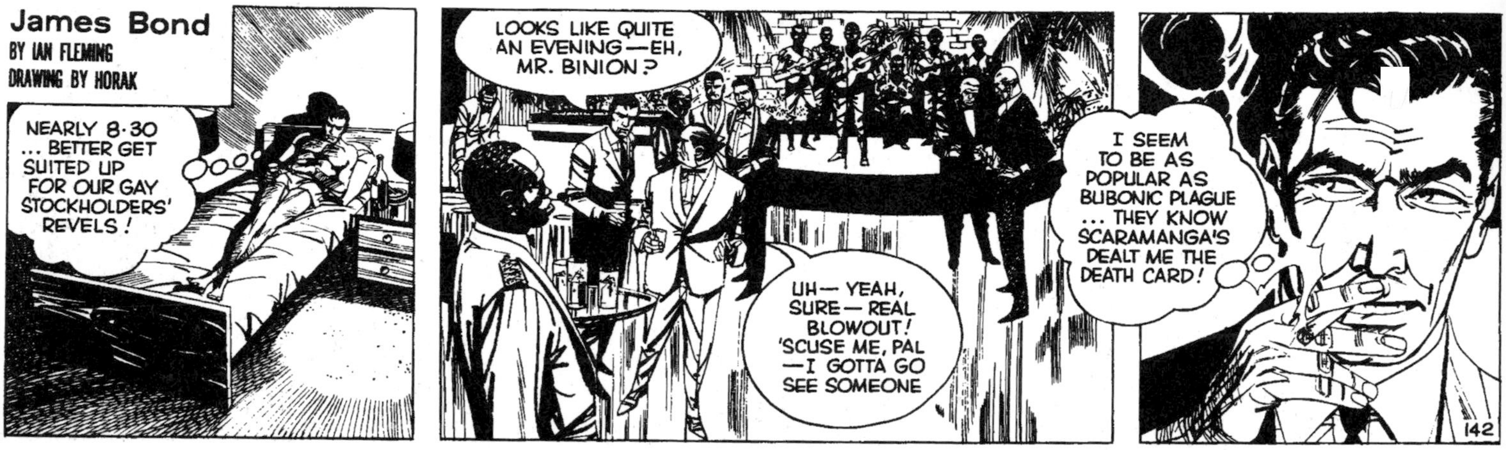
James Bond
BY IAN FLEMING
DRAWING BY HORAK
NEARLY 8·30 ... BETTER GET SUITED UP FOR OUR GAY STOCKHOLDERS' REVELS!
LOOKS LIKE QUITE AN EVENING—EH, MR. BINION?
UH— YEAH, SURE— REAL BLOWOUT! 'SCUSE ME, PAL —I GOTTA GO SEE SOMEONE
I SEEM TO BE AS POPULAR AS BUBONIC PLAGUE ... THEY KNOW SCARAMANGA'S DEALT ME THE DEATH CARD!
142

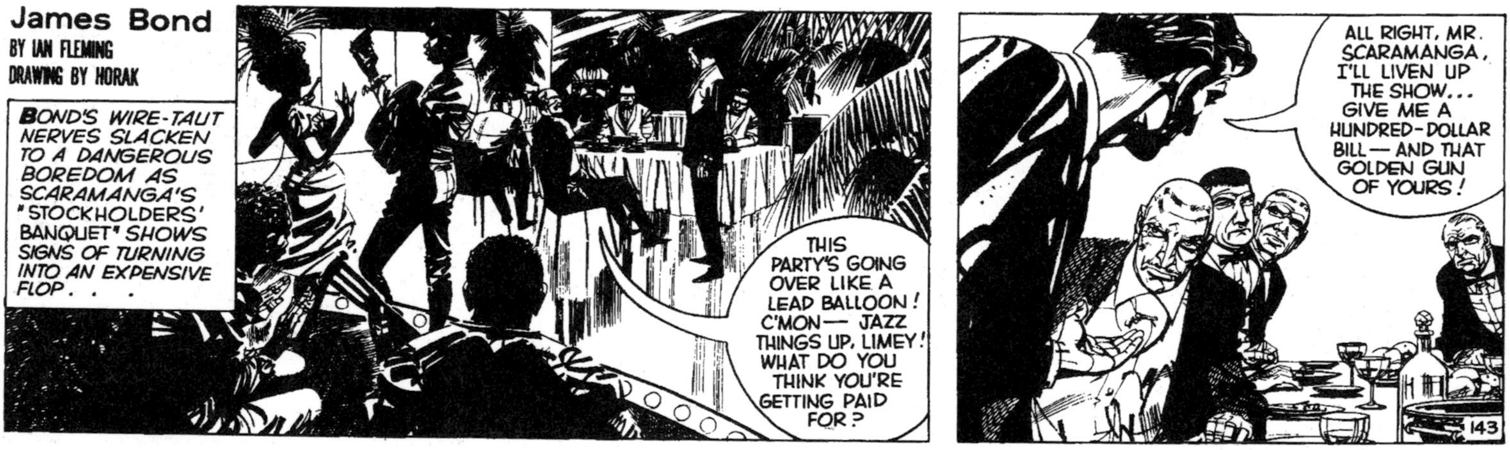
James Bond
BY IAN FLEMING
DRAWING BY HORAK
BOND'S WIRE-TAUT NERVES SLACKEN TO A DANGEROUS BOREDOM AS SCARAMANGA'S "STOCKHOLDERS' BANQUET" SHOWS SIGNS OF TURNING INTO AN EXPENSIVE FLOP . . .
THIS PARTY'S GOING OVER LIKE A LEAD BALLOON! C'MON— JAZZ THINGS UP, LIMEY! WHAT DO YOU THINK YOU'RE GETTING PAID FOR?
ALL RIGHT, MR. SCARAMANGA, I'LL LIVEN UP THE SHOW... GIVE ME A HUNDRED-DOLLAR BILL — AND THAT GOLDEN GUN OF YOURS!
143

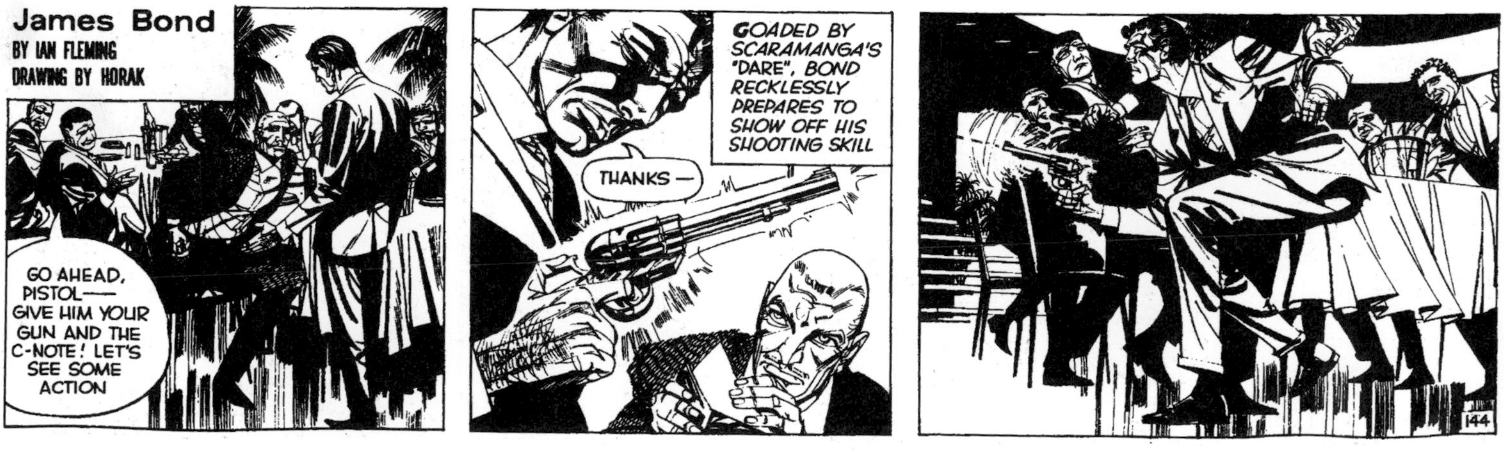
James Bond
BY IAN FLEMING
DRAWING BY HORAK
GO AHEAD, PISTOL— GIVE HIM YOUR GUN AND THE C-NOTE! LET'S SEE SOME ACTION
GOADED BY SCARAMANGA'S "DARE", BOND RECKLESSLY PREPARES TO SHOW OFF HIS SHOOTING SKILL
THANKS —
144

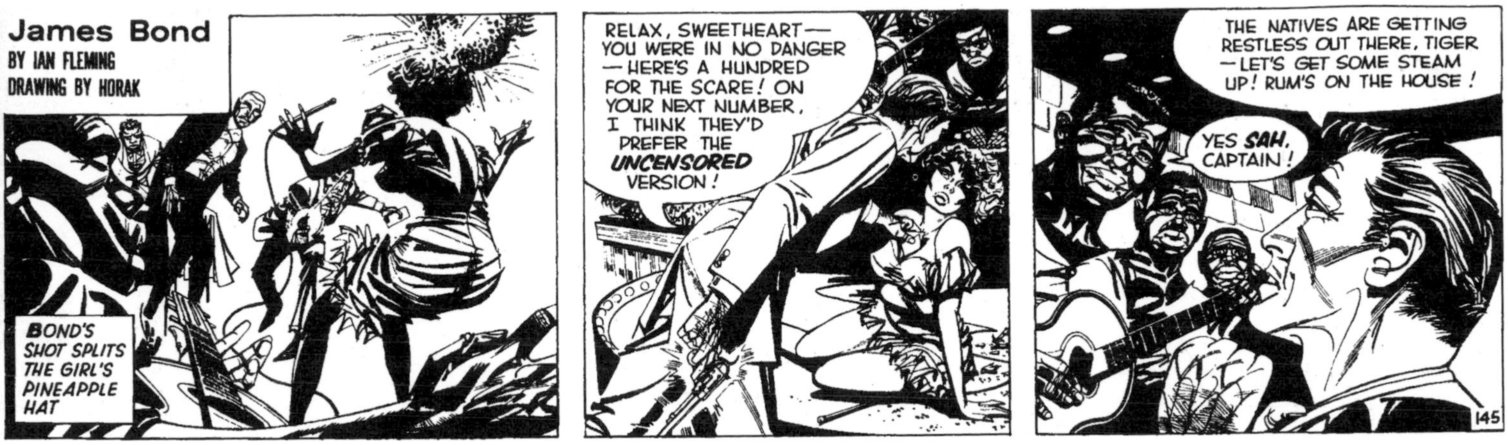
James Bond
BY IAN FLEMING
DRAWING BY HORAK
BOND'S SHOT SPLITS THE GIRL'S PINEAPPLE HAT
RELAX, SWEETHEART— YOU WERE IN NO DANGER —HERE'S A HUNDRED FOR THE SCARE! ON YOUR NEXT NUMBER, I THINK THEY'D PREFER THE UNCENSORED VERSION!
THE NATIVES ARE GETTING RESTLESS OUT THERE, TIGER —LET'S GET SOME STEAM UP! RUM'S ON THE HOUSE!
YES SAH, CAPTAIN!
145

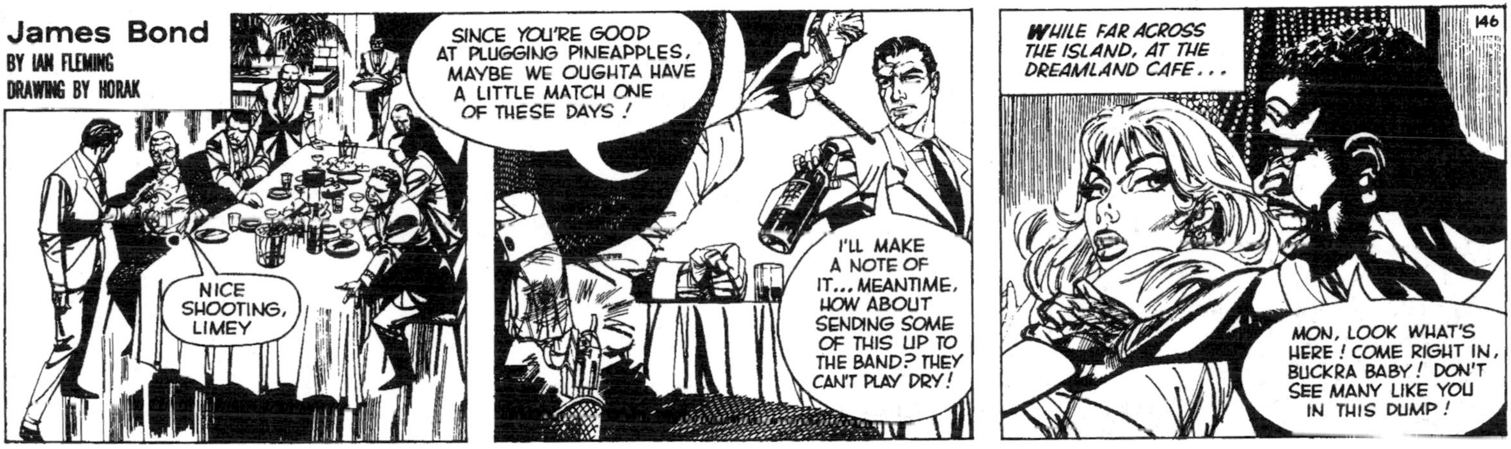
James Bond
BY IAN FLEMING
DRAWING BY HORAK
NICE SHOOTING, LIMEY
SINCE YOU'RE GOOD AT PLUGGING PINEAPPLES, MAYBE WE OUGHTA HAVE A LITTLE MATCH ONE OF THESE DAYS!
I'LL MAKE A NOTE OF IT... MEANTIME, HOW ABOUT SENDING SOME OF THIS UP TO THE BAND? THEY CAN'T PLAY DRY!
WHILE FAR ACROSS THE ISLAND, AT THE DREAMLAND CAFE...
146
MON, LOOK WHAT'S HERE! COME RIGHT IN, BUCKRA BABY! DON'T SEE MANY LIKE YOU IN THIS DUMP!

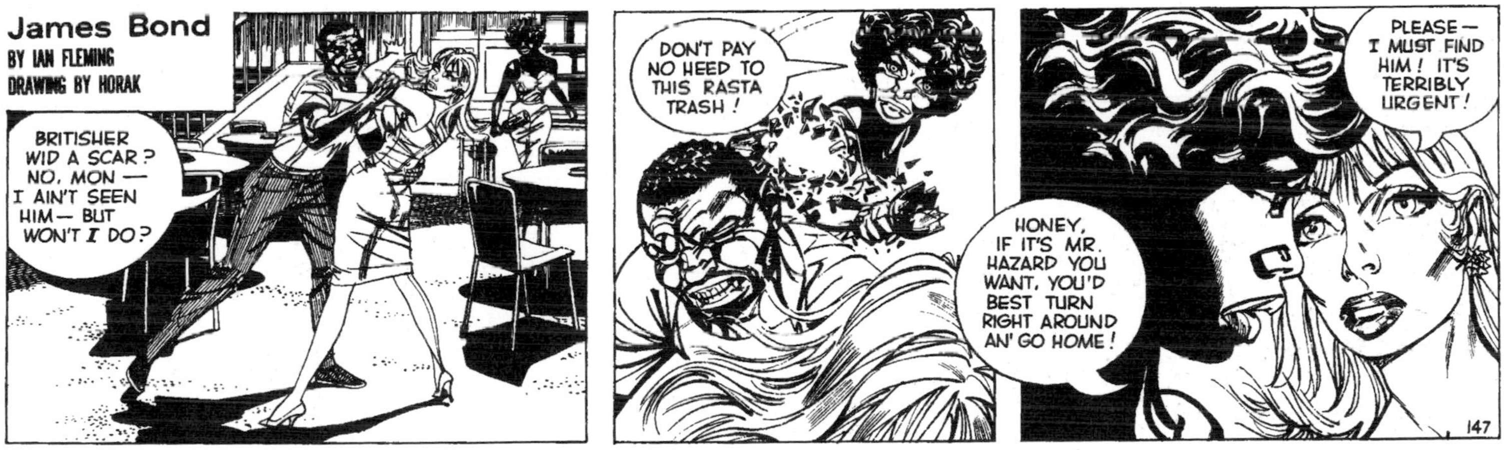
James Bond
BY IAN FLEMING
DRAWING BY HORAK
BRITISHER WID A SCAR? NO, MON — I AIN'T SEEN HIM— BUT WON'T I DO?
DON'T PAY NO HEED TO THIS RASTA TRASH!
HONEY, IF IT'S MR. HAZARD YOU WANT, YOU'D BEST TURN RIGHT AROUND AN' GO HOME!
PLEASE— I MUST FIND HIM! IT'S TERRIBLY URGENT!
147

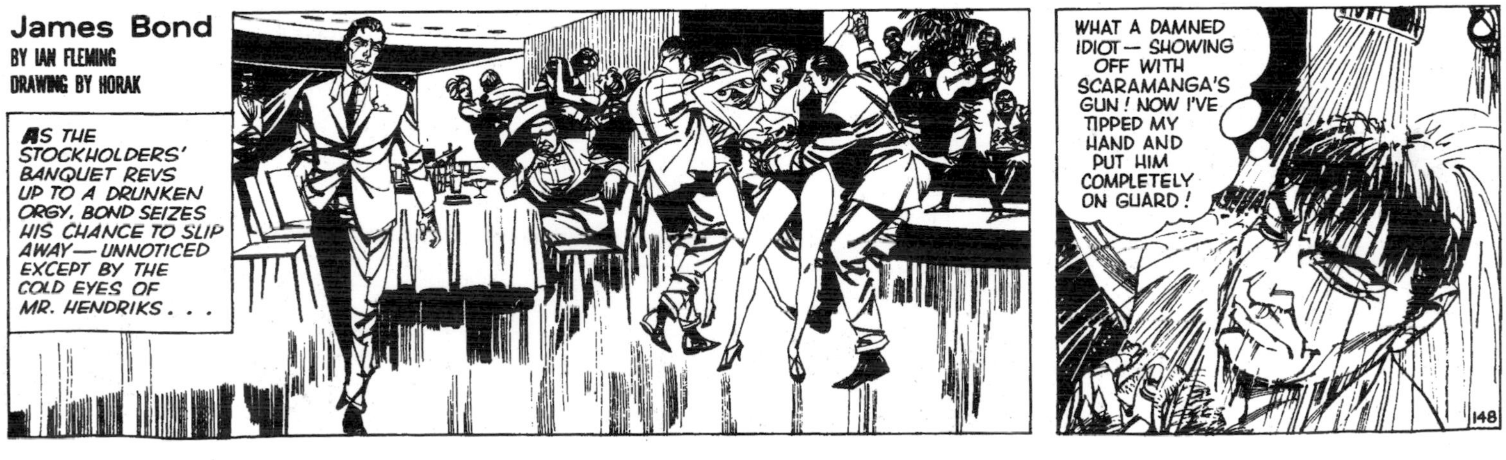
James Bond
BY IAN FLEMING
DRAWING BY HORAK
AS THE STOCKHOLDERS' BANQUET REVS UP TO A DRUNKEN ORGY, BOND SEIZES HIS CHANCE TO SLIP AWAY— UNNOTICED EXCEPT BY THE COLD EYES OF MR. HENDRIKS...
WHAT A DAMNED IDIOT— SHOWING OFF WITH SCARAMANGA'S GUN! NOW I'VE TIPPED MY HAND AND PUT HIM COMPLETELY ON GUARD!
148

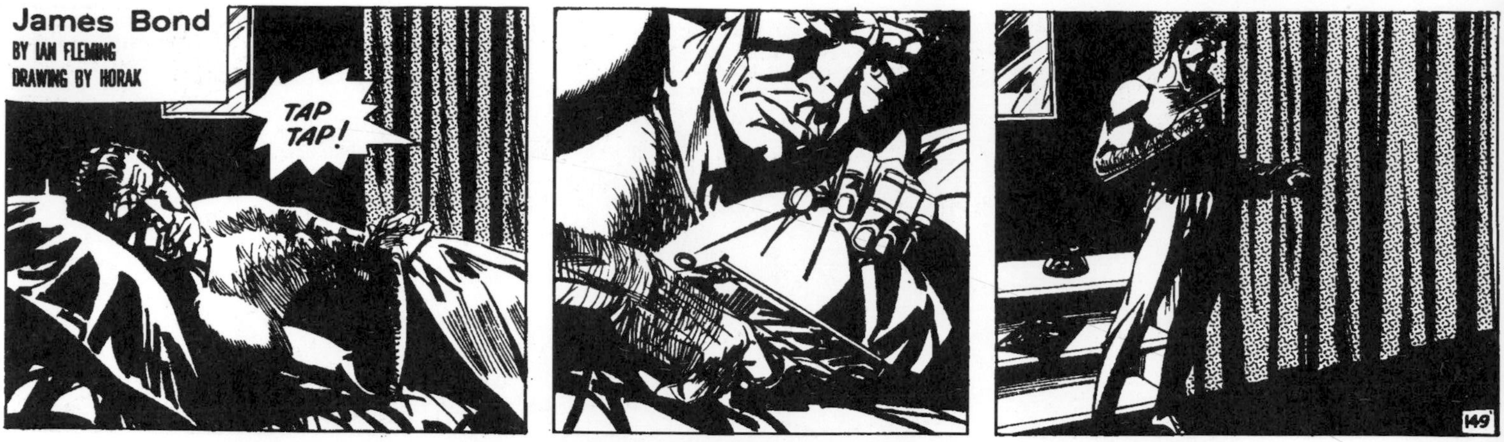
James Bond
BY IAN FLEMING
DRAWING BY HORAK
TAP TAP!
149

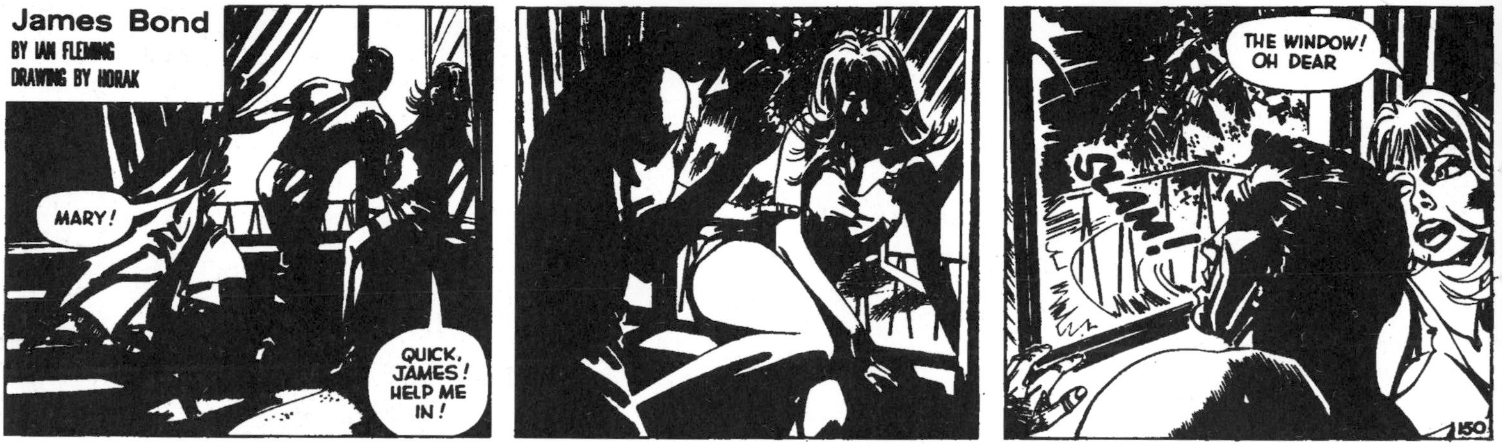
James Bond
BY IAN FLEMING
DRAWING BY HORAK
MARY!
QUICK, JAMES! HELP ME IN!
THE WINDOW! OH DEAR
SLAM!
150

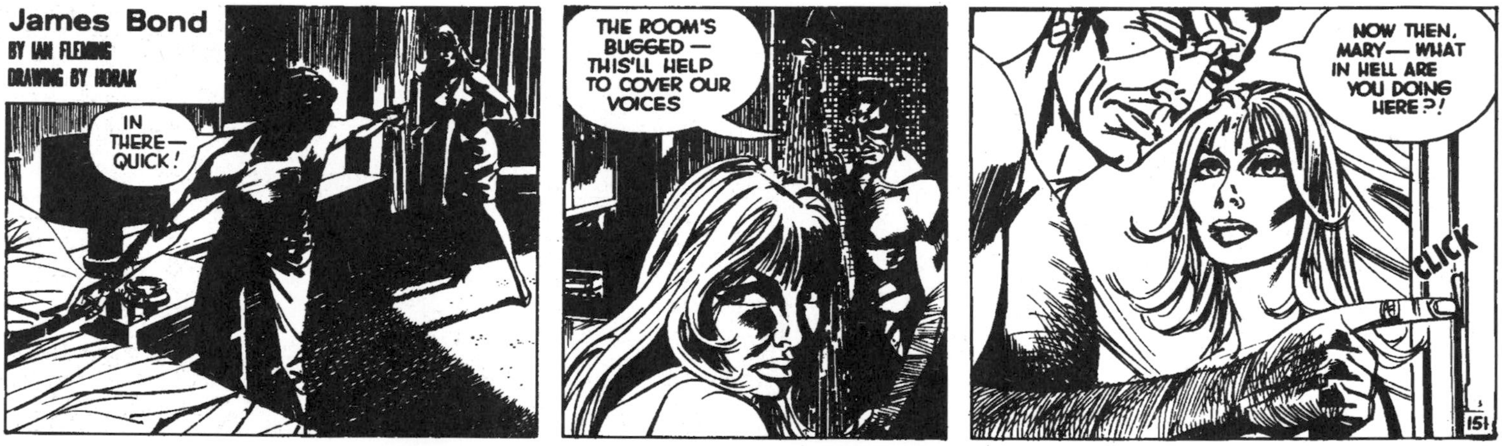
James Bond
BY IAN FLEMING
DRAWING BY HORAK
IN THERE—QUICK!
THE ROOM'S BUGGED—THIS'LL HELP TO COVER OUR VOICES
NOW THEN, MARY— WHAT IN HELL ARE YOU DOING HERE?!
CLICK
151

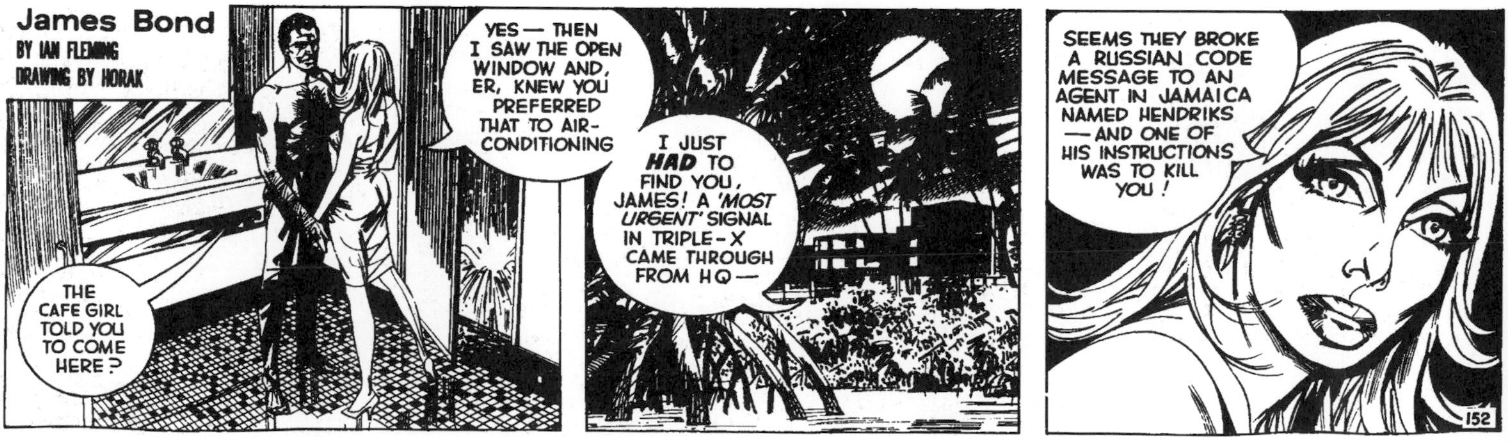
James Bond
BY IAN FLEMING
DRAWING BY HORAK
THE CAFE GIRL TOLD YOU TO COME HERE?
YES— THEN I SAW THE OPEN WINDOW AND, ER, KNEW YOU PREFERRED THAT TO AIR-CONDITIONING
I JUST HAD TO FIND YOU, JAMES! A 'MOST URGENT' SIGNAL IN TRIPLE-X CAME THROUGH FROM HQ—
SEEMS THEY BROKE A RUSSIAN CODE MESSAGE TO AN AGENT IN JAMAICA NAMED HENDRIKS —AND ONE OF HIS INSTRUCTIONS WAS TO KILL YOU!
152

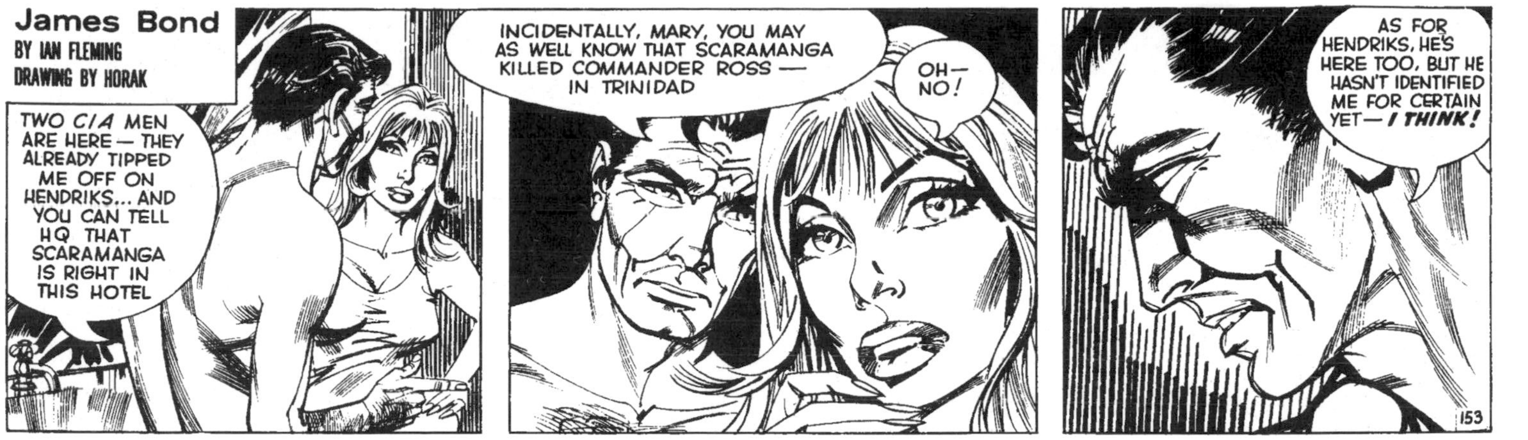
James Bond
BY IAN FLEMING
DRAWING BY HORAK
TWO C/A MEN ARE HERE — THEY ALREADY TIPPED ME OFF ON HENDRIKS... AND YOU CAN TELL HQ THAT SCARAMANGA IS RIGHT IN THIS HOTEL
INCIDENTALLY, MARY, YOU MAY AS WELL KNOW THAT SCARAMANGA KILLED COMMANDER ROSS — IN TRINIDAD
OH— NO!
AS FOR HENDRIKS, HE'S HERE TOO, BUT HE HASN'T IDENTIFIED ME FOR CERTAIN YET— I THINK!
153

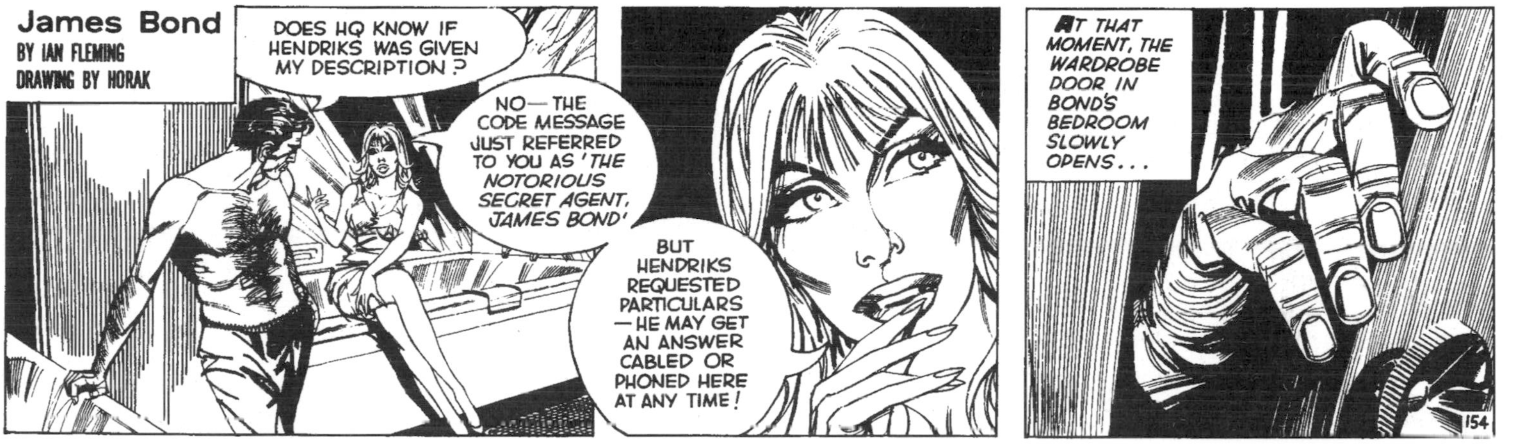
James Bond
BY IAN FLEMING
DRAWING BY HORAK
DOES HQ KNOW IF HENDRIKS WAS GIVEN MY DESCRIPTION?
NO— THE CODE MESSAGE JUST REFERRED TO YOU AS 'THE NOTORIOUS SECRET AGENT, JAMES BOND'
BUT HENDRIKS REQUESTED PARTICULARS —HE MAY GET AN ANSWER CABLED OR PHONED HERE AT ANY TIME!
AT THAT MOMENT, THE WARDROBE DOOR IN BOND'S BEDROOM SLOWLY OPENS...
154

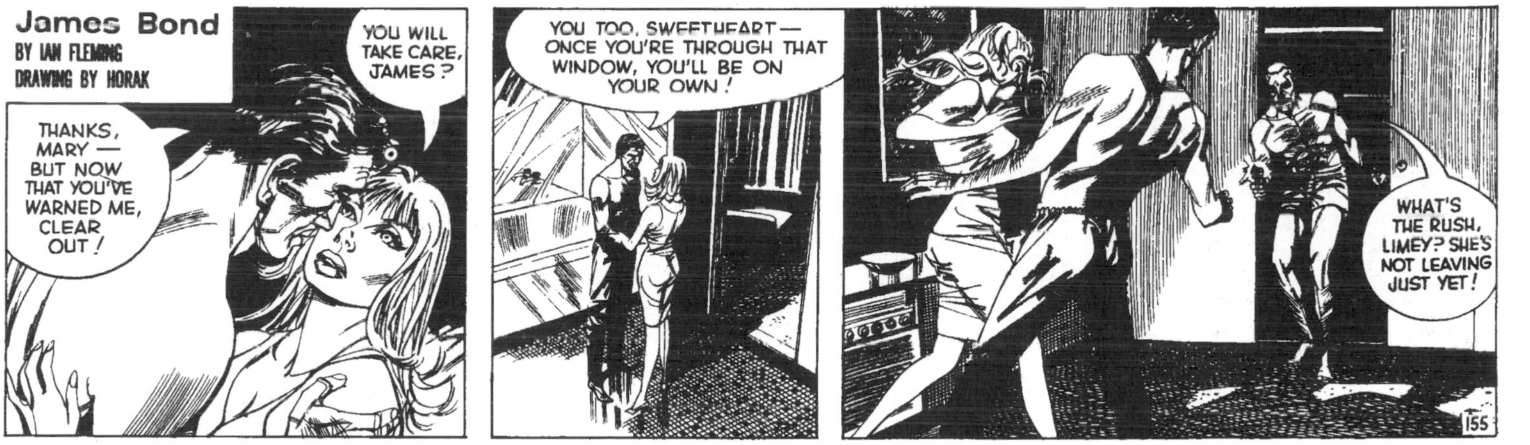
James Bond
BY IAN FLEMING
DRAWING BY HORAK
YOU WILL TAKE CARE, JAMES?
THANKS, MARY — BUT NOW THAT YOU'VE WARNED ME, CLEAR OUT!
YOU TOO, SWEETHEART — ONCE YOU'RE THROUGH THAT WINDOW, YOU'LL BE ON YOUR OWN!
WHAT'S THE RUSH, LIMEY? SHE'S NOT LEAVING JUST YET!
155

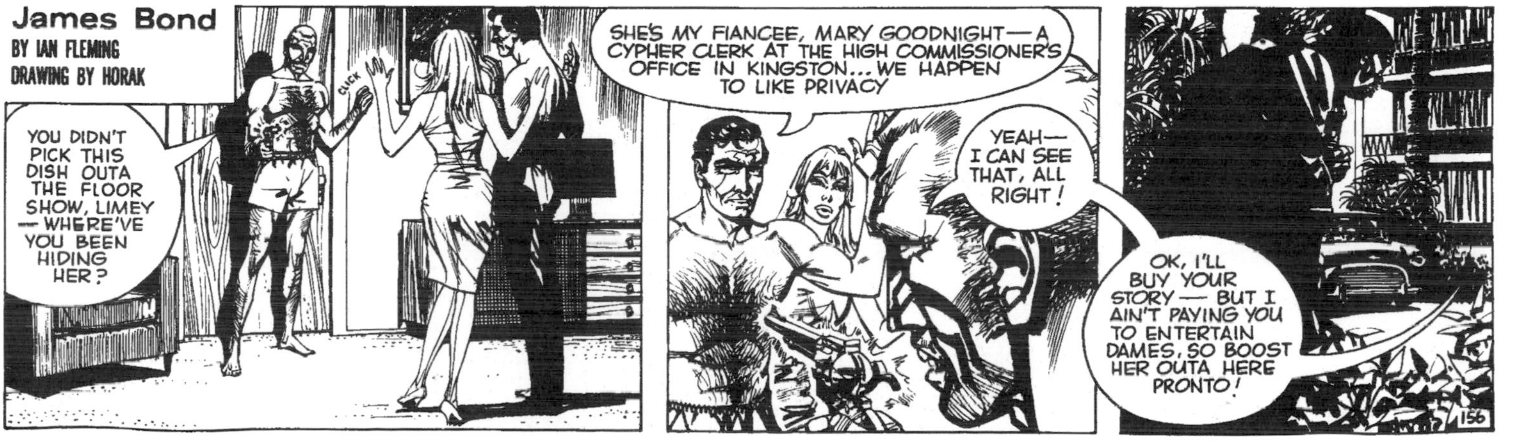
James Bond
BY IAN FLEMING
DRAWING BY HORAK
CLICK
YOU DIDN'T PICK THIS DISH OUTA THE FLOOR SHOW, LIMEY — WHERE'VE YOU BEEN HIDING HER?
SHE'S MY FIANCEE, MARY GOODNIGHT — A CYPHER CLERK AT THE HIGH COMMISSIONER'S OFFICE IN KINGSTON... WE HAPPEN TO LIKE PRIVACY
YEAH— I CAN SEE THAT, ALL RIGHT!
OK, I'LL BUY YOUR STORY — BUT I AIN'T PAYING YOU TO ENTERTAIN DAMES, SO BOOST HER OUTA HERE PRONTO!
156

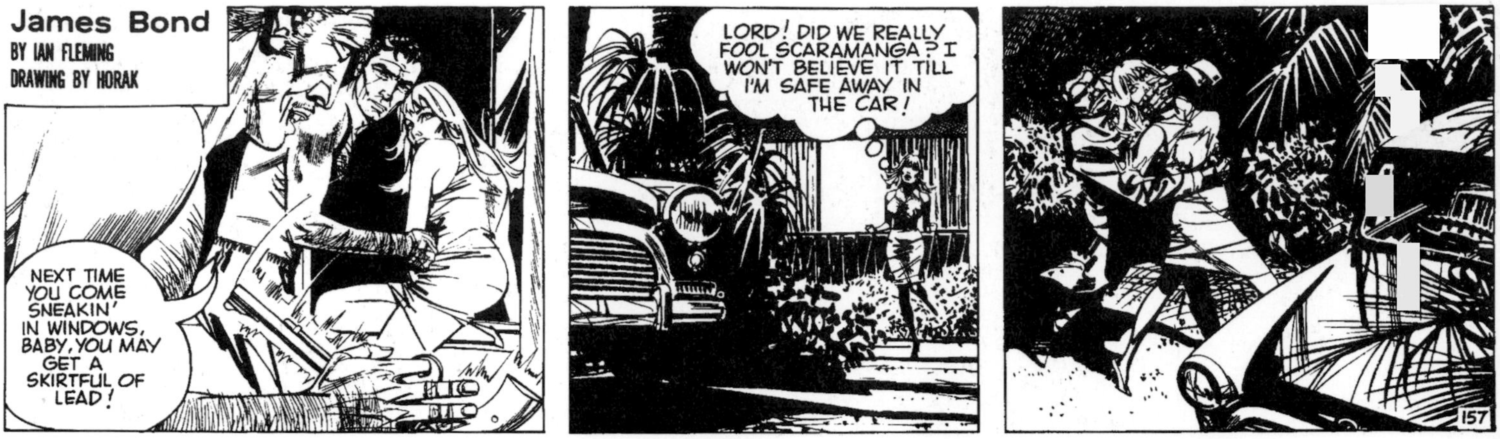
James Bond
BY IAN FLEMING
DRAWING BY HORAK
NEXT TIME YOU COME SNEAKIN' IN WINDOWS, BABY, YOU MAY GET A SKIRTFUL OF LEAD!
LORD! DID WE REALLY FOOL SCARAMANGA? I WON'T BELIEVE IT TILL I'M SAFE AWAY IN THE CAR!
157

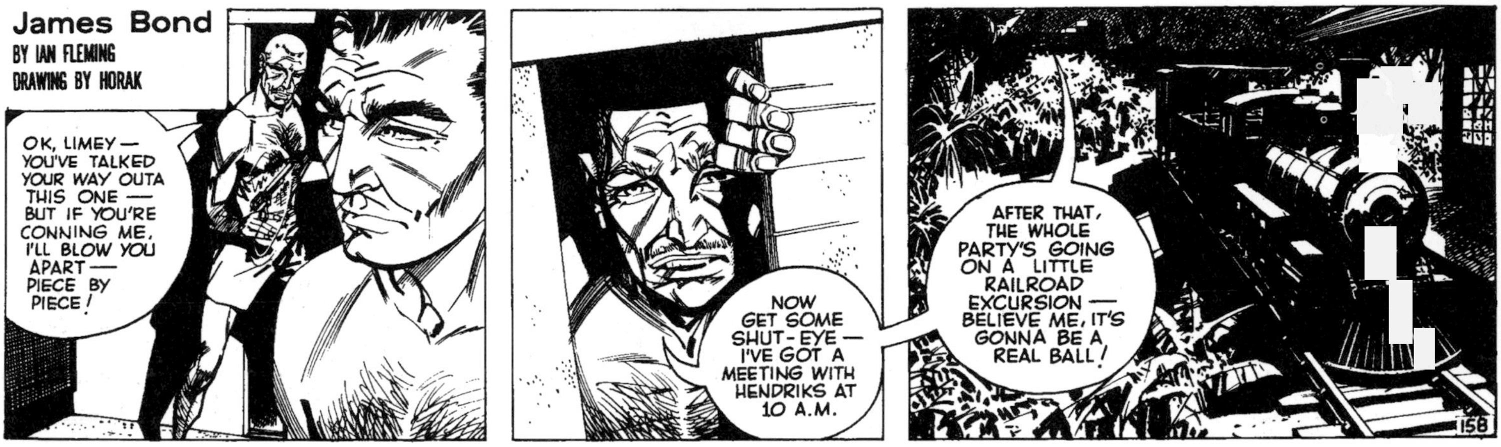
James Bond
BY IAN FLEMING
DRAWING BY HORAK
OK, LIMEY — YOU'VE TALKED YOUR WAY OUTA THIS ONE — BUT IF YOU'RE CONNING ME, I'LL BLOW YOU APART — PIECE BY PIECE!
NOW GET SOME SHUT-EYE — I'VE GOT A MEETING WITH HENDRIKS AT 10 A.M.
AFTER THAT, THE WHOLE PARTY'S GOING ON A LITTLE RAILROAD EXCURSION — BELIEVE ME, IT'S GONNA BE A REAL BALL!
158

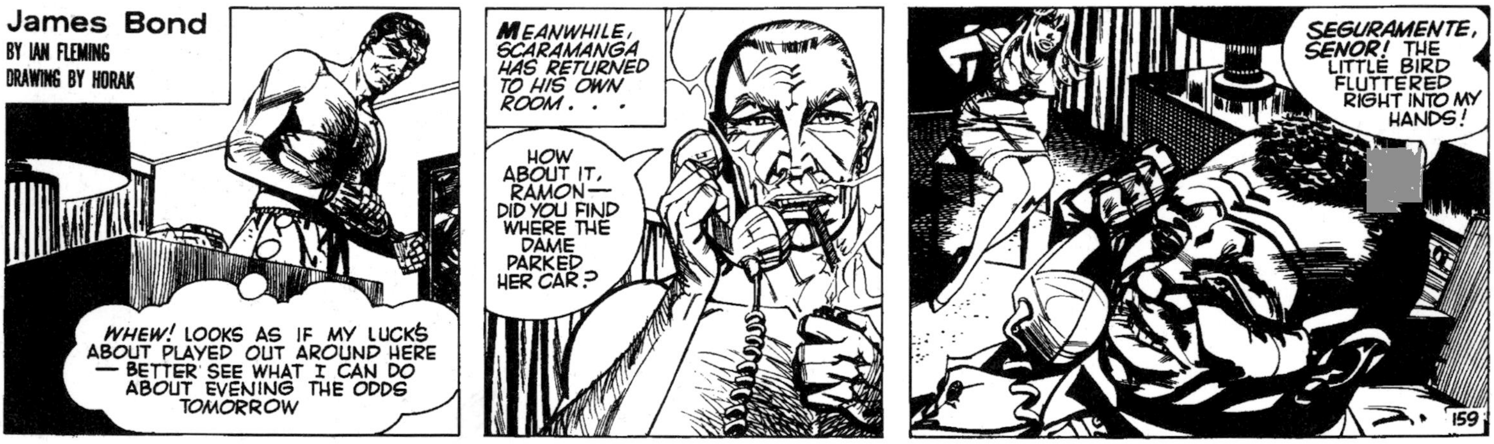
James Bond
BY IAN FLEMING
DRAWING BY HORAK
WHEW! LOOKS AS IF MY LUCK'S ABOUT PLAYED OUT AROUND HERE — BETTER SEE WHAT I CAN DO ABOUT EVENING THE ODDS TOMORROW
MEANWHILE, SCARAMANGA HAS RETURNED TO HIS OWN ROOM . . .
HOW ABOUT IT, RAMON — DID YOU FIND WHERE THE DAME PARKED HER CAR?
SEGURAMENTE, SENOR! THE LITTLE BIRD FLUTTERED RIGHT INTO MY HANDS!
159

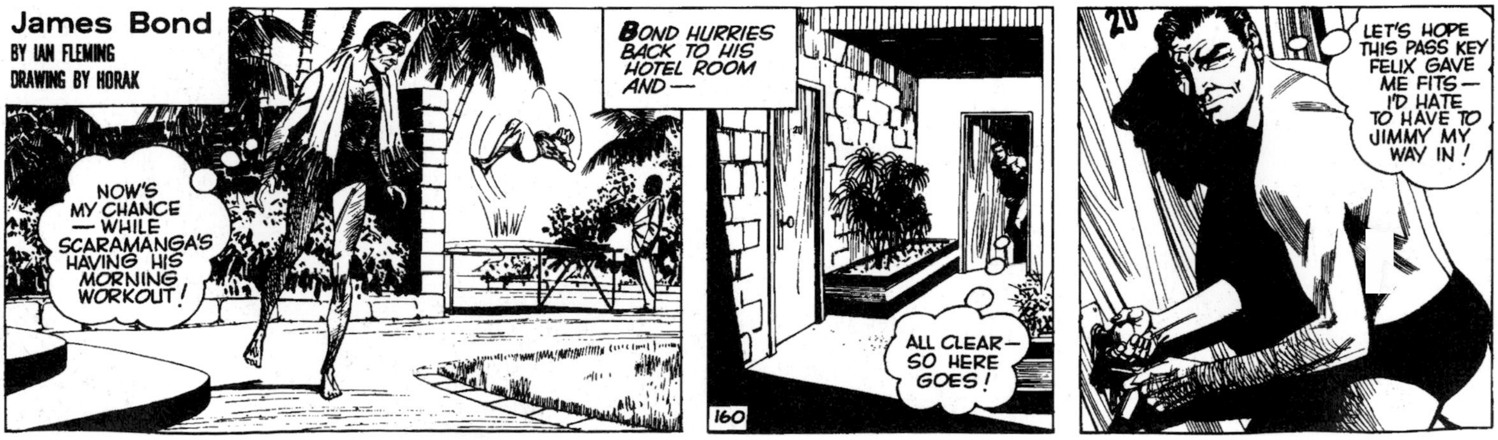
James Bond
BY IAN FLEMING
DRAWING BY HORAK
NOW'S MY CHANCE — WHILE SCARAMANGA'S HAVING HIS MORNING WORKOUT!
BOND HURRIES BACK TO HIS HOTEL ROOM AND —
ALL CLEAR — SO HERE GOES!
160
LET'S HOPE THIS PASS KEY FELIX GAVE ME FITS — I'D HATE TO HAVE TO JIMMY MY WAY IN!

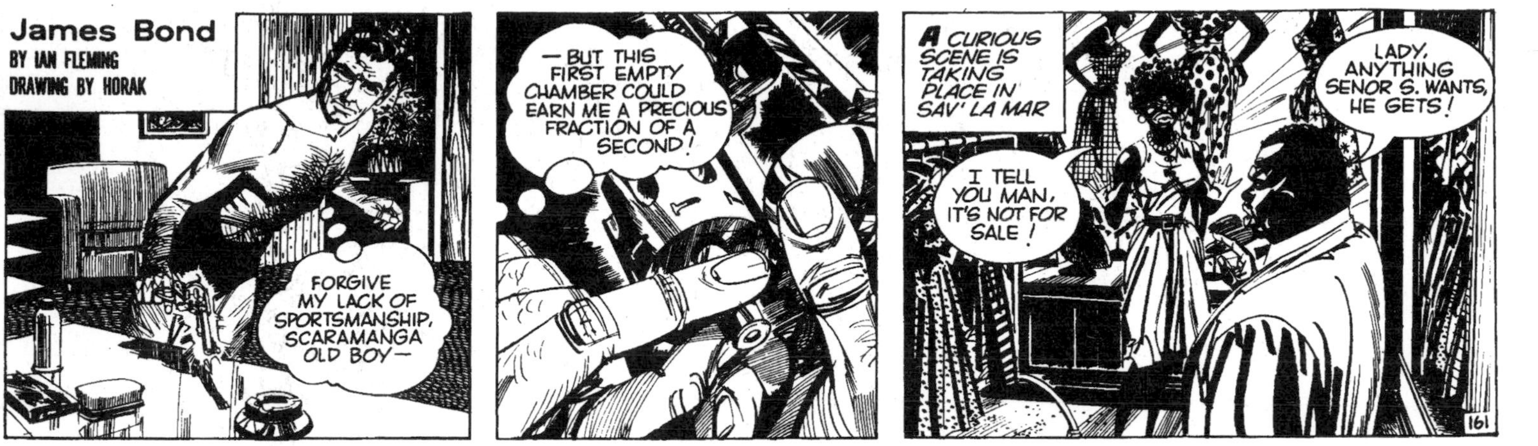
James Bond
BY IAN FLEMING
DRAWING BY HORAK
FORGIVE MY LACK OF SPORTSMANSHIP, SCARAMANGA OLD BOY —
— BUT THIS FIRST EMPTY CHAMBER COULD EARN ME A PRECIOUS FRACTION OF A SECOND!
A CURIOUS SCENE IS TAKING PLACE IN SAV' LA MAR
LADY, ANYTHING SENOR S. WANTS, HE GETS!
I TELL YOU MAN, IT'S NOT FOR SALE!
161

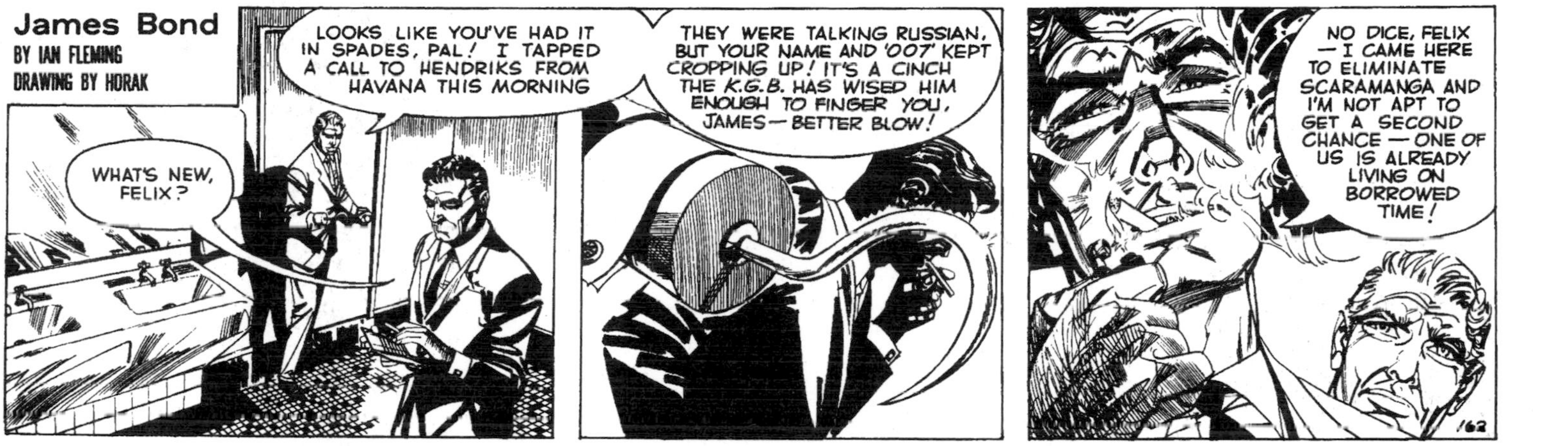
James Bond
BY IAN FLEMING
DRAWING BY HORAK
WHAT'S NEW, FELIX?
LOOKS LIKE YOU'VE HAD IT IN SPADES, PAL! I TAPPED A CALL TO HENDRIKS FROM HAVANA THIS MORNING
THEY WERE TALKING RUSSIAN, BUT YOUR NAME AND '007' KEPT CROPPING UP! IT'S A CINCH THE K.G.B. HAS WISED HIM ENOUGH TO FINGER YOU, JAMES — BETTER BLOW!
NO DICE, FELIX — I CAME HERE TO ELIMINATE SCARAMANGA AND I'M NOT APT TO GET A SECOND CHANCE — ONE OF US IS ALREADY LIVING ON BORROWED TIME!
162

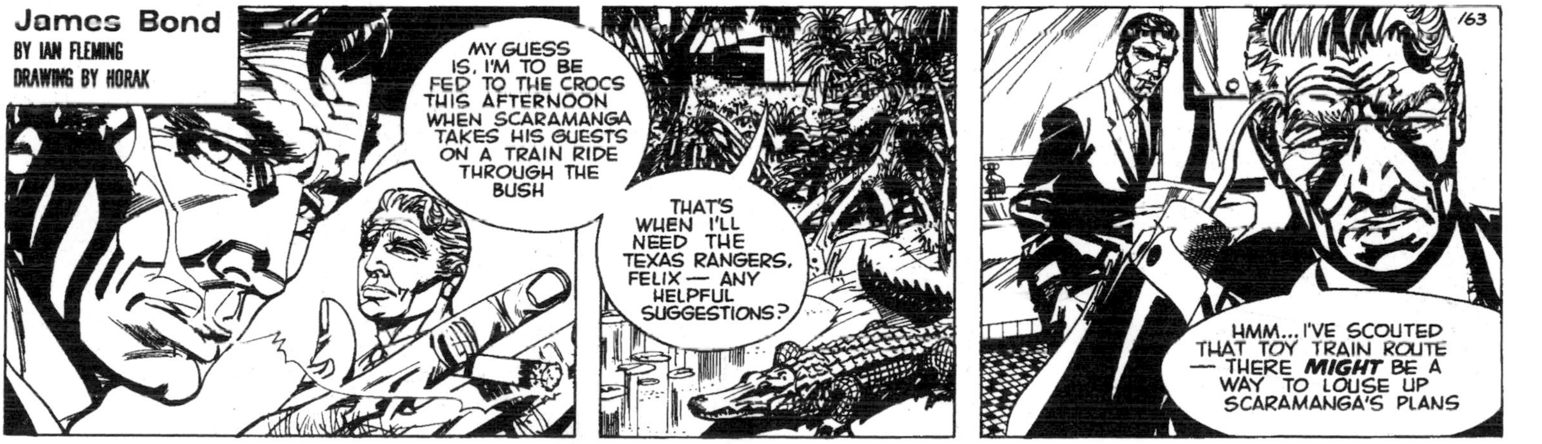
James Bond
BY IAN FLEMING
DRAWING BY HORAK
MY GUESS IS, I'M TO BE FED TO THE CROCS THIS AFTERNOON WHEN SCARAMANGA TAKES HIS GUESTS ON A TRAIN RIDE THROUGH THE BUSH
THAT'S WHEN I'LL NEED THE TEXAS RANGERS, FELIX — ANY HELPFUL SUGGESTIONS?
163
HMM... I'VE SCOUTED THAT TOY TRAIN ROUTE — THERE MIGHT BE A WAY TO LOUSE UP SCARAMANGA'S PLANS

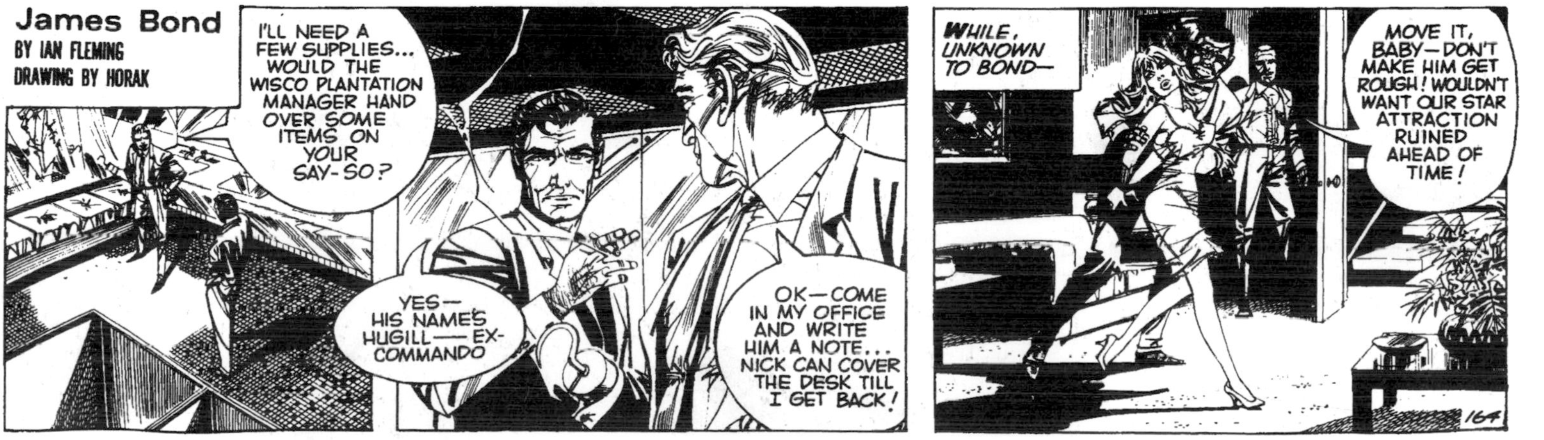
James Bond
BY IAN FLEMING
DRAWING BY HORAK
I'LL NEED A FEW SUPPLIES... WOULD THE WISCO PLANTATION MANAGER HAND OVER SOME ITEMS ON YOUR SAY-SO?
YES — HIS NAME'S HUGILL — EX-COMMANDO
OK — COME IN MY OFFICE AND WRITE HIM A NOTE... NICK CAN COVER THE DESK TILL I GET BACK!
WHILE, UNKNOWN TO BOND —
MOVE IT, BABY — DON'T MAKE HIM GET ROUGH! WOULDN'T WANT OUR STAR ATTRACTION RUINED AHEAD OF TIME!
164

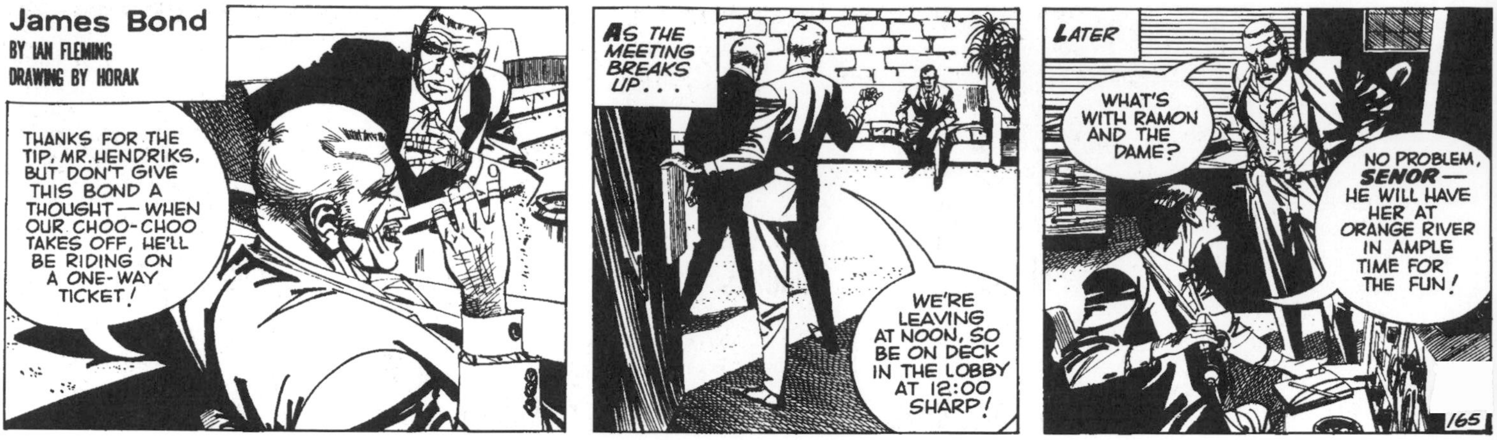
James Bond
BY IAN FLEMING
DRAWING BY HORAK
THANKS FOR THE TIP, MR. HENDRIKS, BUT DON'T GIVE THIS BOND A THOUGHT — WHEN OUR CHOO-CHOO TAKES OFF, HE'LL BE RIDING ON A ONE-WAY TICKET!
AS THE MEETING BREAKS UP...
WE'RE LEAVING AT NOON, SO BE ON DECK IN THE LOBBY AT 12:00 SHARP!
LATER
WHAT'S WITH RAMON AND THE DAME?
NO PROBLEM, SENOR — HE WILL HAVE HER AT ORANGE RIVER IN AMPLE TIME FOR THE FUN!
165

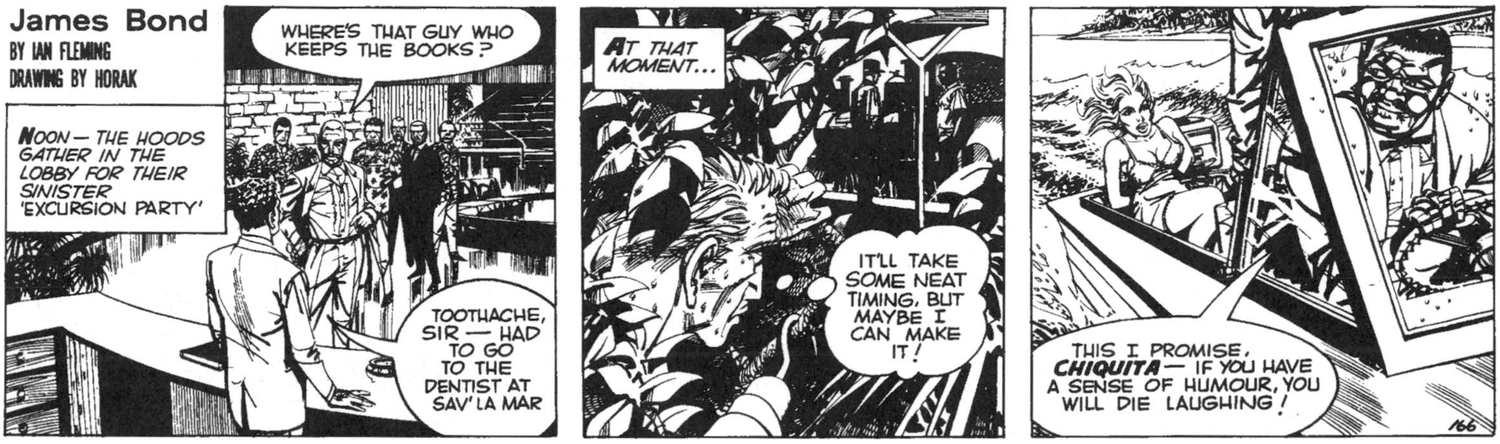
James Bond
BY IAN FLEMING
DRAWING BY HORAK
NOON — THE HOODS GATHER IN THE LOBBY FOR THEIR SINISTER 'EXCURSION PARTY'
WHERE'S THAT GUY WHO KEEPS THE BOOKS?
TOOTHACHE, SIR — HAD TO GO TO THE DENTIST AT SAV' LA MAR
AT THAT MOMENT...
IT'LL TAKE SOME NEAT TIMING, BUT MAYBE I CAN MAKE IT!
THIS I PROMISE, CHIQUITA — IF YOU HAVE A SENSE OF HUMOUR, YOU WILL DIE LAUGHING!
166

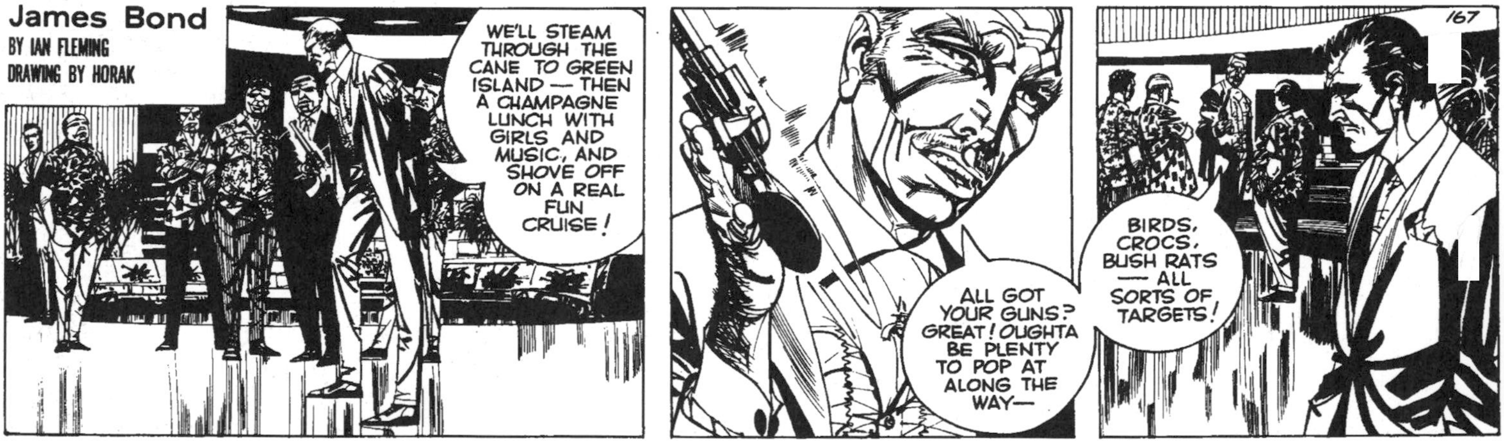
James Bond
BY IAN FLEMING
DRAWING BY HORAK
WE'LL STEAM THROUGH THE CANE TO GREEN ISLAND — THEN A CHAMPAGNE LUNCH WITH GIRLS AND MUSIC, AND SHOVE OFF ON A REAL FUN CRUISE!
ALL GOT YOUR GUNS? GREAT! OUGHTA BE PLENTY TO POP AT ALONG THE WAY—
167
BIRDS, CROCS, BUSH RATS — ALL SORTS OF TARGETS!

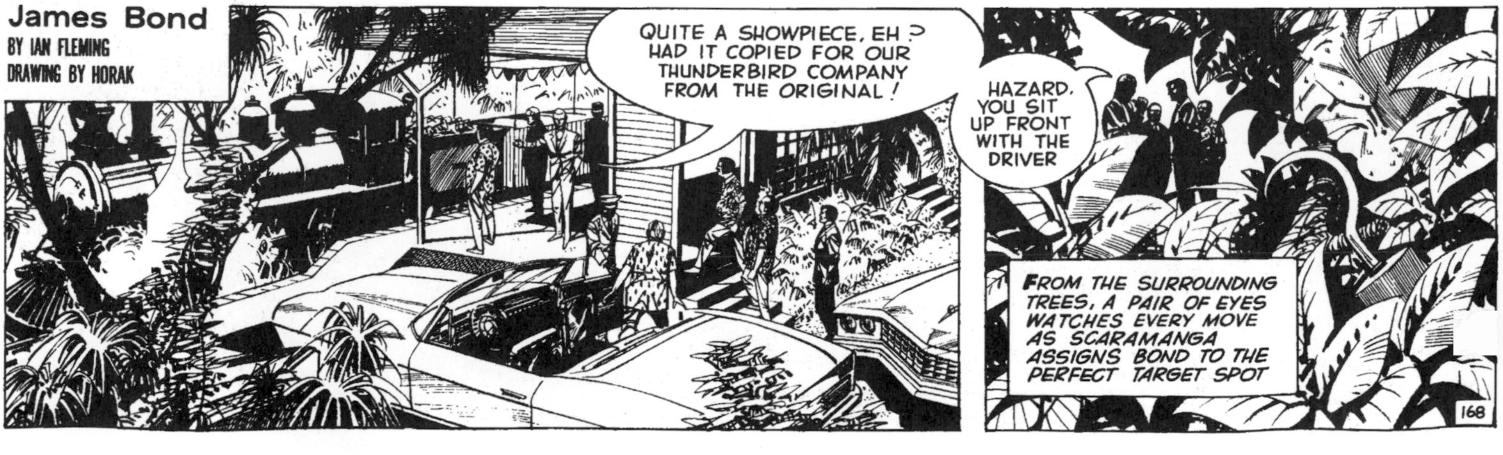
James Bond
BY IAN FLEMING
DRAWING BY HORAK
QUITE A SHOWPIECE, EH? HAD IT COPIED FOR OUR THUNDERBIRD COMPANY FROM THE ORIGINAL!
HAZARD, YOU SIT UP FRONT WITH THE DRIVER
FROM THE SURROUNDING TREES, A PAIR OF EYES WATCHES EVERY MOVE AS SCARAMANGA ASSIGNS BOND TO THE PERFECT TARGET SPOT
168

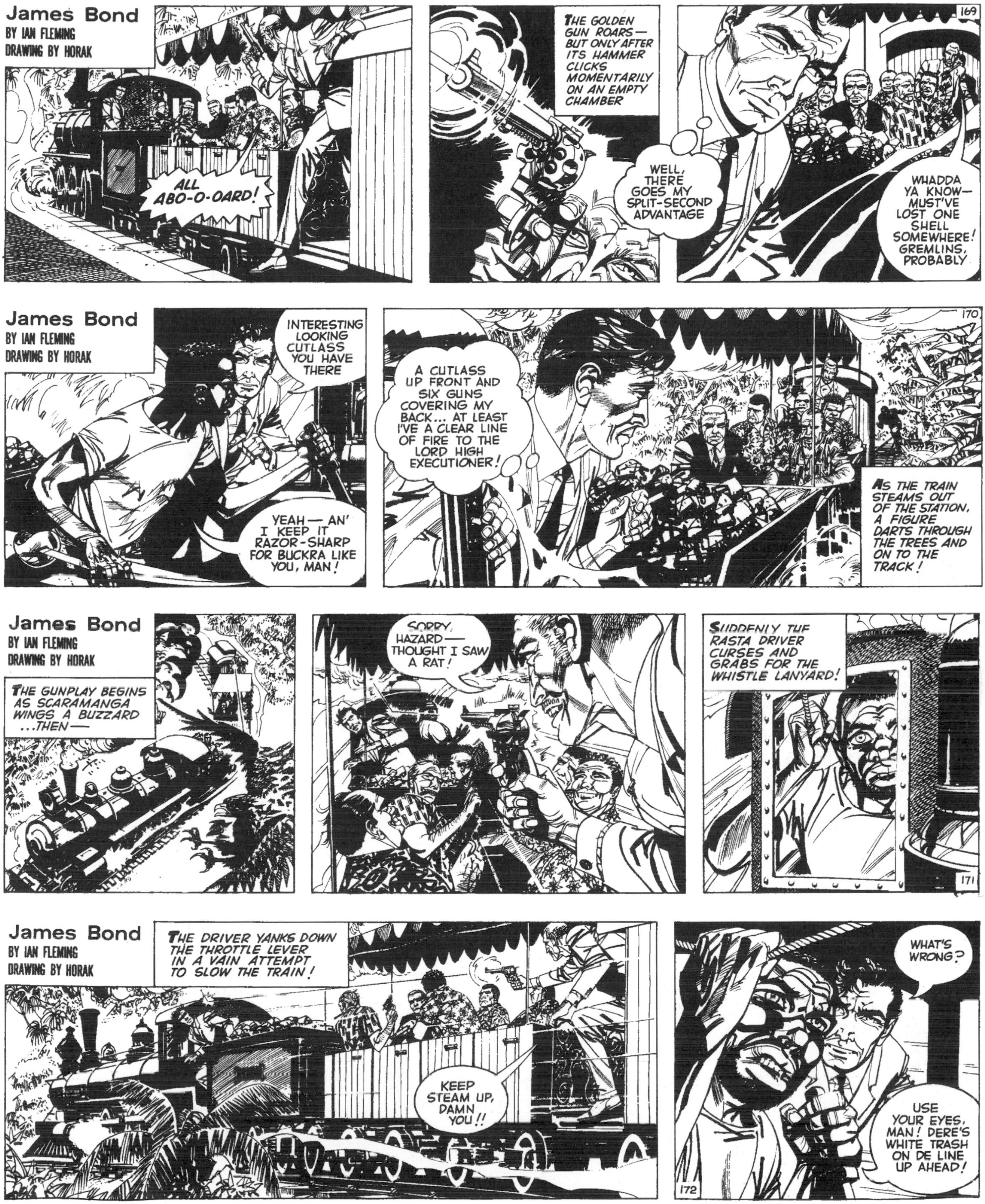

James Bond
BY IAN FLEMING
DRAWING BY HORAK
ALL ABO-O-OARD!
THE GOLDEN GUN ROARS— BUT ONLY AFTER ITS HAMMER CLICKS MOMENTARILY ON AN EMPTY CHAMBER
WELL, THERE GOES MY SPLIT-SECOND ADVANTAGE
169
WHADDA YA KNOW— MUST'VE LOST ONE SHELL SOMEWHERE! GREMLINS, PROBABLY
James Bond
BY IAN FLEMING
DRAWING BY HORAK
INTERESTING LOOKING CUTLASS YOU HAVE THERE
YEAH— AN' I KEEP IT RAZOR-SHARP FOR BUCKRA LIKE YOU, MAN!
170
A CUTLASS UP FRONT AND SIX GUNS COVERING MY BACK... AT LEAST I'VE A CLEAR LINE OF FIRE TO THE LORD HIGH EXECUTIONER!
AS THE TRAIN STEAMS OUT OF THE STATION, A FIGURE DARTS THROUGH THE TREES AND ON TO THE TRACK!
James Bond
BY IAN FLEMING
DRAWING BY HORAK
THE GUNPLAY BEGINS AS SCARAMANGA WINGS A BUZZARD ...THEN—
SORRY, HAZARD— THOUGHT I SAW A RAT!
SUDDENLY THE RASTA DRIVER CURSES AND GRABS FOR THE WHISTLE LANYARD!
171
James Bond
BY IAN FLEMING
DRAWING BY HORAK
THE DRIVER YANKS DOWN THE THROTTLE LEVER IN A VAIN ATTEMPT TO SLOW THE TRAIN!
KEEP STEAM UP, DAMN YOU!!
172
WHAT'S WRONG?
USE YOUR EYES, MAN! DERE'S WHITE TRASH ON DE LINE UP AHEAD!

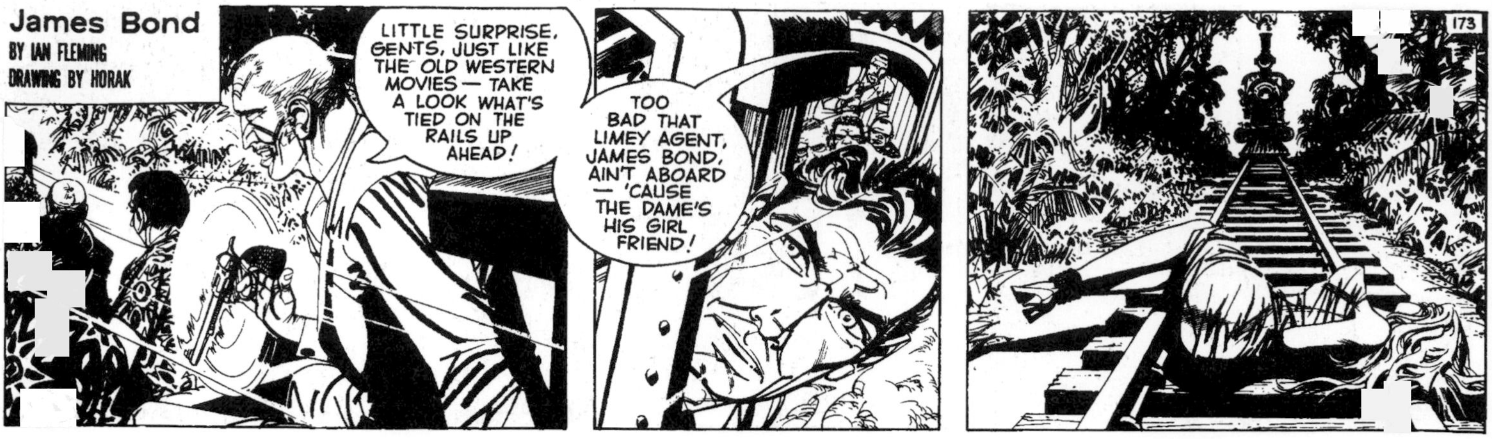
James Bond
BY IAN FLEMING
DRAWING BY HORAK
LITTLE SURPRISE, GENTS, JUST LIKE THE OLD WESTERN MOVIES — TAKE A LOOK WHAT'S TIED ON THE RAILS UP AHEAD!
TOO BAD THAT LIMEY AGENT, JAMES BOND, AIN'T ABOARD — 'CAUSE THE DAME'S HIS GIRL FRIEND!
173

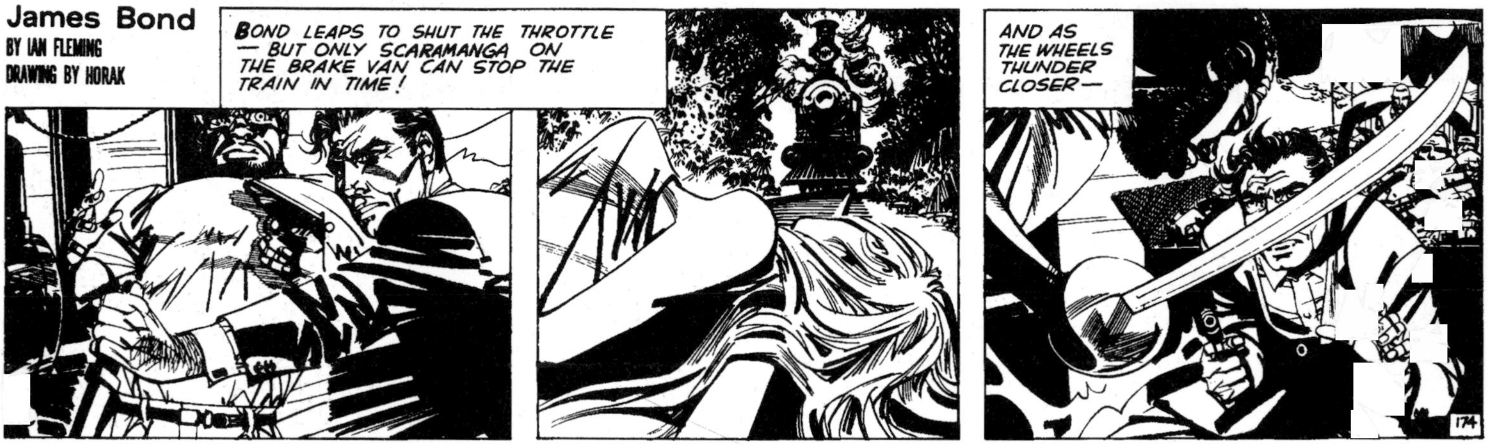
James Bond
BY IAN FLEMING
DRAWING BY HORAK
BOND LEAPS TO SHUT THE THROTTLE — BUT ONLY SCARAMANGA ON THE BRAKE VAN CAN STOP THE TRAIN IN TIME!
AND AS THE WHEELS THUNDER CLOSER—
174

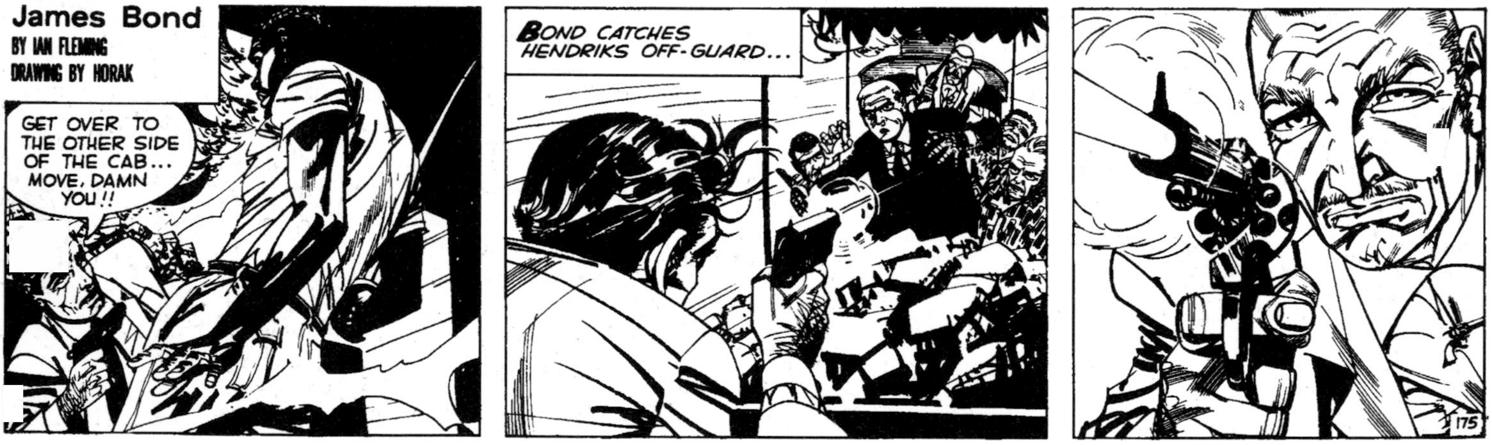
James Bond
BY IAN FLEMING
DRAWING BY HORAK
GET OVER TO THE OTHER SIDE OF THE CAB... MOVE, DAMN YOU!!
BOND CATCHES HENDRIKS OFF-GUARD...
175

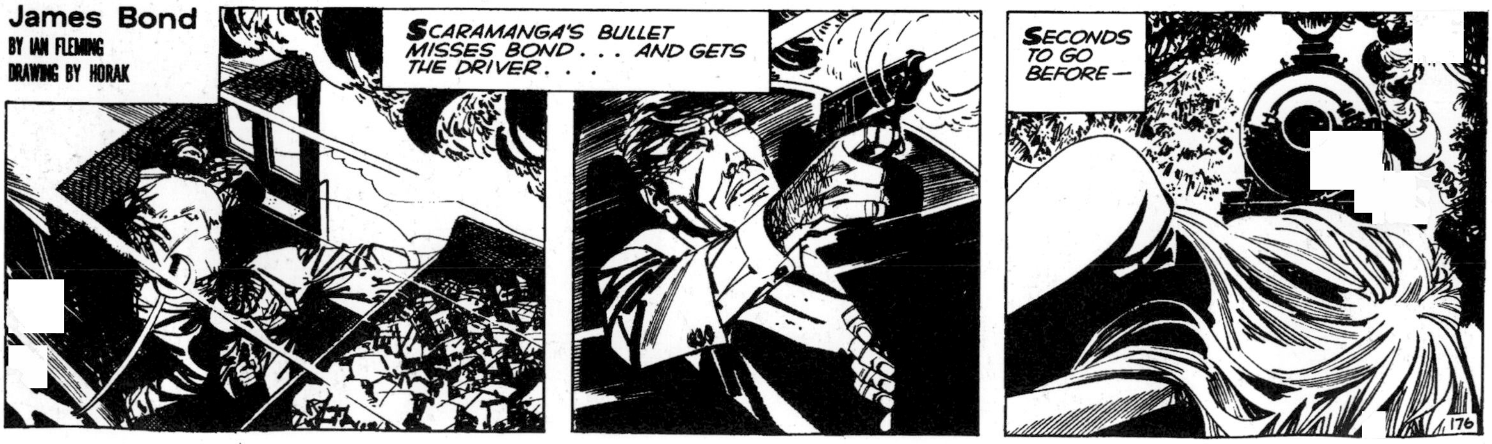
James Bond
BY IAN FLEMING
DRAWING BY HORAK
SCARAMANGA'S BULLET MISSES BOND . . . AND GETS THE DRIVER . . .
SECONDS TO GO BEFORE—
176

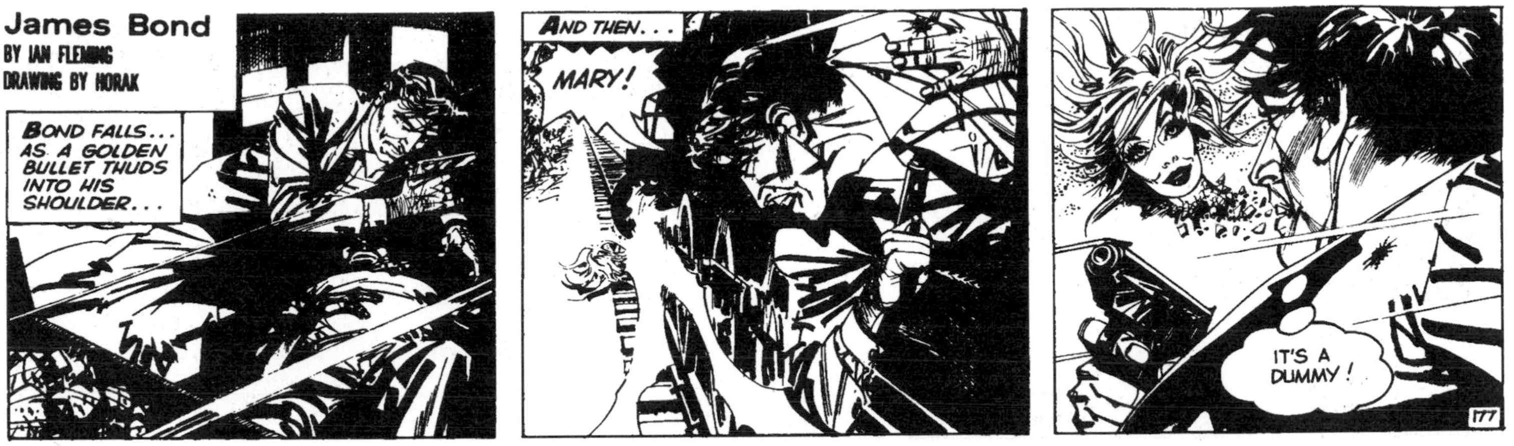
James Bond
BY IAN FLEMING
DRAWING BY HORAK
BOND FALLS... AS A GOLDEN BULLET THUDS INTO HIS SHOULDER...
AND THEN...
MARY!
IT'S A DUMMY!
177

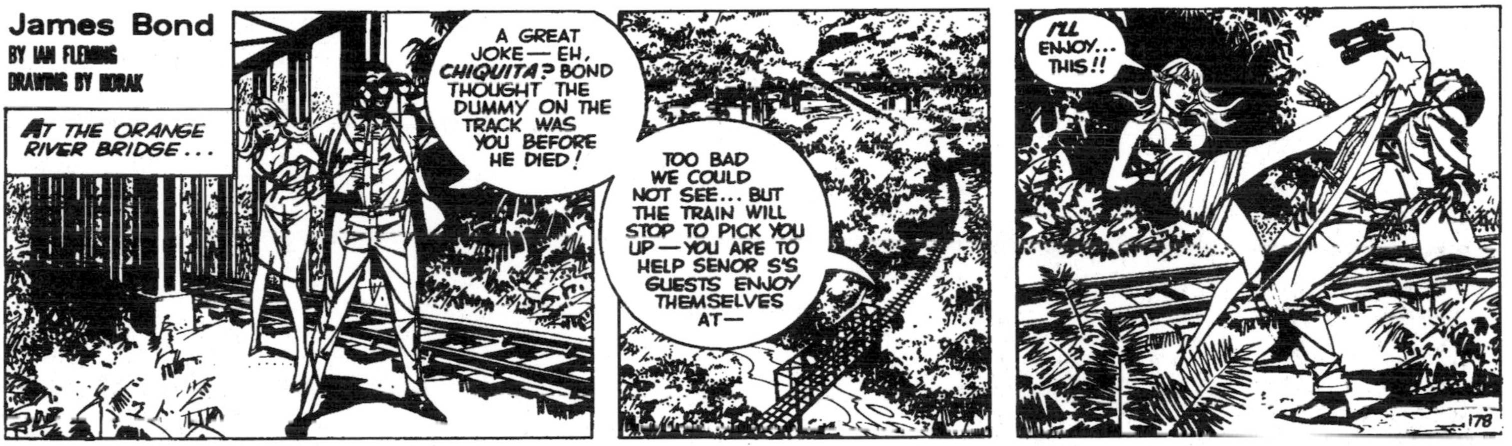
James Bond
BY IAN FLEMING
DRAWING BY HORAK
AT THE ORANGE RIVER BRIDGE...
A GREAT JOKE — EH, CHIQUITA? BOND THOUGHT THE DUMMY ON THE TRACK WAS YOU BEFORE HE DIED!
TOO BAD WE COULD NOT SEE... BUT THE TRAIN WILL STOP TO PICK YOU UP — YOU ARE TO HELP SENOR S'S GUESTS ENJOY THEMSELVES AT—
I'LL ENJOY... THIS!!
178

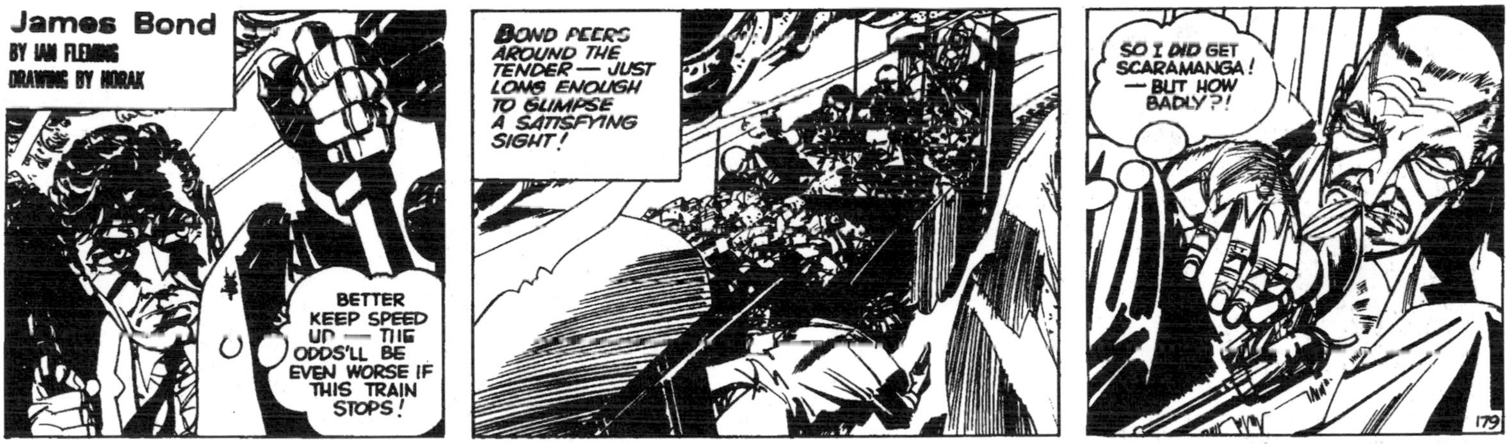
James Bond
BY IAN FLEMING
DRAWING BY HORAK
BETTER KEEP SPEED UP — THE ODDS'LL BE EVEN WORSE IF THIS TRAIN STOPS!
BOND PEERS AROUND THE TENDER — JUST LONG ENOUGH TO GLIMPSE A SATISFYING SIGHT!
SO I DID GET SCARAMANGA! — BUT HOW BADLY?!
179

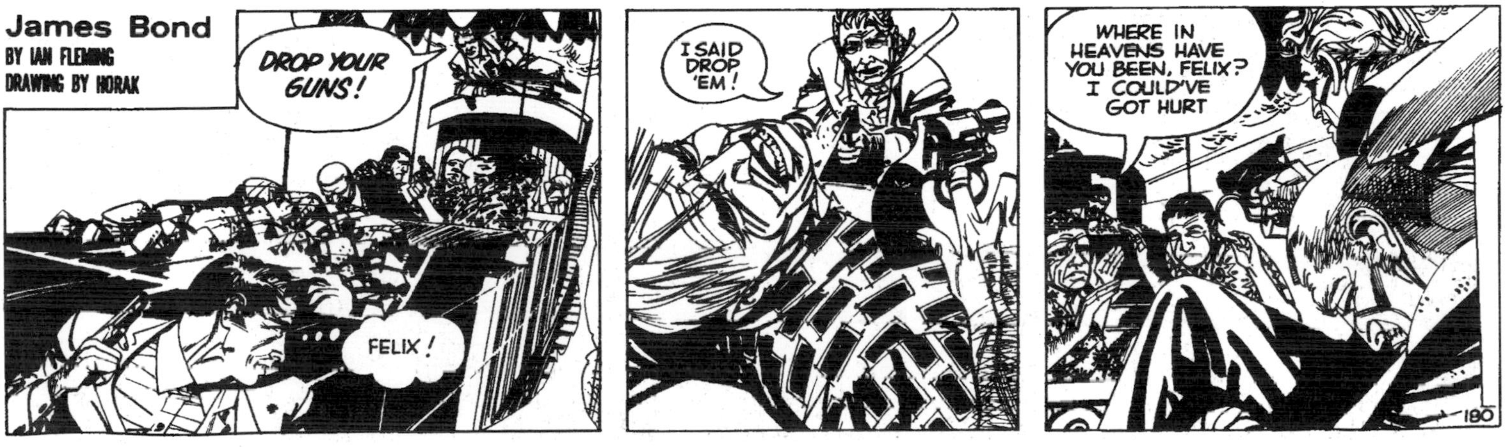
James Bond
BY IAN FLEMING
DRAWING BY HORAK
DROP YOUR GUNS!
FELIX!
I SAID DROP 'EM!
WHERE IN HEAVENS HAVE YOU BEEN, FELIX? I COULD'VE GOT HURT
180

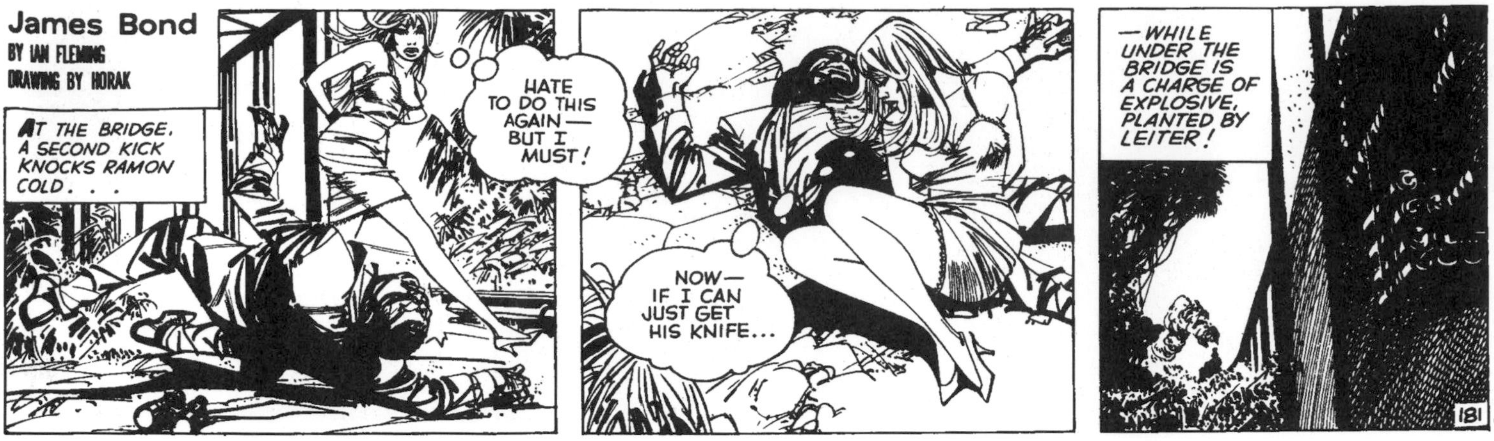
James Bond
BY IAN FLEMING
DRAWING BY HORAK
AT THE BRIDGE, A SECOND KICK KNOCKS RAMON COLD . . .
HATE TO DO THIS AGAIN— BUT I MUST!
NOW— IF I CAN JUST GET HIS KNIFE...
—WHILE UNDER THE BRIDGE IS A CHARGE OF EXPLOSIVE, PLANTED BY LEITER!
181

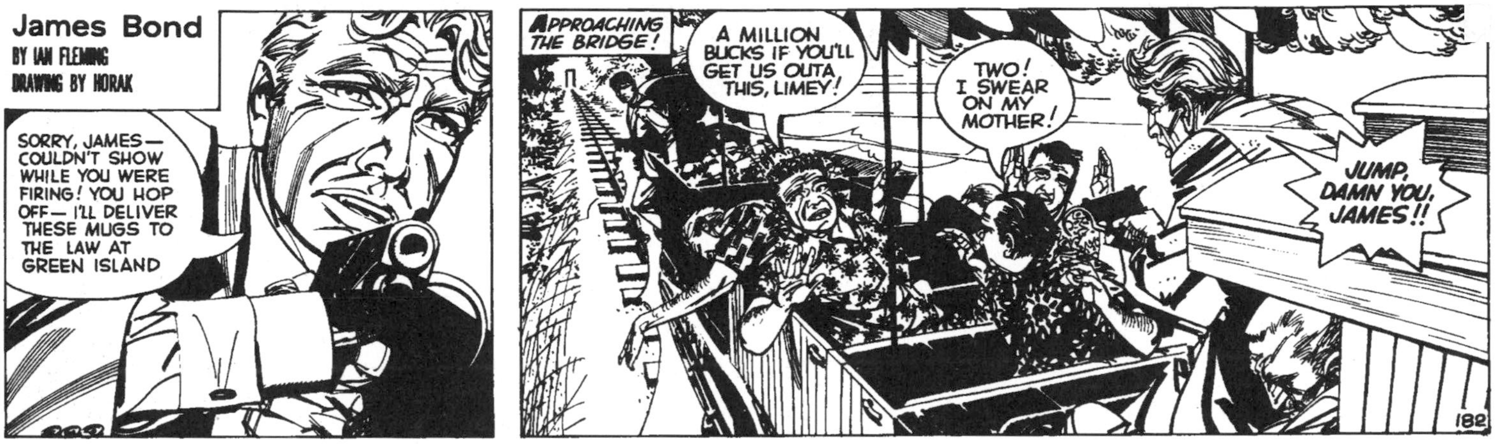
James Bond
BY IAN FLEMING
DRAWING BY HORAK
SORRY, JAMES— COULDN'T SHOW WHILE YOU WERE FIRING! YOU HOP OFF— I'LL DELIVER THESE MUGS TO THE LAW AT GREEN ISLAND
APPROACHING THE BRIDGE!
A MILLION BUCKS IF YOU'LL GET US OUTA THIS, LIMEY!
TWO! I SWEAR ON MY MOTHER!
JUMP, DAMN YOU, JAMES!!
182

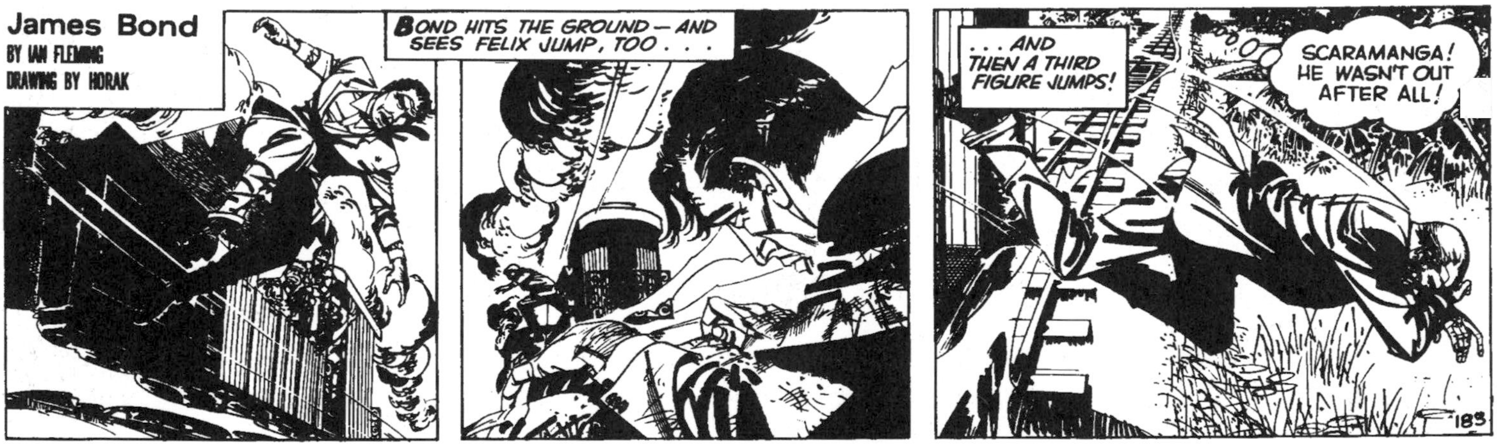
James Bond
BY IAN FLEMING
DRAWING BY HORAK
BOND HITS THE GROUND — AND SEES FELIX JUMP, TOO . . .
. . . AND THEN A THIRD FIGURE JUMPS!
SCARAMANGA! HE WASN'T OUT AFTER ALL!
183

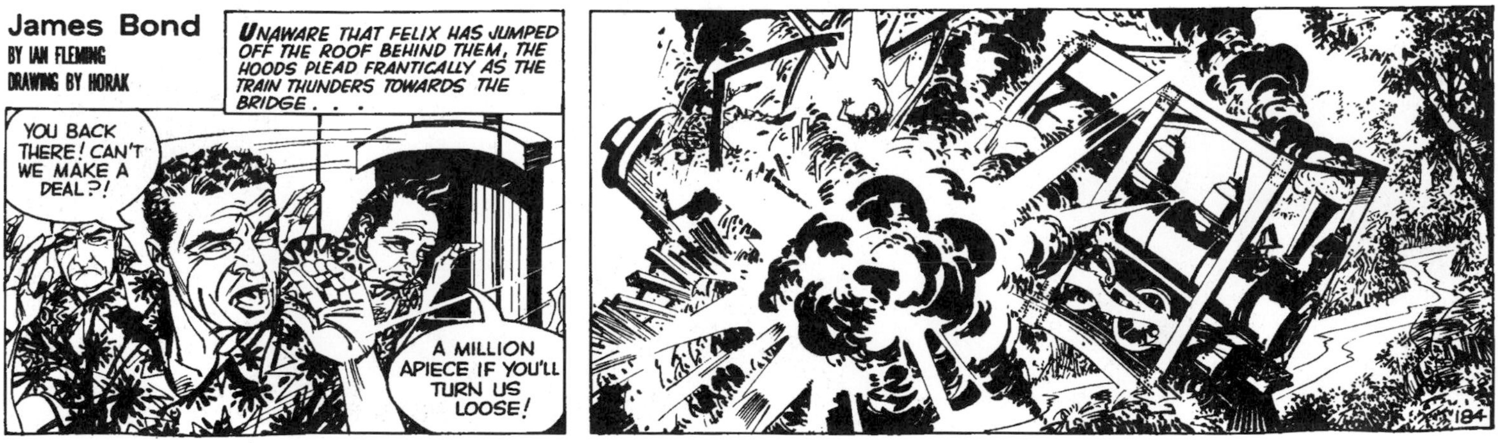
James Bond
BY IAN FLEMING
DRAWING BY HORAK
UNAWARE THAT FELIX HAS JUMPED OFF THE ROOF BEHIND THEM, THE HOODS PLEAD FRANTICALLY AS THE TRAIN THUNDERS TOWARDS THE BRIDGE . . .
YOU BACK THERE! CAN'T WE MAKE A DEAL?!
A MILLION APIECE IF YOU'LL TURN US LOOSE!
184

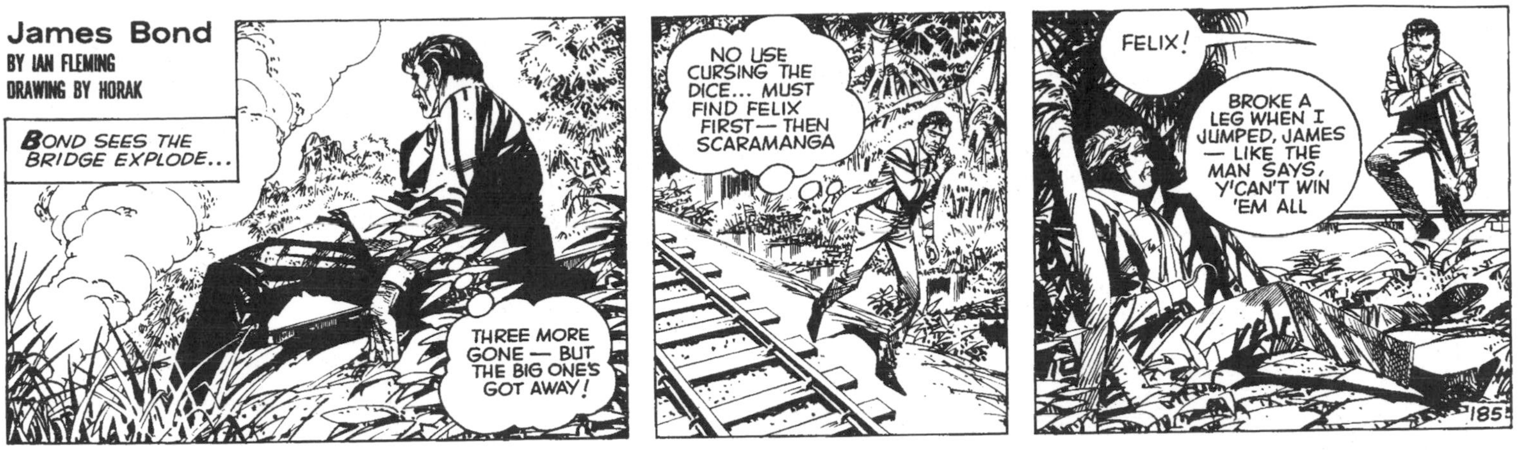
James Bond
BY IAN FLEMING
DRAWING BY HORAK
BOND SEES THE BRIDGE EXPLODE...
THREE MORE GONE — BUT THE BIG ONE'S GOT AWAY!
NO USE CURSING THE DICE... MUST FIND FELIX FIRST — THEN SCARAMANGA
FELIX!
BROKE A LEG WHEN I JUMPED, JAMES — LIKE THE MAN SAYS, Y'CAN'T WIN 'EM ALL
185

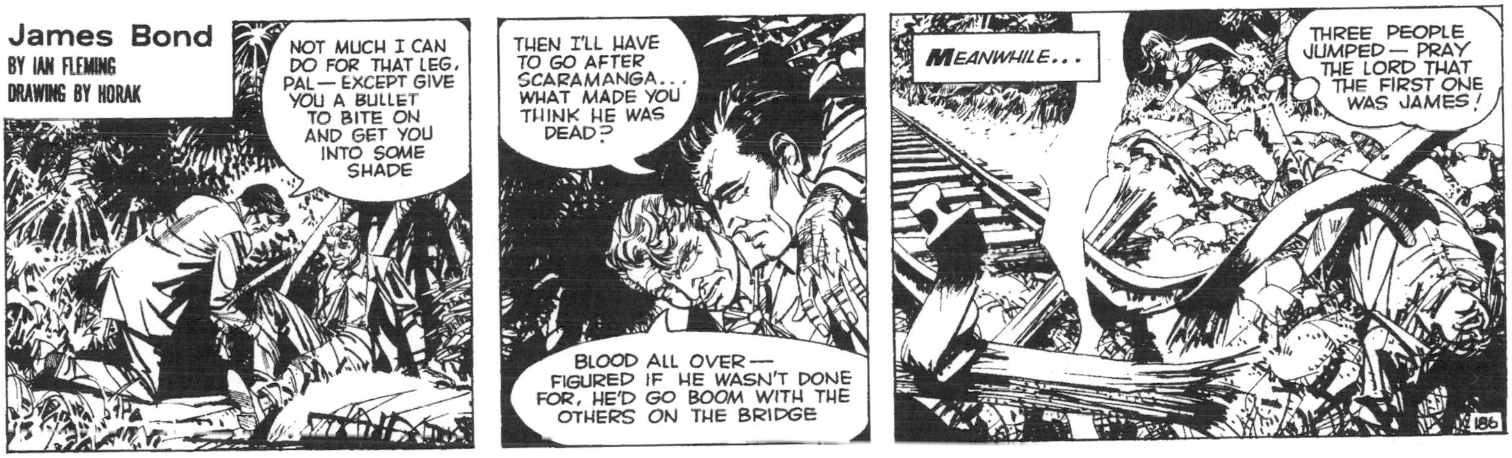
James Bond
BY IAN FLEMING
DRAWING BY HORAK
NOT MUCH I CAN DO FOR THAT LEG, PAL — EXCEPT GIVE YOU A BULLET TO BITE ON AND GET YOU INTO SOME SHADE
THEN I'LL HAVE TO GO AFTER SCARAMANGA... WHAT MADE YOU THINK HE WAS DEAD?
BLOOD ALL OVER — FIGURED IF HE WASN'T DONE FOR, HE'D GO BOOM WITH THE OTHERS ON THE BRIDGE
MEANWHILE...
THREE PEOPLE JUMPED — PRAY THE LORD THAT THE FIRST ONE WAS JAMES!
186

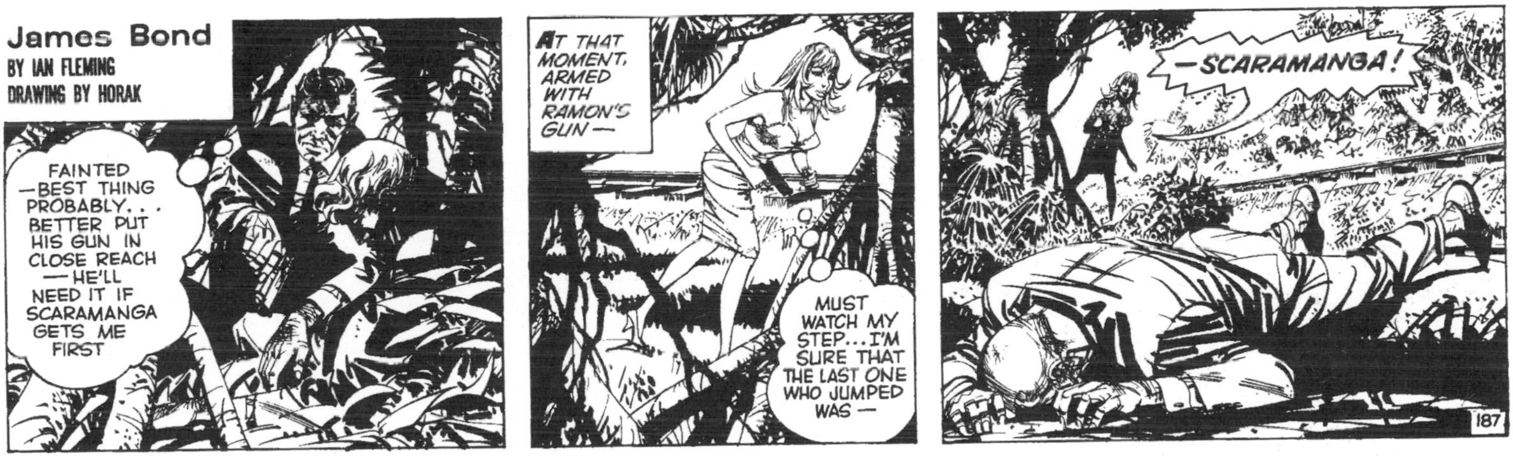
James Bond
BY IAN FLEMING
DRAWING BY HORAK
—FAINTED —BEST THING PROBABLY... BETTER PUT HIS GUN IN CLOSE REACH —HE'LL NEED IT IF SCARAMANGA GETS ME FIRST
AT THAT MOMENT, ARMED WITH RAMON'S GUN —
MUST WATCH MY STEP... I'M SURE THAT THE LAST ONE WHO JUMPED WAS —
—SCARAMANGA!
187

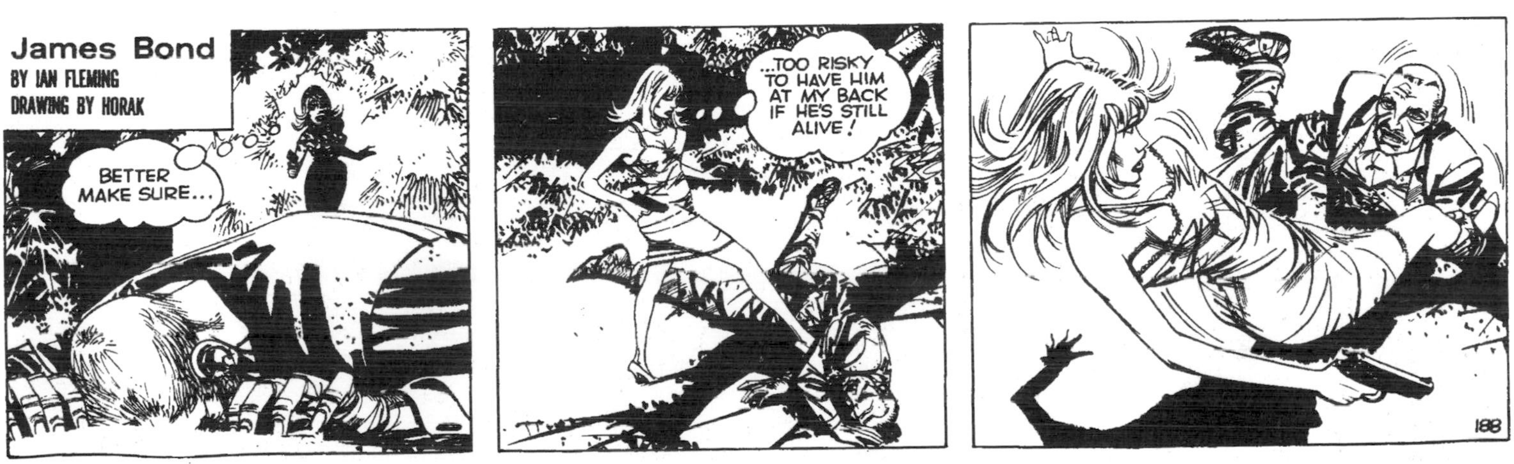
James Bond
BY IAN FLEMING
DRAWING BY HORAK
BETTER MAKE SURE...
...TOO RISKY TO HAVE HIM AT MY BACK IF HE'S STILL ALIVE!
188

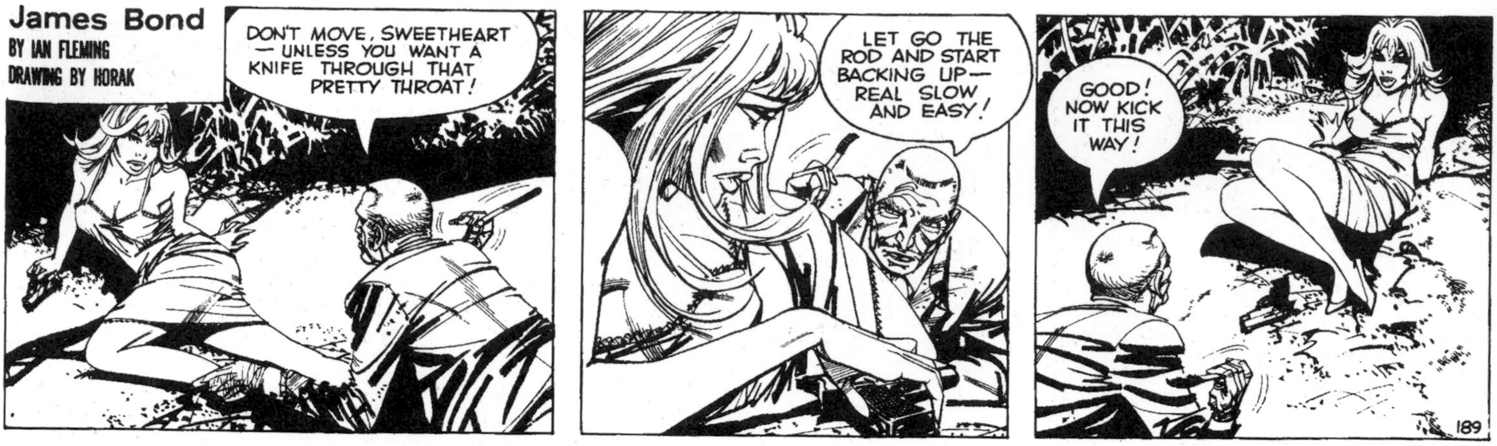
James Bond
BY IAN FLEMING
DRAWING BY HORAK
DON'T MOVE, SWEETHEART — UNLESS YOU WANT A KNIFE THROUGH THAT PRETTY THROAT!
LET GO THE ROD AND START BACKING UP — REAL SLOW AND EASY!
GOOD! NOW KICK IT THIS WAY!
189

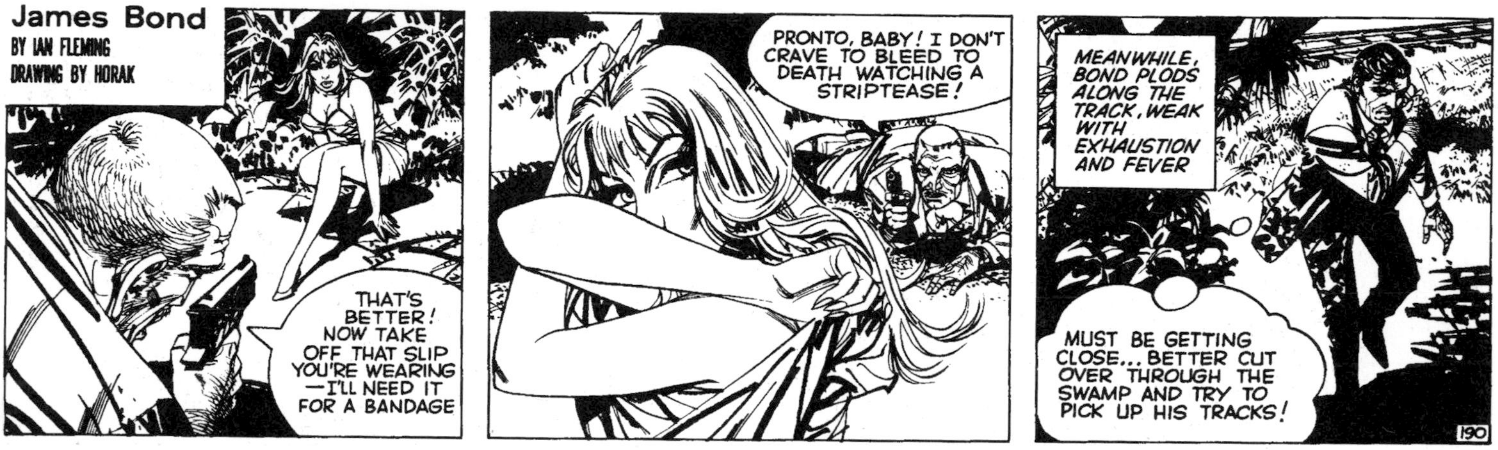
James Bond
BY IAN FLEMING
DRAWING BY HORAK
THAT'S BETTER! NOW TAKE OFF THAT SLIP YOU'RE WEARING — I'LL NEED IT FOR A BANDAGE
PRONTO, BABY! I DON'T CRAVE TO BLEED TO DEATH WATCHING A STRIPTEASE!
MEANWHILE, BOND PLODS ALONG THE TRACK, WEAK WITH EXHAUSTION AND FEVER
MUST BE GETTING CLOSE... BETTER CUT OVER THROUGH THE SWAMP AND TRY TO PICK UP HIS TRACKS!
190

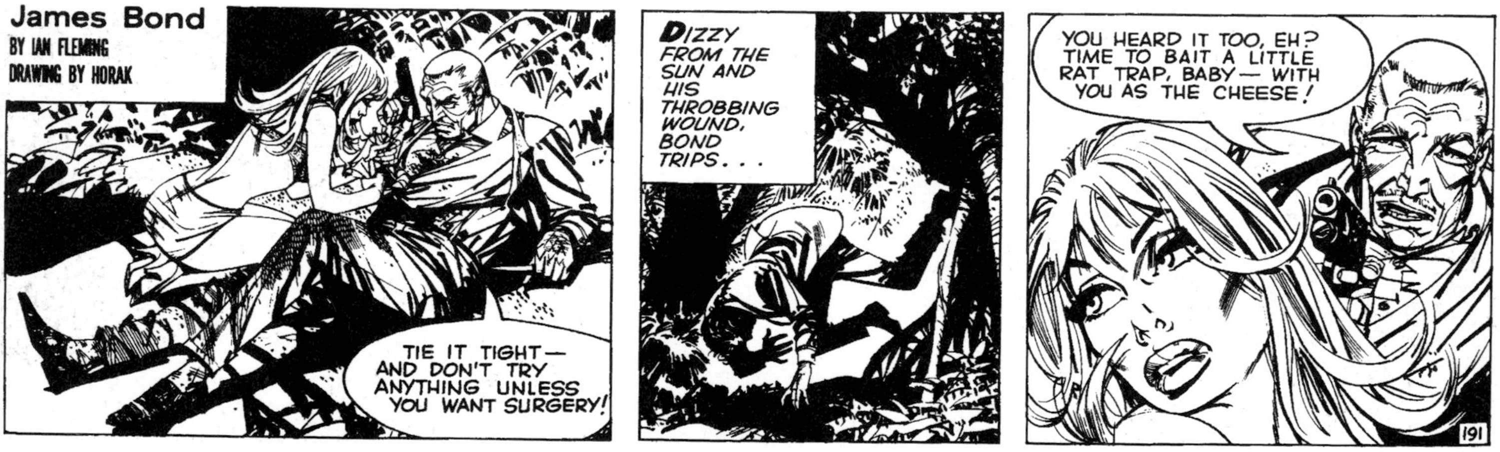
James Bond
BY IAN FLEMING
DRAWING BY HORAK
TIE IT TIGHT— AND DON'T TRY ANYTHING UNLESS YOU WANT SURGERY!
DIZZY FROM THE SUN AND HIS THROBBING WOUND, BOND TRIPS...
YOU HEARD IT TOO, EH? TIME TO BAIT A LITTLE RAT TRAP, BABY — WITH YOU AS THE CHEESE!
191

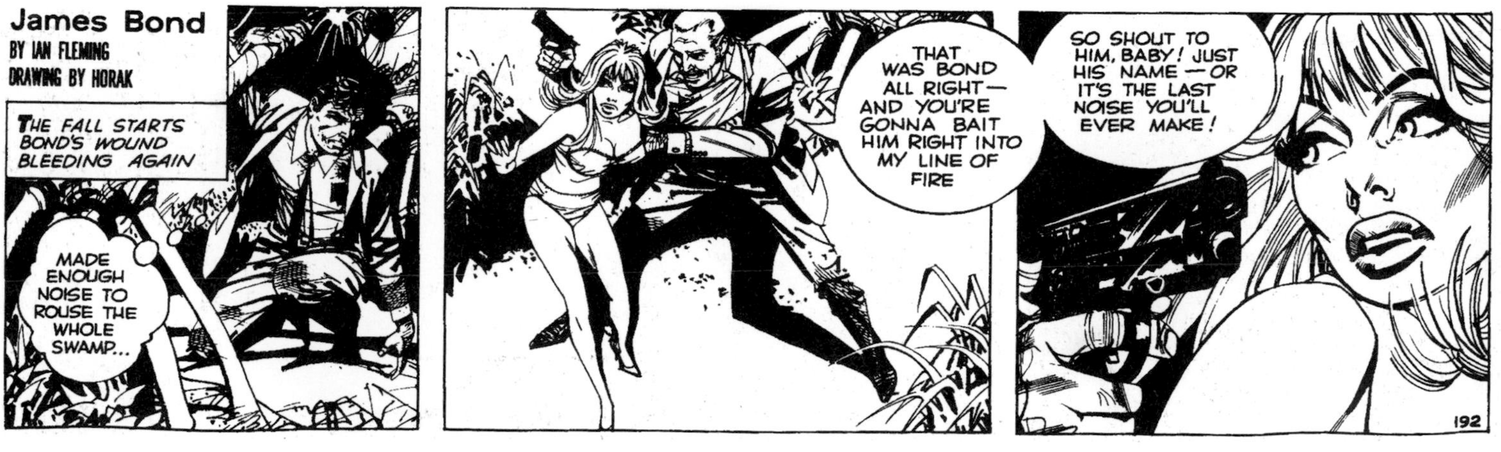
James Bond
BY IAN FLEMING
DRAWING BY HORAK
THE FALL STARTS BOND'S WOUND BLEEDING AGAIN
MADE ENOUGH NOISE TO ROUSE THE WHOLE SWAMP...
THAT WAS BOND ALL RIGHT — AND YOU'RE GONNA BAIT HIM RIGHT INTO MY LINE OF FIRE
SO SHOUT TO HIM, BABY! JUST HIS NAME — OR IT'S THE LAST NOISE YOU'LL EVER MAKE!
192

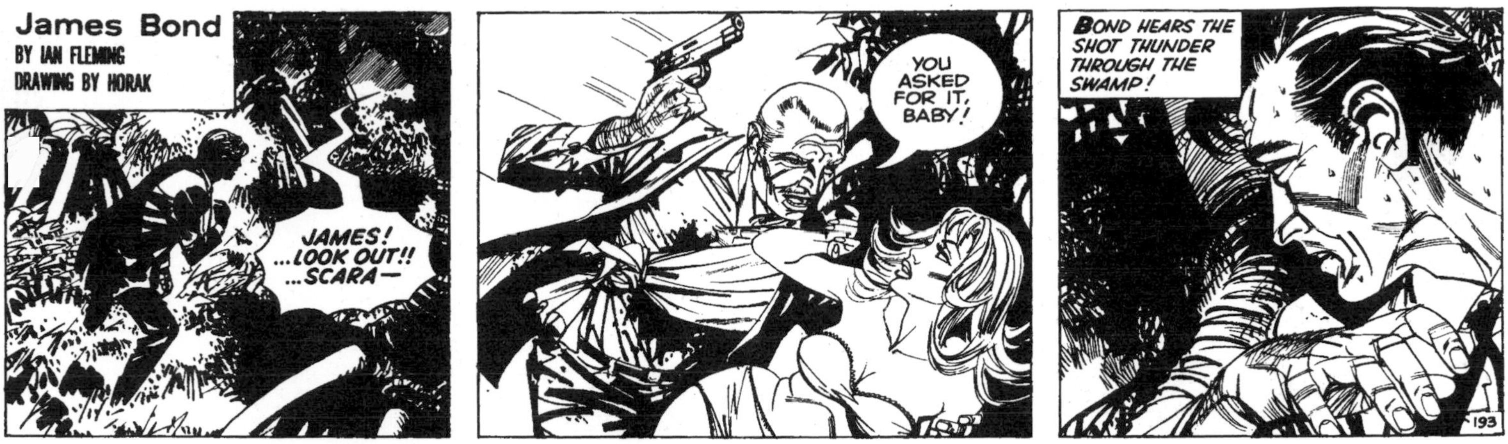
James Bond
BY IAN FLEMING
DRAWING BY HORAK
JAMES! ...LOOK OUT!! ...SCARA—
YOU ASKED FOR IT, BABY!
BOND HEARS THE SHOT THUNDER THROUGH THE SWAMP!
193

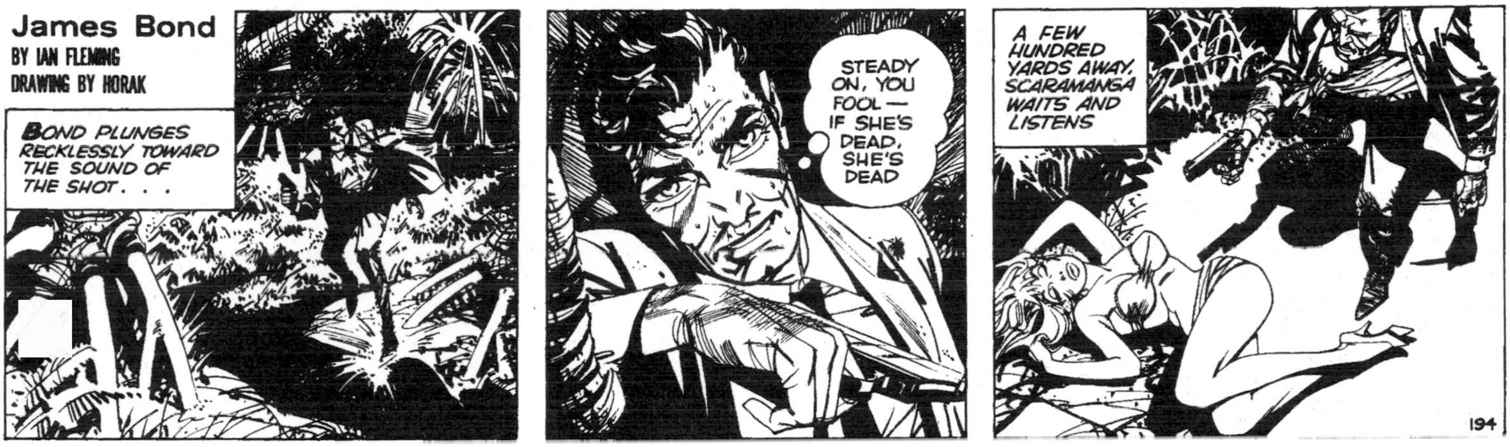
James Bond
BY IAN FLEMING
DRAWING BY HORAK
BOND PLUNGES RECKLESSLY TOWARD THE SOUND OF THE SHOT . . .
STEADY ON, YOU FOOL — IF SHE'S DEAD, SHE'S DEAD
A FEW HUNDRED YARDS AWAY, SCARAMANGA WAITS AND LISTENS
194

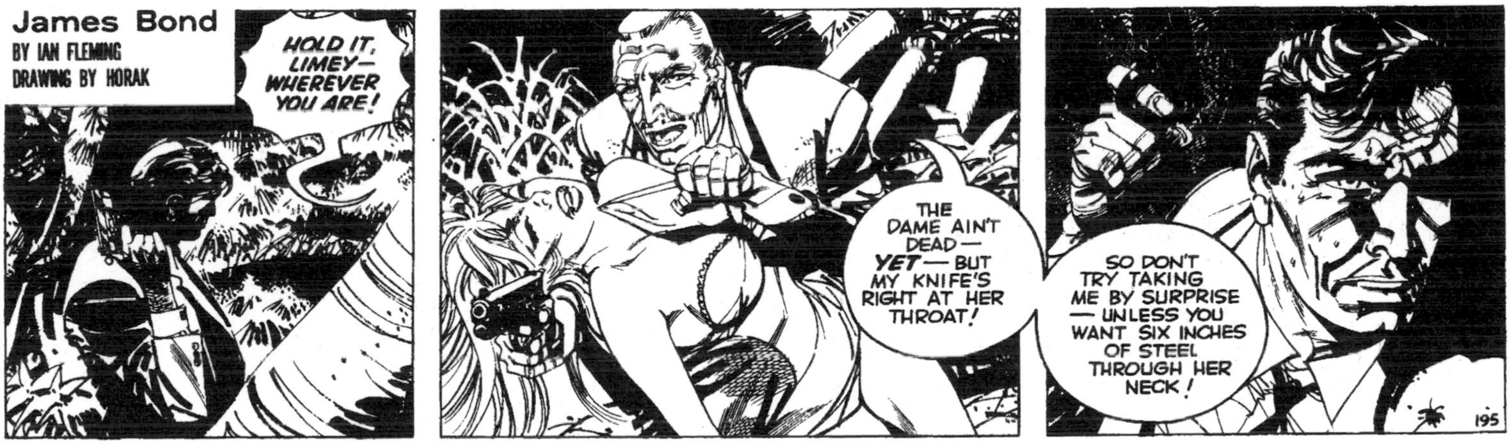
James Bond
BY IAN FLEMING
DRAWING BY HORAK
HOLD IT, LIMEY— WHEREVER YOU ARE!
THE DAME AIN'T DEAD — YET — BUT MY KNIFE'S RIGHT AT HER THROAT!
SO DON'T TRY TAKING ME BY SURPRISE — UNLESS YOU WANT SIX INCHES OF STEEL THROUGH HER NECK!
195

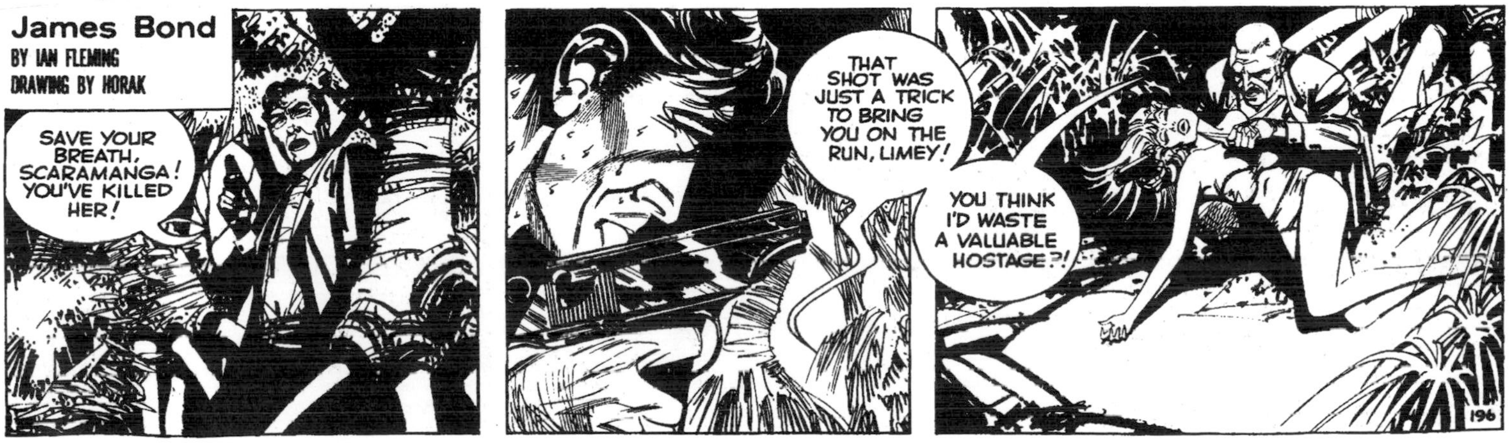
James Bond
BY IAN FLEMING
DRAWING BY HORAK
SAVE YOUR BREATH, SCARAMANGA! YOU'VE KILLED HER!
THAT SHOT WAS JUST A TRICK TO BRING YOU ON THE RUN, LIMEY!
YOU THINK I'D WASTE A VALUABLE HOSTAGE?!
196

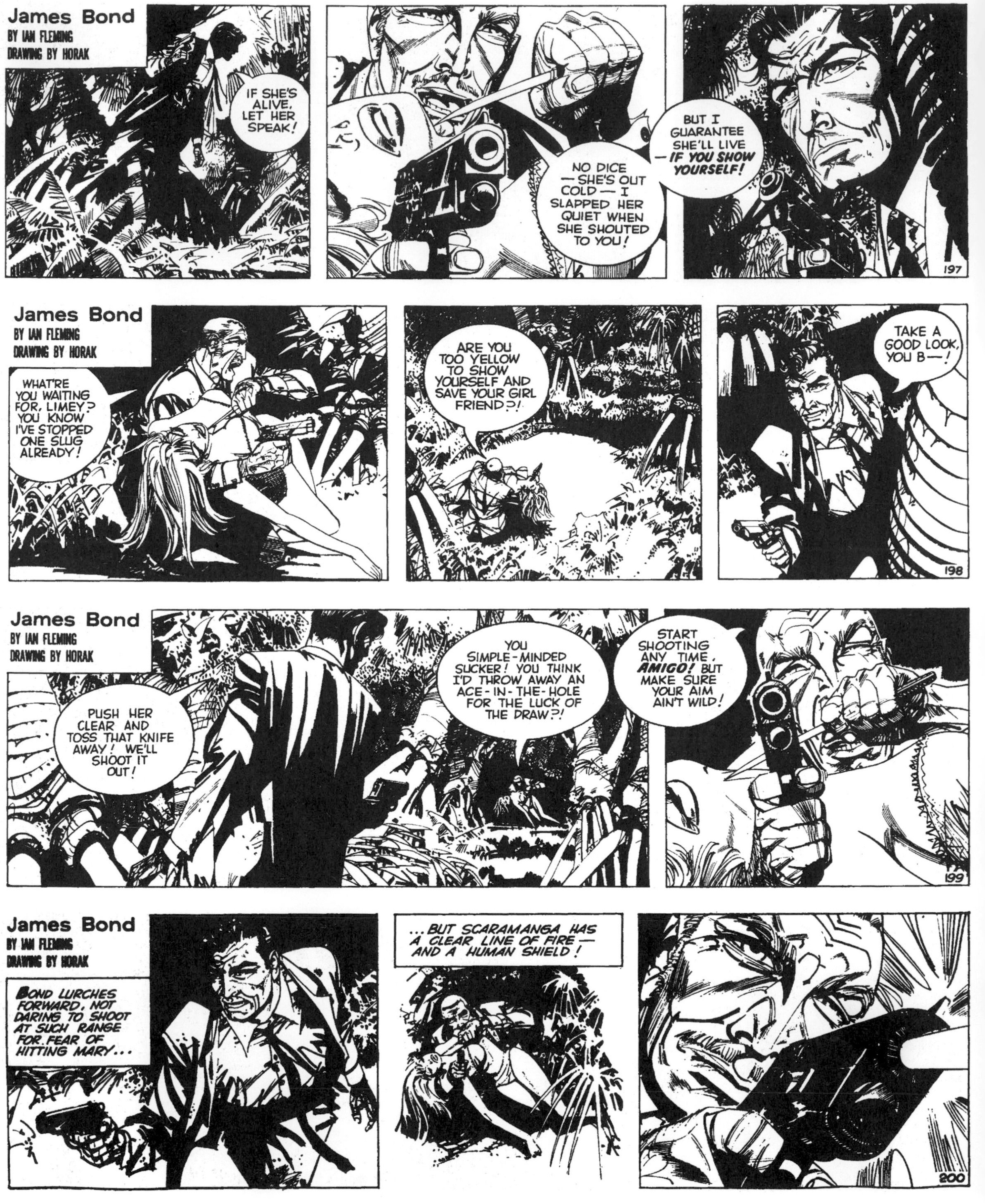
James Bond
BY IAN FLEMING
DRAWING BY HORAK
IF SHE'S ALIVE, LET HER SPEAK!
NO DICE — SHE'S OUT COLD — I SLAPPED HER QUIET WHEN SHE SHOUTED TO YOU!
BUT I GUARANTEE SHE'LL LIVE — IF YOU SHOW YOURSELF!
197
James Bond
BY IAN FLEMING
DRAWING BY HORAK
WHAT'RE YOU WAITING FOR, LIMEY? YOU KNOW I'VE STOPPED ONE SLUG ALREADY!
ARE YOU TOO YELLOW TO SHOW YOURSELF AND SAVE YOUR GIRL FRIEND?!
TAKE A GOOD LOOK, YOU B—!
198
James Bond
BY IAN FLEMING
DRAWING BY HORAK
PUSH HER CLEAR AND TOSS THAT KNIFE AWAY! WE'LL SHOOT IT OUT!
YOU SIMPLE-MINDED SUCKER! YOU THINK I'D THROW AWAY AN ACE-IN-THE-HOLE FOR THE LUCK OF THE DRAW?!
START SHOOTING ANY TIME, AMIGO! BUT MAKE SURE YOUR AIM AIN'T WILD!
199
James Bond
BY IAN FLEMING
DRAWING BY HORAK
BOND LURCHES FORWARD, NOT DARING TO SHOOT AT SUCH RANGE FOR FEAR OF HITTING MARY...
...BUT SCARAMANGA HAS A CLEAR LINE OF FIRE — AND A HUMAN SHIELD!
200

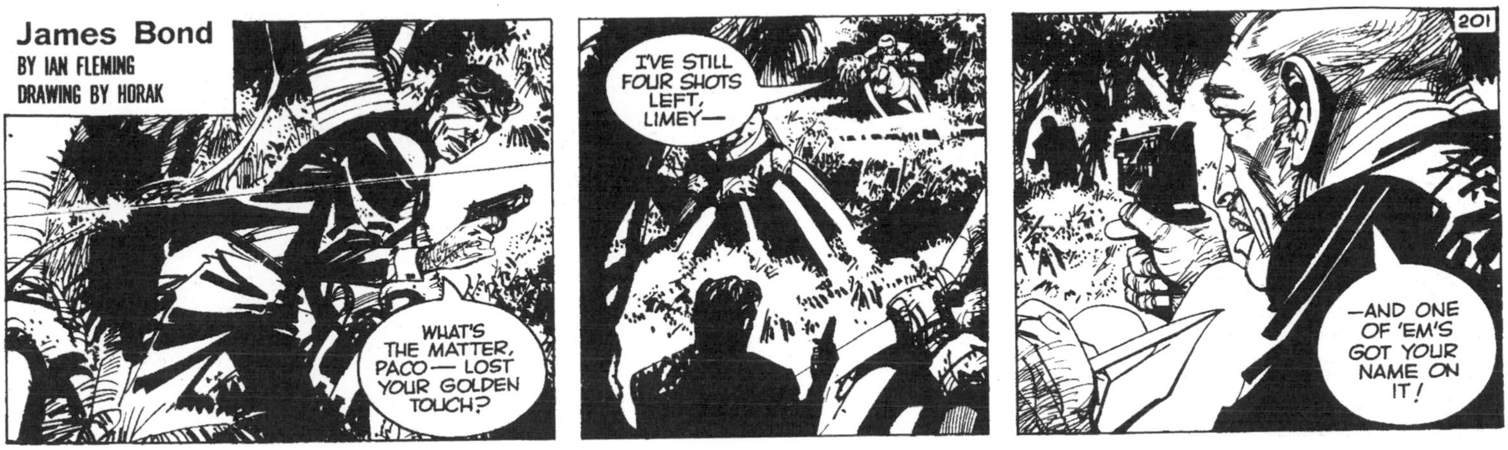
James Bond
BY IAN FLEMING
DRAWING BY HORAK
WHAT'S THE MATTER, PACO— LOST YOUR GOLDEN TOUCH?
I'VE STILL FOUR SHOTS LEFT, LIMEY—
—AND ONE OF 'EM'S GOT YOUR NAME ON IT!
201

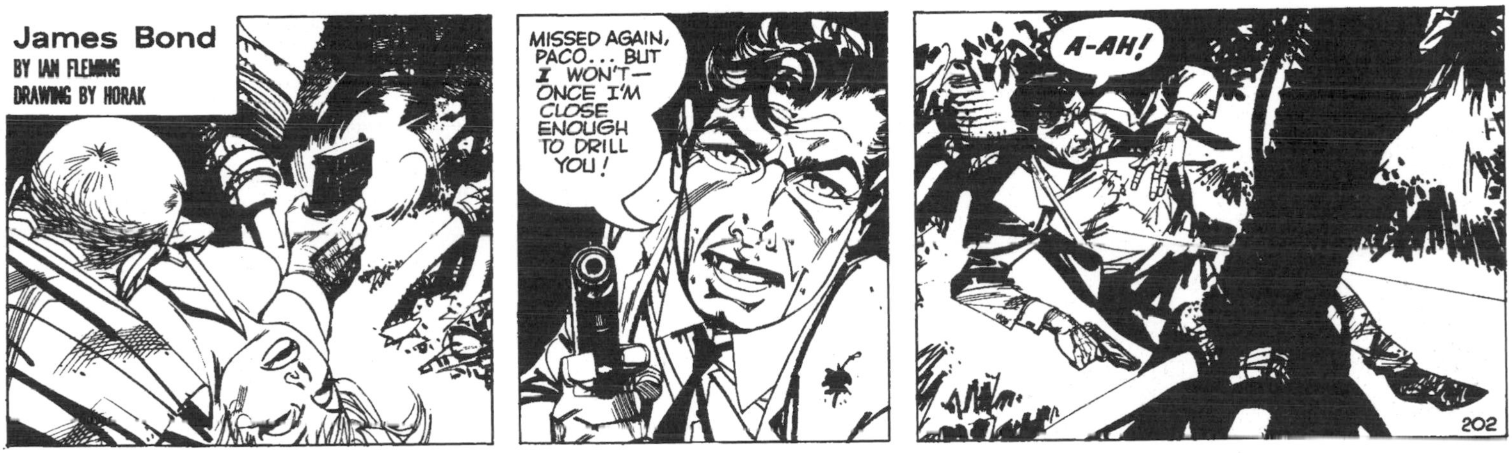
James Bond
BY IAN FLEMING
DRAWING BY HORAK
MISSED AGAIN, PACO... BUT I WON'T— ONCE I'M CLOSE ENOUGH TO DRILL YOU!
A-AH!
202

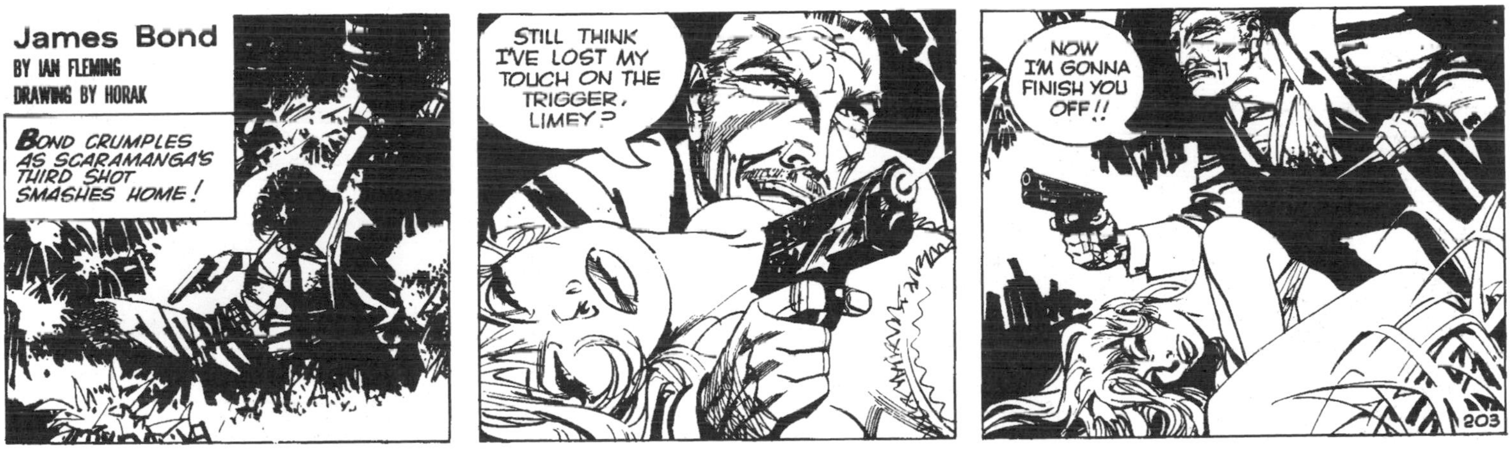
James Bond
BY IAN FLEMING
DRAWING BY HORAK
BOND CRUMPLES AS SCARAMANGA'S THIRD SHOT SMASHES HOME!
STILL THINK I'VE LOST MY TOUCH ON THE TRIGGER, LIMEY?
NOW I'M GONNA FINISH YOU OFF!!
203

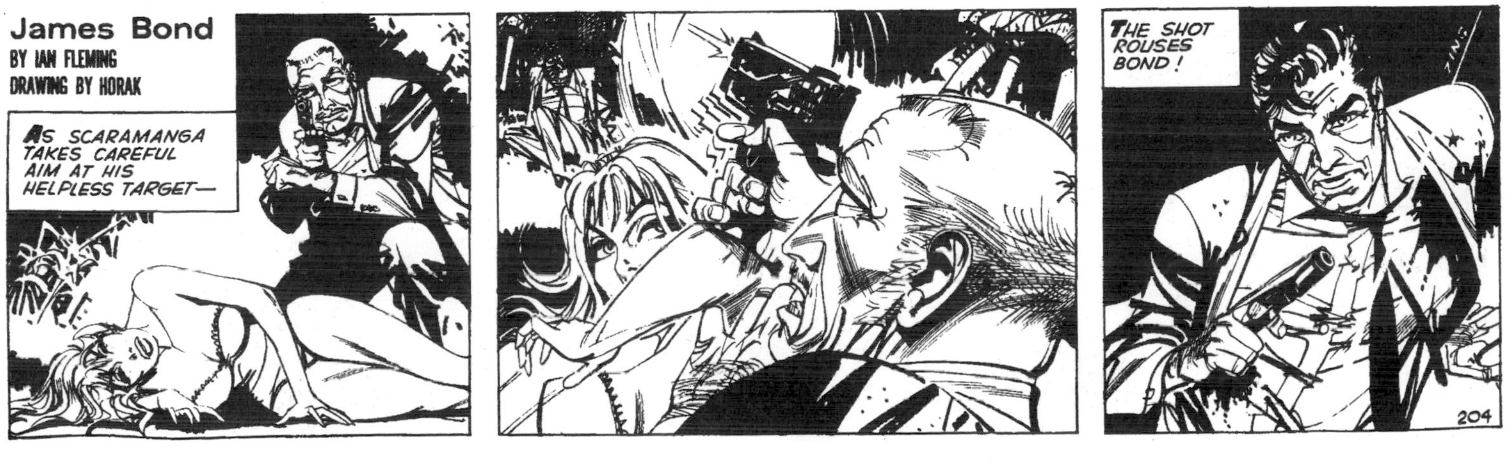
James Bond
BY IAN FLEMING
DRAWING BY HORAK
AS SCARAMANGA TAKES CAREFUL AIM AT HIS HELPLESS TARGET—
THE SHOT ROUSES BOND!
204

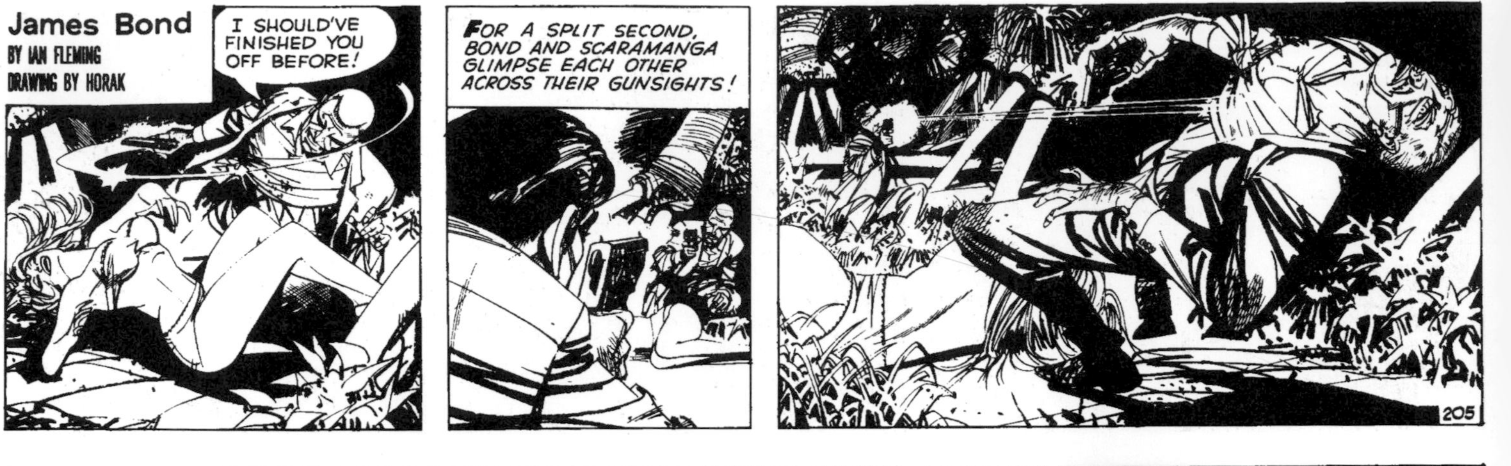
James Bond
BY IAN FLEMING
DRAWING BY HORAK
I SHOULD'VE FINISHED YOU OFF BEFORE!
FOR A SPLIT SECOND, BOND AND SCARAMANGA GLIMPSE EACH OTHER ACROSS THEIR GUNSIGHTS!
205

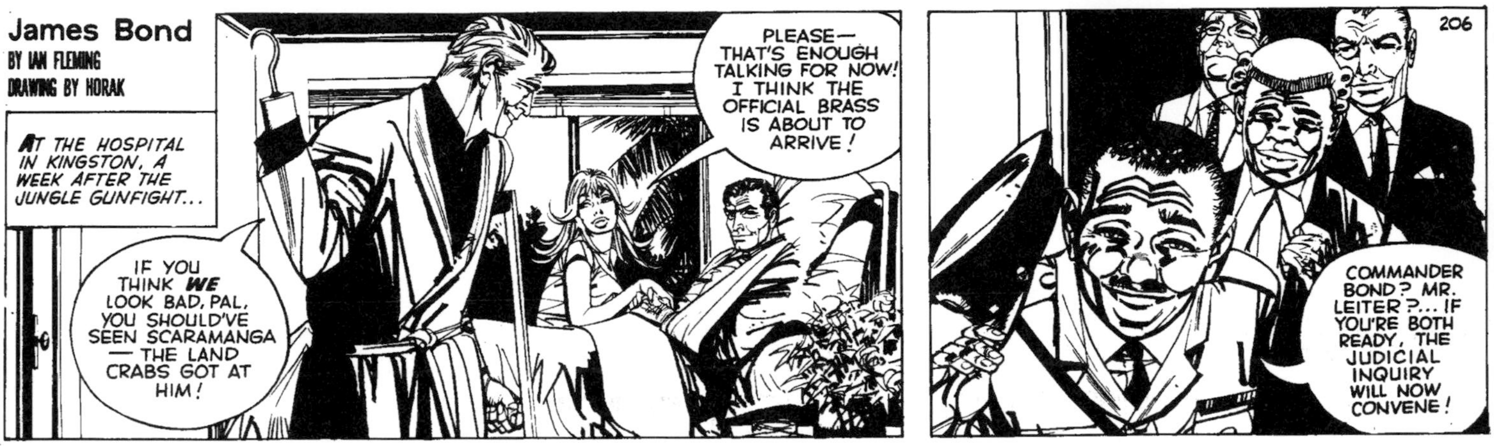
James Bond
BY IAN FLEMING
DRAWING BY HORAK
AT THE HOSPITAL IN KINGSTON, A WEEK AFTER THE JUNGLE GUNFIGHT...
IF YOU THINK WE LOOK BAD, PAL, YOU SHOULD'VE SEEN SCARAMANGA — THE LAND CRABS GOT AT HIM!
PLEASE— THAT'S ENOUGH TALKING FOR NOW! I THINK THE OFFICIAL BRASS IS ABOUT TO ARRIVE!
206
COMMANDER BOND? MR. LEITER?... IF YOU'RE BOTH READY, THE JUDICIAL INQUIRY WILL NOW CONVENE!

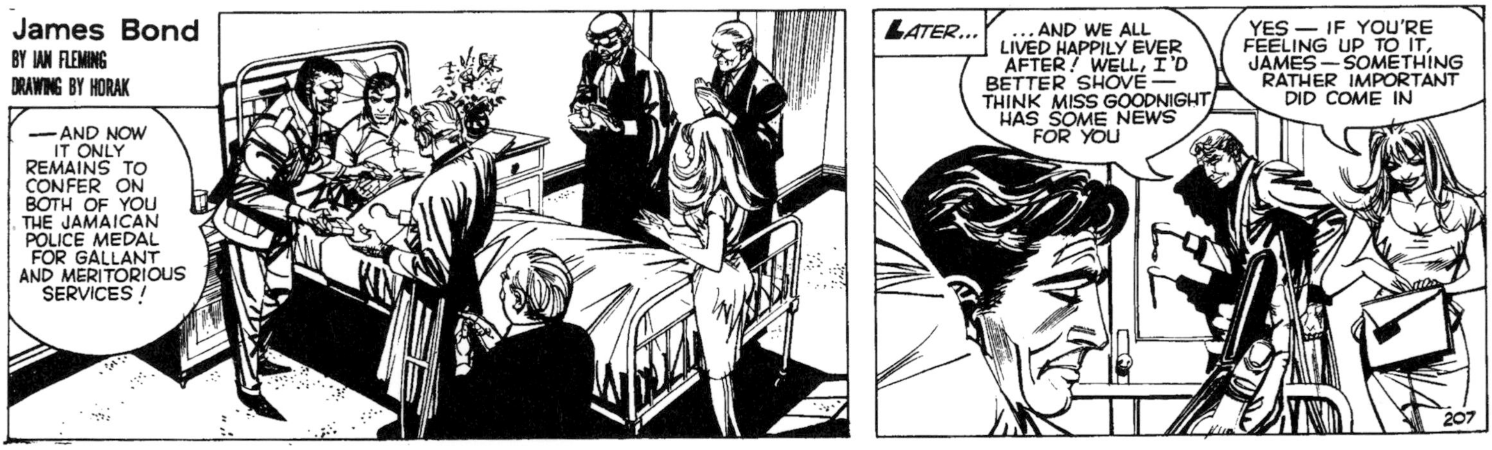
James Bond
BY IAN FLEMING
DRAWING BY HORAK
—AND NOW IT ONLY REMAINS TO CONFER ON BOTH OF YOU THE JAMAICAN POLICE MEDAL FOR GALLANT AND MERITORIOUS SERVICES!
LATER...
...AND WE ALL LIVED HAPPILY EVER AFTER! WELL, I'D BETTER SHOVE— THINK MISS GOODNIGHT HAS SOME NEWS FOR YOU
YES — IF YOU'RE FEELING UP TO IT, JAMES — SOMETHING RATHER IMPORTANT DID COME IN
207

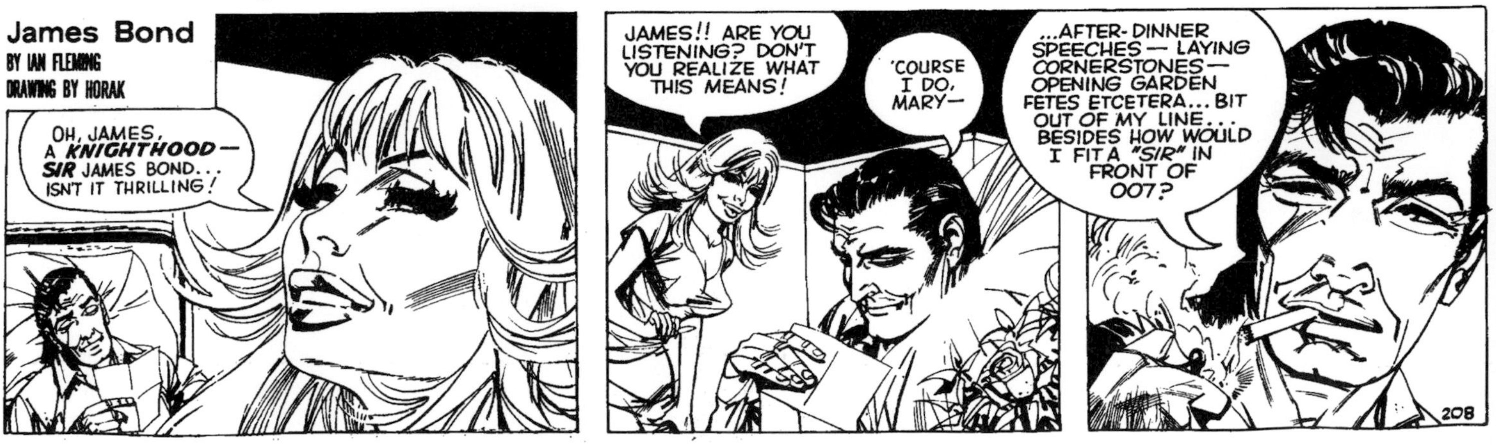
James Bond
BY IAN FLEMING
DRAWING BY HORAK
OH, JAMES, A KNIGHTHOOD— SIR JAMES BOND... ISN'T IT THRILLING!
JAMES!! ARE YOU LISTENING? DON'T YOU REALIZE WHAT THIS MEANS!
'COURSE I DO, MARY—
...AFTER-DINNER SPEECHES — LAYING CORNERSTONES— OPENING GARDEN FETES ETCETERA... BIT OUT OF MY LINE... BESIDES HOW WOULD I FIT A "SIR" IN FRONT OF 007?
208

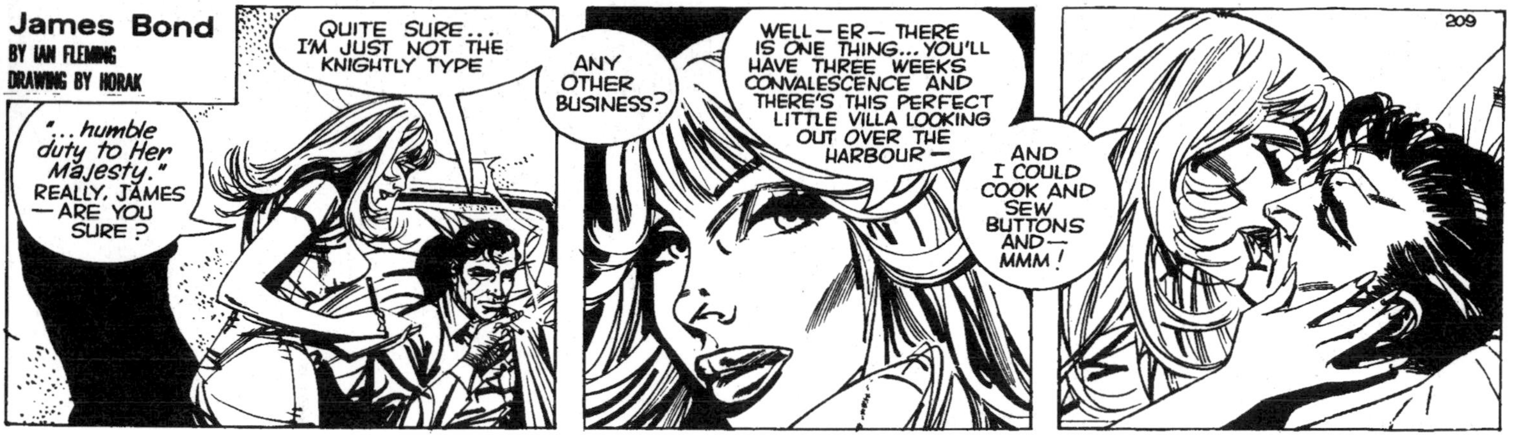

James Bond
BY IAN FLEMING
DRAWING BY HORAK
"... humble duty to Her Majesty." REALLY, JAMES — ARE YOU SURE?
QUITE SURE... I'M JUST NOT THE KNIGHTLY TYPE
ANY OTHER BUSINESS?
WELL — ER — THERE IS ONE THING... YOU'LL HAVE THREE WEEKS CONVALESCENCE AND THERE'S THIS PERFECT LITTLE VILLA LOOKING OUT OVER THE HARBOUR —
AND I COULD COOK AND SEW BUTTONS AND — MMM!
209

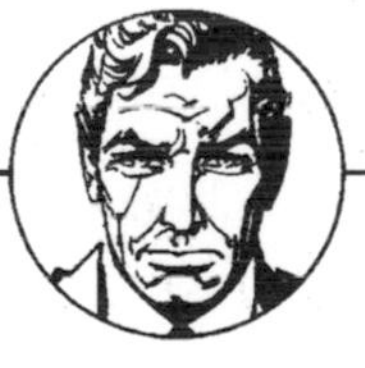

THE LIVING DAYLIGHTS

The Living Daylights followed immediately on from *Golden Gun*, although it's clear that some time has elapsed. The original story first appeared in 1962, and its placement here in the comic strip is odd. Bond is showing the ennui about his profession that made sense at the time of the original publication of the story shortly after *Thunderball*, when Bond had just spent some considerable time pursuing Blofeld fruitlessly around the world. In the comic strip's continuity, he has only just returned to the job and should still be determined to get revenge on the KGB. Lawrence fleshes out the backstory of agent 272's decision to cross the border, and interestingly makes the KGB agent Trigger a mirror of Bond, giving Trigger many of the activities and thoughts that Fleming ascribed to Bond. Lawrence is also more ruthless than Fleming — in his version, Trigger pays the price for failure.

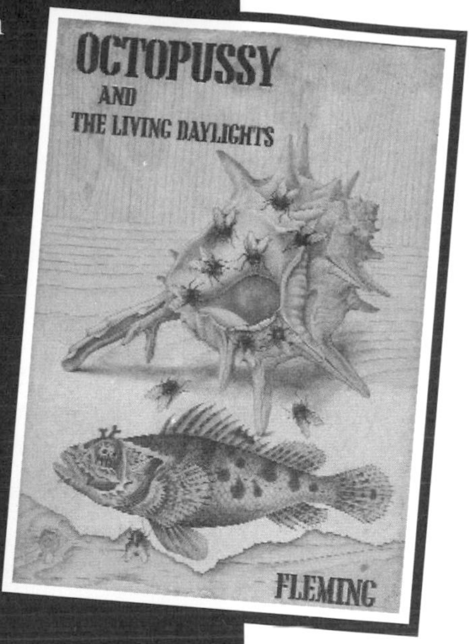
OCTOPUSSY
AND
THE LIVING DAYLIGHTS
FLEMING

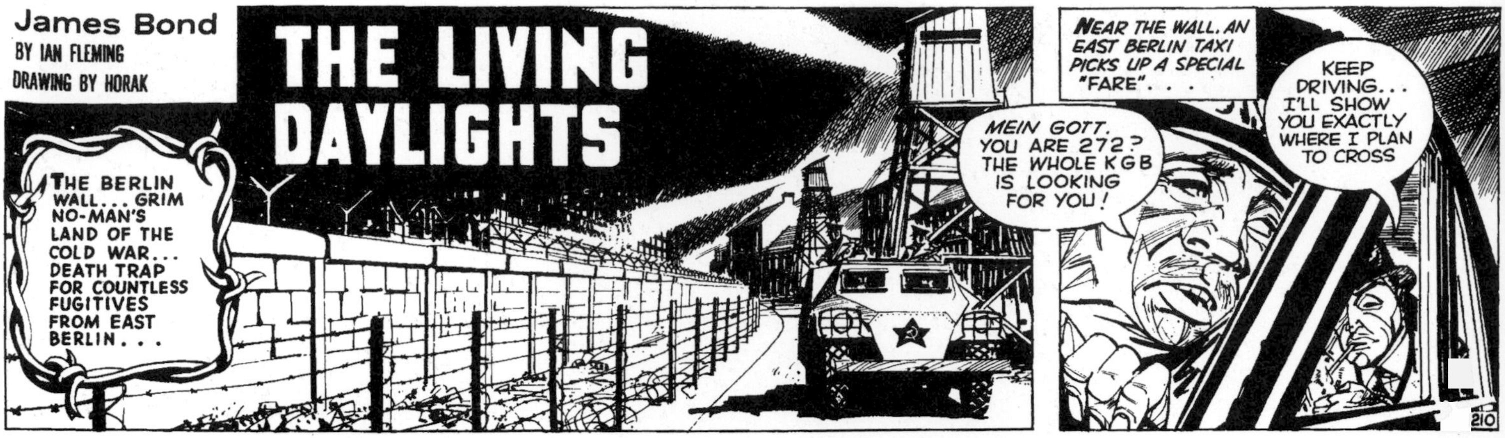
James Bond
BY IAN FLEMING
DRAWING BY HORAK
THE LIVING DAYLIGHTS
THE BERLIN WALL... GRIM NO-MAN'S LAND OF THE COLD WAR... DEATH TRAP FOR COUNTLESS FUGITIVES FROM EAST BERLIN...
NEAR THE WALL, AN EAST BERLIN TAXI PICKS UP A SPECIAL "FARE"...
MEIN GOTT. YOU ARE 272? THE WHOLE KGB IS LOOKING FOR YOU!
KEEP DRIVING... I'LL SHOW YOU EXACTLY WHERE I PLAN TO CROSS
210

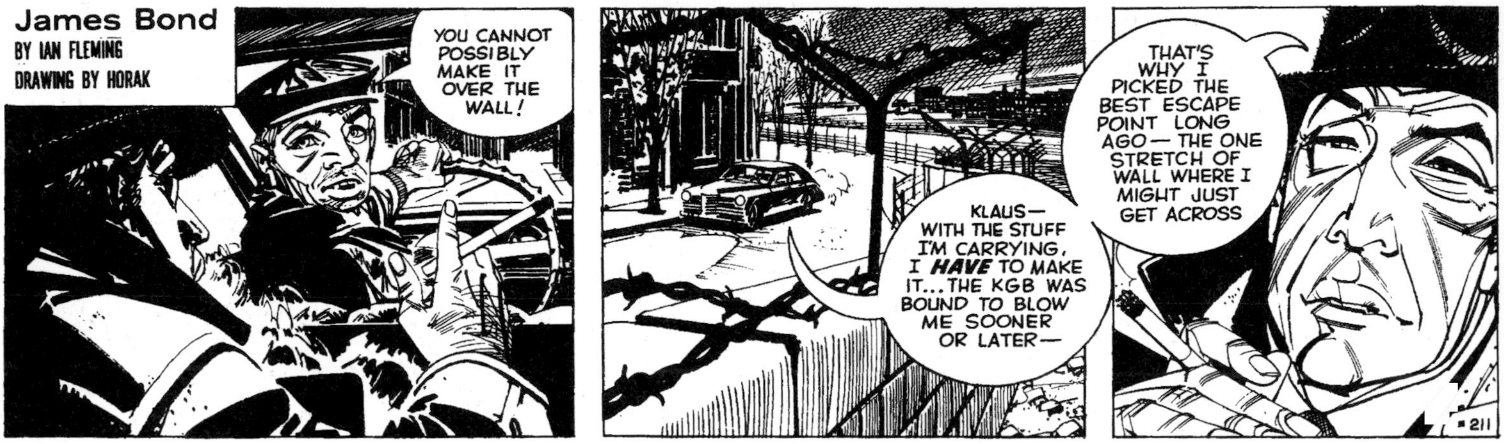
James Bond
BY IAN FLEMING
DRAWING BY HORAK
YOU CANNOT POSSIBLY MAKE IT OVER THE WALL!
KLAUS— WITH THE STUFF I'M CARRYING, I HAVE TO MAKE IT... THE KGB WAS BOUND TO BLOW ME SOONER OR LATER—
THAT'S WHY I PICKED THE BEST ESCAPE POINT LONG AGO— THE ONE STRETCH OF WALL WHERE I MIGHT JUST GET ACROSS
211

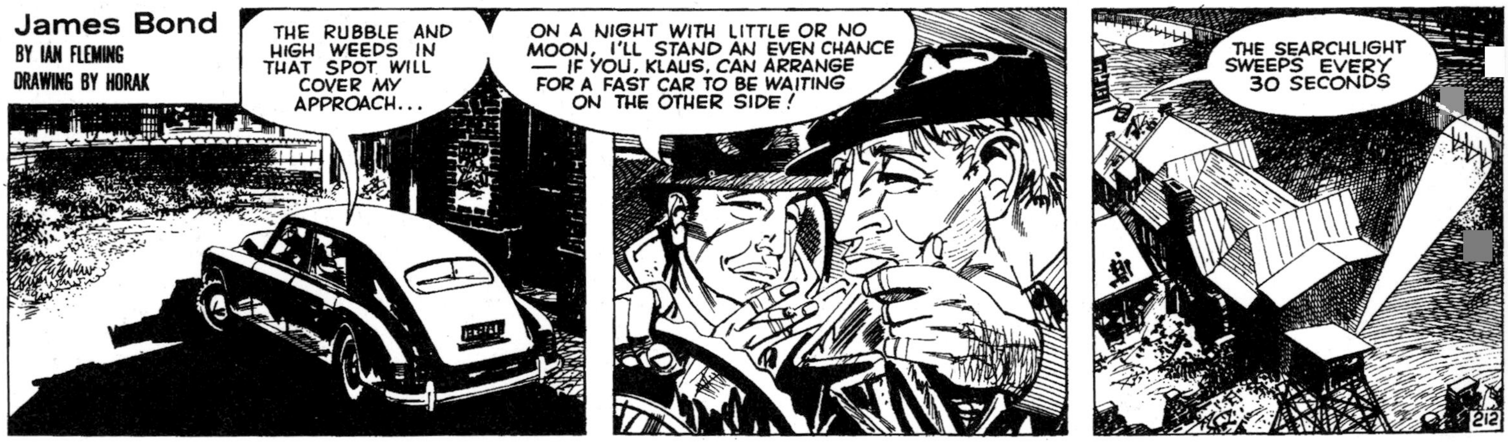
James Bond
BY IAN FLEMING
DRAWING BY HORAK
THE RUBBLE AND HIGH WEEDS IN THAT SPOT WILL COVER MY APPROACH...
ON A NIGHT WITH LITTLE OR NO MOON, I'LL STAND AN EVEN CHANCE — IF YOU, KLAUS, CAN ARRANGE FOR A FAST CAR TO BE WAITING ON THE OTHER SIDE!
THE SEARCHLIGHT SWEEPS EVERY 30 SECONDS
212

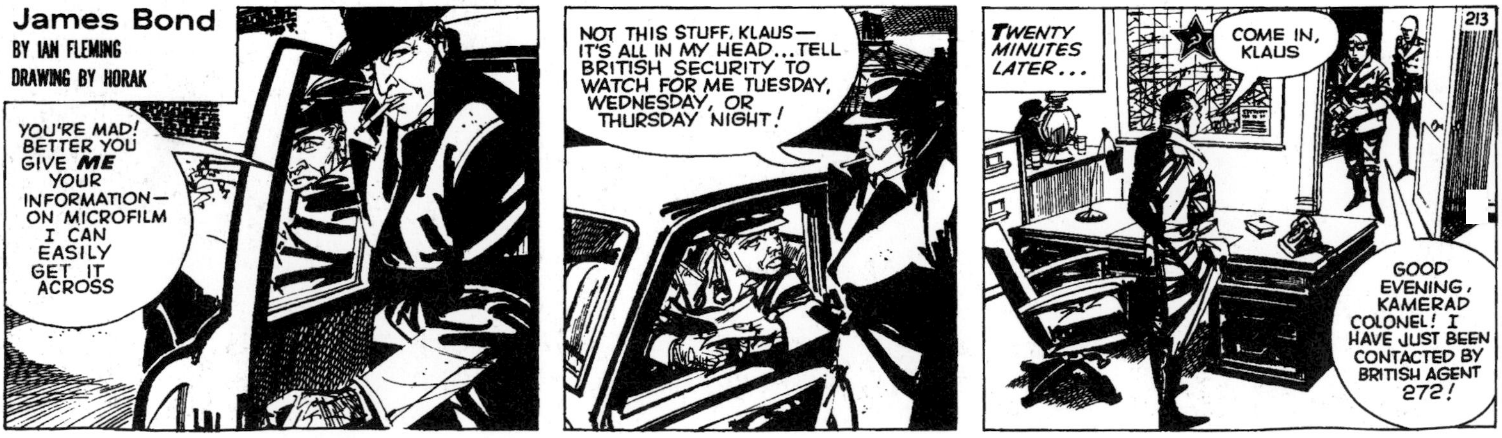
James Bond
BY IAN FLEMING
DRAWING BY HORAK
YOU'RE MAD! BETTER YOU GIVE ME YOUR INFORMATION— ON MICROFILM I CAN EASILY GET IT ACROSS
NOT THIS STUFF, KLAUS— IT'S ALL IN MY HEAD... TELL BRITISH SECURITY TO WATCH FOR ME TUESDAY, WEDNESDAY, OR THURSDAY NIGHT!
TWENTY MINUTES LATER...
COME IN, KLAUS
GOOD EVENING, KAMERAD COLONEL! I HAVE JUST BEEN CONTACTED BY BRITISH AGENT 272!
213

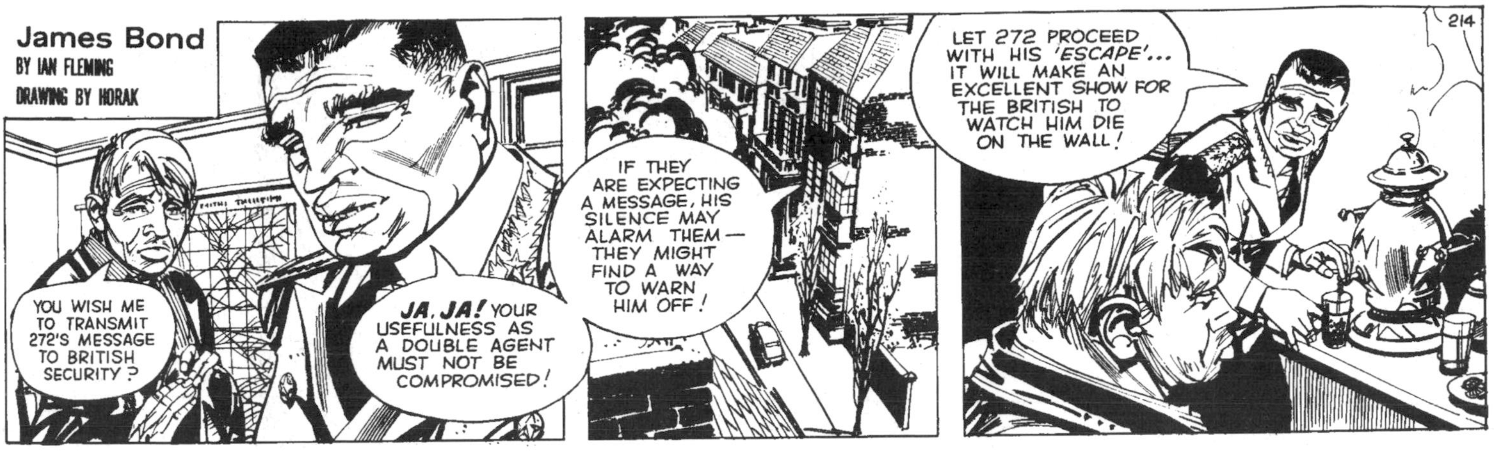
James Bond
BY IAN FLEMING
DRAWING BY HORAK
YOU WISH ME TO TRANSMIT 272'S MESSAGE TO BRITISH SECURITY?
JA, JA! YOUR USEFULNESS AS A DOUBLE AGENT MUST NOT BE COMPROMISED!
IF THEY ARE EXPECTING A MESSAGE, HIS SILENCE MAY ALARM THEM— THEY MIGHT FIND A WAY TO WARN HIM OFF!
LET 272 PROCEED WITH HIS 'ESCAPE'... IT WILL MAKE AN EXCELLENT SHOW FOR THE BRITISH TO WATCH HIM DIE ON THE WALL!
214

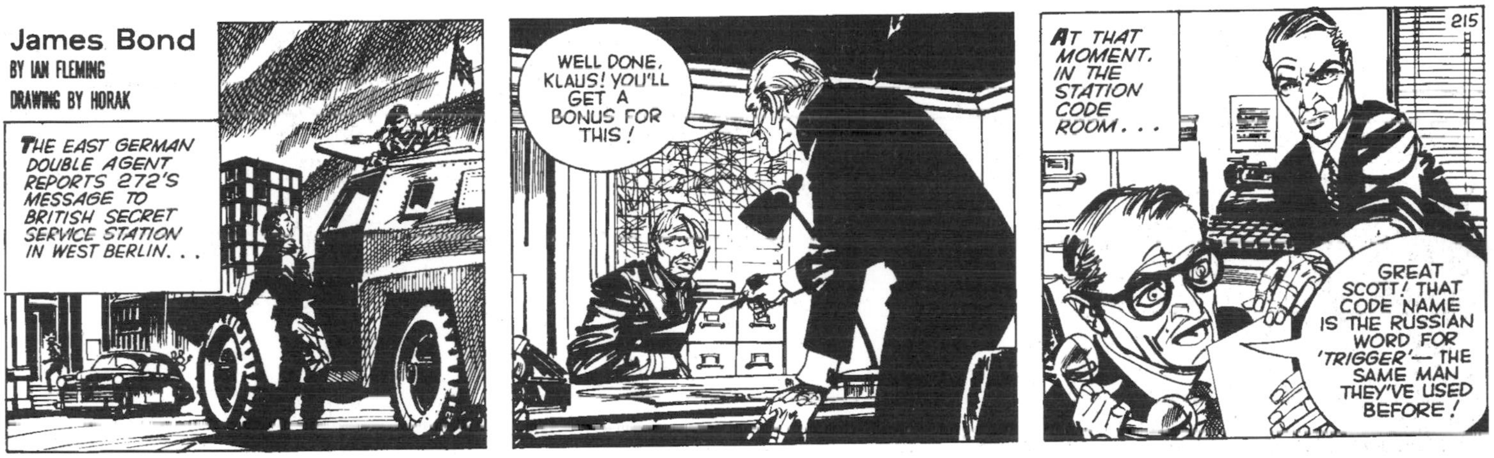
James Bond
BY IAN FLEMING
DRAWING BY HORAK
THE EAST GERMAN DOUBLE AGENT REPORTS 272'S MESSAGE TO BRITISH SECRET SERVICE STATION IN WEST BERLIN...
WELL DONE, KLAUS! YOU'LL GET A BONUS FOR THIS!
AT THAT MOMENT, IN THE STATION CODE ROOM...
215
GREAT SCOTT! THAT CODE NAME IS THE RUSSIAN WORD FOR 'TRIGGER'— THE SAME MAN THEY'VE USED BEFORE!

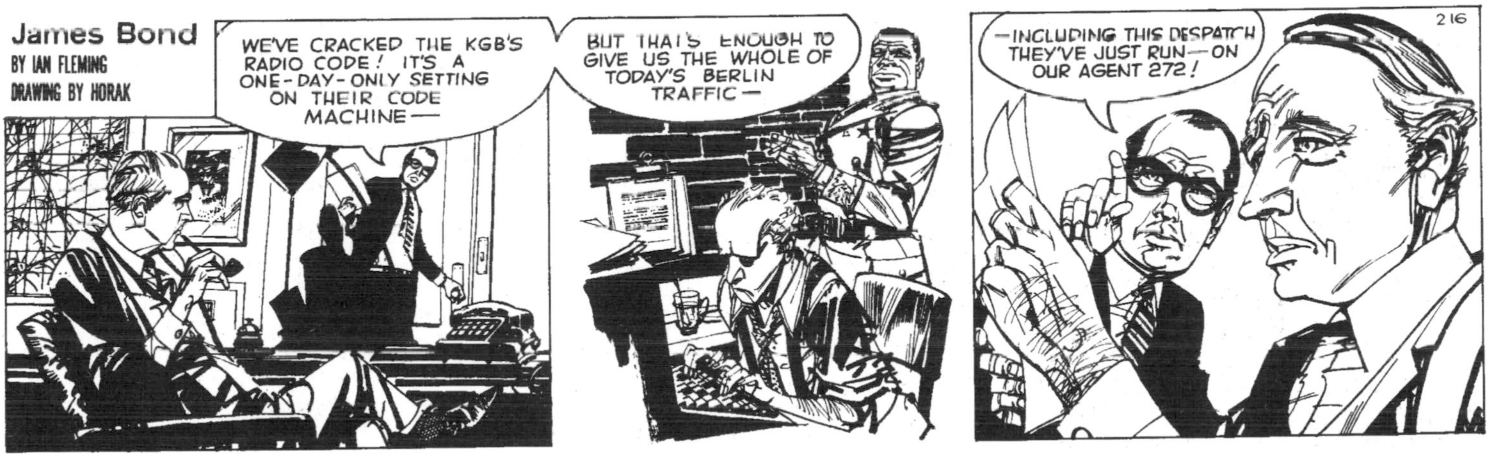
James Bond
BY IAN FLEMING
DRAWING BY HORAK
WE'VE CRACKED THE KGB'S RADIO CODE! IT'S A ONE-DAY-ONLY SETTING ON THEIR CODE MACHINE—
BUT THAT'S ENOUGH TO GIVE US THE WHOLE OF TODAY'S BERLIN TRAFFIC—
—INCLUDING THIS DESPATCH THEY'VE JUST RUN—ON OUR AGENT 272!
216

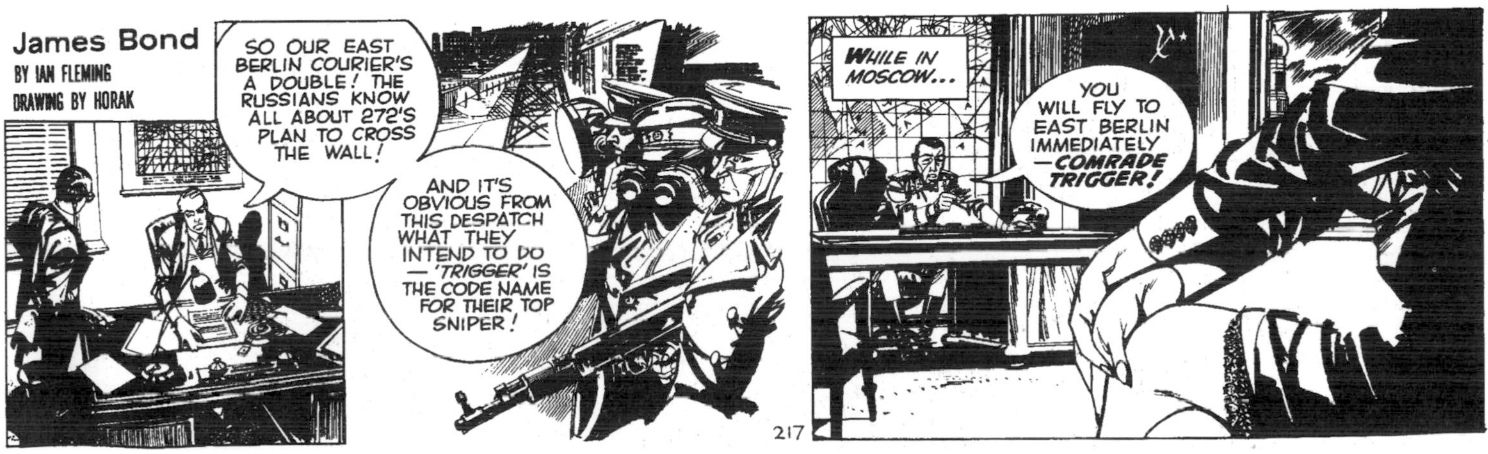
James Bond
BY IAN FLEMING
DRAWING BY HORAK
SO OUR EAST BERLIN COURIER'S A DOUBLE! THE RUSSIANS KNOW ALL ABOUT 272'S PLAN TO CROSS THE WALL!
AND IT'S OBVIOUS FROM THIS DESPATCH WHAT THEY INTEND TO DO — 'TRIGGER' IS THE CODE NAME FOR THEIR TOP SNIPER!
WHILE IN MOSCOW...
YOU WILL FLY TO EAST BERLIN IMMEDIATELY —COMRADE TRIGGER!

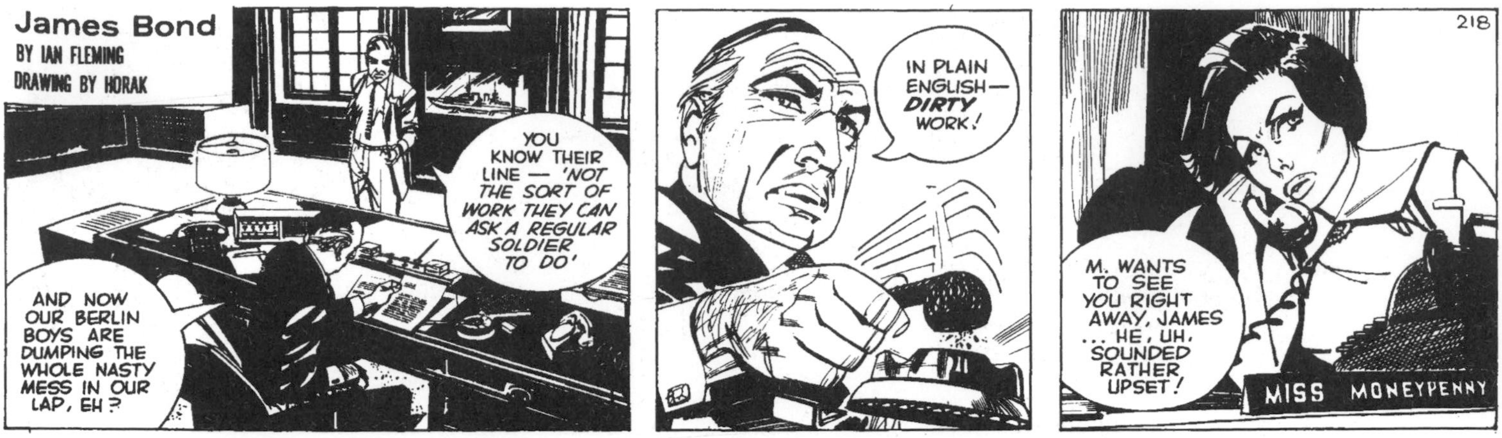

James Bond
BY IAN FLEMING
DRAWING BY HORAK
AND NOW OUR BERLIN BOYS ARE DUMPING THE WHOLE NASTY MESS IN OUR LAP, EH?
YOU KNOW THEIR LINE — 'NOT THE SORT OF WORK THEY CAN ASK A REGULAR SOLDIER TO DO'
IN PLAIN ENGLISH— DIRTY WORK!
218
M. WANTS TO SEE YOU RIGHT AWAY, JAMES ... HE, UH, SOUNDED RATHER UPSET!
MISS MONEYPENNY

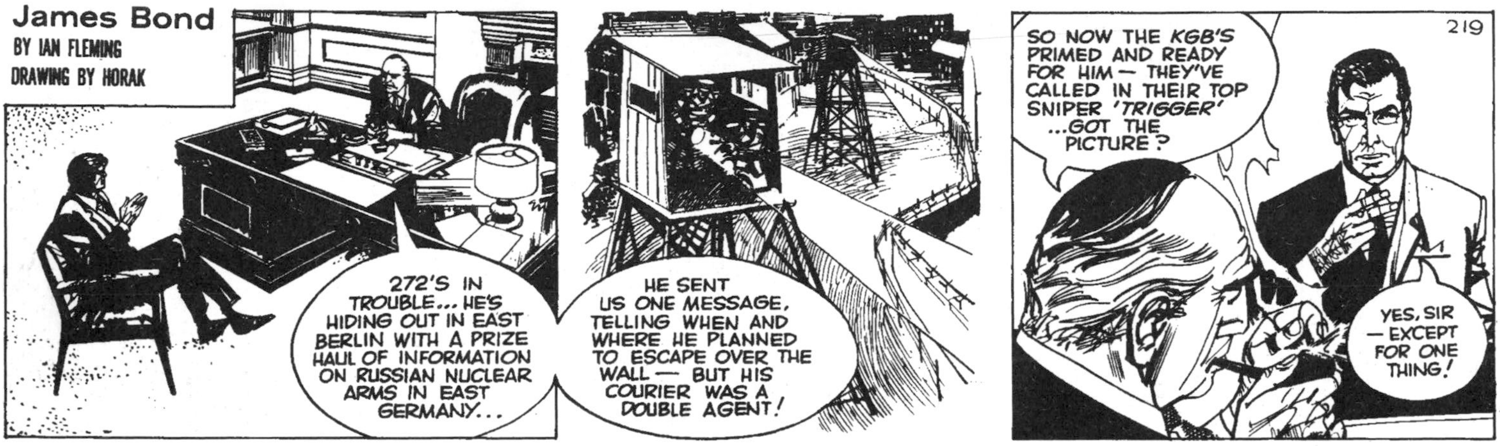

James Bond
BY IAN FLEMING
DRAWING BY HORAK
272'S IN TROUBLE... HE'S HIDING OUT IN EAST BERLIN WITH A PRIZE HAUL OF INFORMATION ON RUSSIAN NUCLEAR ARMS IN EAST GERMANY...
HE SENT US ONE MESSAGE, TELLING WHEN AND WHERE HE PLANNED TO ESCAPE OVER THE WALL— BUT HIS COURIER WAS A DOUBLE AGENT!
219
SO NOW THE KGB'S PRIMED AND READY FOR HIM— THEY'VE CALLED IN THEIR TOP SNIPER 'TRIGGER' ...GOT THE PICTURE?
YES, SIR — EXCEPT FOR ONE THING!

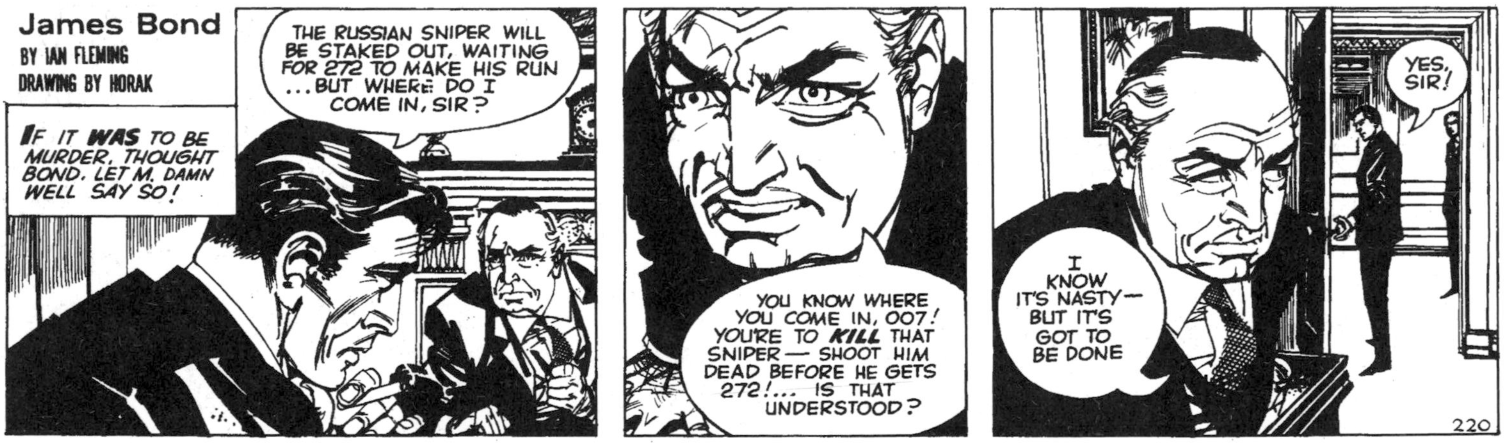

James Bond
BY IAN FLEMING
DRAWING BY HORAK
IF IT WAS TO BE MURDER, THOUGHT BOND, LET M. DAMN WELL SAY SO!
THE RUSSIAN SNIPER WILL BE STAKED OUT, WAITING FOR 272 TO MAKE HIS RUN ...BUT WHERE DO I COME IN, SIR?
YOU KNOW WHERE YOU COME IN, 007! YOU'RE TO KILL THAT SNIPER— SHOOT HIM DEAD BEFORE HE GETS 272!... IS THAT UNDERSTOOD?
I KNOW IT'S NASTY— BUT IT'S GOT TO BE DONE
YES, SIR!
220

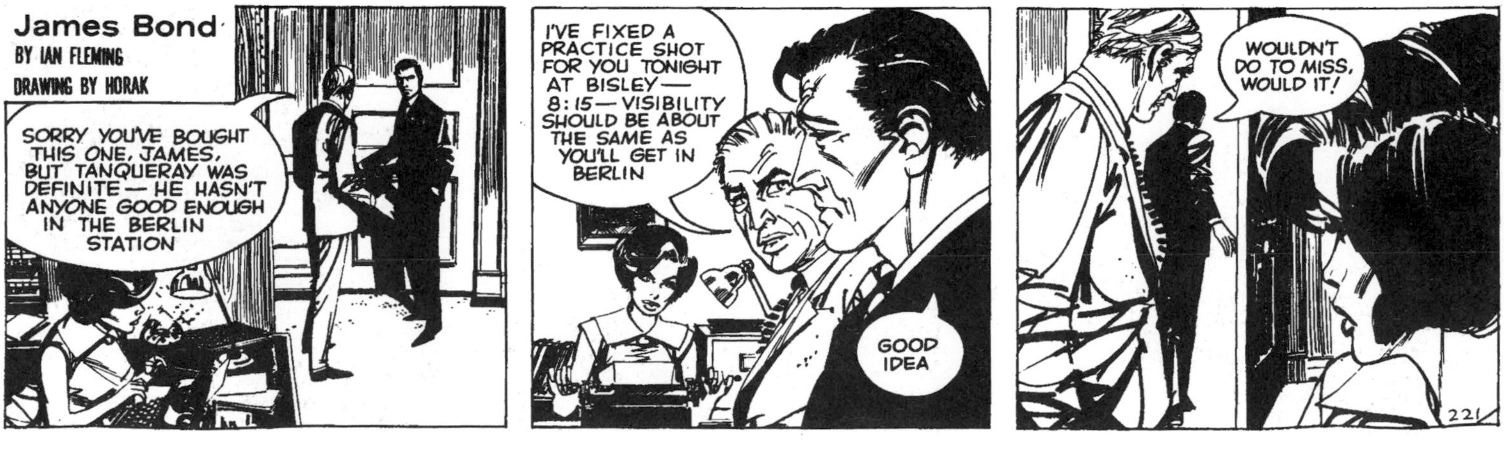

James Bond
BY IAN FLEMING
DRAWING BY HORAK
SORRY YOU'VE BOUGHT THIS ONE, JAMES, BUT TANQUERAY WAS DEFINITE— HE HASN'T ANYONE GOOD ENOUGH IN THE BERLIN STATION
I'VE FIXED A PRACTICE SHOT FOR YOU TONIGHT AT BISLEY— 8:15— VISIBILITY SHOULD BE ABOUT THE SAME AS YOU'LL GET IN BERLIN
GOOD IDEA
WOULDN'T DO TO MISS, WOULD IT!
221

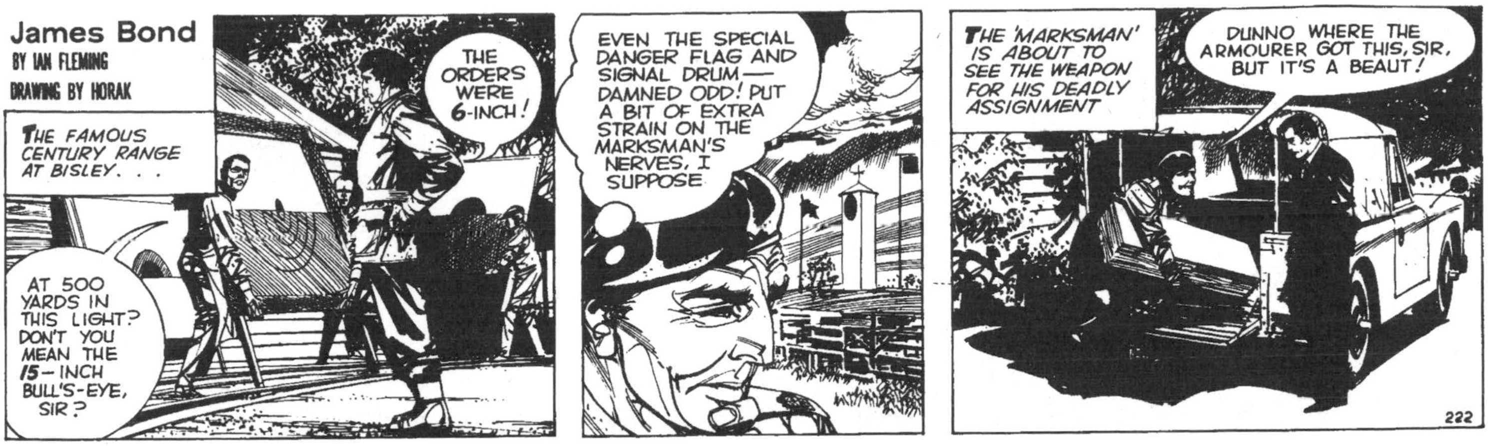
James Bond
BY IAN FLEMING
DRAWING BY HORAK
THE FAMOUS CENTURY RANGE AT BISLEY. . .
AT 500 YARDS IN THIS LIGHT? DON'T YOU MEAN THE 15-INCH BULL'S-EYE, SIR?
THE ORDERS WERE 6-INCH!
EVEN THE SPECIAL DANGER FLAG AND SIGNAL DRUM— DAMNED ODD! PUT A BIT OF EXTRA STRAIN ON THE MARKSMAN'S NERVES, I SUPPOSE
THE 'MARKSMAN' IS ABOUT TO SEE THE WEAPON FOR HIS DEADLY ASSIGNMENT
DUNNO WHERE THE ARMOURER GOT THIS, SIR, BUT IT'S A BEAUT!
222

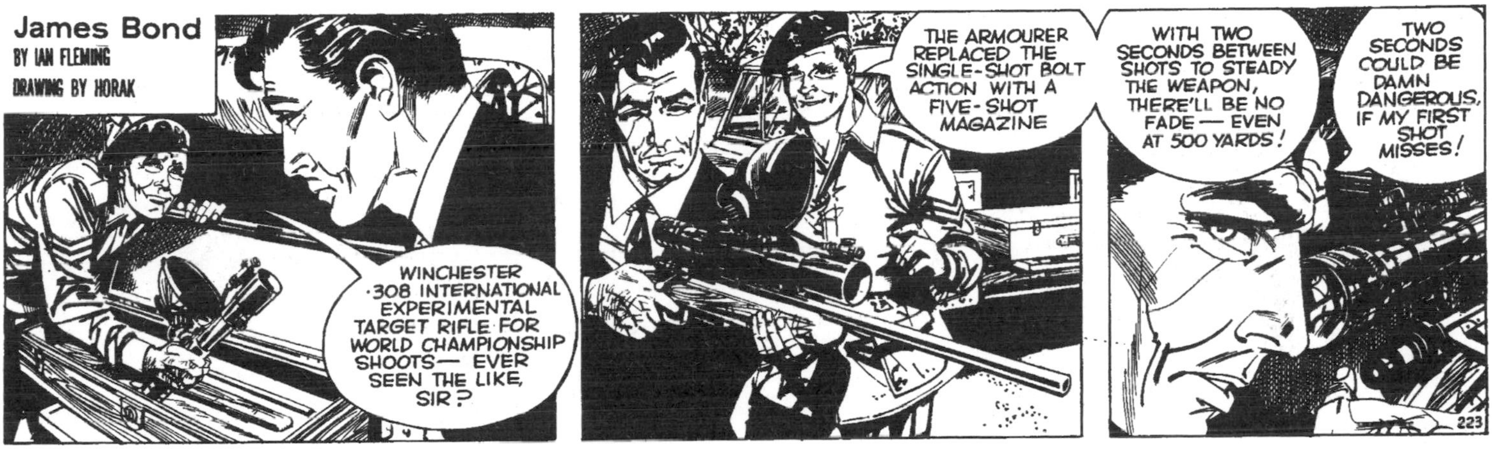
James Bond
BY IAN FLEMING
DRAWING BY HORAK
WINCHESTER ·308 INTERNATIONAL EXPERIMENTAL TARGET RIFLE FOR WORLD CHAMPIONSHIP SHOOTS— EVER SEEN THE LIKE, SIR?
THE ARMOURER REPLACED THE SINGLE-SHOT BOLT ACTION WITH A FIVE-SHOT MAGAZINE
WITH TWO SECONDS BETWEEN SHOTS TO STEADY THE WEAPON, THERE'LL BE NO FADE— EVEN AT 500 YARDS!
TWO SECONDS COULD BE DAMN DANGEROUS, IF MY FIRST SHOT MISSES!
223

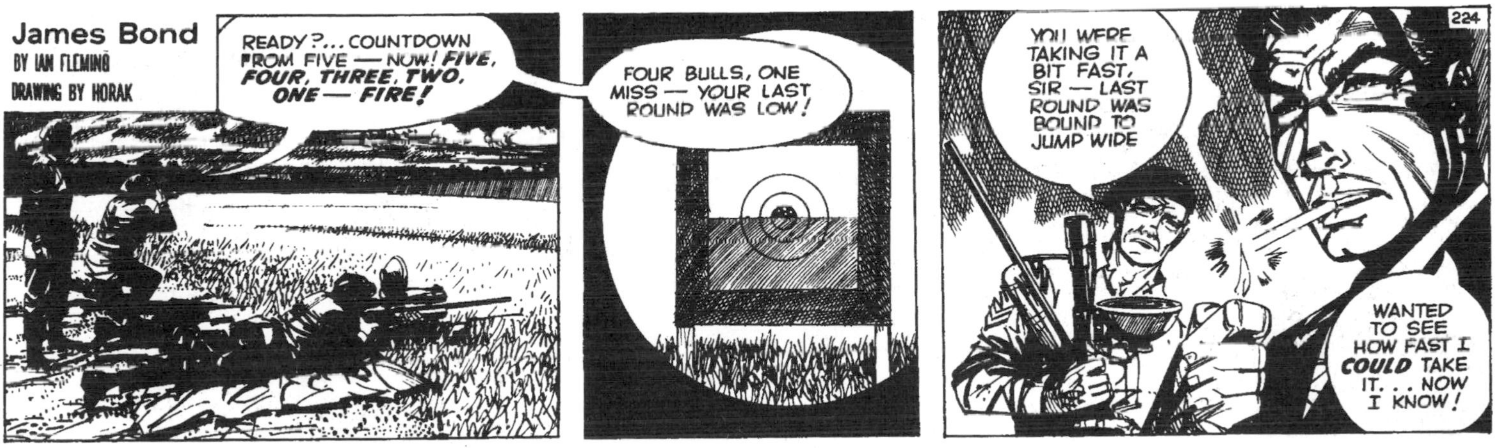
James Bond
BY IAN FLEMING
DRAWING BY HORAK
READY?... COUNTDOWN FROM FIVE — NOW! FIVE, FOUR, THREE, TWO, ONE — FIRE!
FOUR BULLS, ONE MISS — YOUR LAST ROUND WAS LOW!
224
YOU WERE TAKING IT A BIT FAST, SIR — LAST ROUND WAS BOUND TO JUMP WIDE
WANTED TO SEE HOW FAST I COULD TAKE IT. . . NOW I KNOW!

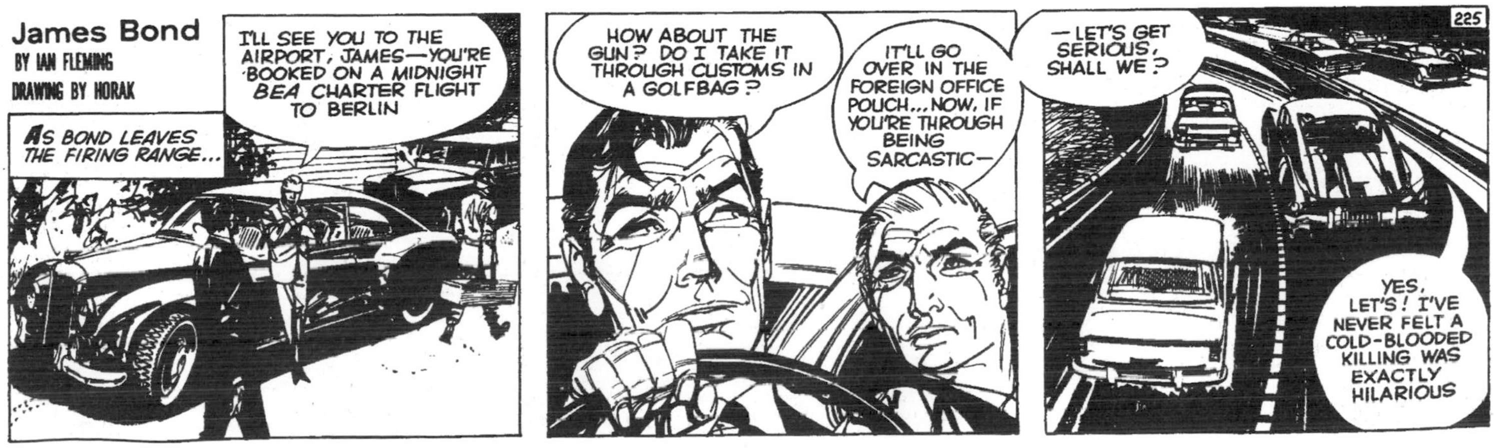
James Bond
BY IAN FLEMING
DRAWING BY HORAK
AS BOND LEAVES THE FIRING RANGE...
I'LL SEE YOU TO THE AIRPORT, JAMES—YOU'RE BOOKED ON A MIDNIGHT BEA CHARTER FLIGHT TO BERLIN
HOW ABOUT THE GUN? DO I TAKE IT THROUGH CUSTOMS IN A GOLFBAG?
IT'LL GO OVER IN THE FOREIGN OFFICE POUCH... NOW, IF YOU'RE THROUGH BEING SARCASTIC—
225
—LET'S GET SERIOUS, SHALL WE?
YES, LET'S! I'VE NEVER FELT A COLD-BLOODED KILLING WAS EXACTLY HILARIOUS

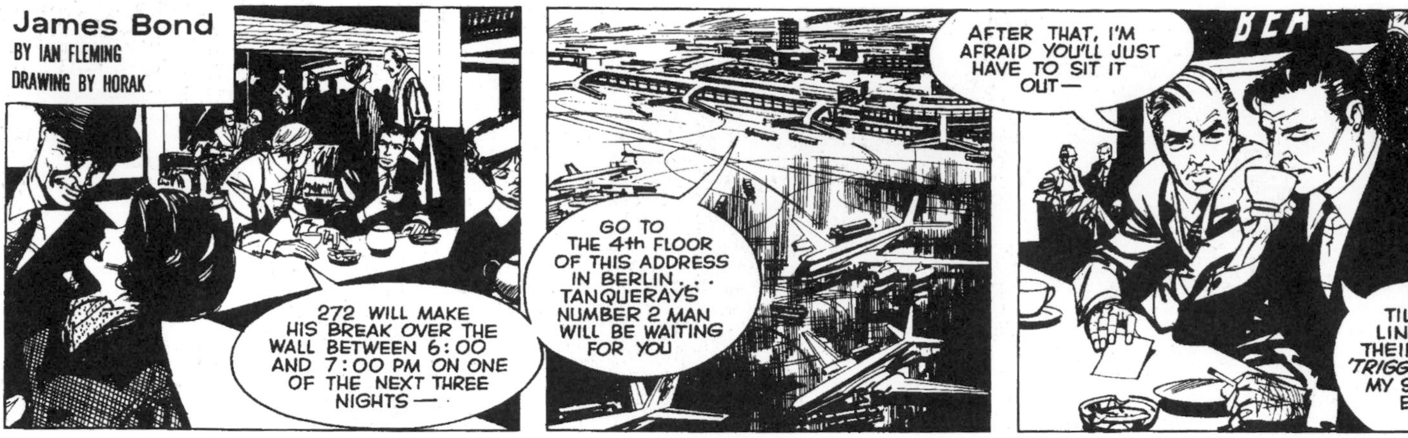
James Bond
BY IAN FLEMING
DRAWING BY HORAK
272 WILL MAKE HIS BREAK OVER THE WALL BETWEEN 6:00 AND 7:00 PM ON ONE OF THE NEXT THREE NIGHTS—
GO TO THE 4th FLOOR OF THIS ADDRESS IN BERLIN... TANQUERAY'S NUMBER 2 MAN WILL BE WAITING FOR YOU
AFTER THAT, I'M AFRAID YOU'LL JUST HAVE TO SIT IT OUT—
TILL I LINE UP THEIR BOY 'TRIGGER' IN MY SIGHTS, EH?
BEA
226

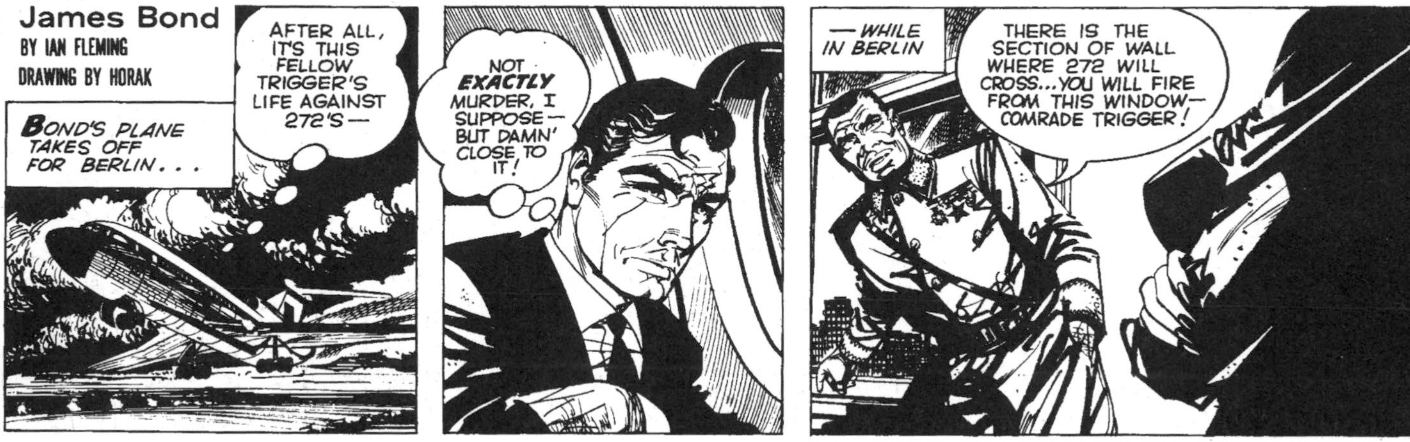
James Bond
BY IAN FLEMING
DRAWING BY HORAK
BOND'S PLANE TAKES OFF FOR BERLIN...
AFTER ALL, IT'S THIS FELLOW TRIGGER'S LIFE AGAINST 272'S—
NOT EXACTLY MURDER, I SUPPOSE— BUT DAMN' CLOSE TO IT!
—WHILE IN BERLIN
THERE IS THE SECTION OF WALL WHERE 272 WILL CROSS... YOU WILL FIRE FROM THIS WINDOW— COMRADE TRIGGER!
227

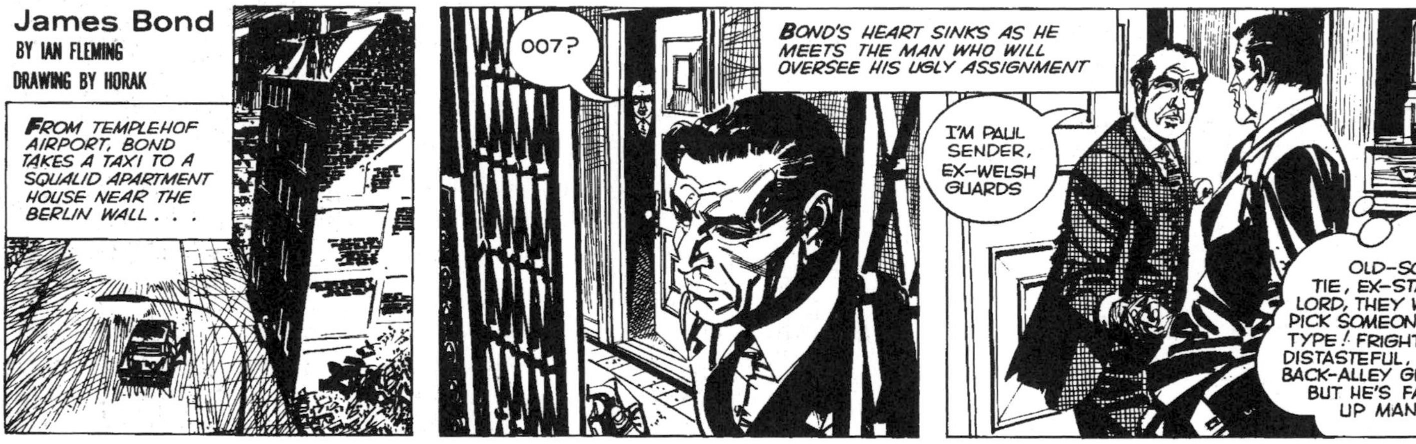
James Bond
BY IAN FLEMING
DRAWING BY HORAK
FROM TEMPLEHOF AIRPORT, BOND TAKES A TAXI TO A SQUALID APARTMENT HOUSE NEAR THE BERLIN WALL...
007?
BOND'S HEART SINKS AS HE MEETS THE MAN WHO WILL OVERSEE HIS UGLY ASSIGNMENT
I'M PAUL SENDER, EX-WELSH GUARDS
OLD-SCHOOL-TIE, EX-STAFF— LORD, THEY WOULD PICK SOMEONE HIS TYPE! FRIGHTFULLY DISTASTEFUL, THIS BACK-ALLEY GUNPLAY, BUT HE'S FACING UP MANFULLY!
228

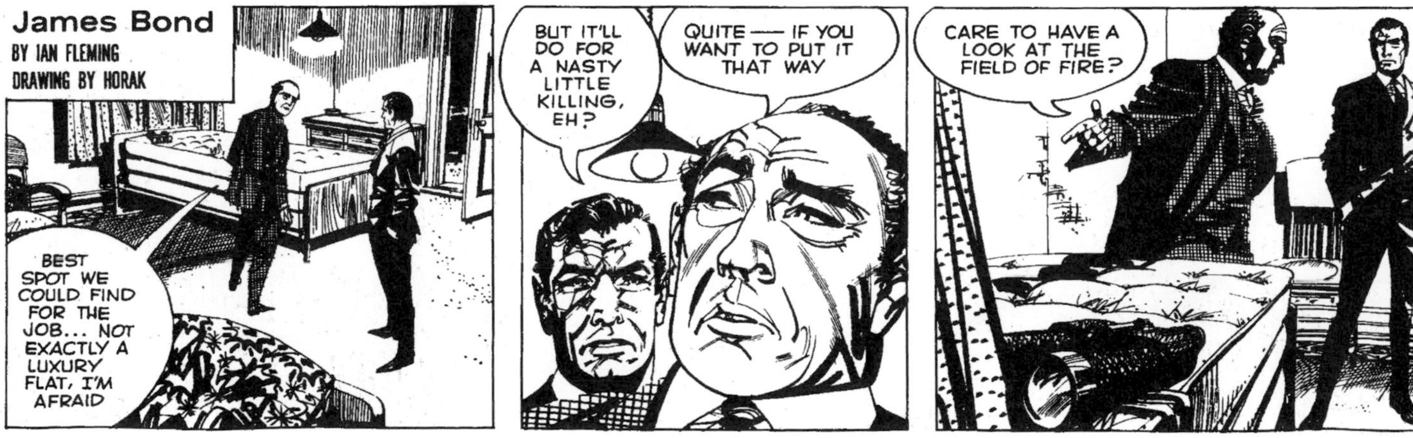
James Bond
BY IAN FLEMING
DRAWING BY HORAK
BEST SPOT WE COULD FIND FOR THE JOB... NOT EXACTLY A LUXURY FLAT, I'M AFRAID
BUT IT'LL DO FOR A NASTY LITTLE KILLING, EH?
QUITE — IF YOU WANT TO PUT IT THAT WAY
CARE TO HAVE A LOOK AT THE FIELD OF FIRE?
229

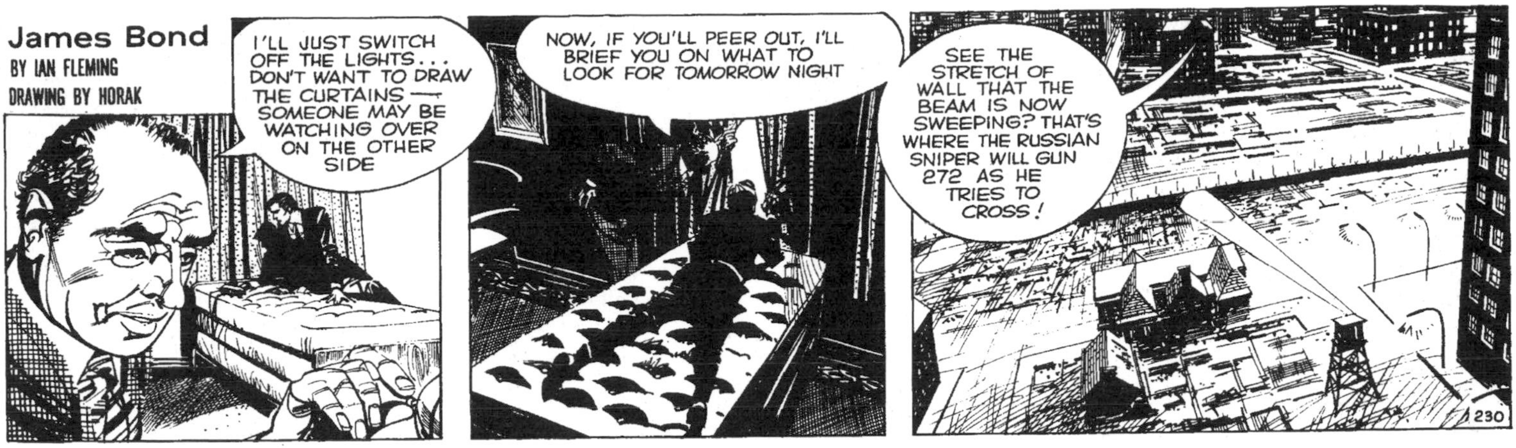
James Bond
BY IAN FLEMING
DRAWING BY HORAK
I'LL JUST SWITCH OFF THE LIGHTS... DON'T WANT TO DRAW THE CURTAINS — SOMEONE MAY BE WATCHING OVER ON THE OTHER SIDE
NOW, IF YOU'LL PEER OUT, I'LL BRIEF YOU ON WHAT TO LOOK FOR TOMORROW NIGHT
SEE THE STRETCH OF WALL THAT THE BEAM IS NOW SWEEPING? THAT'S WHERE THE RUSSIAN SNIPER WILL GUN 272 AS HE TRIES TO CROSS!
230

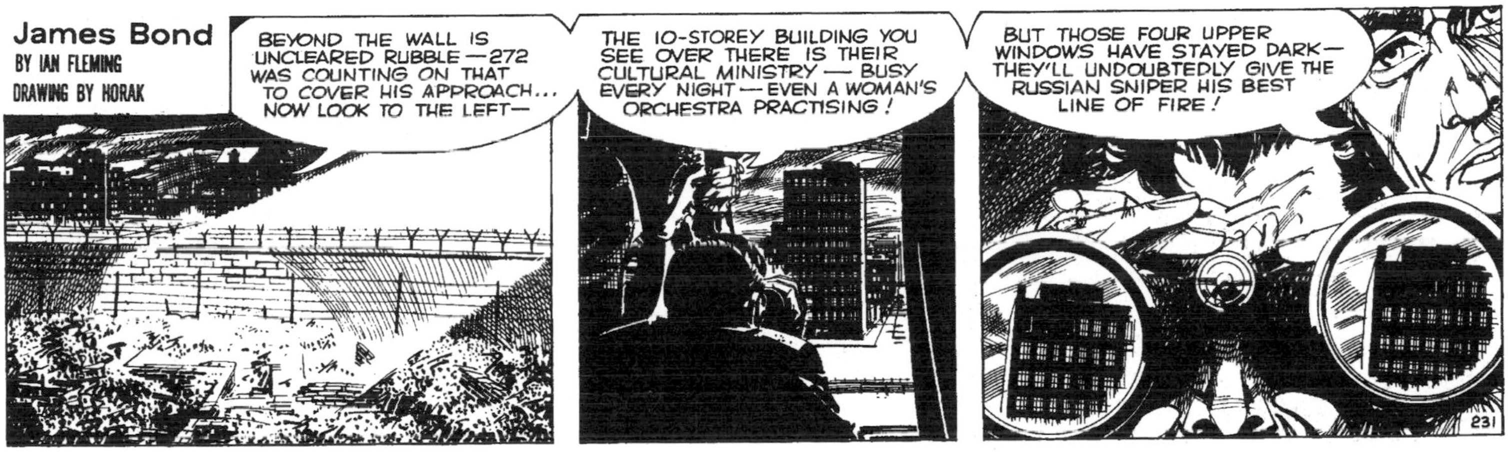
James Bond
BY IAN FLEMING
DRAWING BY HORAK
BEYOND THE WALL IS UNCLEARED RUBBLE — 272 WAS COUNTING ON THAT TO COVER HIS APPROACH... NOW LOOK TO THE LEFT—
THE 10-STOREY BUILDING YOU SEE OVER THERE IS THEIR CULTURAL MINISTRY — BUSY EVERY NIGHT — EVEN A WOMAN'S ORCHESTRA PRACTISING!
BUT THOSE FOUR UPPER WINDOWS HAVE STAYED DARK— THEY'LL UNDOUBTEDLY GIVE THE RUSSIAN SNIPER HIS BEST LINE OF FIRE!
231

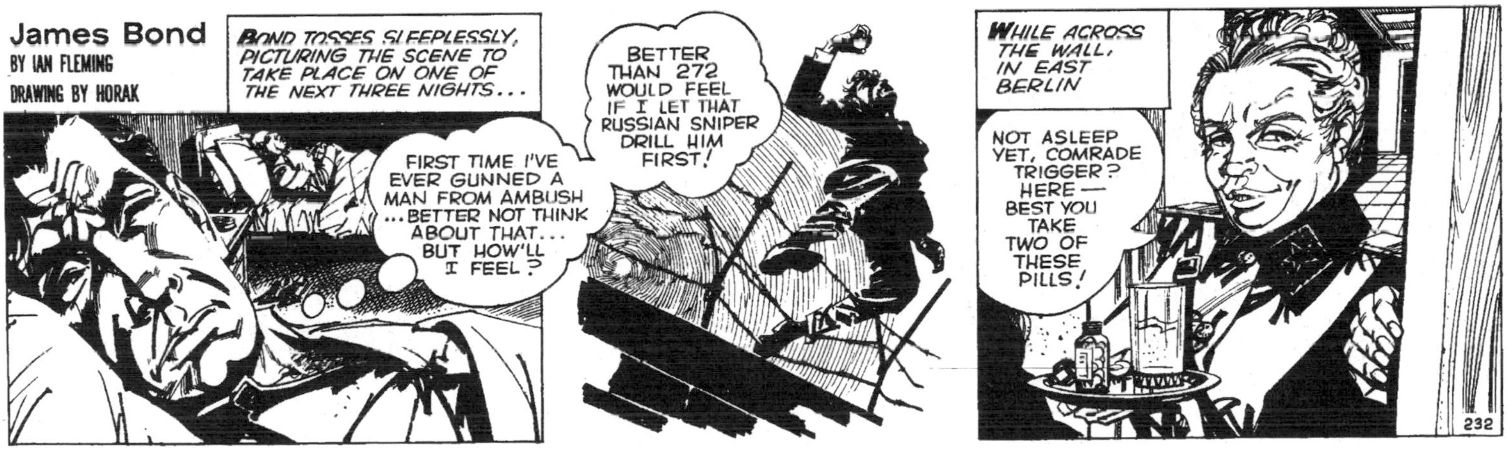
James Bond
BY IAN FLEMING
DRAWING BY HORAK
BOND TOSSES SLEEPLESSLY, PICTURING THE SCENE TO TAKE PLACE ON ONE OF THE NEXT THREE NIGHTS...
FIRST TIME I'VE EVER GUNNED A MAN FROM AMBUSH ...BETTER NOT THINK ABOUT THAT... BUT HOW'LL I FEEL?
BETTER THAN 272 WOULD FEEL IF I LET THAT RUSSIAN SNIPER DRILL HIM FIRST!
WHILE ACROSS THE WALL, IN EAST BERLIN
NOT ASLEEP YET, COMRADE TRIGGER? HERE — BEST YOU TAKE TWO OF THESE PILLS!
232

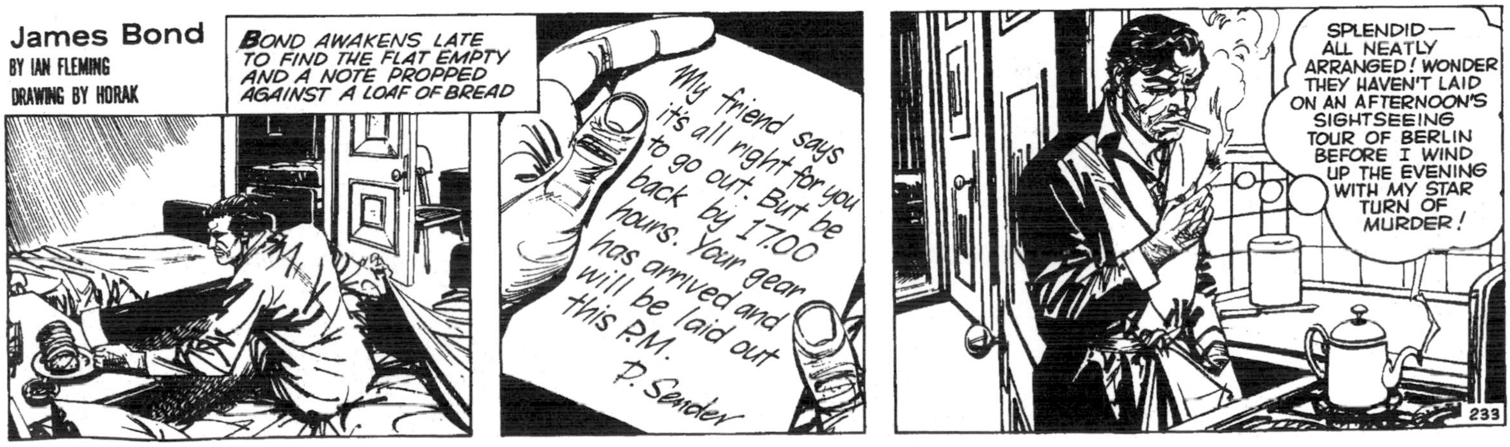
James Bond
BY IAN FLEMING
DRAWING BY HORAK
BOND AWAKENS LATE TO FIND THE FLAT EMPTY AND A NOTE PROPPED AGAINST A LOAF OF BREAD
My friend says it's all right for you to go out. But be back by 17.00 hours. Your gear has arrived and will be laid out this P.M.
P. Sender
SPLENDID— ALL NEATLY ARRANGED! WONDER THEY HAVEN'T LAID ON AN AFTERNOON'S SIGHTSEEING TOUR OF BERLIN BEFORE I WIND UP THE EVENING WITH MY STAR TURN OF MURDER!
233

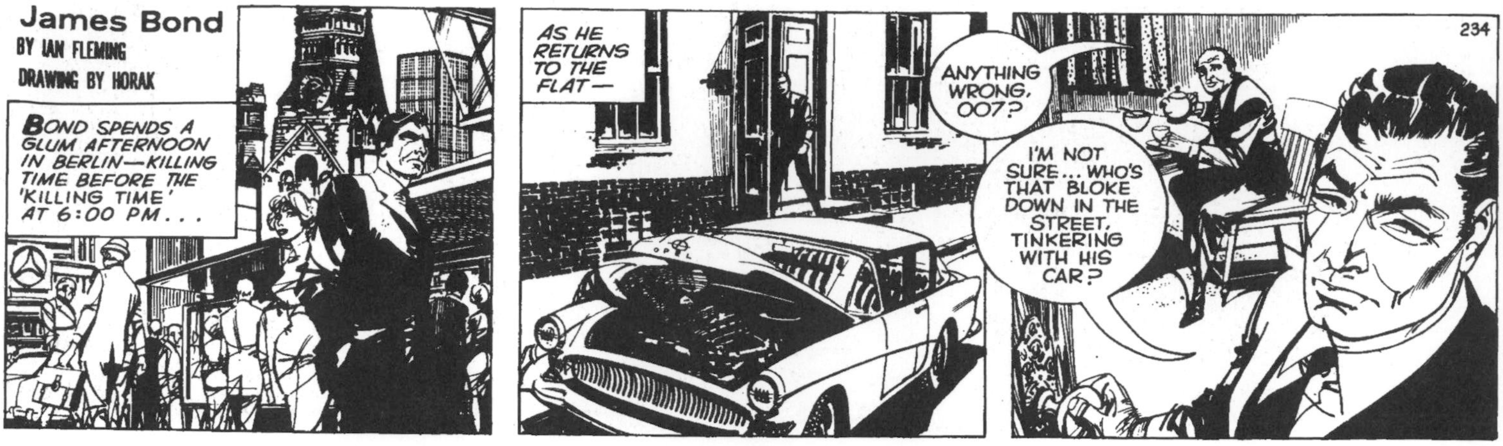
James Bond
BY IAN FLEMING
DRAWING BY HORAK
BOND SPENDS A GLUM AFTERNOON IN BERLIN—KILLING TIME BEFORE THE 'KILLING TIME' AT 6:00 PM . . .
AS HE RETURNS TO THE FLAT—
234
ANYTHING WRONG, 007?
I'M NOT SURE . . . WHO'S THAT BLOKE DOWN IN THE STREET, TINKERING WITH HIS CAR?

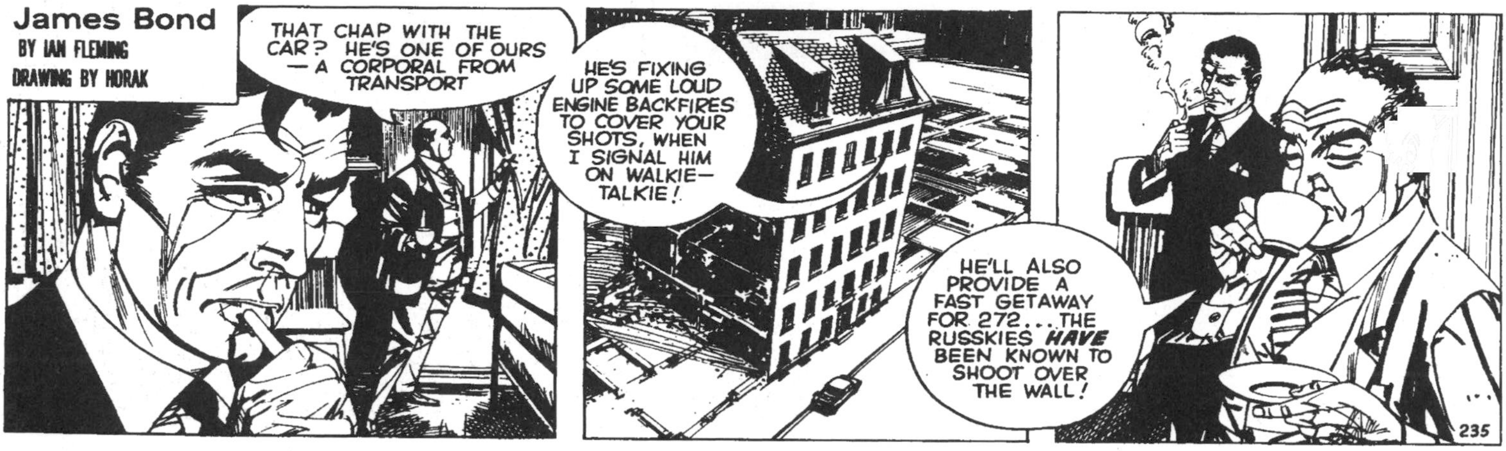
James Bond
BY IAN FLEMING
DRAWING BY HORAK
THAT CHAP WITH THE CAR? HE'S ONE OF OURS —A CORPORAL FROM TRANSPORT
HE'S FIXING UP SOME LOUD ENGINE BACKFIRES TO COVER YOUR SHOTS, WHEN I SIGNAL HIM ON WALKIE-TALKIE!
HE'LL ALSO PROVIDE A FAST GETAWAY FOR 272 . . . THE RUSSKIES HAVE BEEN KNOWN TO SHOOT OVER THE WALL!
235

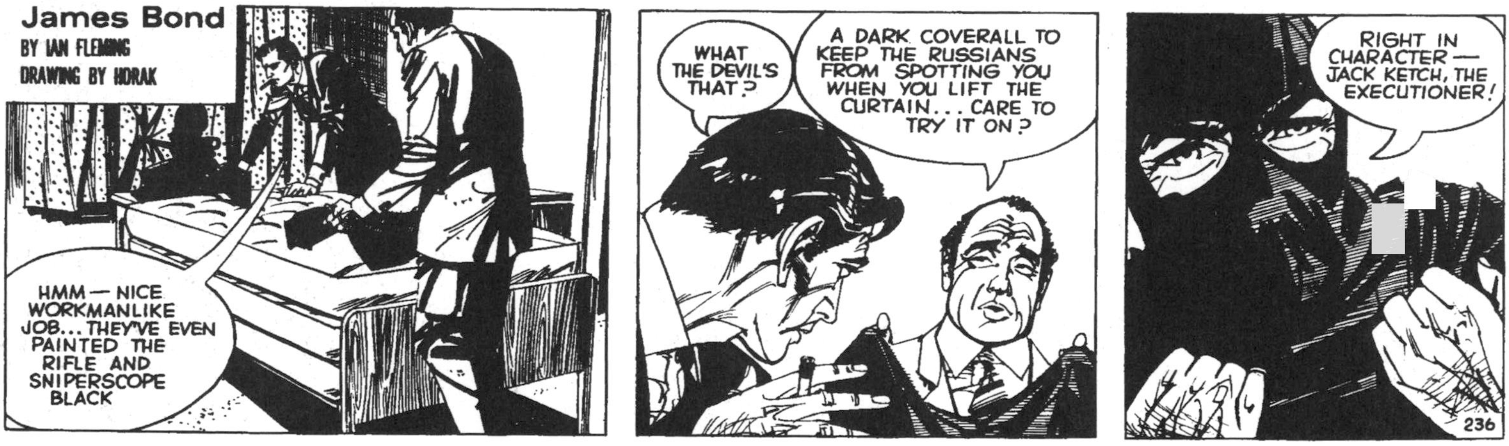
James Bond
BY IAN FLEMING
DRAWING BY HORAK
HMM—NICE WORKMANLIKE JOB . . . THEY'VE EVEN PAINTED THE RIFLE AND SNIPERSCOPE BLACK
WHAT THE DEVIL'S THAT?
A DARK COVERALL TO KEEP THE RUSSIANS FROM SPOTTING YOU WHEN YOU LIFT THE CURTAIN . . . CARE TO TRY IT ON?
RIGHT IN CHARACTER—JACK KETCH, THE EXECUTIONER!
236

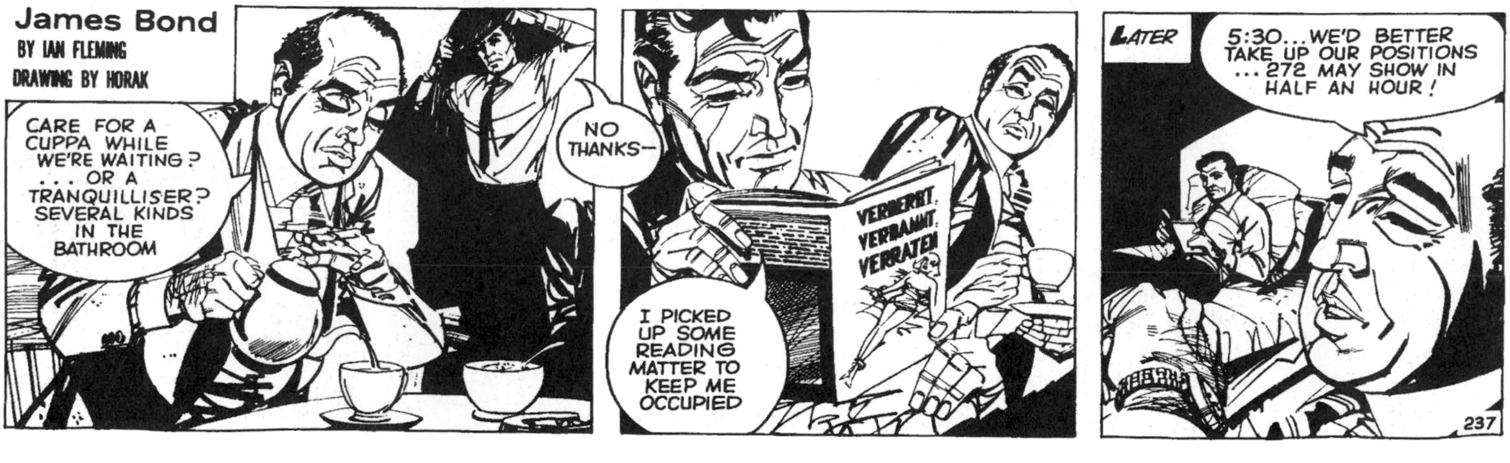
James Bond
BY IAN FLEMING
DRAWING BY HORAK
CARE FOR A CUPPA WHILE WE'RE WAITING? . . . OR A TRANQUILLISER? SEVERAL KINDS IN THE BATHROOM
NO THANKS—
VERDERBT, VERDAMMT, VERRATEN
I PICKED UP SOME READING MATTER TO KEEP ME OCCUPIED
LATER
5:30 . . . WE'D BETTER TAKE UP OUR POSITIONS . . . 272 MAY SHOW IN HALF AN HOUR!
237

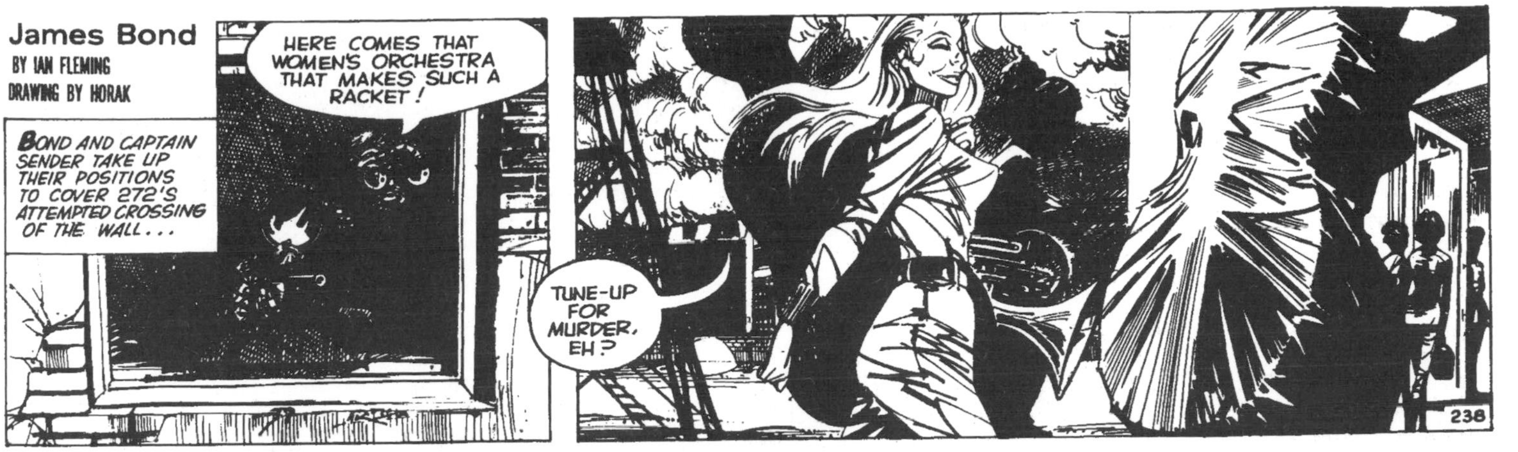
James Bond
BY IAN FLEMING
DRAWING BY HORAK
BOND AND CAPTAIN SENDER TAKE UP THEIR POSITIONS TO COVER 272'S ATTEMPTED CROSSING OF THE WALL...
HERE COMES THAT WOMEN'S ORCHESTRA THAT MAKES SUCH A RACKET!
TUNE-UP FOR MURDER, EH?
238

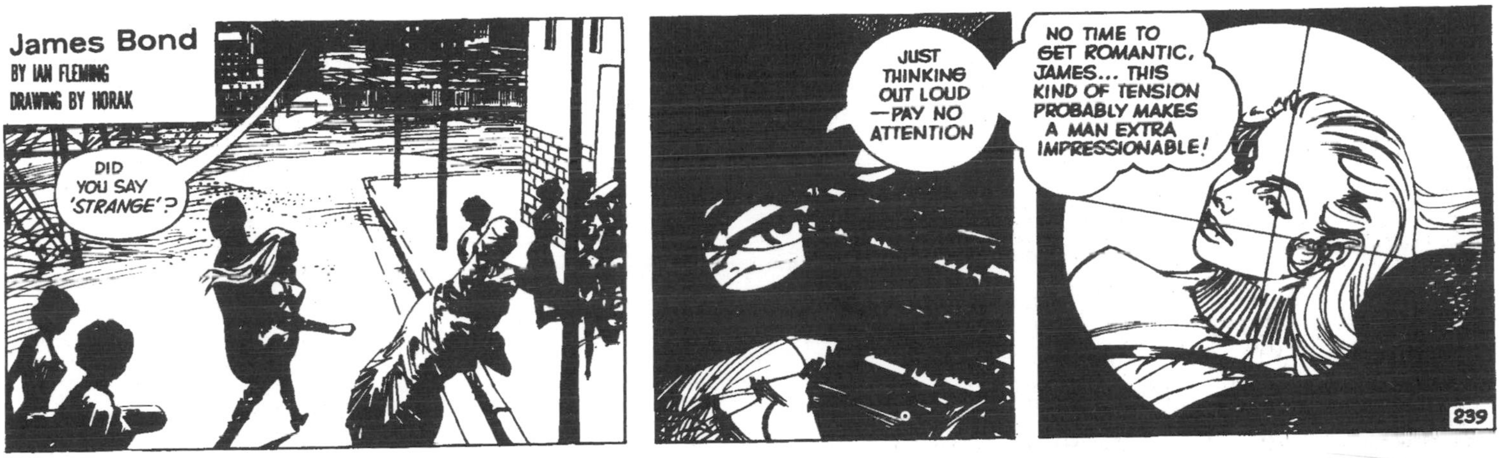
James Bond
BY IAN FLEMING
DRAWING BY HORAK
DID YOU SAY 'STRANGE'?
JUST THINKING OUT LOUD —PAY NO ATTENTION
NO TIME TO GET ROMANTIC, JAMES... THIS KIND OF TENSION PROBABLY MAKES A MAN EXTRA IMPRESSIONABLE!
239

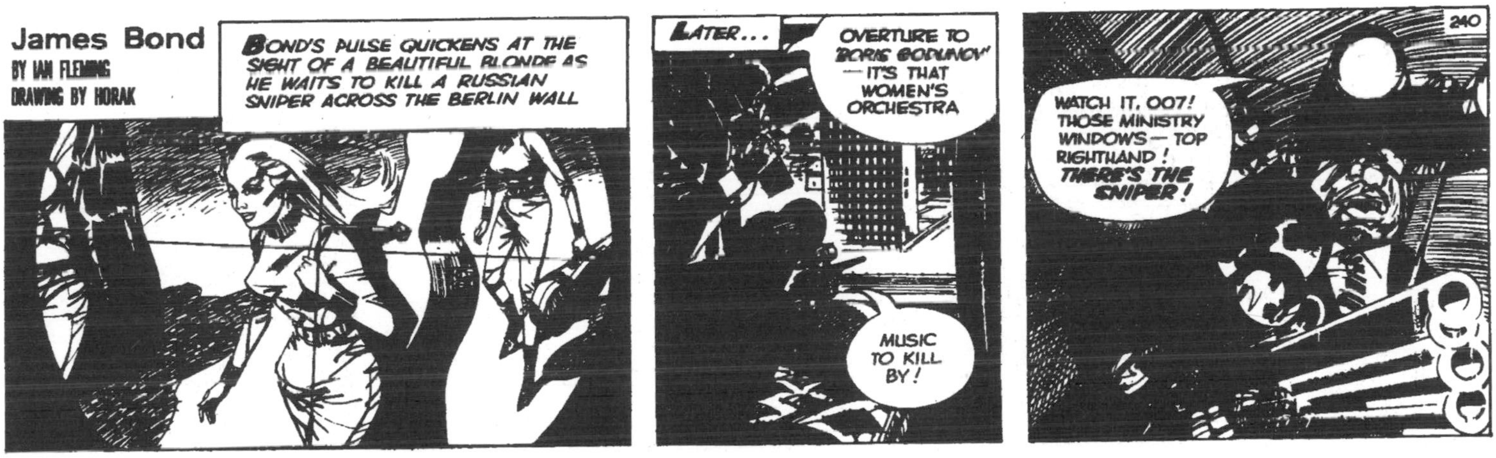
James Bond
BY IAN FLEMING
DRAWING BY HORAK
BOND'S PULSE QUICKENS AT THE SIGHT OF A BEAUTIFUL BLONDE AS HE WAITS TO KILL A RUSSIAN SNIPER ACROSS THE BERLIN WALL
LATER...
OVERTURE TO 'BORIS GODUNOV' —IT'S THAT WOMEN'S ORCHESTRA
MUSIC TO KILL BY!
240
WATCH IT, 007! THOSE MINISTRY WINDOWS — TOP RIGHTHAND! THERE'S THE SNIPER!

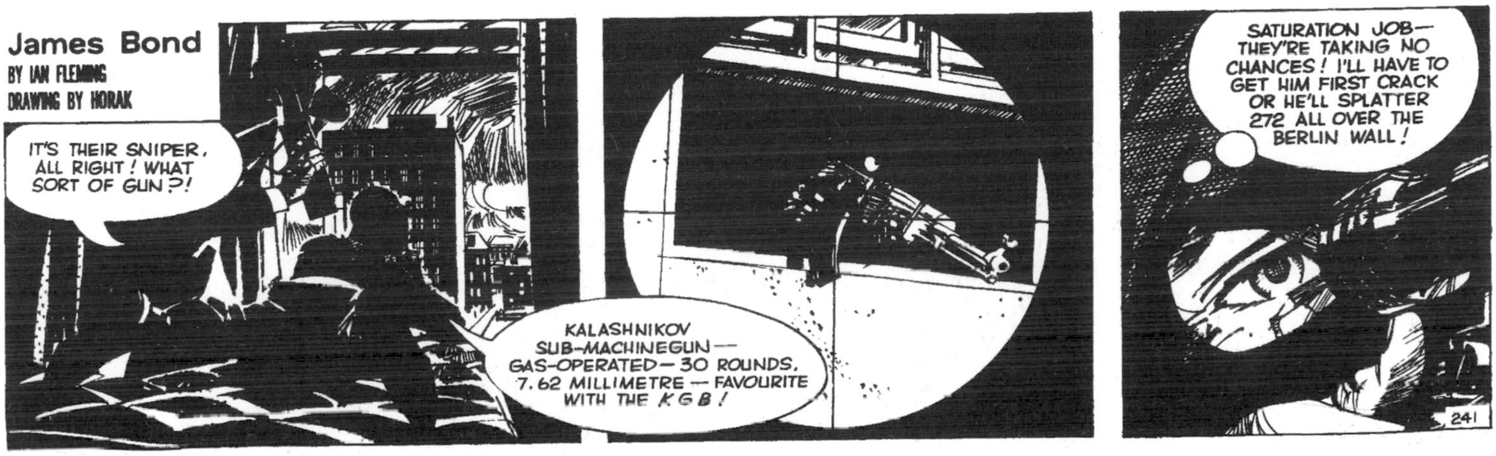
James Bond
BY IAN FLEMING
DRAWING BY HORAK
IT'S THEIR SNIPER, ALL RIGHT! WHAT SORT OF GUN?!
KALASHNIKOV SUB-MACHINEGUN— GAS-OPERATED—30 ROUNDS, 7.62 MILLIMETRE — FAVOURITE WITH THE KGB!
SATURATION JOB— THEY'RE TAKING NO CHANCES! I'LL HAVE TO GET HIM FIRST CRACK OR HE'LL SPLATTER 272 ALL OVER THE BERLIN WALL!
241

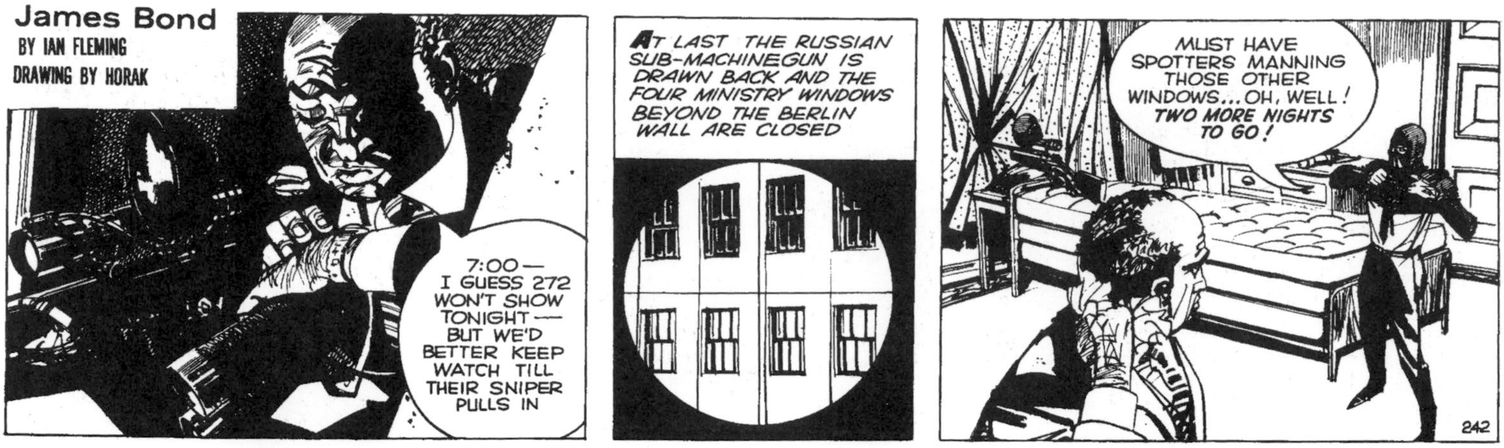
James Bond
BY IAN FLEMING
DRAWING BY HORAK
7:00— I GUESS 272 WON'T SHOW TONIGHT— BUT WE'D BETTER KEEP WATCH TILL THEIR SNIPER PULLS IN
AT LAST THE RUSSIAN SUB-MACHINEGUN IS DRAWN BACK AND THE FOUR MINISTRY WINDOWS BEYOND THE BERLIN WALL ARE CLOSED
MUST HAVE SPOTTERS MANNING THOSE OTHER WINDOWS...OH, WELL! TWO MORE NIGHTS TO GO!
242

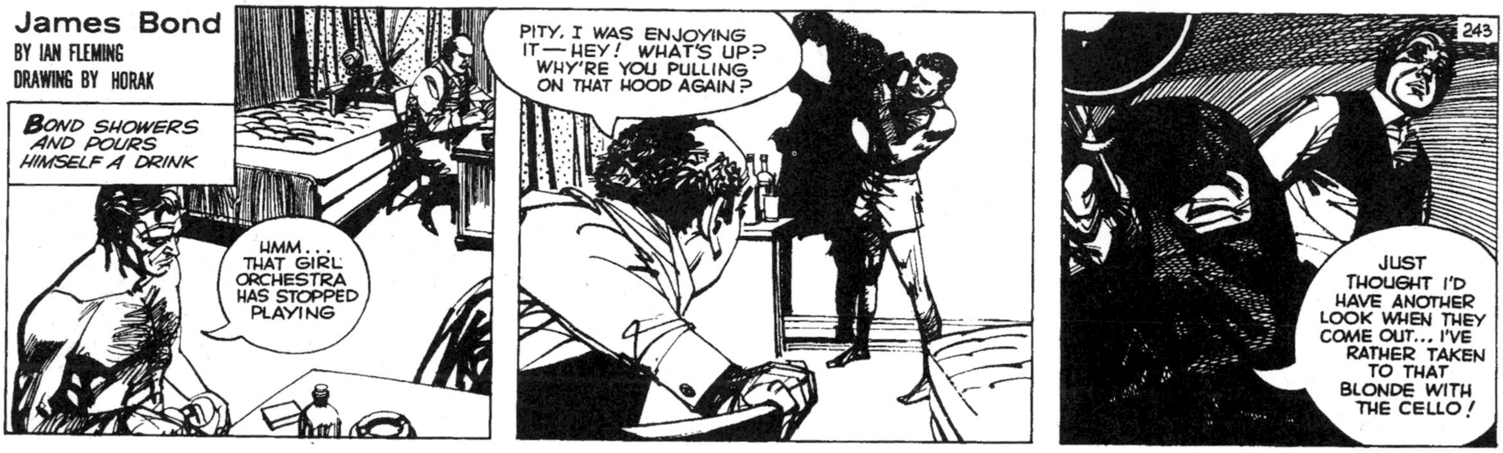
James Bond
BY IAN FLEMING
DRAWING BY HORAK
BOND SHOWERS AND POURS HIMSELF A DRINK
HMM... THAT GIRL ORCHESTRA HAS STOPPED PLAYING
PITY, I WAS ENJOYING IT—HEY! WHAT'S UP? WHY'RE YOU PULLING ON THAT HOOD AGAIN?
243
JUST THOUGHT I'D HAVE ANOTHER LOOK WHEN THEY COME OUT... I'VE RATHER TAKEN TO THAT BLONDE WITH THE CELLO!

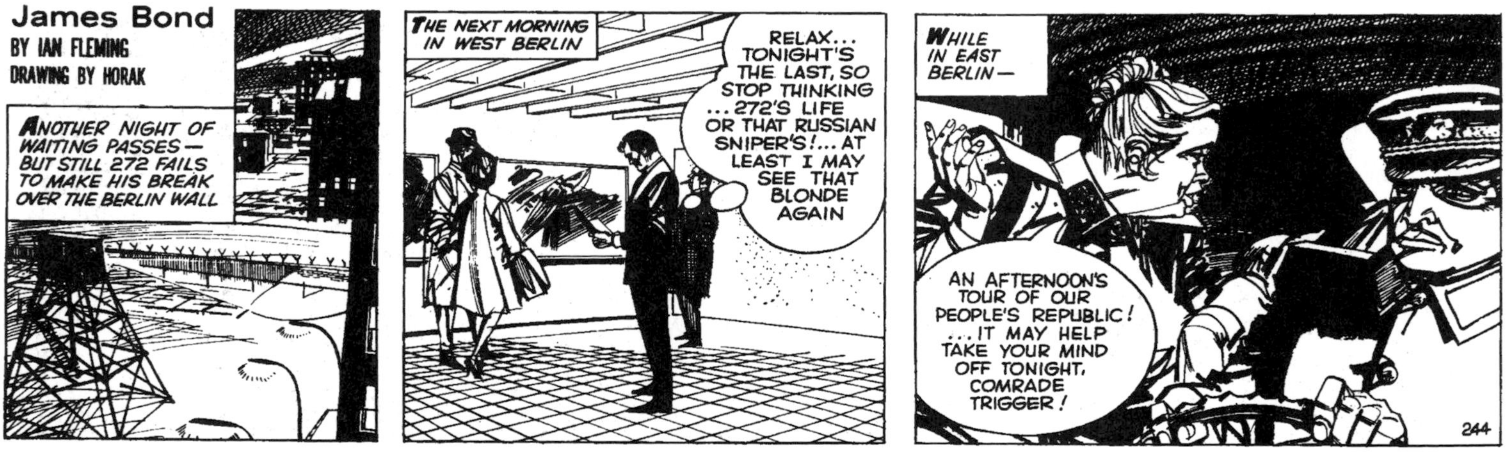
James Bond
BY IAN FLEMING
DRAWING BY HORAK
ANOTHER NIGHT OF WAITING PASSES— BUT STILL 272 FAILS TO MAKE HIS BREAK OVER THE BERLIN WALL
THE NEXT MORNING IN WEST BERLIN
RELAX... TONIGHT'S THE LAST, SO STOP THINKING ...272'S LIFE OR THAT RUSSIAN SNIPER'S!... AT LEAST I MAY SEE THAT BLONDE AGAIN
WHILE IN EAST BERLIN—
AN AFTERNOON'S TOUR OF OUR PEOPLE'S REPUBLIC! ...IT MAY HELP TAKE YOUR MIND OFF TONIGHT, COMRADE TRIGGER!
244

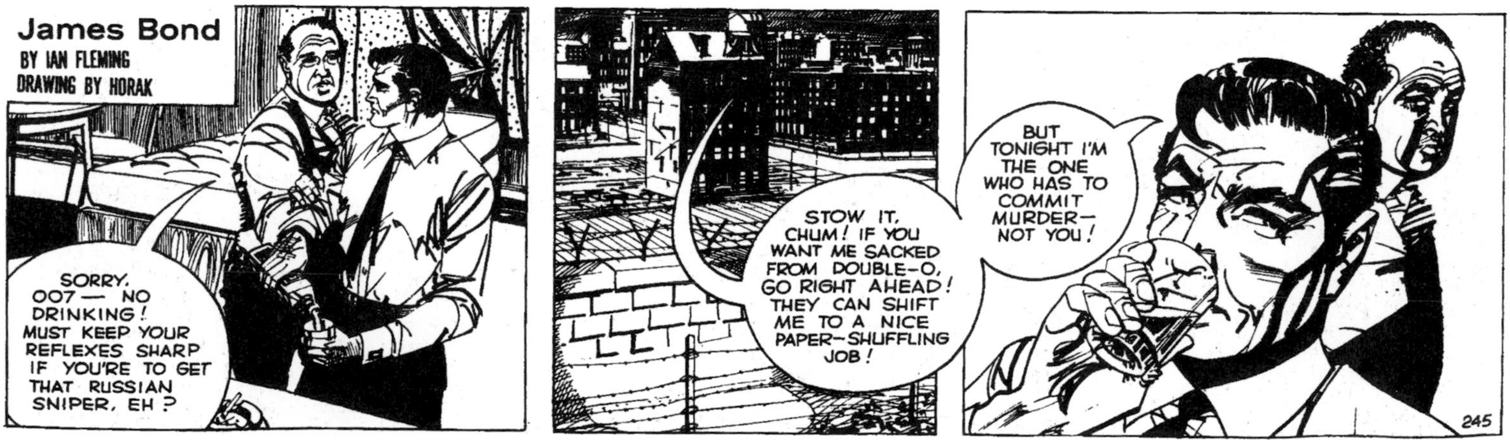
James Bond
BY IAN FLEMING
DRAWING BY HORAK
SORRY, 007— NO DRINKING! MUST KEEP YOUR REFLEXES SHARP IF YOU'RE TO GET THAT RUSSIAN SNIPER, EH?
STOW IT, CHUM! IF YOU WANT ME SACKED FROM DOUBLE-O, GO RIGHT AHEAD! THEY CAN SHIFT ME TO A NICE PAPER-SHUFFLING JOB!
BUT TONIGHT I'M THE ONE WHO HAS TO COMMIT MURDER— NOT YOU!
245

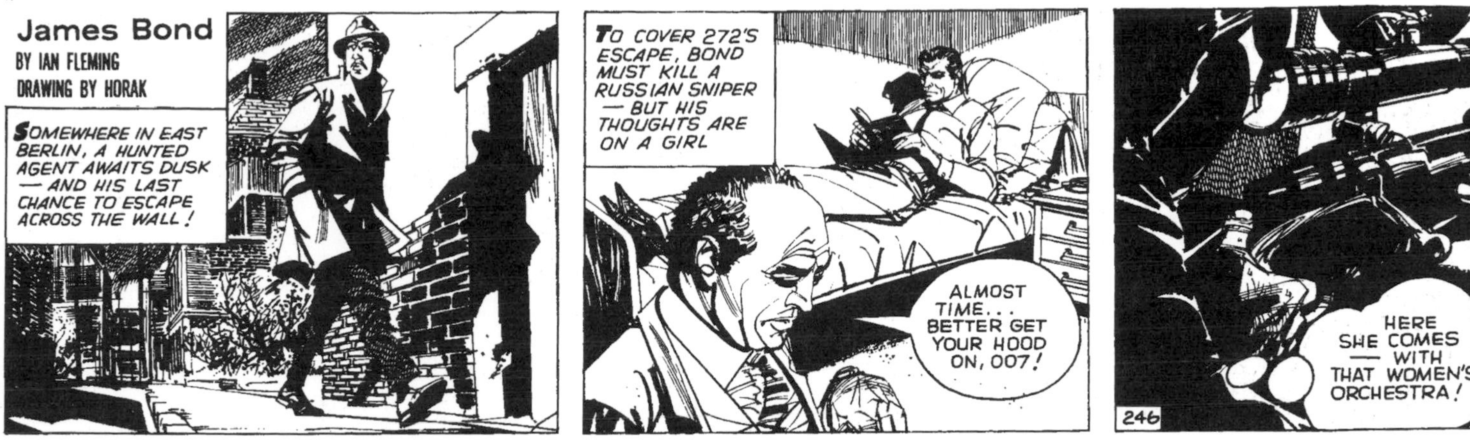
James Bond
BY IAN FLEMING
DRAWING BY HORAK
SOMEWHERE IN EAST BERLIN, A HUNTED AGENT AWAITS DUSK — AND HIS LAST CHANCE TO ESCAPE ACROSS THE WALL!
TO COVER 272'S ESCAPE, BOND MUST KILL A RUSSIAN SNIPER — BUT HIS THOUGHTS ARE ON A GIRL
ALMOST TIME... BETTER GET YOUR HOOD ON, 007!
HERE SHE COMES — WITH THAT WOMEN'S ORCHESTRA!
246

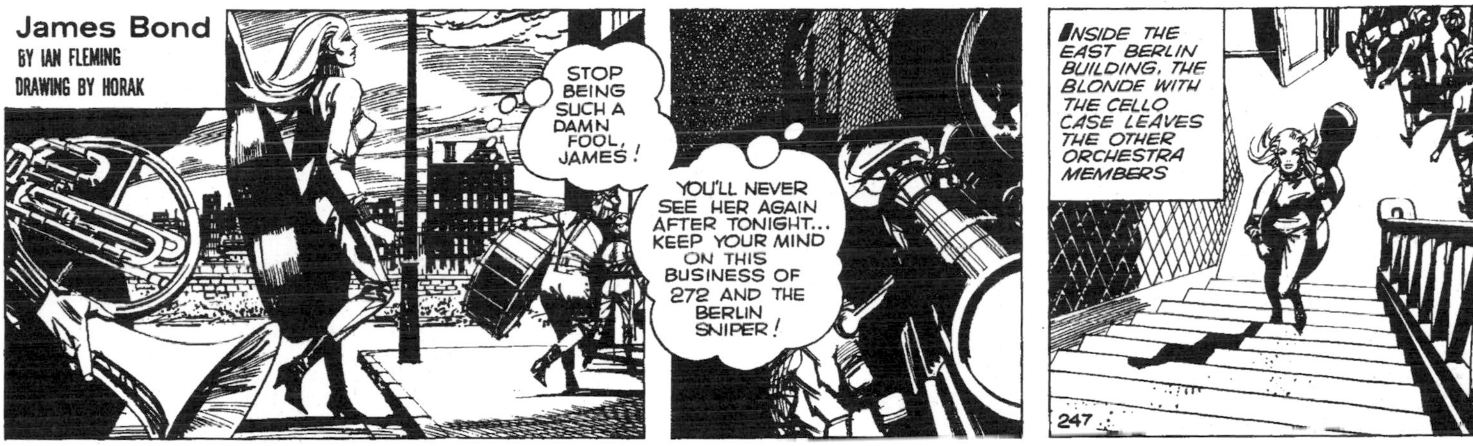
James Bond
BY IAN FLEMING
DRAWING BY HORAK
STOP BEING SUCH A DAMN FOOL, JAMES!
YOU'LL NEVER SEE HER AGAIN AFTER TONIGHT... KEEP YOUR MIND ON THIS BUSINESS OF 272 AND THE BERLIN SNIPER!
INSIDE THE EAST BERLIN BUILDING, THE BLONDE WITH THE CELLO CASE LEAVES THE OTHER ORCHESTRA MEMBERS
247

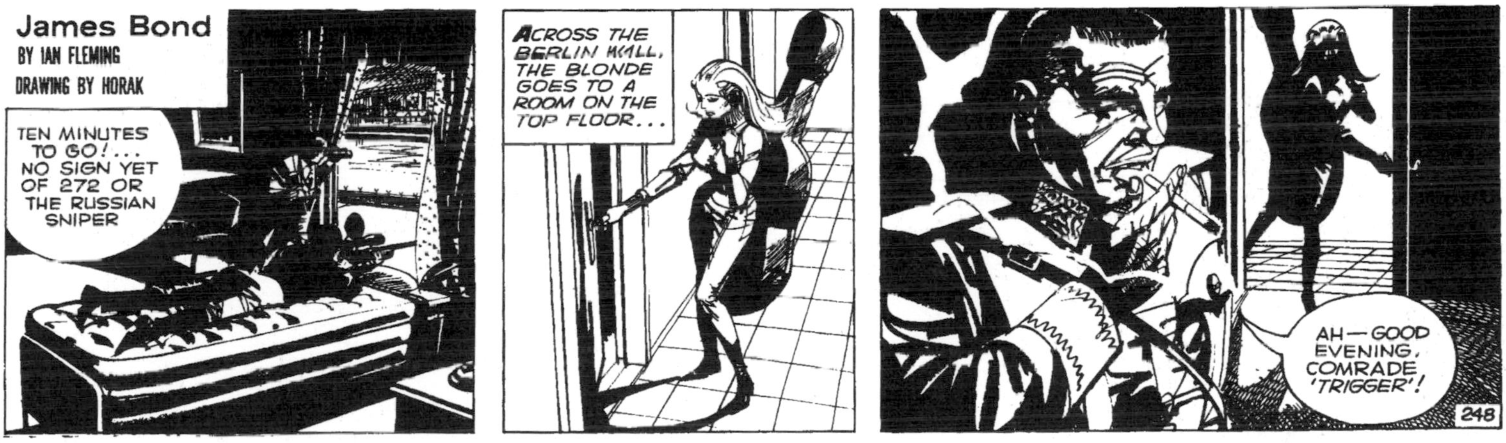
James Bond
BY IAN FLEMING
DRAWING BY HORAK
TEN MINUTES TO GO!... NO SIGN YET OF 272 OR THE RUSSIAN SNIPER
ACROSS THE BERLIN WALL, THE BLONDE GOES TO A ROOM ON THE TOP FLOOR...
AH—GOOD EVENING, COMRADE 'TRIGGER'!
248

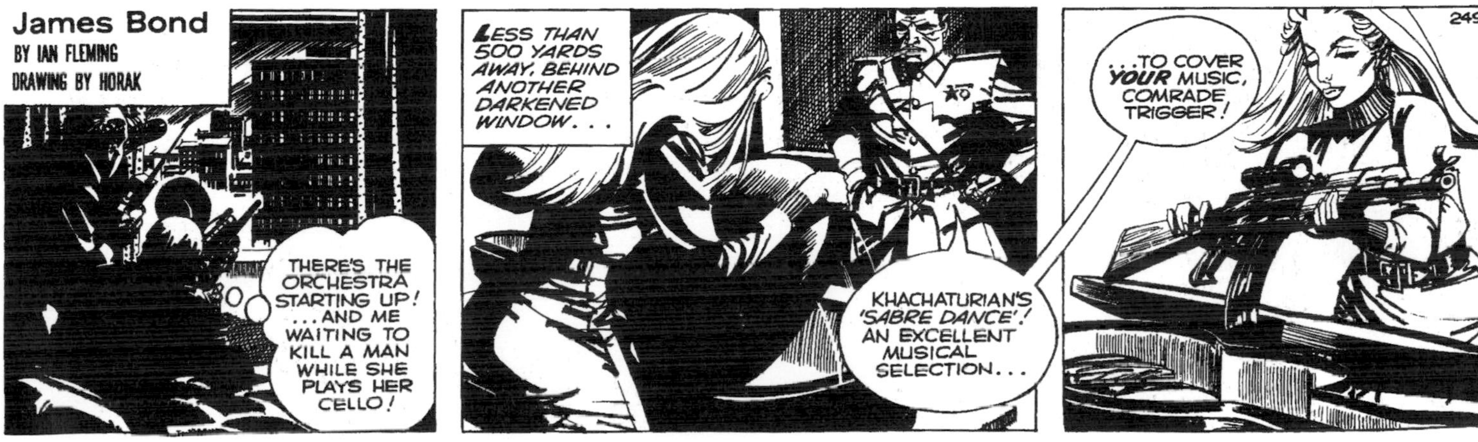
James Bond
BY IAN FLEMING
DRAWING BY HORAK
THERE'S THE ORCHESTRA STARTING UP! ...AND ME WAITING TO KILL A MAN WHILE SHE PLAYS HER CELLO!
LESS THAN 500 YARDS AWAY, BEHIND ANOTHER DARKENED WINDOW...
KHACHATURIAN'S 'SABRE DANCE'! AN EXCELLENT MUSICAL SELECTION...
...TO COVER YOUR MUSIC, COMRADE TRIGGER!
249

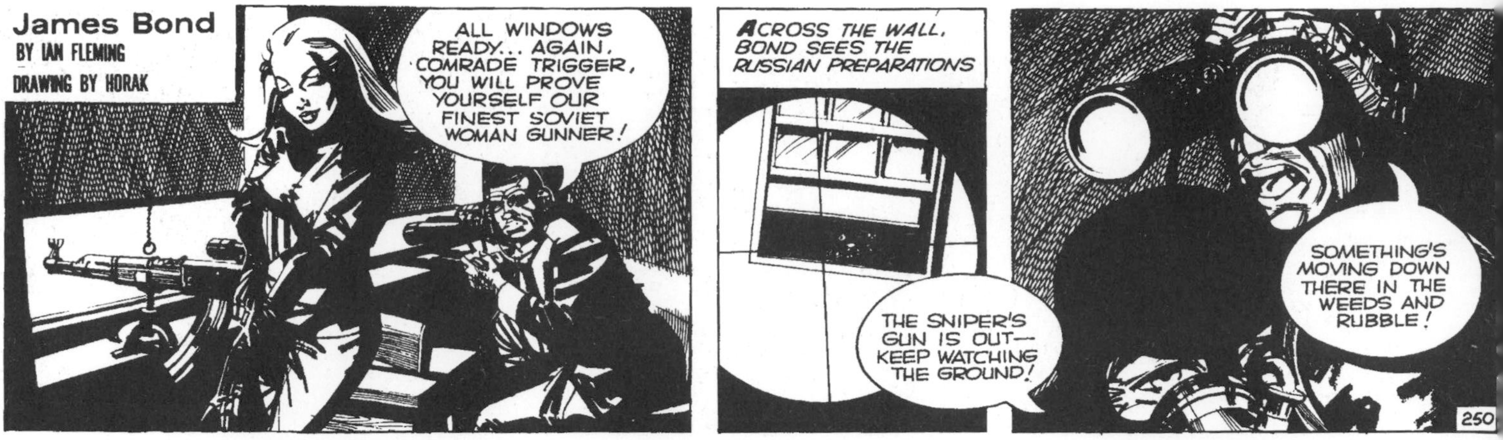
James Bond
BY IAN FLEMING
DRAWING BY HORAK
ALL WINDOWS READY... AGAIN, COMRADE TRIGGER, YOU WILL PROVE YOURSELF OUR FINEST SOVIET WOMAN GUNNER!
ACROSS THE WALL, BOND SEES THE RUSSIAN PREPARATIONS
THE SNIPER'S GUN IS OUT— KEEP WATCHING THE GROUND!
SOMETHING'S MOVING DOWN THERE IN THE WEEDS AND RUBBLE!
250

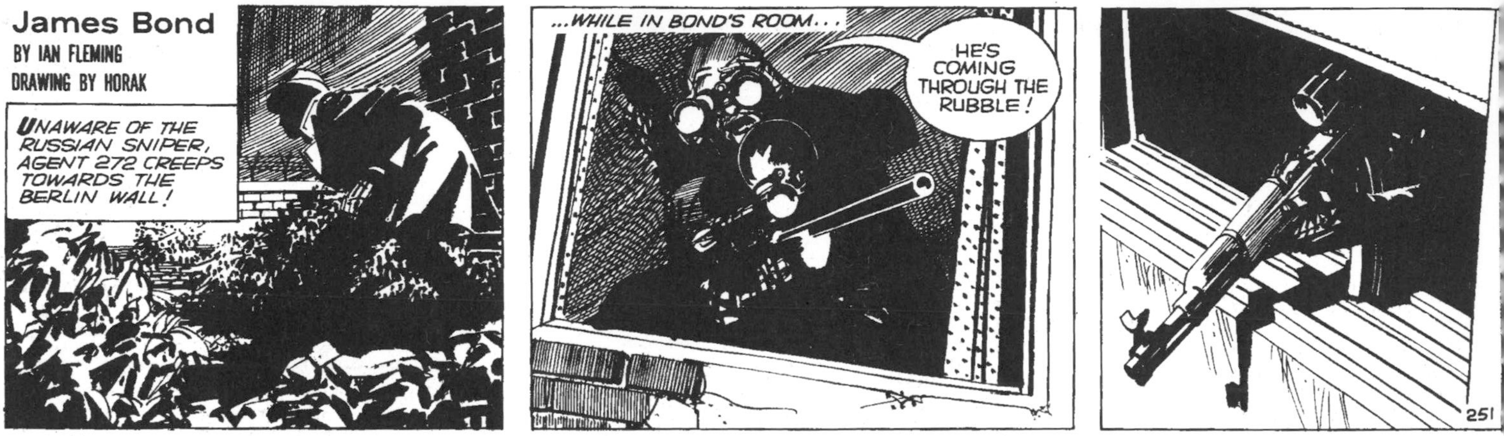
James Bond
BY IAN FLEMING
DRAWING BY HORAK
UNAWARE OF THE RUSSIAN SNIPER, AGENT 272 CREEPS TOWARDS THE BERLIN WALL!
...WHILE IN BOND'S ROOM...
HE'S COMING THROUGH THE RUBBLE!
251

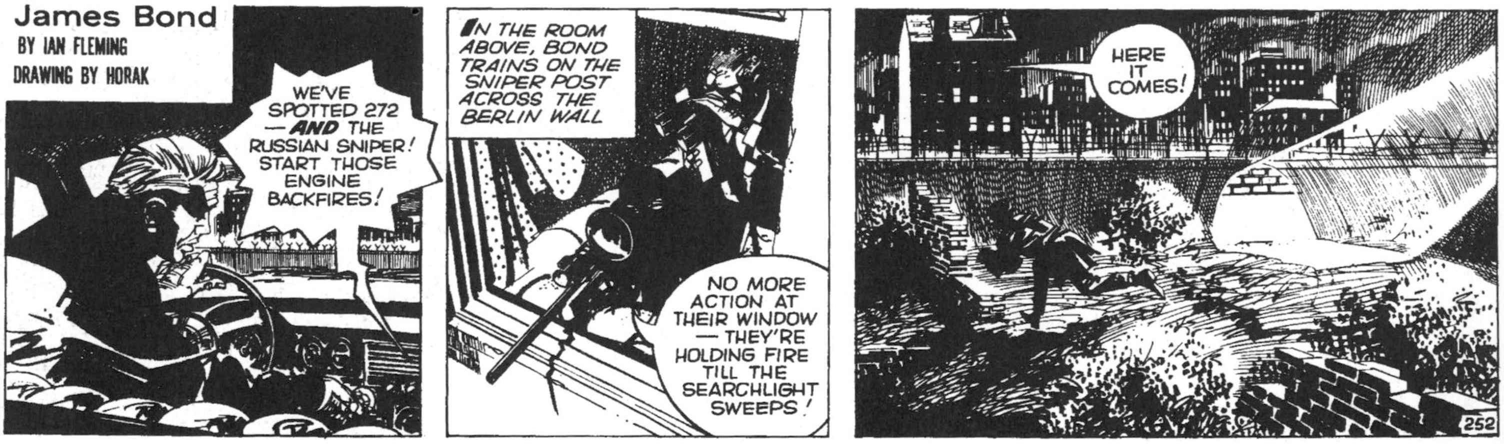
James Bond
BY IAN FLEMING
DRAWING BY HORAK
WE'VE SPOTTED 272 —AND THE RUSSIAN SNIPER! START THOSE ENGINE BACKFIRES!
IN THE ROOM ABOVE, BOND TRAINS ON THE SNIPER POST ACROSS THE BERLIN WALL
NO MORE ACTION AT THEIR WINDOW — THEY'RE HOLDING FIRE TILL THE SEARCHLIGHT SWEEPS!
HERE IT COMES!
252

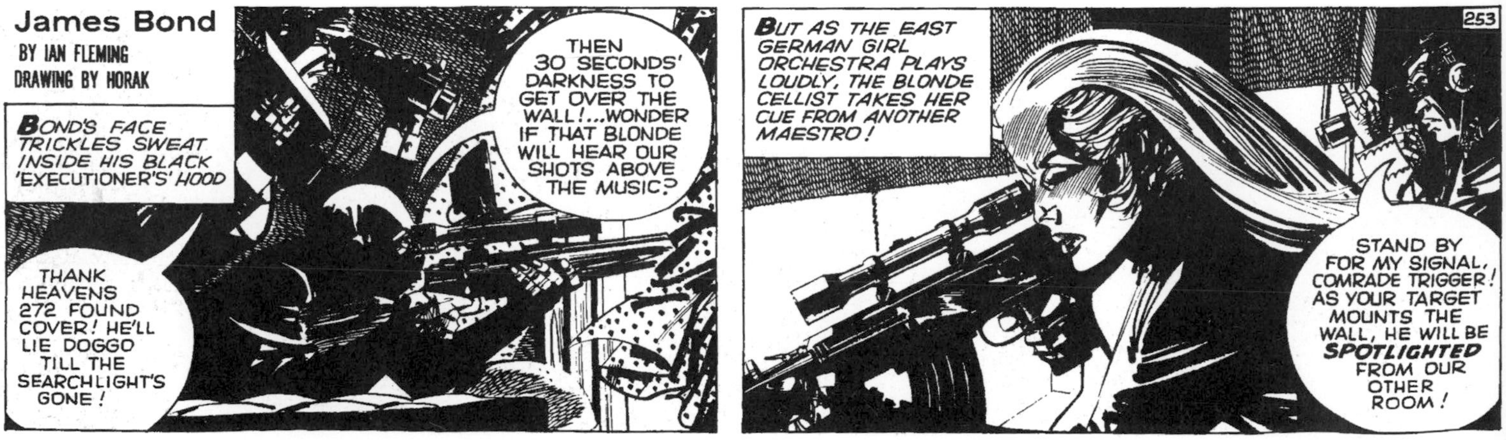
James Bond
BY IAN FLEMING
DRAWING BY HORAK
BOND'S FACE TRICKLES SWEAT INSIDE HIS BLACK 'EXECUTIONER'S' HOOD
THEN 30 SECONDS' DARKNESS TO GET OVER THE WALL!...WONDER IF THAT BLONDE WILL HEAR OUR SHOTS ABOVE THE MUSIC?
THANK HEAVENS 272 FOUND COVER! HE'LL LIE DOGGO TILL THE SEARCHLIGHT'S GONE!
253
BUT AS THE EAST GERMAN GIRL ORCHESTRA PLAYS LOUDLY, THE BLONDE CELLIST TAKES HER CUE FROM ANOTHER MAESTRO!
STAND BY FOR MY SIGNAL, COMRADE TRIGGER! AS YOUR TARGET MOUNTS THE WALL, HE WILL BE SPOTLIGHTED FROM OUR OTHER ROOM!

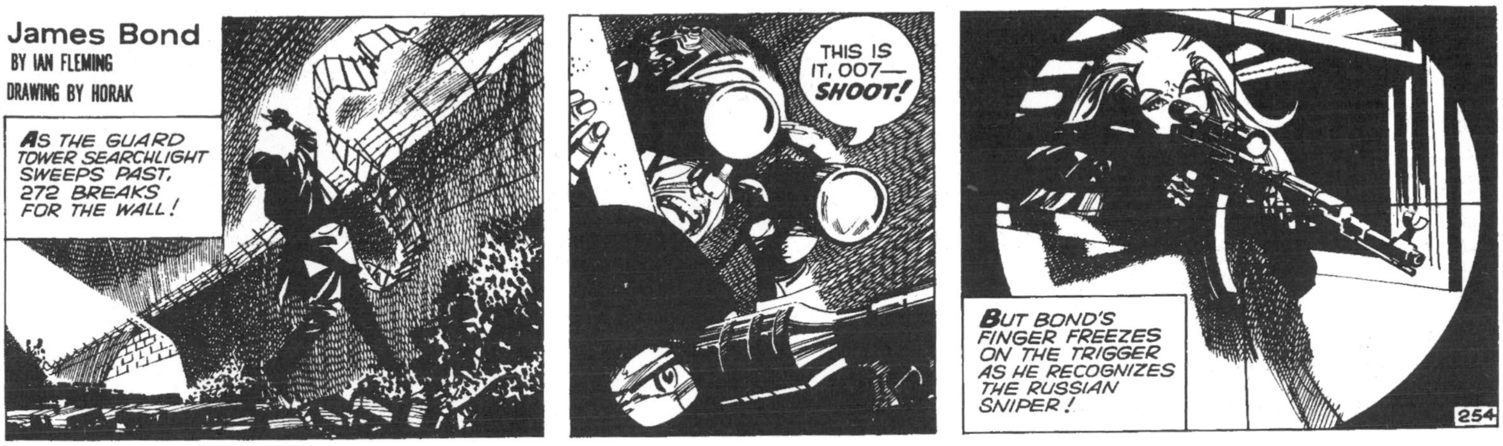
James Bond
BY IAN FLEMING
DRAWING BY HORAK
AS THE GUARD TOWER SEARCHLIGHT SWEEPS PAST, 272 BREAKS FOR THE WALL!
THIS IS IT, 007— SHOOT!
BUT BOND'S FINGER FREEZES ON THE TRIGGER AS HE RECOGNIZES THE RUSSIAN SNIPER!
254

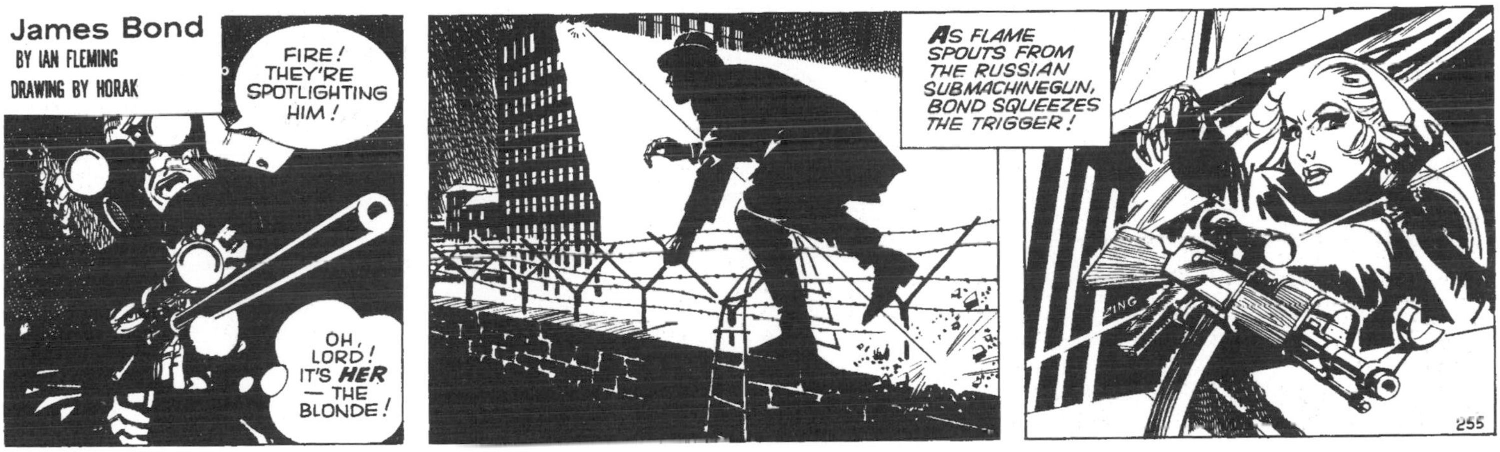
James Bond
BY IAN FLEMING
DRAWING BY HORAK
FIRE! THEY'RE SPOTLIGHTING HIM!
OH, LORD! IT'S HER — THE BLONDE!
AS FLAME SPOUTS FROM THE RUSSIAN SUBMACHINEGUN, BOND SQUEEZES THE TRIGGER!
ZING
255

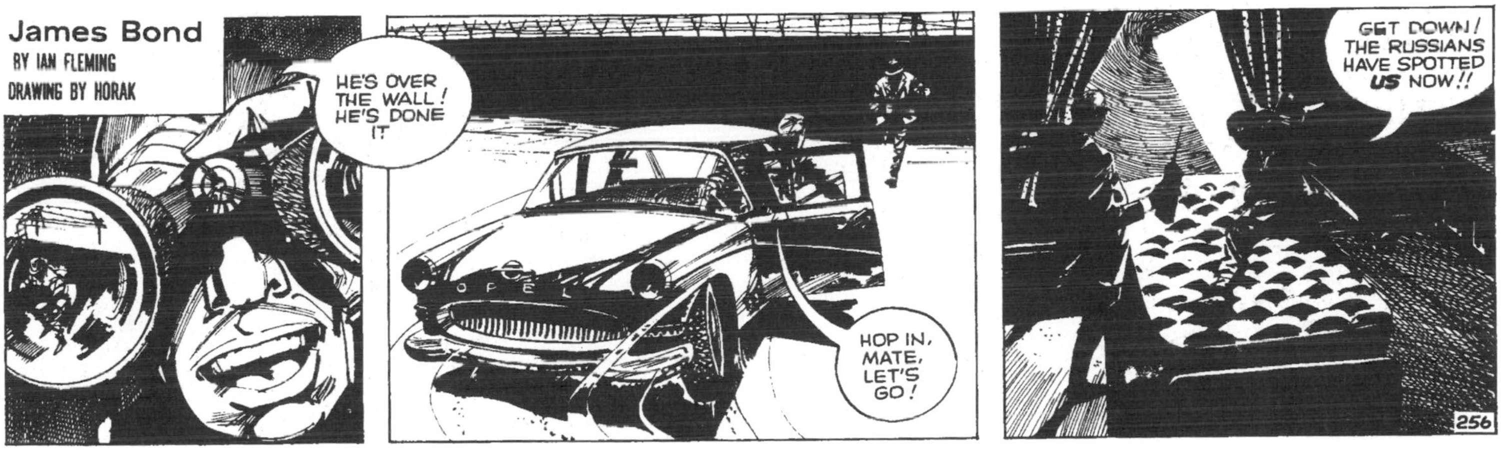
James Bond
BY IAN FLEMING
DRAWING BY HORAK
HE'S OVER THE WALL! HE'S DONE IT
OPEL
HOP IN, MATE, LET'S GO!
GET DOWN! THE RUSSIANS HAVE SPOTTED US NOW!!
256

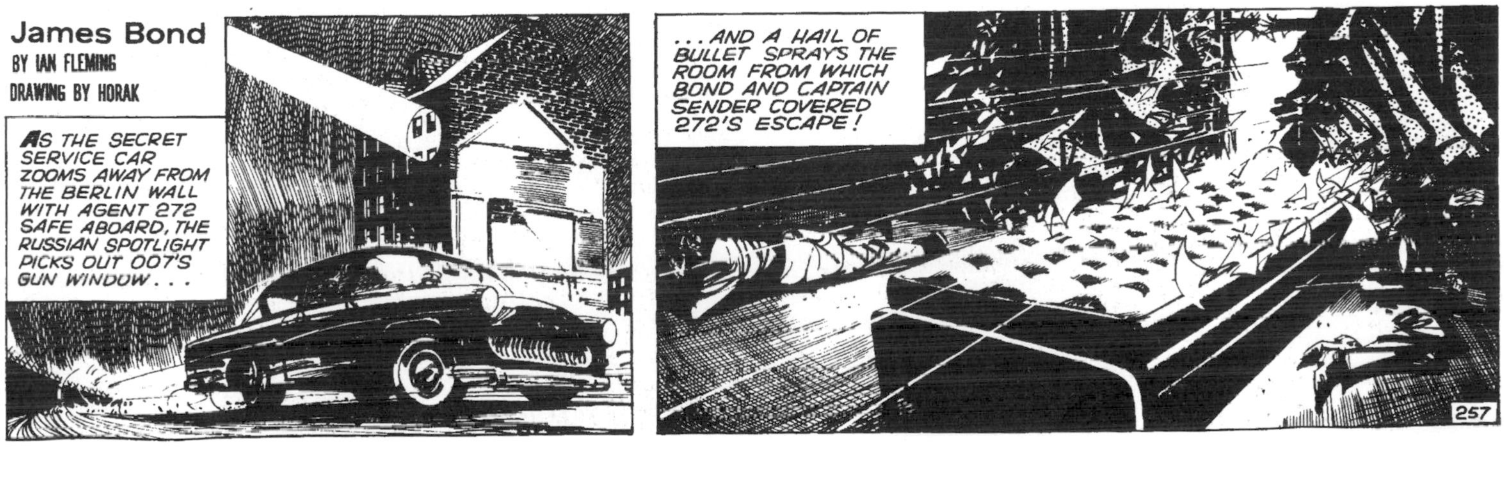
James Bond
BY IAN FLEMING
DRAWING BY HORAK
AS THE SECRET SERVICE CAR ZOOMS AWAY FROM THE BERLIN WALL WITH AGENT 272 SAFE ABOARD, THE RUSSIAN SPOTLIGHT PICKS OUT 007'S GUN WINDOW . . .
. . . AND A HAIL OF BULLET SPRAYS THE ROOM FROM WHICH BOND AND CAPTAIN SENDER COVERED 272'S ESCAPE!
257

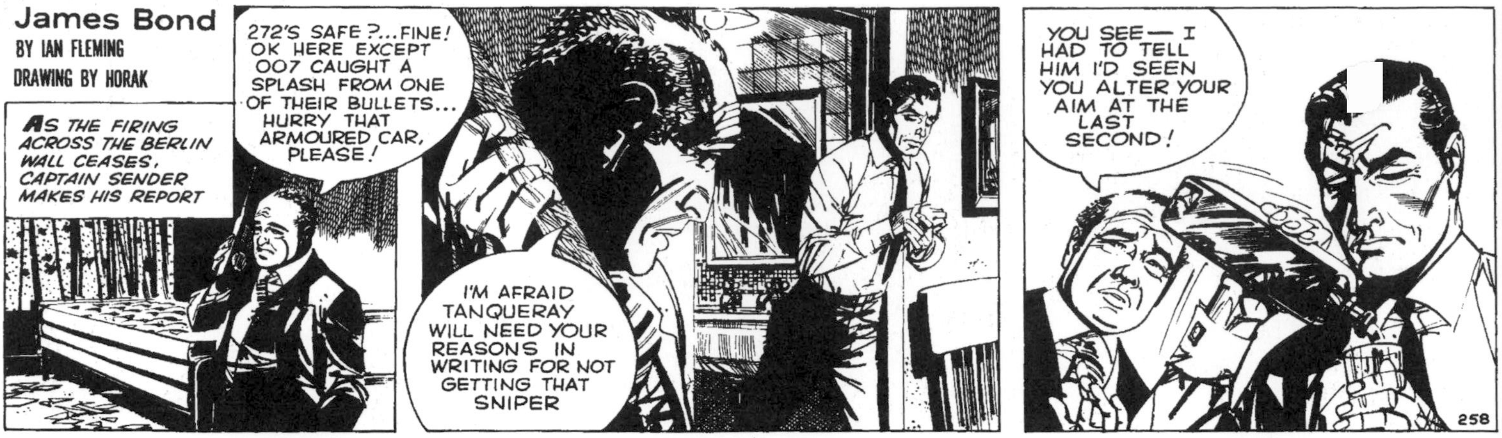
James Bond
BY IAN FLEMING
DRAWING BY HORAK
AS THE FIRING ACROSS THE BERLIN WALL CEASES, CAPTAIN SENDER MAKES HIS REPORT
272'S SAFE?...FINE! OK HERE EXCEPT 007 CAUGHT A SPLASH FROM ONE OF THEIR BULLETS... HURRY THAT ARMOURED CAR, PLEASE!
I'M AFRAID TANQUERAY WILL NEED YOUR REASONS IN WRITING FOR NOT GETTING THAT SNIPER
YOU SEE— I HAD TO TELL HIM I'D SEEN YOU ALTER YOUR AIM AT THE LAST SECOND!
258

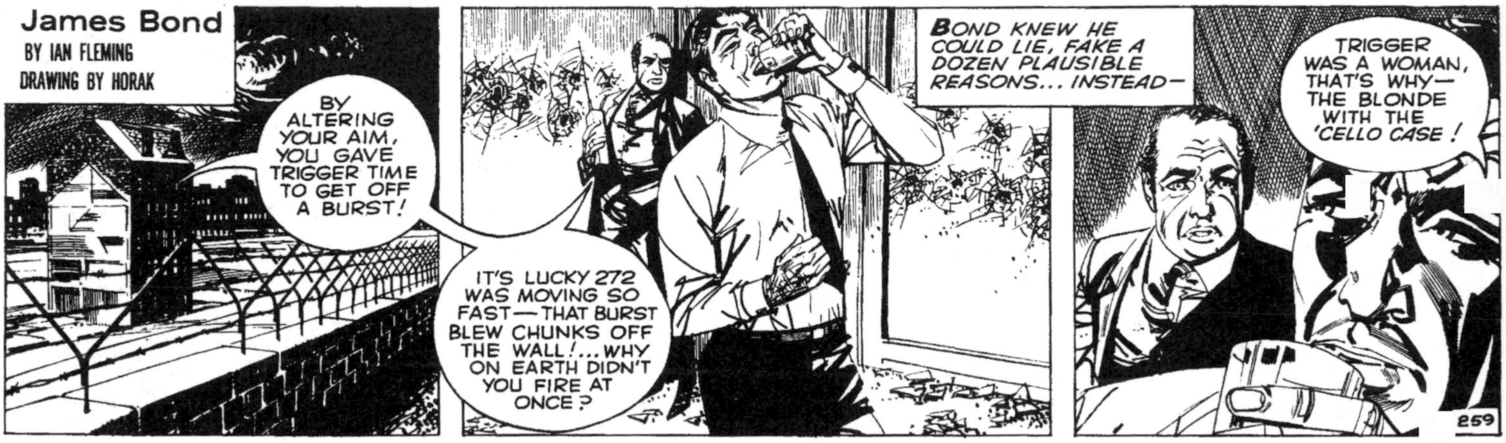
James Bond
BY IAN FLEMING
DRAWING BY HORAK
BY ALTERING YOUR AIM, YOU GAVE TRIGGER TIME TO GET OFF A BURST!
IT'S LUCKY 272 WAS MOVING SO FAST—THAT BURST BLEW CHUNKS OFF THE WALL!...WHY ON EARTH DIDN'T YOU FIRE AT ONCE?
BOND KNEW HE COULD LIE, FAKE A DOZEN PLAUSIBLE REASONS... INSTEAD—
TRIGGER WAS A WOMAN, THAT'S WHY— THE BLONDE WITH THE 'CELLO CASE!
259

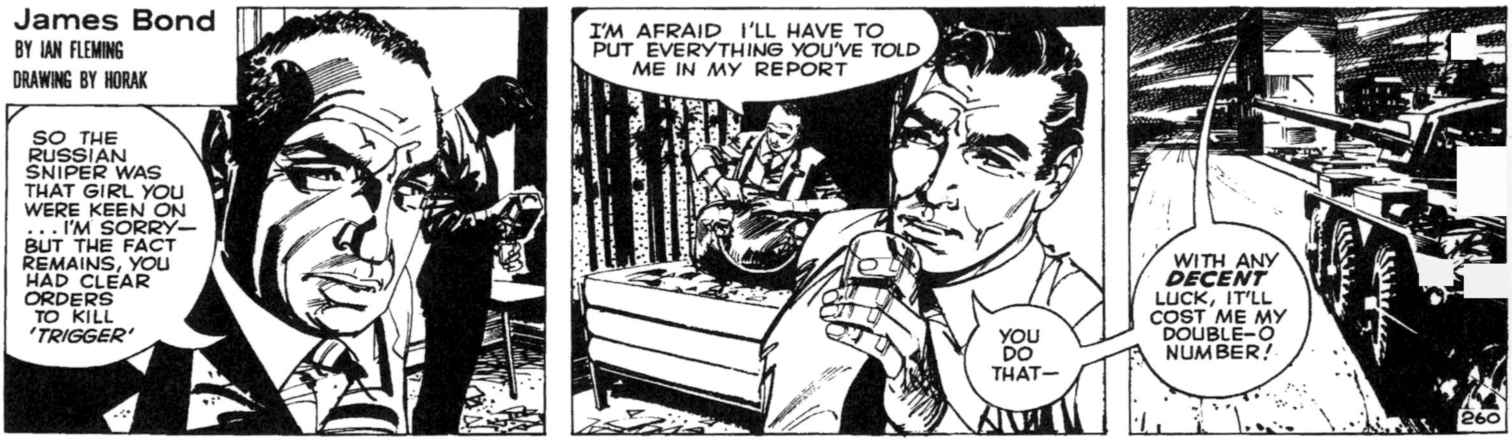
James Bond
BY IAN FLEMING
DRAWING BY HORAK
SO THE RUSSIAN SNIPER WAS THAT GIRL YOU WERE KEEN ON ... I'M SORRY— BUT THE FACT REMAINS, YOU HAD CLEAR ORDERS TO KILL 'TRIGGER'
I'M AFRAID I'LL HAVE TO PUT EVERYTHING YOU'VE TOLD ME IN MY REPORT
YOU DO THAT—
WITH ANY DECENT LUCK, IT'LL COST ME MY DOUBLE-O NUMBER!
260

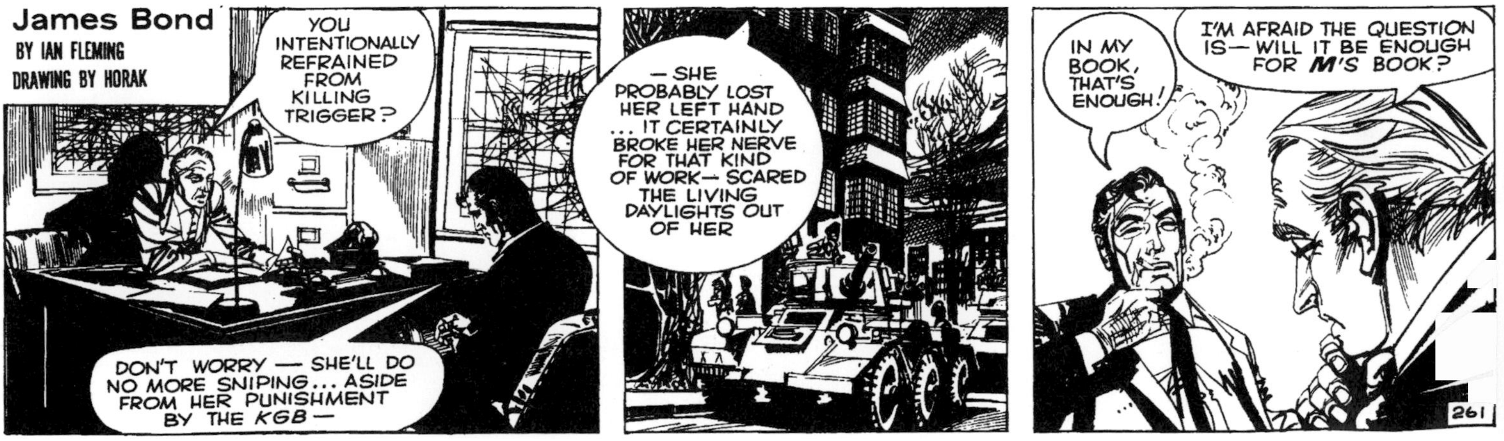
James Bond
BY IAN FLEMING
DRAWING BY HORAK
YOU INTENTIONALLY REFRAINED FROM KILLING TRIGGER?
DON'T WORRY — SHE'LL DO NO MORE SNIPING... ASIDE FROM HER PUNISHMENT BY THE KGB —
—SHE PROBABLY LOST HER LEFT HAND ... IT CERTAINLY BROKE HER NERVE FOR THAT KIND OF WORK— SCARED THE LIVING DAYLIGHTS OUT OF HER
IN MY BOOK, THAT'S ENOUGH!
I'M AFRAID THE QUESTION IS— WILL IT BE ENOUGH FOR M'S BOOK?
261

James Bond
BY IAN FLEMING
DRAWING BY HORAK

BOND FLIES HOME TO LONDON, STILL HAUNTED BY THE MEMORY OF THE RUSSIAN GIRL SNIPER

POOR LITTLE B—! SHE'S IN WORSE TROUBLE THAN I AM!

WHILE AT M.I.5

M. WANTS TO SEE YOU... IT'S ABOUT JAMES, I THINK

COME IN, CHIEF OF STAFF... I EXPECT YOU'VE SEEN THIS SIGNAL FROM BERLIN

262

James Bond
BY IAN FLEMING
DRAWING BY HORAK

WELCOME BACK, JAMES! SEEN THE PAPER?

LET'S NOT BEAT AROUND THE BUSH, BILL— WHAT'S MY FATE WITH M.?

HMM, WELL — INASMUCH AS 272 ESCAPED SAFELY, HE SEES NO REASON TO DISCIPLINE AN OFFICER SUFFERING FROM DELUSIONS OF ROMANTIC CHIVALRY TOWARDS WOMEN

263

SO THE MATTER'S CLOSED— SINCE IN YOUR CASE THE MALADY APPEARS INCURABLE!

World champion Russian woman marksman repor killed in shooting nge accident

End of story

THE COMPLETE JAMES BOND SYNDICATED NEWSPAPER CHECKLIST

The following is the first complete checklist of *James Bond* strips to have appeared in the *Express* newspapers and been syndicated in non-UK newspapers.

STORY	WRITER	ARTISTS	DATE	SERIAL No.
Serialised in the *Daily Express*				
Casino Royale	IF/AH	JM	7.7.58–13.12.58	1–138
Live and Let Die	IF/HG	JM	15.12.58–28.3.59	139-225
Moonraker	IF/HG	JM	30.3.59–8.8.59	226-339
Diamonds Are Forever	IF/HG	JM	10.8.59–30.1.60	340–487
From Russia With Love	IF/HG	JM	3.2.60–21.5.60	488–583
Dr. No	IF/PO	JM	23.5.60–1.10.60	584–697
Goldfinger	IF/HG	JM	3.10.60–1.4.61	698–849
Risico	IF/HG	JM	3.4.61–24.6.61	850–921
From A View To A Kill	IF/HG	JM	25.6.61–9.9.61	922–987
For Your Eyes Only	IF/HG	JM	11.9.61–9.12.61	988–1065
Thunderball	IF/HG	JM	11.12.61–10.2.62	1066–1128*

**Series aborted prematurely*

STORY	WRITER	ARTISTS	DATE	SERIAL No.
(Series Two)				
On Her Majesty's Secret Service	IF/HG	JM	29.6.64–17.5.65	1–274
You Only Live Twice	IF/HG	JM	18.5.65–8.1.66	275–475
(Series Three)				
The Man With the Golden Gun	IF/JL	YH	10.1.66–10.9.66	1–209
The Living Daylights	IF/JL	YH	12.9.66–12.11.66	210–263
Octopussy	IF/JL	YH	14.11.66–27.5.67	264–428
The Hildebrand Rarity	IF/JL	YH	29.5.67–16.12.67	429–602
The Spy Who Loved Me	IF/JL	YH	18.12.67–3.10.68	603–815
The Harpies	JL	YH	4.10.68–23.6.69	816–1037
River of Death	JL	YH	24.6.69–29.11.69	1038–1174
Colonel Sun	KA/JL	YH	1.12.69–20.8.70	1175–1393
The Golden Ghost	JL	YH	21.8.70–16.1.71	1394–1519
Fear Face	JL	YH	18.1.71–20.4.71	1520–1596
Double Jeopardy	JL	YH	21.4.71–28.8.71	1597–1708
Starfire	JL	YH	30.8.71–24.12.71	1709–1809
Trouble Spot	JL	YH	28.12.71–10.6.72	1810–1951
Isle of Condors	JL	YH	12.6.72–21.10.72	1952–2065
The League of Vampires	JL	YH	25.10.72–28.2.73	2066–2172
Die With My Boots On	JL	YH	1.3.73–18.6.73	2173–2256
The Girl Machine	JL	YH	19.6.73–3.12.73	2257–2407
Beware of Butterflies	JL	YH	4.12.73–11.5.74	2408–2541
The Nevsky Nude	JL	YH	13.5.74–21.9.74	2542–2655
The Phoenix Project	JL	YH	23.9.74–18.2.75	2656–2780
The Black Ruby Caper	JL	YH	19.2.75–15.7.75	2781–2897
Till Death Do Us Part	JL	YH	7.7.75–14.10.75	2898–2983
The Torch–Time Affair	JL	YH	15.10.75–15.1.76	2984–3060
Hot-Shot	JL	YH	16.1.76–1.6.76	3061–3178
Nightbird	JL	YH	2.6.76–4.11.76	3179–3312
Ape of Diamonds	JL	YH	5.11.76–22.1.77	3313–3437

STORY	WRITER	ARTISTS	DATE	SERIAL No.
Serialised in the *Sunday Express*				
(Series Four)				
When The Wizard Awakes	JL	YH	30.1.77–22.5.77	1–54
Syndicated strips not featured in newspapers in the UK				
Sea Dragon	JL	YH	not applicable	55–192
Death Wing	JL	YH	not applicable	193–354
The Xanadu Connection	JL	YH	not applicable	355–468
Shark Bait	JL	YH	not applicable	469–636
Serialised in the *Daily Star*				
(Series Five)				
Doomcrack	JL	HN	2.2.81–19.8.81	1–174
The Paradise Plot	JL	JM	20.8.81–4.6.82	175–378
Deathmask	JL	JM	7.6.82–8.2.83	379–552
Flittermouse	JL	JM	9.2.83–20.5.83	553–624
Polestar	JL	JM	23.5.83–15.7.83	625–719*

**Series stopped publishing in the* Daily Star *at 673*

STORY	WRITER	ARTISTS	DATE	SERIAL No.
Syndicated strips not featured in UK newspapers				
The Scent of Danger	JL	JM	not applicable	720–821
Snake Goddess	JL	YH	not applicable	822–893
Double Edge	JL	YH	not applicable	894–965

GLOSSARY

KEY TO CREATORS

IF: IAN FLEMING
AH: ANTHONY HERN
HG: HENRY GAMMIDGE
PO: PETER O'DONNELL
JL: JIM LAWRENCE
KA: KINGSLEY AMIS
(under pseudonym Robert Markham)
JM: JOHN MCLUSKY
YH: YAROSLAV HORAK
HN: HARRY NORTH

SERIAL NUMBERS

Each serial number represents a day. However, in Scotland, some strips were published in the *Daily Express* on days when there were Bank Holidays in England and Wales; these were designated by the suffix 'a' after the serial number on the strips.

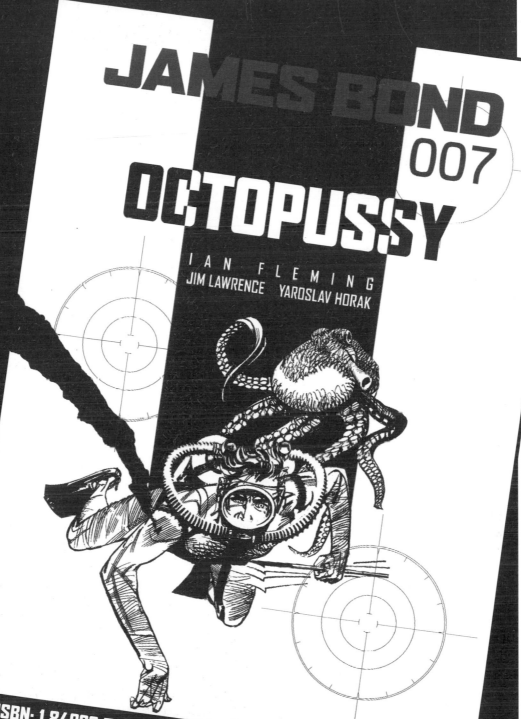